Jan Jürjens

Secure Systems Development with UML

T0180778

Jan Jürjens

Secure Systems Development with UML

With 79 Figures

 Springer

Jan Jürjens
Dep. of Informatics
Software and Systems Engineering
Technische Universität München
Boltzmannstr. 3
85748 München/Garching
e-mail: juerjens@in.tum.de

ACM Computing Classification (1998): D.2.2, D.2.4

ISBN 978-3-642-05635-2

e-ISBN 978-3-540-26494-1

Springer is a part of Springer Science+Business Media

springeronline.com

© Springer-Verlag Berlin Heidelberg 2010
Printed in Germany

Cover design: KünkelLopka, Heidelberg

Printed on acid-free paper 45/3142/YL - 5 4 3 2 1 0

to Li

Foreword

Those who spend their professional life developing and deploying – or observing – new information technology systems may believe that the security issues raised in this process are a direct consequence of developments in technology. This is not quite so. New technologies create opportunities for new applications, sometimes not even foreseen when the technology was first fielded. Pertinent examples are e-mail, the first major application of the Internet and its precursors (rather than the "serious" scientific collaborations originally intended), or the success of SMS (Short Messaging Service), which was initially perceived as a minor addition to the services offered by second-generation mobile telecommunications systems.

At the same time, new technologies and the applications they are facilitating also open up new opportunities for creating mischief of various hues, which in turn trigger a demand for "security technologies" that should prevent – or at least reduce – unwelcome use of those new applications. To stay with the example of e-mail, spam has today become a major nuisance, to the extent that some see success in the battle against spam as essential for e-mail to survive as a useful service.

For software systems, the release of the Internet for commercial use in the early 1990s was an incisive event, whose implications have still not been fully digested. It first led to the development of distributed applications in closed environments that use the Internet as an open communications network. In this domain, security requirements are mainly, but not exclusively, related to communications security. Virtual Private Networks may serve as an example. However, today we are also dealing with open environments without central points of control or authority, which require novel ways of approaching security. Indeed, the fact that in different applications fundamentally different security requirements have to be met is one of the reasons why the design of security protocols is difficult and error prone.

All of which brings us to security. Security professionals like to state that security must not be treated as an add-on feature, and that systems cannot be made secure by adding some so-called security features in the later design stages. To the extent that security requirements depend on the application, it is then the task of the application designer to include those requirements in the specification early on, and the task of the design process to make sure that adequate protection mechanisms are implemented. There is thus an obvious demand for design methodologies that help in specifying security requirements, and in making sure that suitable security mechanisms are implemented.

To add a second general statement on security, there are hardly ever correct answers to security challenges, only answers that are better or worse than others. When proposing design methodologies for security, we are walking a tightrope if security-unaware application writers are asked to decide on matters of security. In application areas where security requirements are well understood and met by a fairly standardized set of security mechanisms, we may justifiably hope that such methodologies can be put to good use. However, particularly in novel kinds of applications, we will not always know the security requirements in advance, and prudent engineering practices may change over time. As an example, robustness against denial-of-service attacks and identity protection (plausible deniability) have become new aspects in the design of key establishment protocols in recent years, as witnessed in the discussions about a successor to the Internet Key Exchange protocol (IKE).

This book makes valuable contributions towards the development of well-founded design methodologies for security engineering. By building on a widely adopted specification language like UML, consideration of security aspects fits into the design process in a natural way. The proposed methodology has solid theoretical foundations so that it is possible to verify in a precise setting whether a design has its desired security properties. The definition of these foundations would in itself constitute a substantial piece of work, but the book goes further. For any design methodology striving to have practical impact, the proverbial saying that "the proof of the pudding is in the eating" applies. The book does not fall short on this count either, covering several case studies the methodology has been applied to, and presenting the tools that have been developed to support this approach.

To say that this book is a first step in a promising direction would thus seriously underrate what has already been achieved. The reader may treat this book as an exemplary demonstration of how formal methods for the design of secure systems could be made accessible to application software designers in general, and wait with interest for further developments as the methodology matures.

Hamburg,   *Dieter Gollmann*
                                                                          May 2004

Preface

Attacks against computer networks, which modern society and modern economies rely on for communication, finance, energy distribution, and transportation, can threaten the economical and physical well-being of people and organizations. Due to the increasing interconnection of systems, such attacks can be waged anonymously and from a safe distance. Thus networked computers need to be secure.

The high-quality development of security-critical systems is difficult. Many systems are developed, deployed, and used that do not satisfy their criticality requirements, sometimes giving rise to spectacular attacks.

Part of the difficulty of secure systems development is that the goal of correctness is often in conflict with that of low development cost. Where thorough methods of system design pose high cost through personnel training and use, they are all too often avoided.

The Unified Modeling Language (UML) offers an unprecedented opportunity for high-quality and cost- and time-efficient secure systems development:

- As the de facto standard in industrial modeling, a large number of developers are trained in UML.
- Compared to previous notations with a user community of comparable size, UML is relatively precisely defined.
- A variety of tools exist that provide the basic functionality required to use UML (such as the drawing of UML diagrams).

To exploit this opportunity, however, some challenges remain: One needs to adapt the UML to the application domain of security-critical systems and advance its correct use in this application domain. One has to develope advanced tool support for secure systems development with UML, such as automatic analysis of UML specifications with respect to security requirements. This requires dealing with conflicts between flexibility and unambiguity in the meaning of UML models. This book aims to contribute to overcoming these challenges.

We present the UML extension UMLsec for secure systems development, using the standard UML extension mechanisms. The possibility of a high degree of abstraction, and diagrams offering different views of a system, allow the modeling of security-critical components in the system context. One can thus automatically evaluate UML specifications for vulnerabilities using the UMLsec tool support based on a formal semantics of a simplified core of UML 1.5 which we also provide.[1] One may also encapsulate established rules of prudent security engineering and make them available to developers. Our method thus aims to be useful both to security experts and to developers who may not be experts in security. We demonstrate the adequacy of UMLsec by using it in several case studies. For example, we develop a secure channel specification and uncover flaws in a published variant of the Internet protocol TLS and in the Common Electronic Purse Specifications, propose corrections, and verify them. We use UMLsec in the context of banking applications and of Java security. We present the concepts and technologies needed for constructing tool support for analyzing UML models for sophisticated requirements, such as the constraints included in UMLsec specifications. The tool support is based on an XML dialect called XMI which allows interchange of UML models.

This book is based on a PhD thesis, several invited talks and summer school lectures, a series of about thirty tutorials at international conferences and feedback from many of their participants, and about thirty articles in international journals and at conferences by the author, as well as on feedback from projects with industrial partners (including a major German bank, car manufacturer, and telecommunications company), and on discussions at international workshops organized on the topic of model-based security engineering with UML, as well as the supervision of about thirty Master's and Bachelor theses and advanced study projects on related topics and seven courses given at the University of Oxford and TU München which included part of the topics covered in this book. Additional material is given on the website [Jür04] associated with this book which is continuously being updated. It includes the following material:

- Slides and audio recordings from the tutorials and courses mentioned above.
- Other learning and teaching materials, including exercises and answers.
- A web interface for a tool which analyzes UMLsec models written using an industrial UML modeling tool (which one can upload over the Internet) for security requirements.[2]

Note that although the UML extension proposed in this book aims to also offer assistance to developers who are not security experts (for example, by enabling them to use security mechanisms in a secure way), parts of the book are

---

[1] In the appendix, we explain how to adjust our approach to the upcoming version UML 2.0.

[2] The tool is currently being made available as open-source.

concerned with advanced applications (such as the analysis of cryptographic protocols) for which background knowledge in security would be helpful.

I would like to express my sincerest gratitude to all of the people involved in some way or another with the above undertakings, and with the compilation of this book in particular. These include my advisor for the PhD thesis on which this book is based, Samson Abramsky (for his insights and advice, encouragement, and patience), as well as Manfred Broy, head of my subsequent affiliation being the Software & Systems Engineering group at TU Munich (for interesting discussions, for sharing his profound experience in formal methods and software engineering, and for providing a very stimulating working environment), various people who provided encouragement to pursue the idea to write a book based on the thesis, my coauthors and colleagues (for fruitful collaborations, and inspiring discussions on security or UML), my students (for helpful collaborations on tool support and for questions on dubious parts of the material), several people reading various portions of the draft and offering useful comments and advice, as well as the many reviewers of the papers on which this book is based, altogether several hundred participants of my tutorials, as well as the audiences of my other talks related to security or UML, many of whom contributed comments and questions. I would also like to thank the members of different organizations in which I am involved (including the working group for Formal Methods and Software Engineering for Safety and Security (FoMSESS) within the German Society for Informatics (GI), the Division of Safety and Security within the GI, the Bavarian Competence Center for Safety and Security, the working group on e-Security of the Bavarian regional government, and the IFIP Working Group 1.7 "Theoretical Foundations of Security Analysis and Design") for interesting discussions about security, the technical support at TU Munich (including the system administrators and the student assistants, in particular Britta Liebscher). Last but not at all least I would like to thank my editor at Springer-Verlag, Ralf Gerstner, for his interest in the book project and his enduring and understanding patience. Apologizing to those who currently manage to escape my mind, I would like to name in particular the following: Martín Abadi, Lionel Van Aertryck, Ewgeny Alter, Axelle Apvrille, David Basin, Peter Braun, Matthias Braun, Ruth Breu, Alexander Chatzigeorgiou, Dominique Chauveau, Pierpaolo Degano, Martin Deubler, Rik Eshuis, Andreas Fedrizzi, Eduardo B. Fernandez, Robert France, Onno Garms, Geri Georg, Andreas Gilg, Dieter Gollmann, Roberto Gorrieri, Susanne Graf, Johannes Grünbauer, Joshua Guttman, Sebastian Höhn, Helia Hollmann, Siv Hilde Houmb, Anna Ioshpe, Gergely Kokavecz, Dimitri Kopjev, Thomas Kuhn, Simon Kulla, Markus Lehrhuber, Britta Liebscher, Wolfgang Linsmeier, Volkmar Lotz, Gavin Lowe, Frank Marschall, Shasha Meng, Carlo Montangero, Haris Mouratidis, Gerhard Popp, Max Raith, Jan Romberg, Bernhard Rumpe, Robert Sandner, Robert Schmidt, Marillyn Schwaiger, Stephan Schwarzmüller, Bran Selic, Pasha Shabalin, Shunwei Shen, Oscar Slotosch, Perdita Stevens, Martin Strecker, Guido Wimmel, and Bo Zhang.

Finally, I particularly thank my parents and my brother for their continued moral support.

This work was financially supported in part by the Studienstiftung des deutschen Volkes, Laboratory for Foundations of Computer Science (University of Edinburgh), Bell Laboratories (Lucent Technologies), Computing Laboratory (University of Oxford), Software & Systems Engineering (TU Munich), the FairPay project (German Ministry of Economy), the HypoVereinsbank (Munich), and the Verisoft project (German Ministry of Education and Research). The support is greatly appreciated.

Comments or questions regarding the content of this book are always welcome, and can be made through the book's website [Jür04].

München,   *Jan Jürjens*
August 2004

> Two roads diverged in a wood, and I,
> I took the one less traveled by,
> And that has made all the difference.
>
> Robert Frost, The Road Not Taken

Contents

List of Figures

Part I

Prologue

1

Introduction

A Need for Security

Modern society and modern economies rely on infrastructures for communication, finance, energy distribution, and transportation. These infrastructures depend increasingly on networked information systems. Attacks against these systems can threaten the economical or even physical well-being of people and organizations. There is widespread interconnection of information systems via the Internet, which is becoming the world's largest public electronic marketplace, while being accessible to untrusted users. Attacks can be waged anonymously and from a safe distance. If the Internet is to provide the platform for commercial transactions, it is vital that sensitive information (like credit card numbers or cryptographic keys) is stored and transmitted securely.

Problems

Developing secure software systems correctly is difficult and error-prone. Many flaws and possible sources of misunderstanding have been found in protocol or system specifications, sometimes years after their publication or use. For example, the observations in [Low95] were made 17 years after the well-known Needham–Schroeder authentication protocol had been published in [NS78]. Many vulnerabilities in deployed security-critical systems have been exploited, sometimes leading to spectacular attacks. For example, as part of a 1997 exercise, an NSA hacker team demonstrated how to break into US Department of Defense computers and the US electric power grid system, among other things simulating a series of rolling power outages and 911 emergency telephone overloads in Washington, DC, and other cities [Sch99a]. While there are of course many more recent examples of security breaches, this particular example also shows that there is more to be concerned about than website defacements and creditcard misuse.

Computer breaches do significant damage, as a study by the Computer Security Institute shows: Ninety percent of the respondents detected computer security breaches within the last 12 months. Forty-four percent of them were willing and able to quantify the damage. These 223 firms reported $455,848,000 in financial losses [Ric03].

Causes

Firstly, enforcing security requirements is intrinsically subtle, because one has to take into account the interaction of the system with motivated adversaries that act independently. Thus security mechanisms, such as security protocols, are notoriously hard to design correctly, even for experts. Also, a system is only as secure as its weakest part or aspect.

Secondly, risks are very hard to calculate: security-critical systems are characterized by the fact that the occurrence of a successful attack at one point in time on a given system dramatically increases the likelihood that the attack will be launched subsequently at another system. This problem is made worse by the existence of the Internet as a mass communication medium that is currently largely uncontrolled and enables fast and anonymous distribution of information on successful exploits.

Thirdly, many problems with security-critical systems arise from the fact that their developers, who employ security mechanisms, do not always have a strong background in computer security. This is problematic since, in practice, security is compromised most often not by breaking dedicated mechanisms such as encryption or security protocols, but by exploiting weaknesses in the way they are being used [And01]: According to A. Shamir, the Israeli state security apparatus is not hampered in its investigations by the fact that suspects may use encryption technology that may be virtually impossible to break. Instead, other weaknesses in overall computer security can be exploited [Sha99]. As another example, the security of Common Electronic Purse Specifications (CEPS) [CEP01] transactions depends on the assumption that it is not feasible for the attacker to act as a relay between an attacked card and an attacked terminal. However, this is not explicitly stated, and it is furthermore planned to use the CEPS over the Internet, where an attacker could easily act as such a relay. This is investigated in Sect. 5.3. As a last example, [Wal00] attributes the failures in the security of the mobile phone protocol GSM among other reasons to the failure to acknowledge limitations of the underlying physical security, such as misplaced trust in terminal identity and the possibility to create false base stations.

Thus it is not enough to ensure correct functioning of security mechanisms used. They cannot be "blindly" inserted into a security-critical system, but the overall system development must take security aspects into account in a coherent way [SS75]. More specifically, one can say that "those who think that their problem can be solved by simply applying cryptography don't understand cryptography and don't understand their problem" (R. Needham). In fact, according to [Sch99a], 85% of Computer Emergency Response Team

(CERT) security advisories [CER] could not have been prevented just by making use of cryptography. Thus, given the current state of software security, just using encryption to protect communication still leaves most weaknesses unresolved, and has been compared to using an armored car to deliver credit card information "from someone living in a cardboard box to someone living on a park bench" [VM02]. Building trustworthy components does not suffice, since the interconnections and interactions of components play a significant role in trustworthiness [Sch99a].

Lastly, while functional requirements are generally analyzed carefully in systems development, security considerations often arise after the fact. Adding security as an afterthought, however, often leads to problems [Gas88, And01]. Also, security engineers get little feedback about the secure functioning of their products in practice, since security violations are often kept secret for fear of harming a company's reputation.

It has remained true over the last 30 years since the seminal paper [SS75] that no coherent and complete methodology to ensure security in the construction of large general-purpose systems exists yet, in spite of very active research and many useful results addressing particular subgoals [Sch99a], as well as a large body of security engineering knowledge accumulated [And01]. Such a methodology would allow the computer security engineer to construct a system in a way similar to how a civil engineer would build a bridge. In contrast, today ad hoc development leads to many deployed systems that do not satisfy important security requirements. Thus a sound methodology supporting secure systems development is needed.

Traditional Approaches

In practice, the traditional strategy for security assurance has been "penetrate and patch": It has been accepted that deployed systems contain vulnerabilities. Whenever a penetration of the system is noticed and the exploited weakness can be identified, the vulnerability is removed. Sometimes this is supported by employing friendly teams trained in penetrating computer systems, the so-called "tiger teams" [Wei95, McG98].

For many systems, this approach is not ideal: Each penetration using a new vulnerability may already have caused significant damage, before the vulnerability can be removed. For systems that offer strong incentives for attack, such as financial applications, the prospect of being able to exploit a discovered weakness only once may already be enough motivation to search for such a weakness. System administrators are often hesitant to apply patches, *especially* in critical systems, since applying the patch may disrupt the service [And01]. Having to create and distribute patches costs money and leads to loss of customer confidence. Patches may contain security threats themselves, such as the FunLove virus in a Microsoft hotfix distributed in April 2001 [Mic01, The01].

It would thus be preferable to consider security aspects more seriously in earlier phases of the system life-cycle, before a system is deployed, or even implemented, because late correction of requirements errors costs up to 200 times as much as early correction [Boe81].

The difficulty of designing security mechanisms correctly has motivated quite successful research using mathematical concepts and tools to ensure correct design of small security-critical components such as security proto- cols, including [MCF87, BAN89, Mea91, Low96, Pau98b, AG99]. The goal is to establish crucial requirements on the specification level through formaliza- tion and proof, which may be mechanically assisted or even automated. Note that it is not possible to actually prove a system secure in an absolute sense: Proofs can only be performed with respect to models which are necessarily abstractions from reality. Attackers can always try to go beyond the limita- tions of a given model to still attempt an attack. Nevertheless, a model-based security analysis is useful, because certain attacks can be prevented and the required effort for successful attacks increased. Also, often problems with a specification are detected just by trying to make it sufficiently precise for formal analysis [Gol03a].

Unfortunately, due to a perceived high cost in personnel training and use, formal methods have not yet been employed very widely in industrial develop- ment [Hoa96, Hei99, KK04]. To increase industry acceptance in the context of security-critical systems, it would be beneficial to integrate security require- ments analysis with a standard development method, which should be easy to learn and to use [CW96]. Also, security concerns must inform every phase of software development, from requirements engineering to design, implemen- tation, testing, and deployment [DS00b].

Some other challenges for using sound engineering methods for secure sys- tems development exist. Currently a large part of effort both in analyzing and implementing specifications is wasted since these are often formulated impre- cisely and unintelligibly, if they exist at all [Pau98a]. If increased precision by use of a particular notation brings an additional advantage, such as automated tool support for security analysis, this may however be sufficient incentive for providing it. Since software developers cannot expect to learn a particular for- mal method to do this, because of limited resources in time and training, one needs to instead use the artifacts that are at any rate constructed in industrial software development. Examples include specification models in the Unified Modeling Language (UML). Also, the boundaries of the specified components with the rest of the system need to be carefully examined, for example with respect to implicit assumptions on the system context [Gol00, Aba00]. Lastly, a more technical issue is that formalized security properties are not always preserved by refinement, which is the so-called *refinement problem* [RSG$^+$01]. Since an implementation is necessarily a refinement of its specification, an im- plementation of a secure specification may, in such a situation, not be secure, which is clearly undesirable. Also, it hinders the use of stepwise development, where one starts with an abstract specification and refines it in several steps to a concrete specification which is implemented, allowing mistakes to be detected early in the development cycle, and thus leading to considerable savings: Without preservation of security by refinement, developing secure systems in a stepwise manner requires one to redo the security analysis after each refinement step. Hence, we need formalizations of security requirements that are indeed preserved under refinement.

Model-Based Security Engineering with UML

Towards a solution of the problems mentioned in the previous sections, we propose an approach for model-based security engineering using the Unified Modeling Language (UML) [RJB99, UML03]. We explain our motivation firstly for choosing this kind of approach and secondly for using the UML notation.

Generally, in model-based development, as represented in Fig. 1.1, the idea is to first construct a model of a system, which should be as close to human intuition as possible and is typically relatively abstract. In a second step, the implementation is derived from the model: either automatically using code generation, or manually, in which case one can still generate test sequences from the model to establish conformance of the code regarding the model. The goal is to increase the quality of the implemented code while keeping the implementation cost and the time-to-market bounded.

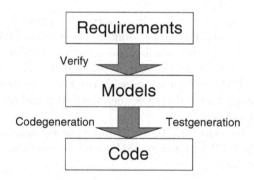

Fig. 1.1. Model-based development

For security-critical systems, this approach allows one to consider security requirements from early of in the development process, within the development context, and in a seamless way throught the development cycle. Using the model-based approach, one can, firstly, establish that the system fulfills the relevant security requirements on the design level, by analyzing the model. Secondly, one can check that the code is also secure by generating test sequences from the model.

UML now offers an, as such probably unprecedented, opportunity as a notation for a high-quality model-based development of security-critical systems that is feasible in an industrial context:

- As the de facto standard in industrial modeling notations, a large number of developers are trained in UML, and this number is still growing because UML is widely taught at universities. Thus, a UML specification may already be available for security analysis, or less difficult to obtain than other notations.
- UML provides graphical, intuitive description techniques with multiple views of a system through different kinds of diagrams. It offers standard extension mechanisms (such as stereotypes, tags, constraints, and profiles) which one can use to tailor the notation to a specific application domain.
- Compared to previous notations with a user community of comparable size, UML is relatively precisely defined, since [UML03] defines syntax and semantics of the UML notation in a relatively high degree of detail, although not entirely formal.
- A variety of tools exist that provide the basic functionality required to use UML, such as the drawing of UML diagrams.

Note that although UML was developed to model object-oriented systems, one may use it just as well to analyze systems that are not object-oriented, by thinking of objects as components and not making use of object-oriented features, such as inheritance.

To exploit this opportunity, however, some challenges remain: One needs to adapt the UML to the application domain of security-critical systems and advance its correct use in this application domain. One has to develope advanced tool support for secure systems development with UML, such as automatic analysis of UML specifications with respect to security requirements. This requires dealing with conflicts between flexibility and unambiguity in the meaning of UML models.

This book aims to contribute to overcoming these challenges. More specifically, it presents the UML extension UMLsec for secure systems development. The UMLsec extension:

- allows one to evaluate UML specifications for security weaknesses on the design level,
- encapsulates established rules of prudent security engineering in the context of a widely known notation, and thus makes them available to developers who may not be security experts,
- allows the developer to consider security requirements from early on in the system development process, and
- involves little additional overhead, since the UML diagrams can serve as system documentation, which is always desirable to have, and sometimes required (for example, for security certifications).

1.1 Overview

The UMLsec extension

We present an extension of the UML [UML03] for secure systems development, called UMLsec. Recurring security requirements (such as secrecy, integrity, and authenticity) are offered as specification elements by the UMLsec extension. The properties are used to evaluate diagrams of various kinds and to indicate possible vulnerabilities. One can thus verify that the stated security requirements, if fulfilled, enforce a given security policy. One can also ensure that the requirements are actually met by the given UML specification of the system. UMLsec encapsulates knowledge on prudent security engineering and thereby makes it available to developers who may not be experts in security.

The extension is given in form of a UML profile using the standard UML extension mechanisms. *Stereotypes* are used together with *tags* to formulate security requirements and assumptions on the system environment. *Constraints* give criteria that determine whether the requirements are met by the system design, by referring to a precise semantics mentioned below.

The extension has been developed based on experiences on the model-based development of security-critical systems in industrial projects involving German government agencies and major banks, insurance companies, smart card and car manufacturers, and other companies. Note that an extension of UML to an application domain such as security-critical systems that aims to include requirements from that application domain as stereotypes, as opposed to just adding specific architectural primitives, can probably never be fully complete: It would then have to incorporate all existing design knowledge on security-critical computing systems, which fills countless books. Therefore, here we focus on providing a core profile that includes the main security requirements. We expect this to be extended with additional, more specific concepts (for example, from more specialized application domains such as mobile security).

We list the requirements on a UML extension for secure systems development and discuss how far our extension meets these requirements. We explain the details of the extension by means of examples, demonstrate how to employ the extension for enforcing established rules of secure systems design and show how to use UMLsec to apply security patterns.

Applications

To validate our approach using UMLsec for secure systems development, we investigate the degree to which it is suitable for enforcing established rules of prudent security engineering. We consider several case studies:

- We demonstrate stepwise development of a security-critical system with UMLsec as the example of a secure channel design, together with a mathematically precise verification.

- We uncover a flaw in a variant of the handshake protocol of the Internet protocol TLS proposed in [APS99], suggest a correction, and verify the corrected protocol.
- We apply UMLsec to a security analysis of CEPS, a candidate for a globally interoperable electronic purse standard. We discover flaws in the two central parts of the specifications (the purchase and the load protocol), propose corrections, and give a verification of the corrected versions.
- We show how to use UMLsec to correctly employ advanced Java 2 security concepts such as guarding objects in a way that allows formal verification of the specifications.
- We also report on a project with a major German bank, where we applied our ideas about model-based development of security-critical systems to a web-based banking application.

There are further applications in industrial development projects which because of space limitations can only shortly be mentioned.

Tool Support

For the ideas that we present in this book to be of benefit in practice, it is important to have advanced tool support to assist in using them. We present the necessary background to construct such tool support, as well as the tool suite that has been developed [JSA+04]. The developed tools can be used to check the constraints associated with UMLsec stereotypes mechanically, based on XMI output of the diagrams from the UML drawing tool in use, and using sophisticated analysis engines that as model-checkers and automated theorem provers. For this, the developer creates a model using a UML drawing tool capable of XMI export and stores it as an XMI file. The file is imported by the UMLsec analysis tool (for example, through its web interface) which analyses the UMLsec model with respect to the security requirements that are included. The results of the analysis are given back to the developer, together with a modified UML model, where the weaknesses that were found are highlighted.

We also explain a framework for implementing verification routines for the constraints associated with the UMLsec stereotypes. The goal is that advanced users of the UMLsec approach should be able to use this framework to implement verification routines for the constraints of self-defined stereotypes. In particular, the framework includes the UMLsec tool web interface, so that new routines are also accessible over this interface. The idea behind the framework is to provide a common programming framework for the developers of different verification modules. A tool developer should be able to concentrate on the implementation of the verification logic and not be required to implement the user interface.

Furthermore, we present research on linking the UMLsec approach with the automated analysis of security-critical data arising at runtime. Specifically, we present research on the construction of a tool which automatically checks the SAP R/3 configuration for security policy rules, such as separation of duty. The permissions are given as input in an XML format through an interface from the SAP R/3 system, the rules are formulated as UML specifications in a standard UML CASE tool and output as XMI, as part of the UMLsec framework mentioned above. The tool then checks the permissions against the rules using an analyzer written in Prolog. Because of its modular architecture and its standardized interfaces, the tool can be adapted to check security constraints in other kinds of application software, such as firewalls or other access control configurations.

As noted, for example, in [Fow04], the ultimate benefit in software development is not "pretty pictures", but the running implementation of a system. We present some approaches for linking UML models to implementations, such as model-based testing. The aim is to ensure that the benefits gained from the model-based approach on the level of the system model, such as increased confidence in satisfaction of critical requirements, actually carry over to the implemented system.

To provide tool support for analyzing UMLsec models with respect to the security properties included as predefined constraints, tool developers need to formulate the properties in a mathematically precise way. This is only possible if the UML specification they refer to also has a mathematically precise meaning. In particular, this concerns the behavioral aspects, since many security requirements refer to the system behavior. For this goal, we provide a precise execution semantics for a simplified part of UML using so-called *UML Machines*. These are based on Abstract State Machines which give a mathematically rigorous yet rather flexible framework for modeling computing systems [Gur95]. *UML Machine Systems* allow us then to build up UML Machine specifications in a modular way and to treat external influences on the system beyond the planned interaction, such as attacks on insecure communication links. This allows a rather natural modeling of potential adversary behavior and to define different kinds of adversary strengths. On this basis, important security requirements such as secrecy, integrity, authenticity, and secure information flow are defined. To support stepwise development, we show secrecy, integrity, authenticity, and secure information flow to be *preserved* under refinement. Because of the modular way UML Machines are defined, they give a formal framework for formally analyzing security-critical systems in their own right, independently of the UML notation.

Based on this, we provide a precise semantics for a simplified core of UML that allows one to use a more focussed kind of UML subsystems to group together several diagrams. The precise semantics for a restricted version of subsystems incorporates the precise semantics of the diagrams contained in a subsystem in a way that allows them to interact by exchanging messages. The statechart semantics which is part of it is based on part of the statechart semantics from [BCR00]. The motivation is to concentrate on a core of UML for which it is feasible to construct and use advanced tool support. The UMLsec case studies mentioned above demonstrate that our choice of a subset of UML is useful. We also consider some helpful concepts, such as consistency between diagrams, different kinds of refinement of and equivalence between UML specifications, and the use of rely-guarantee specifications.

Via UML Machines and UML Machine Systems we make use of the presented treatment of security-critical systems. In particular, UML specifications can be evaluated using the attacker model, which incorporates the possible attacker behaviors, to find vulnerabilities.

1.2 Outline

Here is an outline of the following chapters:

Chapter 2: For a short "walk-through" to highlight the UMLsec approach, we consider a simplified model of an Internet-based business application as a running example.

Chapter 3: Some background information is recalled that is needed in the remainder of the book.

Chapter 4: After discussing requirements on a UML extension for secure systems development, we present the UMLsec profile. We show how to formulate security requirements on a system and security assumptions on the underlying layer in UMLsec. It is explained how to evaluate the system specification against the security requirements, by referring to the precise semantics sketched in Chap. 3. We demonstrate how to employ the extension for enforcing established rules of secure systems design and how to use UMLsec in order to apply security patterns.

Chapter 5: At the example of a secure channel design, we demonstrate stepwise development of a security-critical system with UMLsec. We uncover a flaw in a variant of the handshake protocol of the Internet protocol TLS proposed in [APS99], suggest a correction, and verify the corrected protocol. Furthermore, we use UMLsec for a security analysis of CEPS, a candidate for a globally interoperable electronic purse standard. We discover three flaws in the two central parts of the specifications, propose corrections, and give a verification. We show how to use UMLsec to correctly employ advanced Java 2 security concepts such as guarded objects.

Chapter 6: The necessary background for developing tool support for UMLsec is explained. We present a tool which automatically checks a UMLsec model with respect to the security requirements associated with the UMLsec stereotypes, based on XML output of industrial UML drawing tools. A framework is presented which allows advanced users to conveniently include verification routines for the constraints of self-defined stereotypes. As an instance of this framework, we present a tool which links the UMLsec approach with the automated analysis of security-critical data arising at runtime, such as permissions in SAP R/3 systems. We explain approaches for linking UML models to implementations, such as model-based testing.

Chapter 7: We introduce *UML Machines* and *UML Machine Systems* and define notions of refinement and rely-guarantee specifications. We explain how we use UML Machines to specify security-critical systems. In particular, we give definitions for secrecy, integrity, authenticity, and secure information flow, and give equivalent internal characterizations to simplify verification. We show secrecy, integrity, authenticity, and secure information flow to be preserved under refinement.

Chapter 8: We use UML Machines and UML Machine Systems to give a precise semantics for a simplified part of UML. This semantics is used to give consistency conditions for different diagrams in a UML specification. Also, we define notions of refinement and behavioral equivalence, and investigate structural properties, such as substitutivity. We consider rely-guarantee properties for UML specifications and their structural properties.

Chapter 9: An account of other approaches to security engineering with a similarly sound basis is given.

Chapter 10: We conclude with a critical evaluation of the approach we presented and an outlook on future developments.

Appendices: We explain how to adjust our approach to the upcoming version UML 2.0, give the formal definition of UML Machine rules and the proofs for the statements from Chaps. 5, 7, and 8.

1.3 How to Use this Book

Being the first book on the topic of secure systems development with UML, this book was written with two audiences in mind:

- researchers and graduate students interested in UML, computer-aided software engineering or formal methods, and IT security, who may use the book as background reading for their own research in using UML for critical systems development, or in building advanced tool support for UML
- advanced software developing professionals as the intended users of the approach proposed in this book.

Some basic knowledge in computer security and UML would be helpful. This knowledge is recalled in Sections 3.1 and 3.2, and pointers to background reading are given.

For the benefit of the second group, we deferred the material on the semantics of UML to the end of the book in Chaps. 7 and 8. These can then be left out by people who are not interested in constructing advanced tool support for UML by themselves. The information in Sect. 3.3 about the used semantics of UML is sufficient to understand the remaining chapters.

Note that the UML extension proposed in this book aims to offer assistance also to developers who are not security experts, for example, by enabling them to use security mechanisms in a secure way. Nevertheless, parts of the book are concerned with advanced applications, such as cryptoprotocol analysis, for which some background knowledge in security would be helpful.

The material in this book has been used extensively for teaching students, as well as researchers and software developers. For example, full-day tutorials for practitioners have been delivered based on the material in Chaps. 3 and 4 and Sects. 6.2 and 6.4. For a two-day course, one can also include Chap. 5. A Masters-level student course could also cover Chaps. 7 and 8.

Additional material is given on a website [Jür04] associated with this book which is continuously being updated. It includes the following material:

- Slides and audio recordings from the tutorials and courses based on this book.
- Other learning and teaching material, including exercises and answers.
- A web interface for a tool which analyzes UMLsec models for security requirements. These models can be written using an industrial UML modeling tool and uploaded over the Internet.

Walk-through: Using UML for Security

For a quick impression of what this book is about, we give a short "walk-through" through a small part of the UMLsec notation to highlight the UMLsec approach, considering a simplified model of an Internet-based business application as a running example. For readers who find themselves lacking background on computer security and on the Unified Modeling Language (UML), it is briefly recalled in Chap. 3. The UMLsec extension is then defined and explained in more detail in Chap. 4, as well as the examples shown in this chapter.

A central idea of the UMLsec extension is to define labels for UML model elements, the so-called *stereotypes*, which, when attached, add security-relevant information to these model elements. This security-relevant information can be of the following kinds:

- Security assumptions on the physical level of the system, such as the « Internet » stereotype shown below.
- Security requirements on the logical structure of the system (such as the « secrecy » stereotype) or on specific data values (such as the « critical » stereotype).
- Security policies that system parts are supposed to obey, such as the « fair exchange », « secure links », « data security », or « no down − flow » stereotypes.

In the first two cases, the stereotypes simply add some additional information to a model. They can be attached to any diagram of the relevant kind. In the third case, there are constraints associated with a stereotype that have to be fulfilled by a diagram so that it can justifiably carry the stereotype. If such a stereotype is attached to a diagram which does not meet this constraints, this results in an incorrect model, as in the case of the « secure links », « data security », and « no down − flow » stereotypes below. This prompts the tool support available for UMLsec [JSA+04], described in Chap. 6, to automatically point out the mistake, which should then be corrected by the developer.

2.1 Security Requirements Capture with Use Case Diagrams

Use case diagrams are commonly used to describe typical interactions between a user and a computer system in requirements elicitation. They may also be used to capture security requirements.

To start with our example, Fig. 2.1 shows a use case diagram describing the following situation: a customer buys a good from a business. The trade should be performed in a way that prevents both parties from cheating. We include this requirement in the diagram by adding a stereotype « fair exchange» to the subsystem containing the use case diagram. A more detailed explanation of what the requirement represented by this stereotype means in this specific situation, and of the activities associated with the use cases, is given in the following subsection.

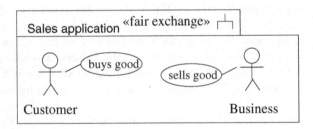

Fig. 2.1. Use case diagram for business application

2.2 Secure Business Processes with Activity Diagrams

Activity diagrams can be used to model workflow and to explain use cases in more detail. Similarly, they can be used to make security requirements more precise.

Following our example, Fig. 2.2 explains the use case in more detail by giving the business process realizing the above two use cases. The requirement «fair exchange» is now formulated by referring to the activities in the diagram. Intuitively, the actions listed in the tags {start} and {stop} should be linked in the sense that if one of the former is executed then eventually one of the latter will be. This property can be checked automatically.

This would entail that, once the customer has paid, either the order is delivered to the customer by the due date, or the customer is able to reclaim the payment on that date.

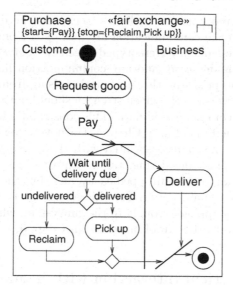

Fig. 2.2. Purchase activity diagram

2.3 Physical Security Using Deployment Diagrams

Deployment diagrams are used to describe the physical layer of a system. We use them to check whether the security requirements on the logical level of the system are enforced by the level of physical security, or whether additional security mechanisms (such as encryption) have to be employed.

Continuing with our example, the business application is part of an e-commerce system, which is supposed to be realized as a web application. The payment transaction involves transmission of data to be kept secret (such as credit card numbers) over Internet links. This information on the physical layer and the security requirement is reflected in the UML model in Fig. 2.3.

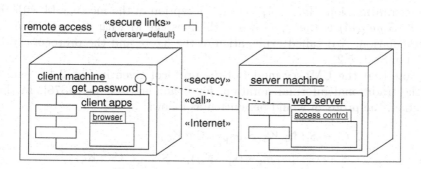

Fig. 2.3. Example *secure links* usage

We then use the stereotype «secure links» to express the demand that security requirements on the communication are met by the physical layer. More precisely, for each dependency stereotyped «secrecy» between subsystems or classes on different nodes n, m, and any communication link between n and m with some stereotype s, the threat scenario arising from the stereotype s with regard to an adversary of a given strength should not violate the secrecy requirement on the communicated data. This constraint will be defined more precisely and explained in detail in Chap. 4. For now we only note that in the given diagram, this constraint associated with the stereotype «secure links» is already violated when considering standard adversaries, because plain Internet connections can be eavesdropped easily, and thus the data that is communicated does not remain secret. For this adversary type, the stereotype «secure links» is thus applied wrongly to the subsystem, which is pointed out automatically by the UMLsec tool presented in Chap. 6.

2.4 Security-Critical Interaction with Sequence Diagrams

Sequence diagrams are used to specify interaction between different parts of a system. Using UMLsec stereotypes, we can extend them with information giving the security requirements relevant to that interaction. For example, this enables one to see whether cryptographic session keys exchanged in a key exchange protocol remain confidential from possible adversaries.

With regard to our example, based on the security analysis in the previous subsection we decide to create a secure channel for the sensitive data that has to be sent over the untrusted networks, by making use of encryption. As usual, we first exchange symmetric session keys for this purpose. Let us assume that, for technical reasons, we decide not to use a standard and well-examined protocol such as SSL but instead a customized key exchange protocol such as the simplified one in Fig. 2.4. The goal is to exchange a secret session key K, using public keys K_C and K_S, which is then used to encrypt the secret data s before transmission. Here $\{M\}_K$ is the encryption of the message M with the key K, $Sign_K(M)$ is the signature of the message M with K, and :: denotes concatenation. A detailed explanation of the figure and the protocol can be found in Sect. 5.2.

Note that the UMLsec model of the protocol given in Fig. 2.4 is similar to the traditional informal notation, for example, used in [NS78]. In that notation, the protocol would be written as follows:

$$C \rightarrow S : N_i, K_C, Sign_{K_C^{-1}}(C :: K_C)$$
$$S \rightarrow C : \{Sign_{K_S^{-1}}(k_j :: N_i)\}_{K_C}, Sign_{K_{CA}^{-1}}(S :: K_S)$$
$$C \rightarrow S : \{s_i\}_{k_j}.$$

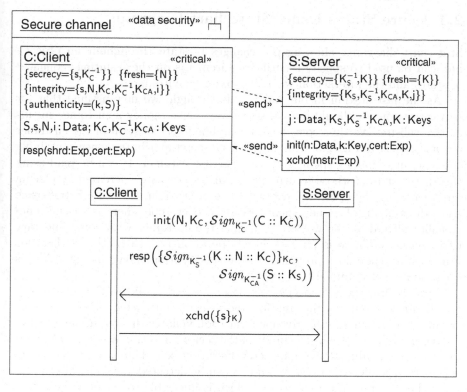

Fig. 2.4. Key exchange protocol

We argue in Sect. 5.2 that the traditional notation needs to be interpreted with care and that the UMLsec notation can be seen to be more precise and to lead over more easily to an implementation.

One can now again use stereotypes to include important security requirements on the data that is involved. Here, the stereotype « critical » labels classes containing sensitive data and has the associated tags {secrecy}, {integrity}, {authenticity}, and {fresh} to denote the respective security requirements on the data. The constraint associated with « data security » then requires that these requirements are met with respect to the given adversary model. We assume that the standard adversary is not able to break the encryption used in the protocol, but can exploit any design flaws that may exist in the protocol, for example by attempting so-called "man-in-the-middle" attacks. This is made precise for a generic adversary model in Sect. 3.3.4. Technically, the constraint then enforces that there are no successful attacks of that kind. Note that it is highly non-trivial to see whether the constraint holds for a given protocol. However, using well-established concepts from formal methods applied to computer security in the context of UMLsec, it is possible to verify this automatically.

2.5 Secure States Using Statechart Diagrams

Statechart diagrams, showing the changes in state throughout an object's life, can be used to specify security requirements on the resulting sequences of states and the interaction with the object's environment.

As the last station in our quick walk-through, we now assume that for privacy reasons, it should remain secret how much money a customer spends at the website. We thus consider the simplified specification of the customer account object in Fig. 2.5. The object has a secret attribute money containing the amount of money spent so far by a given customer. It can be read using the operation rm() whose return value is also secret, and increased by placing an order using the operation wm(x). If the object is in the state ExtraService since the amount of money spent already is over 1000, there is special functionality offered at the website providing the customer with complimentary extra services. There is an associated operation rx() to check whether this functionality should be provided. In the specification shown in Fig. 2.5, this operation is not assumed to be secret.

Now we use the stereotype « no down-flow » to indicate that the object should not leak out any information about secret data, such as the money attribute. Unfortunately, the given specification violates this requirement, since partial information about the input of the secret operation wm() is leaked out via the return value of the non-secret operation rx(). Thus the model carries the stereotype illegitimately. Again this can be detected automatically, and it is another example for a constraint which is infeasible to verify without tool support, for specifications of the size arising in practice.

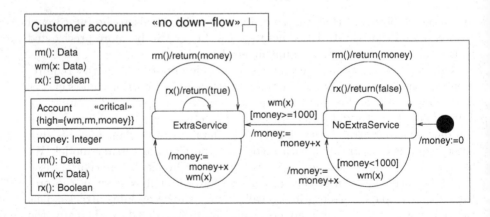

Fig. 2.5. Customer account data object

3

Background

We briefly present some important concepts used in the course of this book and give references to more comprehensive background reading.

Some previous knowledge of computer security and of UML may be helpful since an in-depth introduction has to be omitted. Below, we give some suggestions for background reading. Of course, there are many more good introductory references on these topics. We also briefly recall the main concepts needed for our purposes.

3.1 Security Engineering

We now explain some issues in computer security engineering that will play a role in this book. For background reading on these topics, good textbooks include [Gol99, And01], as well as [VM02] with an emphasis on software.[1] [APG95] contains interesting essays on the topic. "Classic" references on security engineering include [SS75, Gas88, AN96]. A good introduction to cryptography can be found, for example, in [MvOV96, GB99]. A classic book on database security and integrity is [ERW81].

Communication over open, unprotected networks is often prone to attacks. In the case of the Internet, it is relatively easy to read or delete messages that are exchanged, or to insert other messages. In wireless networks, it is even easier at least to read or insert messages, in physical proximity of the network. Secure communication over untrusted networks thus requires specific mechanisms such as encryption and cryptographic protocols. A *cryptographic protocol* is a description of a message exchange, which includes cryptographic data, for establishing a secure relationship between the protocol participants, such as a secure communication channel. As pointed out in the introduction, cryptographic protocols are very difficult to design and prone to very subtle errors.

---

[1] For the German-speaking audience, we also recommend [Eck03].

Apart from attacking the communication links in a distributed system, an adversary may also try to directly attack the physical system nodes, if physical access is possible. Given sufficient time, it is also usually easy to get access to data or to manipulate the data or the behavior of unprotected system components which lack special protection. In systems, where adversaries may get in possession of security-critical nodes (for example, if adversaries may be system users), one therefore often uses specially protected hardware such as smart-cards assumed to be tamper-proof.

The model-based security engineering approach presented in this book has been designed for object-oriented and component-oriented systems. In particular, object-orientation is suitable as a conceptual basis for secure systems: they are equipped with a general mechanism for controlling access to data, namely *method calls*, and offer *information hiding* by encapsulating data in objects. The data encapsulated in an object can only be accessed through objects, and messages are the only way to communicate. Note, however, that to offer protection, these mechanisms have to be implemented within the object-oriented execution environment in a way that can withstand motivated attacks and so that the mechanisms cannot be circumvented. More information on this can be found in [Gol99, ch. 17].

A *security policy* summarizes the protection requirements of a system. We recall below some important security requirements and concepts which will be considered in the course of this book.

Fair Exchange

When trading goods electronically, the *fair exchange* requirement postulates that the trade is performed in a way that prevents the participating parties from cheating. If for example buyer has to make a prepayment, the buyer should be able to prove having made the payment and to reclaim the money if that good is subsequently not delivered.

Non-repudiation

One way of providing fair exchange is by using the security requirement of *non-repudiation* of some action, which means that this action cannot subsequently be successfully denied. That is, the action is *provable*, usually with respect to some trusted third party.

Role-based Access Control

An important mechanism for controlling access to protected resources is the concept of *role-based access control*. In order to keep permissions manageable, especially in systems with a large or frequently changing user-base, they are not directly assigned to users. Instead, users can have one or more *roles* often related to their function within an organisation, and then permissions are assigned to roles.

Secure Communication Link

Sensitive communication between different parts of a system needs to be protected. The relevant requirement of a *secure communication link* is here assumed to preserve secrecy and integrity for the data in transit.

Secrecy and Integrity

Two of the main data security requirements are *secrecy* (or *confidentiality*) and *integrity*. Secrecy of data means that the data should be *read* only by legitimate parties. Integrity of data means that it should be *modified* only by legitimate parties.

Authenticity

There are different variants of this third main security requirement. Two important ones are message authenticity and entity authenticity. *Message authenticity* (or *data origin authenticity*) means that one can trace back some piece of data to what its original source was, at some point in the past. *Entity authenticity* ensures that one can identify a participant in a protocol, and in particular make sure that the party has actually actively participated in the protocol at the time. The process providing authenticity is called *authentication*.

Freshness

A message is *fresh* if it has been created during the current execution round of the system under consideration (for example, during the current protocol iteration) and therefore cannot be a replay of an older message by the adversary. A *nonce* is a random value that is supposed to be used only once (hence the name), for example to establish that a certain message containing a recently created nonce is itself freshly constructed.

Secure Information Flow

A traditional way of ensuring security in computer systems is to design *multi-level secure* systems [LB73]. In such systems, there are different levels of sensitivity of data. For simplicity, one usually considers two security levels: *high*, meaning highly sensitive or highly trusted, and *low*, meaning less sensitive or less trusted. Where trusted parts of a system interact with untrusted parts, one has to ensure that there is no indirect leakage of sensitive information from a trusted to an untrusted part. To ensure this, one enforces the "no down-flow" policy: *low* data may influence *high* data, but not vc. vs.. The opposite of this condition, "no up-flow", enforces that untrusted parts of a system may not indirectly manipulate high data: *high* data may influence *low* data, but not vc. vs.. These security requirements, called *secure information flow* or *non-interference* [GM84], are rather stringent definitions of secrecy and integrity which can detect implicit flows of information that are called *covert channels* [Lam73].

Guarded Access

One of the main security mechanisms is *access control*, which ensures that only legitimate parties have access to a security-relevant part of the system. Sometimes, access control is enforced by *guards*: in the case of the *Java Security Architecture*, *guard objects* control access to protected objects; similarly for the *access decision objects* in *CORBA*.

3.2 Unified Modeling Language

The Unified Modeling Language (UML) [RJB99] is the de facto industry standard for specifying object-oriented software systems, also suitable for component-oriented systems. It is a graphical language that may be used to specify architectural and behavioral aspects of software. Good introductions to UML can for example be found in [SP99, Fow04].[2] Here, we consider its current version UML 1.5 [UML03][3].

UML diagrams describe various views on different parts of a system design. There are several kinds of diagrams, describing different aspects of a system at varying degrees of abstraction. In this book, we use the following kinds:

Use case diagrams describe an abstract view of the functionality offered by a system by specifying typical interactions with the user. They are often used in an informal way for negotiation with a customer before a system is designed.

Class diagrams define the static class structure of the system: classes with attributes, operations, and signals and relationships between classes. On the instance level, the corresponding diagrams are called *object diagrams*.

Statechart diagrams (or *state diagrams*) give the dynamic behavior of an individual object or component: events may cause a change in state or an execution of actions. They are an adaptation of Harel's statecharts [HG97].

Sequence diagrams describe interaction between objects or system components via message exchange, in particular method calls.

Activity diagrams specify the control flow between several components within the system, usually at a higher degree of abstraction than statecharts and sequence diagrams. They can be used to put objects or components in the context of overall system behavior or to explain use cases in more detail.

Deployment diagrams describe the mapping of the system components to the physical structure of the system.

Subsystems (a certain kind of *packages*) integrate the information between the different kinds of diagrams and between different parts of the system specification.

---

[2] For German-speaking readers, we also recommend [Bre01, Rum04].

[3] Some remarks on the upcoming version UML 2.0 can be found in Appendix A.

In addition to sequence diagrams, there are *collaboration diagrams*, which present similar information. Also, there are *component diagrams*, presenting part of the information contained in deployment diagrams. These two kinds of diagrams are omitted here to simplify the presentation, although they could be used with our approach as well.

For each kind of diagram, we will only need a relatively simple fragment of its various notational elements. In the following few subsections, we will informally explain only those features of the above kinds of diagrams which are needed in this book. There are many other diagram elements. Although they can also be used in the context of our approach, we will not need them in our presentation.

3.2.1 Use Case Diagrams

Use case diagrams can be used to structure the functionality of a system and to represent interactions between a system and a user in an abstract way. Use case diagrams contain *use cases* and *actors*. A use case is a coherent group of interactions belonging to a particular usage of the system. An actor has a name and defines a set of roles of entities. Entities can, for example, be humans or other computer systems. A role of a human could for example be Customer, as in Fig. 3.1. A link from an actor to a use case means that the system that the use case is part of is supposed to provide the service represented by the use case to any entity in the role represented by the actor. The intention is that instances of use cases and instances of actors interact when the services of the described system are used. One uses other kinds of diagrams, such as activity diagrams or sequence diagrams, to specify this interaction in more detail. As with the other diagram kinds, there are many more model elements, and these could also be used with our approach, such as the *extends* and *includes* relationships.

An example of a use case is given in Fig. 3.1. There, a Customer actor is supposed to perform a buys good use case and a Business actor is supposed to perform a sells good use case.

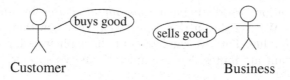

Customer   Business

Fig. 3.1. Use case diagram

3.2.2 Class Diagrams

An *object* is an "entity with a well-defined boundary and identity that en-capsulates state and behavior. State is represented by attributes and relation-ships, behavior is represented by operations, methods, and state machines. An object is an *instance* of a class" [UML03, p. Glos.-10]. A *class* is a "descrip-tion of a set of objects that share the same attributes, operations, methods, relationships, and semantics. A class may use a set of interfaces to specify collections of operations it provides to its environment" [UML03, p. Glos.-4]. We use *class diagrams* to present the classes and their interfaces used in a system, together with their relationships, such as dependencies. A modeling element *depends* on another modeling element if a change to the latter might affect the former.

In the diagrammatic notation, a class is represented by a rectangle with three compartments giving its name, its attributes, and its operations. An object is displayed in the same way, except that the name is underlined. This notational mechanism is also used in other kinds of diagrams to distinguish between the type and instance levels. Dependencies between classes are writ-ten as broken arrows with an open arrow-head. Interfaces are represented by the interface specification, which is a rectangle labeled « Interface » containing the operations and signals offered by the interface, with a broken arrow with a closed head coming from the class implementing the interface. A label set in « » in a UML diagram is called a *stereotype*; see Sect. 3.2.8 for an explanation of the concept of UML stereotypes. As shorthand, one may omit the inter-face specification and instead write a circle attached to the class rectangle. A dependency arrow stereotyped « call » (resp. « send ») from a class *dep* to a class *indep* indicates that instances of class *dep* may call operations of (resp. send signals to) instances of class *indep*. In particular, the instance of class *dep* knows of the instance of class *indep*. If the arrow points to an interface of *indep*, *dep* may only call the operations or send the signals listed in the corre-sponding interface specification. For example, in Fig. 3.2, Sender may send the signal transmit with argument d to Receiver, but an object accessing Receiver through the interface receiving would only be able to call the operation receive with no arguments, and get a return value of type Data.

As a convention, we distinguish *constant attributes* by underlining the attribute type. We use the further convention that constant attributes are named by their value. Thus we can leave out the explicit assignment of initial values to constant attributes. For example, K : **Keys** specifies a constant of value $K \in$ **Keys**.

3.2.3 Statechart Diagrams

UML statechart diagrams are used to describe state machines, which specify the sequences of states that an entity, such as an object or component, can go through in response to events, together with its responding actions [UML03].

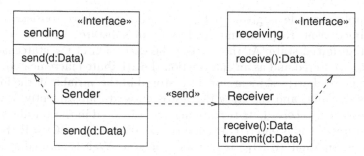

Fig. 3.2. Class diagram

They are derived from the statecharts proposed by Harel [HG97]. They consist of states and transitions between states.

A *state* is "a condition or situation during the life of an object during which it satisfies some condition, performs some activity, or waits for some event" [UML03, p. Glos.-14]. States are indicated by boxes which contain the name of the state. They may contain entry (resp. exit) actions that are executed on entry (resp. exit) of the state. A state may be divided into sequential (resp. concurrent) substates and is then called a *sequential composite state* (resp. a *concurrent composite state*). When a sequential composite state is active, exactly one of its sequential substates is active. When a concurrent state is active, all of its concurrent substates are active. A statechart diagram and its subdiagrams contain each an initial state and may contain one or more final states, denoted by a solid circle and a circle containing a small solid circle, respectively. Final states may not be present in the case of non-terminating behavior, like in Fig. 3.3.

A *transition* with label $e[g]/a$ indicates that an object in the first state will perform the action a and enter the target state when the event e occurs and the *guard* condition g is satisfied, that is, the transition *fires*. The guard can be a logical formula, involving for example equality $=$ and inequality $\neq$ between data expressions and logical connectives such as $\wedge$ (conjunction), $\vee$ (disjunction), $\neg$ (negation), and $\Rightarrow$ (implication). The action could be to call an operation or send a signal, written as $\mathsf{call}(op(args))$ resp. $\mathsf{send}(sig(args))$, or to assign a value to an attribute, written as $att := val$. In the case of an operation call or a signal transmission, the keywords $\mathsf{call()}$ and $\mathsf{send()}$ are usually omitted from the diagram for readability; instead only the operation or signal name and the arguments are given. Generally, the name of a message sent to an object obj has the name obj as a prefix; this may also be omitted if no confusion can arise. Transitions with the same source and target object may be *internal*, which means that they are fired without invoking entry or exit actions and internal activities executed as long as the state is active. The intuition behind internal transitions is that they model a response to an event that does not change the state of an object.

A simple example is given in Fig. 3.3. The statechart consists of three states named Wait, Request, and Send (without substates, actions, or activities) and an initial state. At the start of the execution of the statechart, the Wait state is entered and as an entry action the attribute i incremented. When the message send arrives, its argument is stored in the variable d, the message request is sent out, and the state Request is entered. Subsequently, when the return message is received, its two arguments are stored in the variables K and C and the state Send is entered. Then, if the condition $\mathcal{E}xt_{K_{CA}}(C) = R :: K$ holds, the message transmit($\{d :: i\}_K$) is sent and the state Wait is entered again.[4]

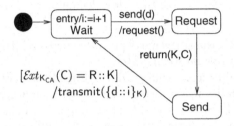

Fig. 3.3. Statechart diagram

3.2.4 Sequence Diagrams

A *sequence diagram* "shows object interactions arranged in time sequence. In particular, it shows the objects participating in the interaction and the sequence of messages exchanged. A sequence diagram can exist in a generic form (describes all possible scenarios) and in an instance form (describes one actual scenario)" [UML03, p. Glos.-13]. Essentially, a sequence diagram specifies interaction among a set of objects or components, the names of which are given in the first line of the diagram. There are vertical lines down from each name, called *life lines*. When the object is active, this is signified by drawing a box rather than a line for that period of time down the sequence diagram. There are arrows, so-called *connections*, with attached messages between the life lines that specify that the attached message is supposed to be sent from the object from whose life-line the arrow emerges to the other object. For readability, the prefix *obj* of the name of a message sent to an object *obj* may be omitted, since it is implicit in the sequence diagram. For each method msg in the diagram and each number n, msg_n represents the nth argument of the operation call msg that was most recently accepted according to the sequence diagram. We do not simply use the expressions appearing as arguments of the messages here, since an adversary may modify the transmitted value. Note

---

[4] Note that the meanings of these cryptographic expressions is irrelevant here but will be explained in Sect. 3.3.3.

that in statechart diagrams this is realized automatically, since the different statecharts have separate namespaces. To increase readability, we allow the definition of syntactic shorthands in the diagram of the form $var ::= exp$ where var is a local variable not used for any other purpose and exp may not contain var. Before assigning a semantics to the diagram, the variable var should be replaced by the expression exp at each occurrence. For example, k is written as a shorthand for the cryptographic expression $\mathbf{fst}(\mathcal{E}xt_{K''}(\mathcal{D}ec_{K_C^{-1}}(c_k)))$ in Fig. 3.4.[5] There may also be conditions associated with arrows, written in square brackets [], which have to be fulfilled when the diagram is executed, otherwise the execution does not proceed at the relevant arrow. Note that the sender or receiver of a message may not be part of the sequence diagram. In that case, the arrows point into or out from the diagram.

An example of a sequence diagram is given in Fig. 3.4. It specifies a security protocol between two permanently active objects, C of class Client and S_i of class Server. The protocol starts with the client C sending the message init with the three arguments N_i, K_C, and $Sign_{K_C^{-1}}(C::K_C)$ to the server S_i. If the condition $\mathbf{snd}(\mathcal{E}xt_{K'}(c_c)) = K'$ is fulfilled, where c_c is a shorthand for init$_3$, the server S_i proceeds by sending the message resp with arguments $\{Sign_{K_S^{-1}}(k_j::N')\}_{K'}$, $Sign_{K_{CA}^{-1}}(S::K_S)$ back to the client C. The client in turn checks the condition on the left hand side of the diagram and, if it holds, finishes the protocol by sending the message xchd back to the server. If any of the conditions are not fulfilled, the execution of the diagram stops at the relevant point. This protocol is explained in more detail in Sect. 5.2.

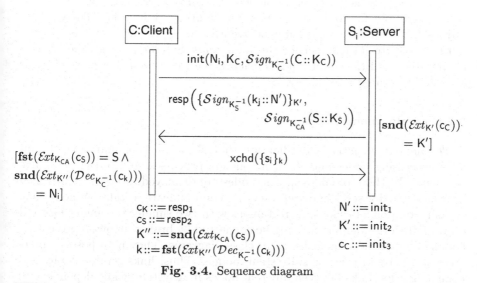

Fig. 3.4. Sequence diagram

<hr />

[5] Again, the meanings of these cryptographic expressions is irrelevant here but will be explained in Sect. 3.3.3.

3.2.5 Activity Diagrams

A UML 1.x *activity diagram* is a special case of a statechart diagram that is used to model processes involving one or more objects or components, whose execution is coordinated by the activity diagram [UML03, p. 3-156].[6] Concurrent composite states are written using *synchronization bars*, such that for each concurrent composite state S, transitions from the initial states of the concurrent substates of S are replaced by transitions from a synchronization bar in the activity diagram, and the lines delineating the concurrent states are omitted. Similarly, transitions to the final states of the concurrent substates of S, where they exist, are replaced by transitions to a synchronization bar.

Activity diagrams can be partitioned into *swimlanes*, each carrying the name of the object and its class, or of the component the behavior of which is modeled by the activities in the swimlane. We assume that the partition is well-defined in the sense that an activity in the swimlane labeled with the component C only accesses the data in C. For readability, we may omit the object name prefixes from attribute names, since they are given as the label of the swimlane.

States in activity diagrams can be of the following kinds. A state without internal activity, internal transitions, exit action, or outgoing non-completion transitions, and with at least one outgoing completion transition, is called an *action state* [UML03, p. 2-171]. A state whose internal activity models the execution of a non-atomic sequence of steps that has some duration is called a *subactivity state* [UML03, p. 2-174]. Action and subactivity states are written as boxes with straight top, and bottom, and convex arcs as sides.

An example for an activity diagram in given in Fig. 3.5. There, three objects C, L and I are executed concurrently. For C, the activity c is iterated until the counter nt has reached the value *limit*. Similarly, for L , the activity l is iterated until the counter n has reached the value *limit*. For I, the activity i is simply iterated indefinitely.

3.2.6 Deployment Diagrams

A *deployment diagram* is a "diagram that shows the configuration of run-time processing nodes and the components, processes, and objects that live on them" [UML03, p. Glos.-6]. The nodes are displayed as boxes, which may be connected by solid lines representing communication links. A node may contain components shown as rectangles with two smaller rectangles inserted on the left side. Components may be connected by broken arrows representing communication dependencies, as in class diagrams. They may possess interfaces and contain class or subsystem models. Thus, links represent physical communication links between different nodes in a system, while dependencies describe logical connections between components.

---

[6] See Appendix A for the changes in the upcoming version UML 2.0.

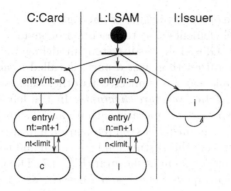

Fig. 3.5. Activity diagram

An example is given in Fig. 3.6. The diagram contains two node instances, client machine and server machine: the node instance client machine contains a component instance client apps with interface get_password, which in turn contains an object browser; the node instance server machine contains a component instance web server, which contains an object access control. The two node instances are connected by a link stereotyped « Internet », and there is a dependency from the web server component to get_password stereotyped « secrecy ». The latter stereotype is already part of the UMLsec extension defined in Sect. 4.1.2. Thus, the web server is specified to be able to communicate with the browser, to request the password, and this is made possible by an Internet connection.

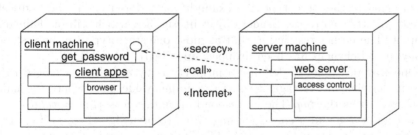

Fig. 3.6. Deployment diagram

3.2.7 Subsystems

A *package* is a notational means of simplifying the presentation of UML diagrams. One can group together parts of a model, represented by diagrams, into a package. Then only the package symbol, and not the represented group of diagrams, has to be shown in the overall diagram.

Here we make use of a specific kind of package called a *subsystem*, which is a "grouping of model elements that represents a behavioral unit in a physical system" [UML03, p. Glos.-15]. A subsystem modeling the complete system under consideration, rather than just a part, is called a *system*. Subsystems can have interfaces and can be connected to other subsystems using dependencies in so-called *static structure diagrams*. In the left upper corner of a subsystem, one can specify the operations that can be called from outside the subsystem. One can distinguish between realization and specification elements in a subsystem; visualizing this distinction is optional and not considered here.

An example for a subsystem is shown in Fig. 3.7. The Channel subsystem instance contains two objects Sender and Receiver, as specified in the class diagram. As the deployment diagram shows, they reside on different node instances. Each has a simple associated statechart diagram specifying its behavior. As specified in the activity diagram, both statecharts are executed concurrently. The Channel subsystem instance offers the operations send and receive to its environment.

3.2.8 UML Extension Mechanisms

UML offers three main "light-weight" language extension mechanisms: stereotypes, tagged values, and constraints [UML03]. We do not consider the "heavy-weight" approach using meta-model extensions here. Stereotypes define new types of modeling elements extending the semantics of existing types or classes in the UML meta-model. Their notation consists of the name of the stereotype written in double angle brackets « », attached to the extended model element. This model element is then interpreted according to the meaning ascribed to the stereotype. An example for a stereotype is the « critical » stereotype attached to the Sender object in Fig. 3.7, which will be defined in Chap. 4. The earlier restriction that at most one stereotype can be assigned to any model element has been dropped since UML 1.4 [UML03].

One way of explicitly defining a property is by attaching a *tagged value* to a model element. A tagged value is a name–value pair, where the name is referred to as the *tag*. The corresponding notation is {*tag* = *value*} with the tag name *tag* and a corresponding *value* to be assigned to the tag. Tags can define either data values, so-called DataTags, or references to other model elements, so-called ReferenceTags. If the value is of type Boolean, one usually omits {*tag* = *false*}, and writes {*tag*} instead of {*tag* = *true*}. An example for a tagged value is the {secrecy} tag with value the set {d} associated with the « critical » stereotype attached to the Sender object in Fig. 3.7.

Another way of adding information to a model element is by attaching *constraints*. These constraints have to be fulfilled by the relevant diagram part. As an example, the « data security » stereotype in Fig. 3.7 has an associated constraint defined in Chap. 4.

Stereotypes can be used to attach tagged values and constraints as pseudo-attributes of the stereotyped model elements. They are called pseudo-

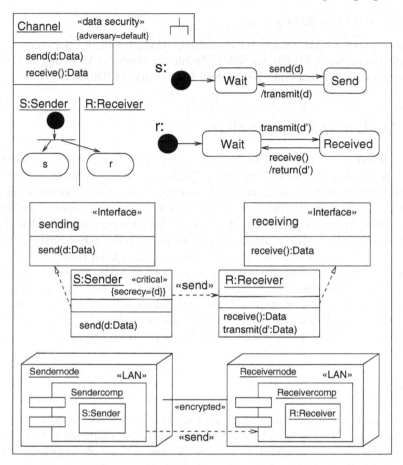

Fig. 3.7. Subsystem

attributes because their semantics is outside the scope of the UML definition. All model elements labeled by a particular stereotype receive the corresponding values and constraints in addition to the attributes, associations, and superclasses that the element has in the standard UML. This usage is new from UML 1.4 [UML03].

To construct an extension of the UML one collects the relevant definitions of stereotypes, tagged values, and constraints into a *profile* [UML03], which is a stereotyped package (alternatively, [CKM+99] suggests the use of so-called *prefaces*). A profile:

- identifies a subset of the UML meta-model,
- gives "well-formedness rules", that is a set of constraints, for this subset,
- gives a semantics in natural language beyond that given by the identified subset, and

- lists common model elements.

Examples for UML extensions include the UML Profile for Software Development Processes [UML03], the UML Profile for Business Modeling [UML03], and extensions for real-time [SR98] and frameworks [FPR00].

3.3 Analyzing UML Models

In the definition of the UMLsec profile, we need to formulate constraints on the UML models that model security requirements that can be rather subtle. To check them mechanically, one needs to refer to an analyzable model of the behavioral semantics of the used fragment of UML. In this section, we define and explain those properties of such a model which we need for formalizing the constraints in the UMLsec profile. For security analysis, the security-relevant information from the security-oriented stereotypes is then incorporated. The complete behavioral semantics of the fragment of UML we use is given in Chap. 8, based on the UML Machines introduced in Chap. 7, together with more explanation and examples. That later chapter is intended for readers interested in building sophisticated tool support for UML themselves; for those mainly interested in using UMLsec, the information in the present section is sufficient.

3.3.1 Notation

We assume the usual definitions from elementary set theory and logic, which may be found for example in [AGM00], including the following definitions.

$\mathbb{N}$ is the set of non-negative integers. $\mathbb{N}_n$ the set of non-negative integers up to and including n, for any $n \in \mathbb{N}$. $\mathcal{P}(X)$ is the set of subsets of a set X.

Given a sequence (or list) $l = (l_1, l_2, l_3, \ldots)$, we write **head**$(l)$ for its *head* l_1 and **tail**(l) for its *tail* $(l_2, l_3, \ldots)$. We write $[\,]$ for the empty list, in particular for the empty string.

A *multi-set* (or *bag*) is a set which may contain multiple copies of an element, with notation $\{\!\{\ \}\!\}$ instead of the usual brackets. For example, $\{\!\{1, 1, 1, 1, 1, 1, 1, 1, 1, 1\}\!\}$ is the multi-set consisting of ten copies of the element 1. For two multi-sets M and N, $M \uplus N$ denotes their union and $M \setminus N$ the subtraction of N from M. For a multi-set M and a set X, we write $M \backslash\!\backslash X$ for the multi-set of those elements in M, preserving their cardinalities, that are also elements of X. Intuitively, in $M \backslash\!\backslash X$, all elements except those in X are filtered out. We write $M \subseteq N$ for two multi-sets M, N if $M \backslash\!\backslash N = M$. We write $\lfloor M \rfloor$ for the set of elements in the multi-set M and $\sharp M$ for the number of elements in M.

3.3.2 Outline of Formal Semantics

In UML, both objects and system components can communicate by exchanging messages from a given set **Events**. The arrival of such a message is called an *event*. They consist of the message name from a given set **MsgNm**, and possibly arguments to the message. Message names may be prefixed with object or subsystem instance names from a given set **UMNames**. The arguments are assumed to be elements of a given set **Exp** of expressions. An example for such a set is defined in Sect. 3.3.3. Each object or component may receive messages in an input queue and release messages to an output queue. Thus in our model, every object or subsystem instance O has associated multi-sets inQu_O, called the input queue, and outQu_O, called the output queue.[7] Our formal semantics models sending a message $msg = op(exp_1, \ldots, exp_n) \in \textbf{Events}$ from an object or subsystem instance S to an object or subsystem instance R as follows:

(1) S places the message $R.msg$ into its multi-set outQu_S.
(2) A scheduler distributes the messages from output queues to the intended input queues, while removing the message head. In particular, $R.msg$ is removed from outQu_S and msg added to inQu_R.
(3) R removes msg from its input queue and processes its content.

In the case of operation calls, we also need to keep track of the sender to allow sending return signals. This way of modeling communication allows for a very flexible treatment. For example, we can modify the behavior of the scheduler to take account of knowledge on the underlying communication layer. This allows us to consider security issues in Sect. 3.3.4, but also other aspects, such as ordering or delay of messages.

At the level of single objects, behavior is modeled using statecharts or sequence diagrams. The internal activities contained as states of these statecharts can, for example, be defined using statecharts or sequence diagrams.

Using subsystems, one can then define the behavior of a system component C by including the behavior of each of the objects or components directly contained in C, and by including an activity diagram that coordinates the respective activities of the various components and objects.

Thus for each object or component C of a given system, our semantics defines a so-called *UML machine* $[\![C]\!]$, which is a state machine that communicates with its environment using messages.

Specifically, the behavioral semantics $[\![D]\!]$ of a statechart diagram D models the run-to-completion semantics of UML statecharts. As a special case, this gives us the semantics for activity diagrams. Any sequence diagram S gives us the behavior $[\![S.C]\!]$ of each contained component C.

Subsystems group together diagrams describing different parts of a system: a system component C given by a subsystem S may contain subcomponents

---

[7] We use multi-sets rather than sets, because several copies of the same message can be received concurrently.

$C_1, \ldots, C_n$. These subcomponents may communicate through the communication links in the corresponding deployment diagram. On the semantical level, each link has a corresponding *link queue* storing the messages that are exchanged along the link while in transit. The behavioral interpretation $[\![S]\!]$ of S is a UML Machine defined as follows:

(1) It takes a multi-set of input events.
(2) The events are distributed from the input multi-set and the link queues connecting the subcomponents and given as arguments to the functions defining the behavior of the intended recipients in S.
(3) The output messages from these functions are distributed to the link queues of the links connecting the sender of a message to the receiver, or given as the output from $[\![S]\!]$ when the receiver is not part of S.

When performing security analysis, after the last step, the adversary model may modify the contents of the link queues in a certain way explained in Sect. 3.3.4.

An *execution* of a UML subsystem S is then a sequence of states and the associated multi-sets of input and output messages of $[\![S]\!]$. In general, UML specifications may be non-deterministic, for example because several transitions in a statechart diagram may be able to fire at a given point in time. A subsystem $\mathcal{T}$ is a *black-box refinement* of a subsystem S if every observable input/output behavior of $\mathcal{T}$ is also an input/output behavior of S. $\mathcal{T}$ is a *delayed black-box refinement* of S if every observable input/output behavior of $\mathcal{T}$ differs from an input/output behavior of S only in that delays may be introduced.

3.3.3 Modeling Cryptography

We introduce some definitions to be used in modeling cryptographic data in a UML specification and its security analysis.

We assume a set **Keys** with a partial injective map $(\ )^{-1} : \textbf{Keys} \to \textbf{Keys}$. The elements in its domain, which may be public, can be used for encryption and for verifying signatures. Those in its range, usually assumed to be secret, are used for decryption and signing. We assume that every key is either an encryption or decryption key, or both: any key k satisfying $k^{-1} = k$ is called *symmetric*; the others are called *asymmetric*. We assume that the numbers of symmetric and asymmetric keys are both infinite. We fix infinite sets **Var** of *variables* and **Data** of *data values*. We assume that **Keys**, **Var**, and **Data** are mutually disjoint and that the set **Data** contains the names: **UMNames** $\cup$ **MsgNm** $\subseteq$ **Data**. **Data** may also include *nonces*, introduced in Sect. 3.1, and other secrets.

We recall that a term algebra generated by a set of elements and operations is the set of terms formed by applying the operations to the elements. A quotient of a term algebra under a given set of equations is derived from the term algebra by imposing these equations, and those that can be derived from them, on the terms. Then the *algebra of cryptographic expressions* **Exp** is the quotient of the term algebra generated from the set **Var** ∪ **Keys** ∪ **Data** with the operations:

- $\_ :: \_$ (concatenation)
- **head**$(\_)$ and **tail**$(\_)$ (head and tail of a concatenation)
- $\{\_\}\_$ (encryption)
- $\mathcal{D}ec\_(\_)$ (decryption)
- $\mathcal{S}ign\_(\_)$ (signing)
- $\mathcal{E}xt\_(\_)$ (extracting from signature)
- $\mathcal{H}ash(\_)$ (hashing)

by factoring out the equations:

- $\mathcal{D}ec_{K^{-1}}(\{E\}_K) = E$ (for all $E \in$ **Exp** and $K \in$ **Keys**)
- $\mathcal{E}xt_K(\mathcal{S}ign_{K^{-1}}(E)) = E$ (for all $E \in$ **Exp** and $K \in$ **Keys**)
- and the usual laws regarding concatenation, **head**(), and **tail**():
  - $(E_1 :: E_2) :: E_3 = E_1 :: (E_2 :: E_3)$ (for all $E_1, E_2, E_3 \in$ **Exp**)
  - **head**$(E_1 :: E_2) = E_1$ (for all expressions $E_1, E_2 \in$ **Exp**) and
  - **tail**$(E_1 :: E_2) = E_2$ (for all expressions $E_1, E_2 \in$ **Exp** such that there exist no E, E' with $E_1 = E :: E'$). For all other cases, **head**() and **tail**() are undefined.

For each $E \in$ **Exp**, we use the following abbreviations:

- **fst**$(E) \stackrel{\text{def}}{=}$ **head**(E)
- **snd**$(E) \stackrel{\text{def}}{=}$ **head**(**tail**(E))
- **thd**$(E) \stackrel{\text{def}}{=}$ **head**(**tail**(**tail**(E))).

We use this abstract model of cryptographic algorithms which abstracts away the details on the level of bit sequences, in order to keep the mechanical analysis feasible. This symbolic model for cryptographic operations, following an established approach initiated by [DY83], implies that we assume cryptography to be perfect, in the sense that an adversary cannot "guess" an encrypted value without knowing the decryption key. In particular, we assume that symmetric encryption is implemented in a way that provides data integrity, for example using Message Authentication Codes (MACs) [MvOV96], since "encryption without integrity-checking is all but useless" [Bel98]. Also, we assume that one can detect whether the correct key is used for decryption. See for example [AJ01] for a formal discussion of these assumptions.

Note also that our model captures the fact that security-critical data such as keys and nonces are usually assumed to be *independent*: This means that no equations should hold between them from which an adversary could derive information, such as $K = K' + 1$ for two different keys $K, K' \in$ **Keys**. This follows from the fact that the algebra of expressions is the quotient of a free algebra under the equations given above, in particular, only equations that follow from these equations hold in **Exp**.

Based on this formalization of cryptographic operations, important conditions on security-critical data (such as freshness, secrecy, integrity, and authenticity) can then be formulated at the level of UML diagrams in a mathematically precise way, explained in Sect. 4.1.

In the following, we will often consider *subalgebras* of **Exp**. These are subsets of **Exp** which are closed under the operations used to define **Exp**, such as concatenation, encryption, decryption, etc.. For each subset E of **Exp** there exists a unique smallest **Exp**-subalgebra $\langle E \rangle$ containing E, which we call **Exp**-*subalgebra generated by* E. Intuitively, it can be constructed from E by iteratively adding all elements in **Exp** reachable by applying the operations used to define **Exp** above. It can be seen as the knowledge one can obtain from a given set E of data by iteratively applying publicly available operations to it and will be used to model the knowledge an attacker may gain from a set E of data obtained for example by eavesdropping on Internet connections.

3.3.4 Security Analysis of UML Diagrams

In this section, we explain the security analysis machinery underlying the UMLsec approach as far as needed in the first half of this book. More details needed for the second half will be given in Sect. 7.5.

Our modular UML semantics allows a rather natural modeling of potential adversary behavior. We can model specific types of adversaries that can attack different parts of the system in a specified way. For example, an attacker of type *insider* may be able to intercept the communication links in a company-wide local area network. We model the actual behavior of the adversary by defining a class of UML Machines that can access the communication links of the system in a specified way. To evaluate the security of the system with respect to the given type of adversary, we consider the joint execution of the system with any UML Machine in this class. This way of reasoning allows an intuitive formulation of many security properties. Since the actual verification is rather indirect this way, we also give alternative intrinsic ways of defining security properties below, which are more manageable, and show that they are equivalent to the earlier ones.

Thus for a security analysis of a UML subsystem specification, we need to model potential adversary behavior. It should be possible to model specific types of adversaries that can attack different parts of the system in a specified way. For this, we firstly define the set of *abstract threats* {delete, read, insert, access} arising from a specification of the physical layer of a system. Following the discussion of possible adversary actions in Sect. 3.1, the delete, read, and insert threats mean that an adversary may delete, read or insert messages on a communication link, respectively. The access threat represents the possibility that an adversary may directly access a physical system node. We then assume a function $\mathsf{Threats}_A(s)$ which takes an *adversary type* A and a stereotype s and returns a subset of {delete, read, insert, access}. In the context of UML, these functions arise from the specification of the physical layer of the system under consideration using deployment diagrams, as explained in Sect. 4.1. The idea is thus that $\text{Threats}_A(s)$ specifies the *threat scenario* associated with an adversary type A against a component or link stereotyped s. On the one hand, the threat scenario determines, which data the adversary can obtain by *accessing* components; on the other hand, it determines, which actions the adversary is permitted by the threat scenario to apply to the concerned links. From the abstract threats we derive the more basic *concrete threats* used for modeling and analyzing the possible adversary behavior. This is done by, firstly, requiring that an adversary needs to have access to the system part to be attacked. For example, to attack a wireless network, the adversary needs to be in physical proximity. Secondly then, the access threat with respect to a node contained in this system part is broken down to the atomic actions delete, read, and insert with respect to the communication links connected to these nodes: If an adversary can access a node, this means that he may delete, read or insert messages on the communication links connected to this node. For a link or node x in a deployment diagram in a UML subsystem specification $\mathcal{S}$, we thus define the set $\text{threats}_A^{\mathcal{S}}(x)$ of concrete threats from adversaries of type A to be the smallest set satisfying the following conditions.

If each node n containing x carries a stereotype s_n with access $\in$ $\text{Threats}_A(s_n)$ then:[8]

- For every stereotype s attached to x, we have $\text{Threats}_A(s) \subseteq \text{threats}_A^{\mathcal{S}}(x)$.
- If x is a link connected to a node that carries a stereotype t with access $\in$ $\text{Threats}_A(t)$ then $\{\text{delete}, \text{read}, \text{insert}\} \subseteq \text{threats}_A^{\mathcal{S}}(x)$.

Then we model the actual behavior of an adversary *adv* of type A as a *type A adversary machine*. Essentially, this is a UML Machine which has the following data, where we give a slightly simplified account sufficient to define the UMLsec notation and semantics:[9]

- A set of *states* State with a control state control $\in$ State.
- A set of *current adversary knowledge* $\mathcal{K}_A \subseteq \mathbf{Exp}$.
- For each possible control state $c \in$ State and set of knowledge $K \subseteq \mathbf{Exp}$, we have:
  - a set $\text{Delete}_{c,K}$ which may contain the name of any link l with delete $\in$ $\text{threats}_A^{\mathcal{S}}(l)$,
  - a set $\text{Insert}_{c,K}$ which may contain any pair (l, E) where l is the name of a link with insert $\in \text{threats}_A^{\mathcal{S}}(l)$, and $E \in \mathcal{K}$, and
  - a set $\text{newState}_{c,k} \subseteq$ State of states.

The machine is executed iteratively from a specified initial state control := control^0 with an *initial adversary knowledge* $\mathcal{K} := \mathcal{K}_A^0$ defined below, where each iteration proceeds according to the following steps:

---

[8] Recall from Sections 3.2.6 and 3.2.7 that nodes and subsystems may be nested one in another.

[9] Readers interested in constructing sophisticated tool support for UML themselves can find the complete technical details in Sect. 7.5.

(1) The contents of all link queues belonging to a link l with read $\in$ threats$_A^S(l)$ are added to $\mathcal{K}$.
(2) The content of any link queue belonging to a link $l \in$ Delete$_{\text{control},\mathcal{K}}$ is mapped to $\emptyset$.
(3) The content of any link queue belonging to a link l is enlarged with all expressions E where $(l, E) \in$ Insert$_{\text{control},\mathcal{K}}$.
(4) The next control state is chosen non-deterministically from the set newState$_{\text{control},\mathcal{K}}$.

The set $\mathcal{K}_A^0$ of *initial knowledge* of an adversary of type A is defined to be the algebra of expressions generated by the sets $\mathcal{K}_A^a$ and $\mathcal{K}_A^p$. Here, the set $\mathcal{K}_A^a$ of *accessible knowledge* contains all data values v given in the UML specification under consideration for which each node n containing v carries a stereotype s_n with access $\in$ Threats$_A(s_n)$. In a given situation, the set $\mathcal{K}_A^p$ of *previous knowledge* can be used to give the adversary access to additional data supposed to be known before start of the execution of the system, such as public keys.

Note that an adversary A able to remove all values sent over the link l, represented by delete$_l \in$ threats$_A^S(l)$, may not be able to selectively remove a value e with known meaning from l. For example, the messages sent over the Internet within a virtual private network are encrypted. Thus, an adversary who is unable to break the encryption may be able to delete all messages indiscriminately, but not a single message whose meaning would be known to the adversary.

For each UML subsystem $\mathcal{S}$ and each adversary A, there exists a *most general adversary machine*, also simply called *the* type A adversary machine. It is the type A adversary machine with the maximal amount of non-determinism in each of its states. Instead of reasoning with respect to all type A adversary machines, it is sufficient to just consider the most general adversary machine, which is often a simplification, and we will usually do this in the following.

To evaluate the security of the system with respect to the given type of adversary, we then define the *execution of the subsystem $\mathcal{S}$ in the presence of an adversary of type A* as the UML Machine $[\![\mathcal{S}]\!]_A$ by extending the definition of $[\![\mathcal{S}]\!]$ from Sect. 3.3.2 with a fourth step (4) as follows:

(1) A multi-set of input events is received.
(2) The events are distributed to the subcomponents.
(3) The output messages from the subcomponents are distributed.
(4) The most general type A adversary machine is applied to the link queues as detailed above.

Thus after each iteration of the system execution, the adversary may non-deterministically change the contents of link queues in a way depending on the level of physical security described in the deployment diagram, as explained in Sect. 4.1.

A subsystem $\mathcal{T}$ is a *black-box refinement in presence of an adversary* of type A of a subsystem $\mathcal{S}$ if every observable input/output behavior of an execution of $\mathcal{T}$ in the presence of an adversary of type A is also an input/output behavior of an execution of $\mathcal{S}$ in the presence of an adversary of type A. $\mathcal{T}$ is a *delayed black-box refinement in presence of an adversary* of type A of $\mathcal{S}$ if $\mathcal{T}$ is a *black-box refinement in presence of an adversary* of type A of a subsystem $\mathcal{S}$, except that delays may be introduced in $\mathcal{T}$.

3.3.5 Important Security Properties

One possibility to specify security requirements is to, firstly, define an idealized system model where the required security property evidently holds. For example, all links and components may be guaranteed to be secure by the physical layer specified in the deployment diagram. Secondly, one would prove that the system model under consideration is behaviorally equivalent to the idealized one, using a notion of behavioral equivalence of UML models. This is explained in detail in Sect. 5.1.

In this subsection, we consider an alternative way of specifying the important security properties of secrecy, integrity, authenticity, and freshness which do not require one to explicitly construct such an idealized system and which are used in the remaining parts of this book. We follow the standard approach of [DY83] which defines security requirements in an intuitive way by incorporating the attacker model. We also explain how to define secure information flow requirements.

Secrecy

The formalization of *secrecy* used in the following relies on the idea that a system specification preserves the secrecy of a piece of data d if the system never sends out any information from which d could be derived by the adversary in interaction with the system. More precisely, d is leaked if there is an adversary of a given adversary type that does not initially know d and an input sequence to the system such that after the execution of the system given the input in presence of the adversary, the adversary knows d, as defined in Sect. 3.3.4. Otherwise, d is said to be kept secret.

Thus we come to the following definition.

Definition 3.1. *We say that a UML subsystem $\mathcal{S}$ preserves the secrecy of an expression E from adversaries of type A if E does not appear in the knowledge set $\mathcal{K}$ of A during any execution of $[\![\mathcal{S}]\!]_A$.*

$\mathcal{S}$ preserves the secrecy of a variable v from adversaries of type A if for every expression E which is a value of the variable v at any point, $\mathcal{S}$ preserves the secrecy of E from adversaries of type A.

Note that, by construction of the adversary knowledge in Sect. 3.3.4, this definition takes into account the fact that the adversary may break up expressions to access a secret subexpression.

This definition is especially convenient to verify if one can give an upper bound for the set of knowledge K, which is often possible when the security-relevant part of the specification of the system S is given as a sequence of commands of the form *await event e – check condition g – output event e'*. For example, this is the case when using UML sequence diagrams or statecharts for the system behavior.

Note that this formalization of secrecy is relatively "coarse" in that it may not prevent implicit information flow, but it is comparatively easy to verify and seems to be sufficient in practice [Aba00]. Also, it fits well with our formalization of cryptographic operations in Sect. 3.3.3: The encryption operations are modeled as deterministic, given a fixed key and a fixed plaintext. Although the basic algorithms for many cryptographic operations, such as RSA, are in fact deterministic, they are usually randomized when implemented in practice, for example by adding extra random data to the plaintext before encrypting it, the so-called "salt" [GB99]. This is done to prevent a guessing attack where an adversary simply encrypts all possible plaintexts with the public encryption key and compares the result to the given ciphertext, which is possible if the set of possible plaintexts is small. In our formalization of cryptographic operations and adversary knowledge, we can abstract from this randomization: Those values that are required to be secret are assumed not to be contained in the adversary knowledge at the start of the system execution, so the adversary cannot use them in the guessing attack mentioned above. For values which are commonly known, but for which it should remain secret whether they are contained in a given encrypted message, one can define a new symbol in **Data** which represents this value in this message. For example, the Boolean value *true* could be represented by PIN_correct in a particular system context, if this is what *true* should signify there.

Examples

- The system that sends the expression $\{m\}_K :: K \in \textbf{Exp}$ over an unprotected Internet link does not preserve the secrecy of m or K against attackers eavesdropping on the Internet, but the system that sends $\{m\}_K$ and nothing else does, assuming that it preserves the secrecy of K against attackers eavesdropping on the Internet.
- A system S that receives a key K encrypted with the public key of S over a dedicated communication link and sends back $\{m\}_K$ over the link does not preserve the secrecy of m against attackers eavesdropping on and inserting messages on the link, but does so against attackers that cannot insert messages on the link.

Integrity

The property *integrity* can be formalized similarly: if during the execution of the considered system, a system variable is assigned a value different from the ones it is supposed to be, then the adversary must have caused this variable to contain the value. In that sense the integrity of the variable is violated. Thus we say that a system preserves the integrity of a variable if there is no adversary such that at some point during the execution of the system in presence of the adversary, the variable has a value different from the ones it should have.

Definition 3.2. *Given a set $E \subseteq$ **Exp** of acceptable expressions, we say that a subsystem S preserves the integrity of an attribute a with respect to E from adversaries of type A with initial knowledge $\mathcal{K}^0$ if during any execution of $[\![S]\!]_A$, at any point the attribute a is undefined or evaluates to an element of E. If $E = $ **Exp** $\setminus \mathcal{K}^0$, we simply say that S preserves the integrity of an attribute a from adversaries of type A with initial knowledge $\mathcal{K}^0$.*

Intuitively, this notion is "dual" to that of secrecy, in the sense that secrecy prevents the flow of information from protected sources to untrusted recipients, while integrity prevents the flow of information in the other direction. Again, it is a relatively simple definition, which may, however, not prevent implicit flows of information. For systems or system parts where, at a given point during the development, nothing is known about the values that a should have, one can still use the above definition by setting $E = $ **Exp** $\setminus \mathcal{K}^0$, where $\mathcal{K}^0$ is the initial knowledge of the adversary. Then no adversary can make a take on a value initially known to the adversary, which offers a certain degree of protection, since in many situations, if the adversary can violate the integrity of an attribute at all, he could in fact make it contain an arbitrary value.

Authenticity

To formalize *message authenticity*, we note that a message has its origin at a system part if during any execution of the system, the message appears at first at that part. To provide authenticity then means to secure the information on the message origin.

Definition 3.3. *Suppose we are given attributes a and o in a subsystem S, where o is supposed to store the origin of the message stored in a. We say that S provides (message) authenticity of the attribute a with respect to its origin o from adversaries of type A with initial knowledge $\mathcal{K}^0$ if during any execution of $[\![S]\!]_A$, at any point the value of the attribute a appeared as a subexpression first within the execution in outQu_o, of all output queues and link queues in S.*

Note that message authenticity is closely related to data integrity [MvOV96, p. 359], [Gol03c]. For example, if messages are communicated via a medium under control of an adversary, data integrity necessitates message authenticity: If the adversary can remove a message from the communication medium and instead insert a different message successfully purporting to originate with the sender of the earlier message, thus breaking data integrity, message authenticity is violated. Differently expressed, to establish for message authenticity the origin of a specific message, it must actually be the message message that originated at the sender, which is only guarantueed where we have data integrity. Thus, message authenticity implies data integrity. If, however, the identity of the sender of a message is part of the message, integrity of the message implies the possibility to authenticate the sender. In this situation, data integrity implies message authenticity.

This observation can be made more precise.

Fact 3.4. *Suppose we are given attributes a and o in a subsystem S, where o is supposed to store the origin of the message stored in a. If S provides (message) authenticity of the attribute a with respect to its origin o from adversaries of type A with initial knowledge $\mathcal{K}^0$, and the origin o is not under control of the adversary, then S preserves the integrity of a from adversaries of type A with initial knowledge $\mathcal{K}^0$.*

The proof of this fact is immediate from the definitions. Note that, as in the statement of this fact, one may need an additional assumption regarding the integrity of the origin o, if this is not a constant within S, because checking authenticity with respect to an identity without verifying integrity of that identity may provide little security.

Note also that the converse of the above fact does not hold since the integrity of a message may be provided although the receipient does not know its first origin. In a sense, integrity amounts to authencity with respect to a non-specified part of the system under consideration.

For more discussions on the relation between message authenticity and data integrity see [Gol03c]. Also, contrary to secrecy, integrity, and message authenticity, the formalization of other kinds of authenticity (such as entity authenticity) seems to be more application-dependent. We therefore do not give a universal definition here, but refer for example to [Gol96, Gol03b] for formalizations of different authenticity properties.

Freshness

Note that freshness of a value may mean the following two properties:[10]

Unpredictability: An attacker cannot guess what its value was.
Newness: The value has never appeared before during the execution of the system.

---

[10] Following a written communication by Gavin Lowe.

Both aspects can be considered with our approach: Unpredictability of *data* is captured by considering a type A of adversary that does not include *data* in its set of previous knowledge $\mathcal{K}_A^p$, defined in Sect. 3.3.4. Freshness in the sense of newness requires an additional definition.

Definition 3.5. *An atomic value data* $\in$ **Data** $\cup$ **Keys** *in a subsystem* S *is fresh within a subsystem instance or object* $\mathcal{D}$ *contained in* S *if the value data appears in the specification* S *only in diagram parts specifying* $\mathcal{D}$, *which are called the* scope *of data in* S.

By the restrictions in Definition 3.5, we only consider freshness of atomic data $d \in$ **Data** $\cup$ **Keys**, not of compound expressions or variables. Note that, as mentioned in Sect. 3.3.3, different elements of **Data** $\cup$ **Keys** are independent. This is why it is sufficient to require of fresh values that they do not appear in the specification outside their scope, as in the above definition.

This definition implies that a value *data* that is fresh within a subsystem instance or object $\mathcal{D}$ in a subsystem S appears as a subexpression in the trace of messages exchanged within S only *after* it has been sent out by $\mathcal{D}$ as a message argument. See Sect. 7.5.5 for a formal argument supporting the last two observations.

Secure Information Flow

We explain an alternative way of specifying secrecy- and integrity-like requirements, which gives protection also against partial flow of information, but can be more difficult to deal with, especially when handling with encryption.

For this definition, one needs to assign to each piece of system data one of two security levels: *high*, meaning highly sensitive or highly trusted, and *low*, meaning less sensitive or less trusted, as explained in Sect. 3.1. The notion is defined by referring to the sequences of input and output values received and generated by the system, using the UML Machine $[\![S]\!]_A$ defined in Sect. 3.3.4.

Given a set of messages H and a sequence **m** of event multi-sets, we write:

- $\mathbf{m}^H$ for the sequence of event multi-sets derived from those in **m** by deleting all events the message names of which are *not* in H, and
- $\mathbf{m}_H$ for the sequence of event multi-sets derived from those in **m** by deleting all events the message names of which *are* in H.

Definition 3.6. *Given a subsystem* S *and a set of* high *messages* H, *we say that:*

- *A prevents down-flow with respect to H if for any two sequences* $\mathbf{i}, \mathbf{j}$ *of event multi-sets and any two output sequences* $\mathbf{o} \in [\![S]\!]_A(\mathbf{i})$ *and* $\mathbf{p} \in [\![S]\!]_A(\mathbf{j})$, $\mathbf{i}_H = \mathbf{j}_H$ *implies* $\mathbf{o}_H = \mathbf{p}_H$ *and*
- *A prevents up-flow with respect to H if for any two sequences* $\mathbf{i}, \mathbf{j}$ *of event multi-sets and any two output sequences* $\mathbf{o} \in [\![S]\!]_A(\mathbf{i})$ *and* $\mathbf{p} \in [\![S]\!]_A(\mathbf{j})$, $\mathbf{i}^H = \mathbf{j}^H$ *implies* $\mathbf{o}^H = \mathbf{p}^H$.

Intuitively, to prevent down-flow means that outputting a *non-high* (or *low*) message does not depend on *high* inputs. This can be seen as a rather stringent secrecy requirement for messages marked as high. Conversely, to prevent up-flow means that outputting a *high* value does not depend on *low* inputs. This can be seen as a stringent integrity requirement for messages marked as high.

This notion of *secure information flow* is a generalization of the original notion of *non-interference* for deterministic systems in [GM82] to system models that are non-deterministic because of underspecification, see [Jür02f] for a more detailed discussion.

Part II

Developing Secure Systems

4

Model-based Security Engineering with UML

In this chapter, we present the extension UMLsec of UML which allows one to express security-related information within the diagrams in a UML system specification. The extension is given in form of a UML profile using the standard UML extension mechanisms. *Stereotypes* are used together with *tags* to formulate security requirements and assumptions on the system environment; *constraints* give criteria that determine whether the requirements are met by the system design, by referring to the execution semantics. These constraints can be checked automatically using the tool support presented in Chap. 6.

We list requirements on a UML extension for secure systems development and discuss how far our extension meets these requirements. The details of the extension are explained by means of examples. We demonstrate the usefulness of the extension for enforcing established rules of secure systems design and indicate with an example how one could use UMLsec in order to apply security patterns.

4.1 UMLsec Profile

For UMLsec, we give validation rules that evaluate a model with respect to listed security requirements, which were introduced in Sect. 3.1. Many security requirements are formulated regarding the behavior of a system in interaction with its environment, in particular, with potential adversaries. To verify these requirements, we use the execution semantics defined in Sect. 3.3.

4.1.1 Requirements on a UML Extension for Development of Security-Critical Systems

We formulate what we consider the necessary properties of an UML extension for secure systems development. Following the format of the OMG Requests for Proposals (RFPs) we distinguish mandatory and optional requirements.

Mandatory Requirements

The following are the main mandatory requirements:

Security requirements: One needs to be able to formulate basic security requirements such as secrecy, integrity, and authenticity of data in a precise way.

Threat scenarios: It should be possible to consider various situations that give rise to different possibilities of attacks.

Security concepts: One should be able to employ important security concepts, such as *tamper-resistant hardware.*

Security mechanisms: One needs to be able to incorporate security mechanisms such as access control and security protocols.

Security primitives: On a more fine-grained level, one needs to model security primitives such as symmetric and asymmetric encryption.

Underlying physical security: It is necessary to take into account the level of security provided by the underlying physical layer.

Security management: Security management questions, such as secure workflow, need to be addressed.

Optional Requirements

It would be very useful to include domain-specific security knowledge, for example, on Java, smart cards, CORBA, etc..

Note that the goal of the extension is not to aim for completeness by including all kinds of security properties as primitives. Instead, we focus on those that have a comparatively intuitive and universally applicable formalization, such as secrecy, integrity, and message authentication. Other properties, such as entity authenticity, have meanings that depend more on the context of their specific use. The idea is that these could be added by more sophisticated users on-the-fly.

4.1.2 The Extension

We give the profile following the structure in [UML03]:

Applicable Subset: The profile concerns all of UML.

Stereotypes, Tagged Values, and Constraints: In Fig. 4.1 we give the list of stereotypes from UMLsec, together with their tags and constraints, following the notation used in [UML03, p. 3-59]. The stereotypes do not have parents. Fig. 4.2 gives the corresponding tags, which are all DataTags. Although the concepts discussed here apply both to the type and the instance level, for simplicity we stay on the instance level in the following. In particular by "subsystem" we mean, more precisely, "subsystem instance".

Prerequisite Profiles: UMLsec requires no prerequisite profiles.

Stereotype	Base Class	Tags	Constraints	Description
fair exchange	subsystem	start, stop, adversary	after start eventually reach stop	enforce fair exchange
provable	subsystem	action, cert, adversary	action is non-deniable	non-repudiation requirement
rbac	subsystem	protected, role, right	only permitted activities executed	enforces role-based access control
Internet	link			Internet connection
encrypted	link			encrypted connection
LAN	link, node			LAN connection
wire	link			wire
smart card	node			smart card node
POS device	node			POS device
issuer node	node			issuer node
secrecy	dependency			assumes secrecy
integrity	dependency			assumes integrity
high	dependency			high sensitivity
critical	object, subsystem	secrecy, integrity, authenticity, high, fresh		critical object
secure links	subsystem	adversary	dependency security matched by links	enforces secure communication links
secure dependency	subsystem		«call», «send» respect data security	structural interaction data security
data security	subsystem	adversary, integ., auth.	provides secrecy, integrity, authenticity, freshness	basic data security requirements
no down-flow	subsystem		prevents down-flow	information flow condition
no up-flow	subsystem		prevents up-flow	information flow condition
guarded access	subsystem		guarded objects accessed through guards	access control using guard objects
guarded	object	guard		guarded object

Fig. 4.1. UMLsec stereotypes

Tag	Stereotype	Type	Multip.	Description
start	fair exchange	state	*	start states
stop	fair exchange	state	*	stop states
adversary	fair exchange	adversary model	1	adversary type
action	provable	state	*	provable action
cert	provable	expression	*	certificate
adversary	provable	adversary model	*	adversary type
protected	rbac	state	*	protected resources
role	rbac	(actor, role)	*	assign role to actor
right	rbac	(role, right)	*	assign right to role
secrecy	critical	data	*	secrecy of data
integrity	critical	(variable, expression)	*	integrity of data
authenticity	critical	(data, origin)	*	authenticity of data
high	critical	message	*	high-level message
fresh	critical	data	*	fresh data
adversary	secure links	adversary model	1	adversary type
adversary	data security	adversary model	1	adversary type
integrity	data security	(variable, expression)	*	integrity of data
authenticity	data security	(data, origin)	*	authenticity of data
guard	guarded	object name	1	guard object

Fig. 4.2. UMLsec tags

Well-formedness Rules

We explain the stereotypes and tags given in Figures 4.1 and 4.2. The constraints use the security-aware interpretation of UML diagrams, defined in Sect. 3.3. Some of them, such as « fair exchange », « provable », « secure links », and « data security », are parameterized over the adversary type with respect to which the security requirements should hold. These stereotypes have an associated {adversary} tag, which may have values of the form (T, C). T is the adversary type, such as $T = default$ for the adversary defined in Fig. 4.6, which may also be self-defined. C is a logical condition on the previous knowledge $\mathcal{K}_A^p$ of the adversary as defined in Sect. 3.3.4. If the type is omitted, this is interpreted as the adversary type $T = default$. If the condition is omitted, we assume the condition C that ensures that data included in the {secrecy} tag of the « critical » stereotype defined below does not appear as subexpressions in $\mathcal{K}_A^p$. For the tag multiplicities in Fig. 4.2, a * represents an arbitrary multiplicity of the tag in a given diagram.

The constraints associated with the stereotypes give a range from structural syntactic conditions, such as « secure links », to relatively deep semantic conditions, such as « no down-flow ». This has the advantage that in an analysis of a system one may start out with the simpler structural conditions, and remove violations against them, before constructing and analyzing the behavioral part of the specification, for which automated mechanical verification is

also available, as presented in Chap. 6. This approach seems to be more efficient than trying to establish the overall security all at once. In an industrial
setting, it also allows a scaling of the necessary costs.

We give short examples for usage of the stereotypes. To keep the presentation concise, we sometimes give only those fragments of subsystems that are
essential to the stereotype in question. Also, we omit proving the stated properties formally, since the examples are just for illustration. More substantial
case-studies for performing security analyses with UMLsec can be found in
Chap. 5.

fair exchange (for use case diagrams)

Intuitively, this stereotype represents the security requirement that any transaction should be performed in a way that prevents both parties from cheating.
When applied to a subsystem containing a use case diagram, it requires that
this subsystem can be refined by another subsystem only if that is also stereotyped « fair exchange ». Note that this usage of the « fair exchange » stereotype
has only an informal meaning, as opposed to the stereotypes below. In particular, "refinement" is meant here in an informal sense. It just serves as an
example how the security requirements included as stereotypes in the other
kinds of diagrams below can also conveniently be included in use case diagrams.

Example The use case diagram in Fig. 4.3 describes the following situation:
a customer buys a good from a shop in a way that is supposed to ensure « fair exchange ». The diagram can be refined to the activity diagram
in Fig. 4.4, because the latter is also stereotyped « fair exchange ». For activity diagrams, the stereotype has a more specific constraint associated, as
explained below.

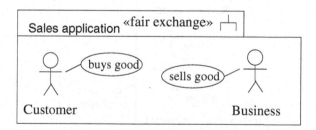

Fig. 4.3. Use case diagram for business application

fair exchange (for activity diagrams)

This stereotype, when applied to subsystems containing an activity diagram,
has associated tags {start}, {stop}, and {adversary}. The tags {start} and

{stop} take pairs (*good*, *state*) as values, where *good* is the name of a good
to be sold and *state* is the name of a state. If there is only one good to be
sold in a given system specification, the value *good* can be omitted. The tag
{adversary} specifies an adversary type relative to which the security requirement should hold. The associated constraint requires that, for every good to
be sold, whenever a {start} state in the contained activity diagram is reached,
then eventually a {stop} state will be reached, when the system is executed in
presence of an adversary of the type A specified in the tag {adversary}. This
is formalized for a given subsystem S as follows. S fulfills the constraint of
«fair exchange» with respect to an adversary type A if for every good to be
sold the following condition holds: For every execution **e** of $[\![S]\!]_A$ there exists
a number $n \in \mathbb{N}$ such that for every sequence $I_1, \ldots, I_n$ of input multi-sets
there exists an execution **e'** which is an extension of **e** and then processes the
inputs in $I_1, \ldots, I_n$, such that there are at least as many {stop} states in **e'**
as there are {start} states in **e**, with respect to the relevant good.

Note that this requirement cannot be ensured for systems which an attacker can stop completely.

Example Figure 4.4 gives a subsystem instance describing the following situation: a customer buys a good from a business. Here the adversary type is
omitted because it is not relevant, since no communication structure is specified. The semantics of the stereotype «fair exchange» is, intuitively, that the
actions listed in the tags {start} and {stop} should be linked in the sense that
if one of the former is executed then eventually one of the latter will be.

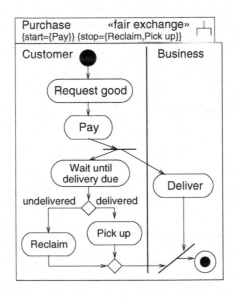

Fig. 4.4. Purchase activity diagram

This would entail that, once the customer has paid, either the order is delivered to the customer by the due date, or the customer is able to reclaim the payment on that date. To avoid illegitimate repayment claims, one could employ the stereotype « provable » with regard to the state Pay, in order to make sure that the Reclaim payment action checks whether the Customer can provide proof of payment.

provable

A subsystem S may be labeled « provable » with associated tags {action}, {cert}, and {adversary}. The tag {cert} contains an expression which serves as proof that the action at the state given in the tag {action} was performed. The tag {adversary} specifies an adversary type relative to which the security requirement should hold. The stereotype « provable » then specifies that S may output the expression $E \in \mathbf{Exp}$ given in {cert} only after the state with name in {action} is reached, when executed in presence of an adversary of the type A that is specified in the tag {adversary}. Here the certificate in {cert} is assumed to be unique for each subsystem instance. More formally, S fulfills the constraint if the following holds for the adversary type A: For every execution $\mathbf{e}$ of $[\![S]\!]_A$, if the expression in {cert} is given as output at a state S in $\mathbf{e}$, the state specified by {action} appears as a current state before S in $\mathbf{e}$.

rbac

This stereotype of subsystems containing an activity diagram enforces *role-based access control* in the business process specified in the activity diagram. It has associated tags {protected}, {role}, and {right}. The tag {protected} has as its values the states in the activity diagram the access to whose activities should be controled. The {role} tag may have as its value a list of pairs (*actor*, *role*) where *actor* is an actor in the activity diagram, and *role* is a role. The tag {right} has as its value a list of pairs (*role*, *right*) where *role* is a role and *right* represents the right to access a protected resource. The associated constraint requires that the actors in the activity diagram only perform activities for which they have the appropriate rights. For a subsystem S, this is formalized as follows: For every actor A in S and every activity a in the swim-lane of A in the activity diagram in S, there exists a role R such that (A, R) is a value of {role} and (R, a) is a value of {right}.

Example Figure 4.5 gives a subsystem instance for an example of the use of role-based access control. It describes a simplified part of a business process where a credit is being set up for a customer of a bank. Usually, there are bank employees who have the right to set up credits. In the case of large credits, their supervisors have to authorize the credit before the money is transferred. For the sake of the example, we assume that the threshold is at 10,000 of the given currency. In the example given, the protected resource is thus the *authorize credit* activity, to which the supervisor in her role of *credit approver* has the appropriate permission, so the diagram is correctly labeled «rbac» because the associated constraint is respected.

Incidentally, this example is an instance of the security principle of *separation of privilege* explained in Sect. 4.2. Note that one also needs to make sure that a given employee is not assigned two roles with associated privileges that are supposed to be separated, for example as a vacation substitute, as explained in Sect. 6.3. How to link access control to the level of the technical security architecture is demonstrated using the stereotype «guarded access» introduced below.

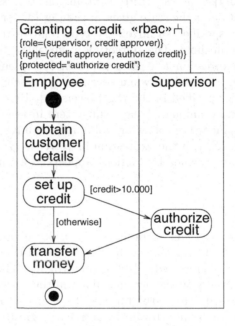

Fig. 4.5. Role-based access control example

Internet, encrypted, LAN, wire, smart card, POS device, issuer node

These stereotypes on links (resp. nodes) in deployment diagrams denote the respective kinds of communication links (resp. system nodes). We require that each link or node carries at most one of these stereotypes. For each adversary type A, we have a function $\text{Threats}_A(s)$ from each stereotype

$$s \in \{\text{«wire»}, \text{«encrypted»}, \text{«LAN»}, \text{«smart card»},$$
$$\text{«POS device»}, \text{«issuer node»}, \text{«Internet»}\}$$

to a set of strings $\text{Threats}_A(s) \subseteq \{\text{delete}, \text{read}, \text{insert}, \text{access}\}$ under the following conditions:

- for a node stereotype s, we have $\mathsf{Threats}_A(s) \subseteq \{\mathsf{access}\}$, and
- for a link stereotype s, we have $\mathsf{Threats}_A(s) \subseteq \{\mathsf{delete}, \mathsf{read}, \mathsf{insert}\}$.

Thus $\mathsf{Threats}_A(s)$ specifies which kinds of actions an adversary of type A can apply to nodes or links stereotyped s. The meanings of the actions are explained in Sect. 3.3.4. Given a UML subsystem $\mathcal{S}$, the function $\mathsf{Threats}_A(s)$ gives rise to a function $\mathsf{threats}_A^A(x)$ that takes a node or link x and a type of adversary A and returns a set of strings $\mathsf{threats}_A^A(x) \subseteq \{\mathsf{delete}, \mathsf{read}, \mathsf{insert}, \mathsf{access}\}$, as defined in Sect. 3.3.4. This way we can evaluate UML subsystems using their execution semantics in Sect. 3.3.2, by referring to the security framework using UML Machine Systems in Sect. 3.3.4. We make use of this for the constraints of the remaining stereotypes of the profile.

Examples for threat sets associated with some common adversary types are given in Figures 4.6 and 4.7.

Figure 4.6 gives the *default* attacker, which represents an outsider adversary with modest capability. This kind of attacker is able to read, delete, and insert messages on an Internet link. On an encrypted Internet link, such as a virtual private network, the attacker might still be able to delete messages, without knowing their encrypted content, by bringing down a network server. However, an average adversary would not be able to read the plaintext messages or insert messages encrypted with the right key. Of course, this assumes that the encryption is set up in a way such that the adversary does not get hold of the secret key. The default attacker is assumed not to have direct access to the local area network (LAN) and therefore not to be able to eavesdrop on those connections,[1] nor on wires connecting security-critical devices (for example, a smart card reader and a display in a point-of-sales (POS) device, as in the case-study in Sect. 5.3). Also, smart cards are assumed to be tamper-resistant against default attackers, although they may not be against more sophisticated attackers [AK96]. Also, the default attacker is assumed not to be able to access POS devices or card issuer systems.

Stereotype	$\mathsf{Threats}_{default}()$
Internet	$\{\mathsf{delete}, \mathsf{read}, \mathsf{insert}\}$
encrypted	$\{\mathsf{delete}\}$
LAN	$\emptyset$
wire	$\emptyset$
smart card	$\emptyset$
POS device	$\emptyset$
issuer node	$\emptyset$

Fig. 4.6. Threats from the *default* attacker

---

[1] With more sophistication, even an external adversary may be able to access local connections, but this is assumed to be beyond "default" capabilities.

Stereotype	Threats$_{insider}()$
Internet	{delete, read, insert}
encrypted	{delete, read, insert}
LAN	{delete, read, insert}
wire	{delete, read, insert}
smart card	$\emptyset$
POS device	$\emptyset$
issuer node	{access}

Fig. 4.7. Threats from the insider attacker *card issuer*

Figure 4.7 defines the *insider* attacker, in the context of the electronic purse system considered in Sect. 5.3. As an insider, the attacker may access the encrypted Internet link, knowing the corresponding key, and the local system components.

secrecy, integrity, high

These stereotypes, which may label dependencies in static structure or component diagrams, denote dependencies that are supposed to provide the respective security requirement for the data that is sent along them as arguments or return values of operations or signals. These stereotypes are used in the constraint for the stereotype « secure links ».

critical

This stereotype labels objects or subsystem instances containing data that is critical in some way, which is specified in more detail using the corresponding tags. These tags are {secrecy}, {integrity}, {authenticity}, {fresh}, and {high}, representing the corresponding security requirements which were introduced in Sections 3.1 and 3.3. The values of the tag {secrecy} are the names of expressions, attributes or message argument variables of the current object the secrecy of which is supposed to be protected. One may also give the name of an operation to require that its arguments and return values should be kept secret. The {integrity} tag has as values pairs (v, E) where v is a variable of the object whose integrity should be protected and E is the set of acceptable expressions that may be assigned to v. The values of the tag {authenticity} are pairs (a, o) of attributes of the « critical » object or subsystem where a stores the data whose authenticity should be provided and o stores the origin of that data. The tag {fresh} has as its values atomic data (that is, elements of the set **Data∪Keys**) that should be freshly generated. These constraints are enforced by the constraint of the stereotype « data security » which labels subsystems that contain « critical » objects, as explained below. The tag {high} has as its values the names of messages that are supposed to be protected with respect to secure information flow, as enforced by the stereotypes « no down-flow » and « no up-flow ». For synchronous operations, the return messages are also required to be protected.

The following stereotypes « secure links », « secure dependencies », and « data security », together with the associated stereotypes « secrecy », « integrity », « high », and « critical » introduced above, describe different conditions for ensuring secure data communication: « secure links » ensures that the security requirements on the communication dependencies between components are supported by the physical situation, relative to the adversary model under consideration. The stereotype « secure dependencies » ensures that the security requirements in different parts of a static structure diagram are consistent. Finally, « data security » ensures that security is enforced on the behavior level. One could for example merge the conditions of « secure links » and « secure dependencies » to give one stereotype. We keep them separate to support the design process suggested above, where one would like to establish security properties as early during the design as possible, before continuing with the next design step.

secure links

This stereotype, which may label subsystems, is used to ensure that security requirements on the communication are met by the physical layer, given the adversary type A that is specified in the tag {adversary} associated with this stereotype. More precisely, when attached to a UML subsystem $\mathcal{S}$, the constraint enforces that for each dependency d with stereotype $s \in \{$« secrecy », « integrity », « high »$\}$ between subsystems or objects on different nodes n, m, we have a communication link l between n and m such that:

- in the case of $s = $ « high », we have $\mathsf{threats}_A^{\mathcal{S}}(l) = \emptyset$,
- in the case of $s = $ « secrecy », we have $\mathsf{read} \notin \mathsf{threats}_A^{\mathcal{S}}(l)$, and
- in the case of $s = $ « integrity », we have $\mathsf{insert} \notin \mathsf{threats}_A^{\mathcal{S}}(l)$.

Example We give an example concerning communication link security in Fig. 4.8. Given the default adversary type as defined in Fig. 4.6, the constraint for the stereotype « secure links » is violated. The model does not provide communication secrecy against the *default* adversary, because the Internet communication link between web server and client does not provide the needed security level according to the $\mathsf{Threats}_{\mathsf{default}}(\mathsf{Internet})$ scenario. Intuitively, the reason is that Internet connections do not provide secrecy against default adversaries. Technically, the constraint is violated because the dependency carries the stereotype « secrecy », but for the stereotype « Internet » of the corresponding link we have $\mathsf{read} \in \mathsf{Threats}_{\mathsf{default}}(\mathsf{Internet})$.

secure dependency

This stereotype, used to label subsystems containing static structure diagrams, ensures that the « call » and « send » dependencies between objects

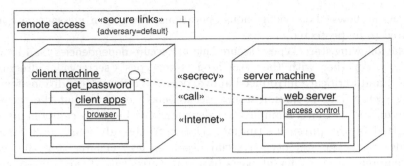

Fig. 4.8. Example *secure links* usage

or subsystems respect the security requirements on the data that may be communicated across them, as given by the tags {secrecy}, {integrity}, and {high} of the stereotype « critical ». More exactly, the constraint enforced by this stereotype is that if there is a « call » or « send » dependency from an object or subsystem C to an interface I of an object or subsystem D then the following conditions are fulfilled:

- For any message name n in I, n appears in the tag {secrecy} (resp. {integrity} resp. {high}) in C if and only if it does so in D.
- If a message name in I appears in the tag {secrecy} (resp. {integrity} resp. {high}) in C then the dependency is stereotyped « secrecy » (resp. « integrity » resp. « high »).

If the dependency goes directly to another object or subsystem without involving an interface, the same requirement applies to the trivial interface containing all messages of the server object.

Example Figure 4.9 shows a key generation subsystem instance with the requirement « secure dependency ». The given specification violates the constraint for this stereotype, since Random generator and the « call » dependency do not provide the security level for the message random required by Key generator. More precisely, the constraint is violated: The message random is required to be of high level by Key generator by the tag {high} in Key generator, but it is not guaranteed to be high level by Random generator. In fact, there are no high messages in Random generator and so the tag {high} is missing.

data security

This stereotype labeling subsystems has the following constraint. The behavior of any subsystem S stereotyped « data security » respects the data security requirements given by the stereotypes « critical » and the associated tags contained in the subsystem, with respect to the threat scenario arising from the

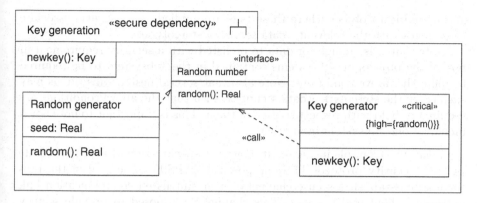

Fig. 4.9. Key generation subsystem instance

deployment diagram and given the adversary type A that is specified in the tag {adversary} associated with this stereotype.

More precisely, the constraint is given by the following four conditions, which use the concepts of secrecy, integrity, authenticity, and freshness defined in Sect. 3.3:

secrecy: The subsystem preserves the secrecy of the data designated by the tag {secrecy} against adversaries of type A.

integrity: Given a tag {integrity} of « critical » with a value (v, E), the subsystem preserves the integrity of the variable v against adversaries of type A, with respect to the sets E of admissible expressions. If the second component E is omitted in the tag {integrity}, the integrity of v should be preserved with respect to the set of expressions that can be constructed from those appearing in the specification of the subsystem S. This means that the adversary should not be able to make the variable v take on a value previously known only to him.

authenticity: For any value (a, o) of the tag {authenticity}, the subsystem provides the authenticity of the attribute a with respect to its origin o against adversaries of type A.

freshness: Within the subsystem S stereotyped « data security », any value $data \in \mathbf{Data} \cup \mathbf{Keys}$ which is tagged {fresh} in the relevant subsystem instance or object $\mathcal{D}$ stereotyped « critical » in S should be fresh in $\mathcal{D}$.

In each case, the initial knowledge of the adversary defined in Sect. 3.3.4 is assumed not to contain the data values that according to the tags of the stereotype « critical » should be guaranteed secrecy, integrity or authenticity: These requirements cannot be achieved if the adversary already knows this data initially. Further assumptions on the initial adversary knowledge can be specified. In case the admissible expressions or the intended origin of data in the {integrity} and {authenticity} tags refer to expressions not locally known

at the «critical» object where these tags are applied, one can also associate
these tages with the relevant «data security» stereotype.

Note that it is enough for data to be listed with a security requirement in
one of the objects or subsystems contained in the subsystem to be required
to fulfill the above conditions. Note also that several nested subsystems may
each carry the stereotype «data security», such that the above conditions are
required to hold with respect to each of them. This is important to note when
including one subsystem in another.

Example The example in Fig. 4.10 shows the specification of a variant of the
Internet security protocol TLS[2] proposed in [APS99]. The goal of the protocol is to establish a secure channel over an untrusted communication link
between a client and a server. This channel is supposed to provide secrecy
and server authenticity, as specified by the {secrecy} and {authenticity} tags.
To achieve this goal, some of the local attributes have to satisfy {integrity} as
well, here in the sense that the adversary should not be able to make these
attributes take on a value in his previous knowledge. The protocol proceeds
as follows: The client initiates the protocol by sending a self-signed certificate
to the server. The sender returns the encrypted session key together with the
certificate $Sign_{K_{CA}^{-1}}(\mathsf{S} :: \mathsf{K_S})$ certifying authenticity of the server public key.
The client finally sends the secret encrypted under the session key. As defined
in Sect. 3.3.3, $\{M\}_K$ is the encryption of the message M with the key K,
$Sign_K(M)$ is the signature of the message M with K, and :: denotes concatenation. Also, $\mathcal{D}ec_K(C)$ is the decryption of the ciphertext C using K and
$\mathcal{E}xt_K(S)$ is the extraction of the data from the signature using K. We recall
that for each method msg in the diagram and each number n, msg_n represents
the nth argument of the operation call msg that was most recently accepted
according to the sequence diagram. Also, we use the notation $\mathsf{S_-}$ to represent
all values S_x, for each x, when specifying data types or security tags, and
similarly for $\mathsf{s_-}$, $\mathsf{N_-}$ etc..

One can now analyze the specification with respect to the default adversary
type using the UMLsec tool support introduced in Chap. 6. In this example,
the default adversary has access to the Internet link between the two nodes
only. It then turns out that the specification violates the constraint of its
stereotype «data security» that the values s_i are kept secret. More details on
the security analysis and how to fix the protocol are given in Sect. 5.2.

Note that in our approach, the properties of secrecy, integrity, and authenticity are taken relative to the considered type of adversary. In case of
the default adversary, this is a principal external to the system; one may, however, consider adversaries that are part of the system under consideration, by
giving the adversary access to the relevant system components. This can be
done by defining $\mathsf{Threats}_A(s)$ to contain access for the relevant stereotype s.
For example, in an e-commerce protocol involving customer, merchant, and

---

[2] TLS (Transport Layer Security) is the current version of the Internet security
protocol SSL (Secure Sockets Layer).

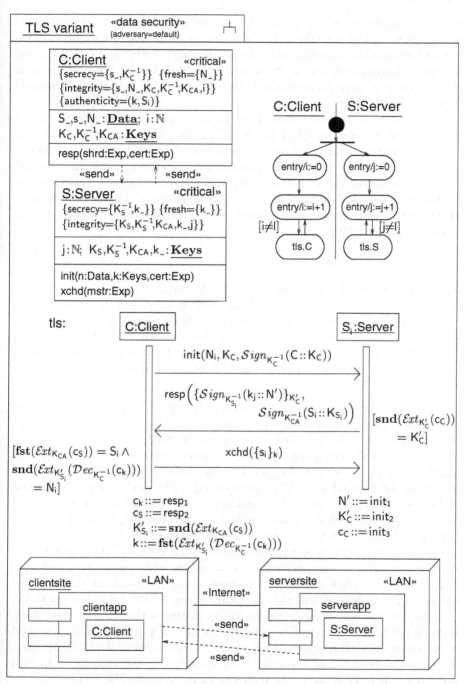

Fig. 4.10. TLS protocol variant

bank, one might want to say that the identity of the goods being purchased is a secret known only to the customer and merchant, and not the bank. This can be formulated by marking the relevant data as "secret" and by performing a security analysis relative to the adversary model "bank". That means that the adversary is given access to the bank component by defining the Threats() function in a suitable way.

Also note that the adversary does not necessarily have access to the input queue of the system. Thus it may be sensible, for example, to apply the {secrecy} tag to a value received by the system from the outside. Of course, the condition associated with the « data security » stereotype only ensures that the component marked with this stereotype keeps the values received by the environment secret. Additionally, one has to make sure that the environment of the system part under consideration does not make these values available to the adversary either.

no down-flow, no up-flow

These stereotypes of subsystems prevents the indirect leakage or corruption of sensitive data: It enforces secure information flow by making use of the tag {high} associated with the stereotype « critical ». More precisely, the constraint for « no down-flow » (resp. « no up-flow ») is that the UML machine **Exec** $[\![S]\!]$ for the subsystem S prevents down-flow (resp. up-flow) with respect to the messages specified in {high} and their return messages, as defined in Sect. 3.3.5.

Example The example in Fig. 4.11 shows the web-based customer account data object from the introductory example in Chap. 2. It allows its secret money attribute to be read using the operation rm(), whose return value is also secret, and written using wm(x). If the money attribute is over 1,000, the object is in a state ExtraService, otherwise in NoExtraService. The state of the object can be queried using the operation rx(). The data object is supposed to be prevented from indirectly leaking out any partial information about high data via non-high data, as specified by the stereotype « no down-flow ». For example for privacy reasons, it may be important that the observable information on the customer account allows no conclusion about the money spent so far. The given specification violates the constraint associated with « no down-flow », since partial information about the input of the high operation wm() is leaked out via the return value of the non-high operation rx(). To see how the underlying formalism captures the security flaw using Definition 3.6, it is sufficient to exhibit sequences $\mathbf{i}, \mathbf{j}$ of input multi-sets and sequences $\mathbf{o} \in [\![A]\!](\mathbf{i})$ and $\mathbf{p} \in [\![A]\!](\mathbf{j})$ of output multi-sets of the UML Machine A giving the behavior of the considered statechart, such that $\mathbf{i}_H = \mathbf{j}_H$ and $\mathbf{o}_H \neq \mathbf{p}_H$, where H is the set of high messages. Consider the sequences

- $\mathbf{i} \stackrel{\text{def}}{=} (\{\!\{ wm(0) \}\!\}, \{\!\{ rx() \}\!\})$ and
- $\mathbf{j} \stackrel{\text{def}}{=} (\{\!\{ wm(0000) \}\!\}, \{\!\{ rx() \}\!\})$.

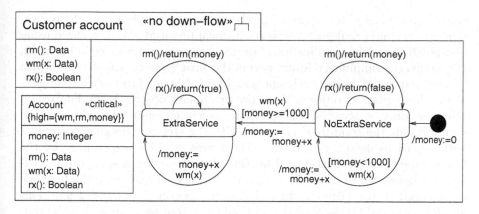

Fig. 4.11. Customer account data object

We have $\mathbf{i}_H = (\{\!\{ \}\!\}, \{\!\{ rx() \}\!\}) = \mathbf{j}_H$. From the definition of the behavioral semantics of statecharts in Sect. 3.3.2, we can see that we have the following output multi-sets:

- $\mathbf{o} \overset{\text{def}}{=} (\{\!\{ \}\!\}, \{\!\{ return(false) \}\!\}) \in [\![A]\!](\imath)$ and
- $\mathbf{p} \overset{\text{def}}{=} (\{\!\{ \}\!\}, \{\!\{ return(true) \}\!\}) \in [\![A]\!](\mathbf{j})$.

But this implies

$$\mathbf{o}_H = (\{\!\{ \}\!\}, \{\!\{ return(false) \}\!\}) \neq (\{\!\{ \}\!\}, \{\!\{ return(true) \}\!\}) = \mathbf{p}_H,$$

meaning that the constraint associated with « **no down-flow** » is violated. Thus the model carries the stereotype illegitimately. Again this can be detected automatically with the tool support provided for UMLsec [JSA+04].

guarded access

This stereotype of subsystems is supposed to mean that each object in the subsystem that is stereotyped « guarded » can only be accessed through the objects specified by the tag {guard} attached to the « guarded » object. An example for this situation is the Java 2 security architecture, as explained in Sect. 5.4. Formally, we assume that we have $name \notin \mathcal{K}_A^p$ for the adversary type A under consideration and each name *name* of an instance of a « guarded » object, meaning that a reference is not publicly available. Also, we assume that for each « guarded » object there is a statechart specification of an object whose name is given in the associated tag {guard}. This way, we model the passing of references. See Sect. 5.4 for more details.

Example We illustrate this stereotype with the example of a web-based financial application. Two institutions offer services over the Internet to local users: an Internet bank, Bankeasy, and a financial advisor, Finance. To make use of these services, a local client needs to grant the applets from the respective sites certain privileges. Access to the local financial data is realized using GuardedObjects. The specification of the local system part is given in Fig. 4.12. It contains the simplified relevant part of the Java Security Architecture which receives requests for object references and forwards them to the guard objects of the three guarded objects. Since the « guarded » objects StoFi, FinEx, and MicSi can only be accessed through their associated guard, the subsystem instance fulfills the condition associated with the stereotype « guarded access » with regard to default adversaries. The access controls are realized by the Guard objects FinGd, ExpGd, and MicGd, whose behavior is specified. For example, applets that are signed by the bank can read and write the financial data stored in the local database, but only between 1 pm and 2 pm. This which is enforced by the FinGd guard object, where we assume that the condition slot is fulfilled if and only if the time is between 1 pm and 2 pm. More details on this example are given in Sect. 5.4.

guarded

This stereotype labels objects in the scope of the stereotype « guarded access » above that are supposed to be guarded, as explained in more detail in Sect. 5.4. It has a tagged value {guard} which defines the name of the corresponding guard object. As an example, in Fig. 4.12, the « guarded » objects StoFi, FinEx, and MicSi are protected by the {guard} objects Guard objects FinGd, ExpGd, and MicGd, respectively.

4.1.3 Addressing the Requirements

We go back to the requirements on an extension of UML for the development of security-critical systems in Sect. 4.1.1 and consider UMLsec in turn with respect to them.

Mandatory Requirements

Security requirements: Formalizations of basic security requirements are provided via stereotypes, such as « secrecy », « integrity », and « authenticity ».

Threat scenarios: Threat scenarios are incorporated using the formal semantics and depending on the modeled underlying physical layer via the sets $\mathsf{Threats}_{adv}(ster)$ of actions available to the adversary of kind adv.

Security concepts: We have shown how to incorporate security concepts such as tamper-resistant hardware using threat scenarios.

Security mechanisms: As an example, in Sect. 5.4 we demonstrate modeling of the Java Security Architecture access control mechanisms.

Security primitives: Security primitives are either built in, such as encryption, or can be treated, such as security protocols.

Underlying physical security: This can be addressed as demonstrated by the stereotype « secure link » in deployment diagrams.

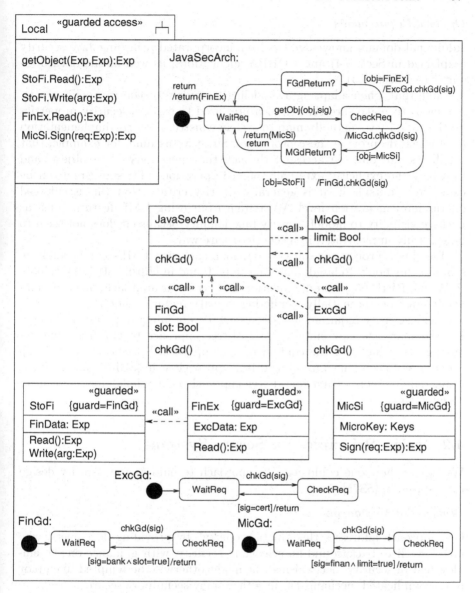

Fig. 4.12. Financial application specification: Local system

Security management: This can be considered in our approach by using activity diagrams, as in Fig. 4.4.

Optional Requirements

Additional domain knowledge has been incorporated regarding Java security (explained in Sect. 5.4) and CORBA applications, as well as smart card security (see Sect. 5.3).

Note that when adapting a modeling language to security requirements, one needs to make sure that the features used to express security properties on the design level actually map to system constructs on the implementation level which do provide these properties. Since we assume, for example, that attributes can only be accessed through the operations of an object, and that only the explicitly externally offered operations of a subsystem can be called from outside it, it is generally security critical that this is enforced on the implementation level. We refrain from using UML features such as package visibility to model security functionality because it does not seem to be generally implemented in a security-aware way.

Defining a process for software development using UMLsec is beyond the scope of this book. Related material can be found in [Jür02j, JPW03, HJ03b, PJWB03, BBH+03]. We only mention that with our approach, one can manage interactions potentially conflicting security requirements in a systematic way. The security requirements are systematically integrated into the design. In particular, one may employ the goal tree approach to non-functional requirements [Chu93] in the context of our approach. Specifically, in [Jür02j] we propose to combine a use-case-driven approach as in [JBR98] for the functional requirements with a goal-driven approach as in [Chu93] for the security requirements.

4.2 Design Principles for Secure Systems

We explain how one could use our approach to enforce the security design rules stated in [SS75].

Economy of Mechanism

Our approach addresses this "meta-property" by providing developers, who may have litte background knowledge in security, with guidance on the employment of security mechanisms who might otherwise be tempted to employ more complicated mechanisms since these may seem more secure.

Fail-safe Defaults

One may verify that a system is fail-safe by showing that certain security-relevant invariants are maintained throughout the execution of the system. In particular, they should hold if the execution is interrupted at some point, possibly due to malicious intent of one of the parties involved. As an example, secure log-keeping for audit control is considered with respect to the unlinked load transaction of the smart-card-based Common Electronic Purse Specifications (CEPS) [CEP01] in Sect. 5.3.2.

Complete Mediation

This principle concerns a strategy for access control where every access is checked. As an example, we show in Sect. 5.4 how to use UMLsec to correctly develop secure Java applications making use of the Java Security Architecture access control mechanisms. With this approach, one can also enforce complete mediation.

More feasibly, one can specify a set of sensitive objects and say that a specification satisfies mediation with respect to these objects if their access is controlled. One may then give a general policy that defines which access restrictions should be enforced.

Open Design

Our approach aims to contribute to the development of a system whose security does not rely on the secrecy of its design.

Separation of Privilege

Separation of privilege gives another strategy for granting access to resources. Again, this can be enforced similarly to the way explained in Sect. 5.4. For example, one can define guard objects that require signatures from two different principals on the applet requesting access to the guarded object.

In this context, a specification satisfies separation of privilege with respect to a certain privilege p if there are two or more principals whose signature is required to be granted p, at every point of the execution.

More generally, one can formulate such requirements on a more abstract level and verify UMLsec specifications with respect to these requirements.

Least Privilege

Given functionality requirements on a system, a system specification satisfies the principle of least privilege if it satisfies these requirements and if every proper diminishing of privileges of the entities in the system leads to a system that does not satisfy the requirements. This has been implemented in the UMLsec tool [JSA+04]. It also includes algorithms that, given functionality requirements, construct the corresponding least privileges for a system.

Least Common Mechanism

Since we follow an object-oriented approach, this principle is automatically enforced in so far as data is encapsulated in objects and the sharing of data between different parts of a system is thus well-defined and can be kept at the minimum of what is necessary.

Psychological Acceptability

With respect to the development process, this principle is addressed by our approach in so far as it aims for ease of use in the development of security-critical systems, and thus for the psychological acceptability of security issues on the side of the developers.

4.3 Applying Security Patterns

There are several conceptual aids for secure systems development using UMLsec. For example, in Chap. 8, we explain how to use tool supported techniques such as refinement and modularity. In this section, we shortly sketch how one could use security patterns in the context of UMLsec.

Patterns [GHJV95] encapsulate the design knowledge of software engineers by presenting recurring design problems and standardized solutions. One can use transformations of UMLsec models to introduce patterns within the design process. A goal of this approach is to ensure that the patterns are introduced in a way that has previously been shown to be useful and correct. Also, having a sound way of introducing patterns using transformations can ease security analysis, since the analysis can be performed on the more abstract and simpler level, and one can derive security properties of the more concrete level, provided that the transformation has been shown to preserve the relevant security properties.

In our approach, the application of a pattern p corresponds to a function f_p which takes a UML specification S and returns a UML specification, namely the one obtained when applying p to S. Technically, such a function can be presented by defining how it should act on certain subsystem instances, and by extending it to all possible UML specifications in a compositional way. Suppose that we have a set S of subsystem instances such that none of the subsystem instances in S is contained in any other subsystem instance in S. Suppose that for every subsystem instance $S \in S$ we are given a subsystem instance $f_p(S)$. Then for any UML specification $\mathcal{U}$, we can define $f_p(\mathcal{U})$ by substituting each occurrence of a subsystem instance $S \in S$ in $\mathcal{U}$ by $f_p(S)$. The challenge then is to define such a function f_p that is applicable as widely as possible. How to do this on a technical level is beyond the scope of this first introduction to UMLsec. Here we just demonstrate the idea by an example.

Consider the problem of communication over untrusted networks, as exemplified in Fig. 4.13. A well-known solution to this problem is to encrypt the traffic over the untrusted link using a key exchange protocol, as demonstrated in Fig. 4.14. A detailed explanation of this pattern is given in Sect. 5.1. The Secure Channel Pattern could thus be formulated intuitively as follows: In a situation such as the one in Fig. 4.13, one can implement the secure channel needed to enforce the security requirements using the system in Fig. 4.14.

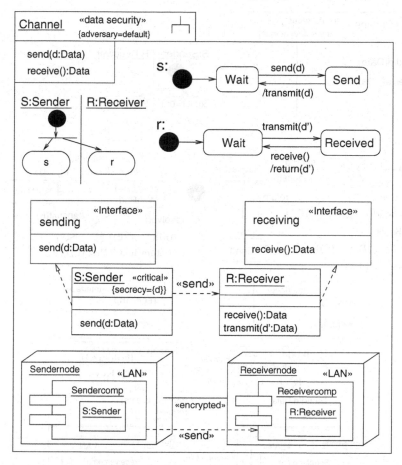

Fig. 4.13. Security pattern example: sender and receiver

To apply this pattern p in a formal way, we consider the set S of subsystems derived from the subsystem in Fig. 4.13 by renaming: This means, we substitute any message, data, state, subsystem instance, node, or component name n by a name m at each occurrence, in a way such that name clashes are avoided. Then f_p maps any subsystem instance $S \in S$ to the subsystem instance derived from that given in Fig. 4.14 by the same renaming. This gives us a presentation of f_p from which the definition of f_p on any UML specification can be derived as indicated above. Since one can show that the subsystem in Fig. 4.14 is secure in a precise sense, as explained in Sect. 5.1, this gives one a convenient way of reusing security engineering knowledge in a well-defined way within the development context.

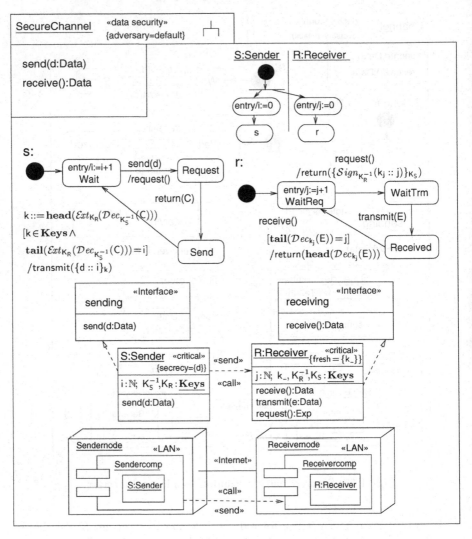

Fig. 4.14. Security pattern example: secure channel

4.4 Notes

Compared to research done using formal methods, less work has been done using software engineering techniques for computer security. Some examples will be presented in Chap. 9.

The basic ideas introduced in this chapter were presented in [Jür01i]. Apart from earlier work on using UML for role-based access control in [FH97], this thus seems to be the first comprehensive and formally based approach to using UML for secure systems development. Since then, interest in secure systems development using UML has quickly grown. An overview on the current lines of work is given in Chap. 9.

In [Jür01e, Jür04c], UMLsec is applied to the security analysis of a smart-card based electronic purse systems. [Jür01h] tailors the methodology to the development of security-critical Java-based systems and [Jür02e] to CORBA-based systems. [Jür01c] presents a business-process centered development, and [JG03] is concerned with applications in the Automotive domain. These applications are explained in detail in Chap. 5, in addition to other applications. A goal-oriented development methodology is presented in [Jür02j]. [Jür01d, Jür02i] explains how to perform security analysis of UMLsec models based on a formal semantics for a suitable fragment of UML. The ideas on how to use UMLsec to enforce established security engineering principles in Sect. 4.2 are taken from [Jür02c]. The material in Sect. 4.3 has been reported in [Jür01j, JPW02]. [PJWB03] defines a use case driven development process with UMLsec and [HJ03b, JH04] explains how to perform model-based risk assessment in the context of UMLsec. UMLsec has been presented in invited conference talks [Jür02b, Jür02g, Jür03c, Jür03g, Jür04d, Jür04f], summer school lectures [Jür04g, Jür04i, Jür05], and a series of tutorials at international conferences [Jür04e]. Other literature on UMLsec will be referred to in the following chapters.

4.5 Discussion

We presented the extension UMLsec of UML for secure systems development, in the form of a UML profile using the standard UML extension mechanisms. Recurring security requirements are written as stereotypes; the associated constraints ensure the security requirements on the level of the formal semantics, by referring to the threat scenario also given as a stereotype. Thus one may evaluate UML specifications to indicate possible vulnerabilities. One can thus verify that the stated security requirements, if fulfilled, enforce a given security policy.

We indicated how one could use UMLsec to model security requirements, threat scenarios, security concepts, security mechanisms, security primitives, underlying physical security, and security management. These are the aspects which were argued to be required for a secure systems extension of UML.

We also considered how UMLsec could be used to encapsulate established rules on prudent security engineering, also by applying security patterns, and thereby to make them available to developers who are not security experts. While UML was developed to model object-oriented systems, one can also use UML and UMLsec to analyze systems that are component-oriented rather than object-oriented, by not making use of OO-specific features and making sure that the underlying assumptions, such as controlled access to data, are ensured.

For defining UMLsec, we made use of experience in the development and analysis of security-critical systems using UML in several industrial projects involving German government agencies and major banks, insurance companies, smart card and car manufacturers, and other companies. Some examples for security designs from these projects will be presented in Chap. 5.

5

Applications

In this chapter, we show how to apply the UMLsec notation in the context of model-based security engineering in several case-studies.

We demonstrate stepwise development of a security-critical system with UMLsec by the example of a secure channel design, together with a formal verification. A flaw is uncovered in a variant of the handshake protocol of the Internet protocol TLS proposed in [APS99], for which we suggest a correction, and verify the corrected protocol.

Next, we apply UMLsec to a security analysis of the Common Electronic Purse Specifications, a candidate for a globally interoperable electronic purse standard. We discover flaws in the two central parts of the specifications (the purchase and the load protocol), propose corrections, and give a verification.

Finally, we show how to use UMLsec to correctly employ advanced Java 2 security concepts such as guarding objects in a way that allows formal verification of the specifications.

These security analyses can be performed using the UMLsec tool support shortly presented in Chap. 6. In addition, the proofs for the statements in this chapter can be found in Appendix C.

5.1 Secure Channels

As an example of the stepwise development of a secure system with UML we give an abstract specification of a secure channel and refine it to a more concrete specification. The abstract specification satisfies secrecy, and by our preservation result the concrete one does as well.

Figure 5.1 gives a high-level system specification in the form of a UML subsystem $\mathcal{C}$ for communication from a sender object to a receiver object, including a class diagram with appropriate interfaces. Note that in this simplified example, which should mainly demonstrate the idea of stepwise development, we are only concerned with fixed participants S and R. Therefore,

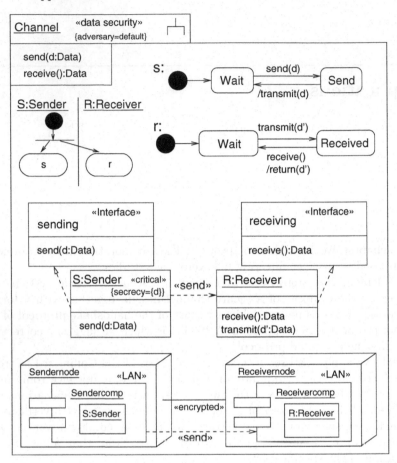

Fig. 5.1. Example subsystem: sender and receiver

authentication is out of scope of our considerations. A more realistic example with a more in-depth security analysis can be found in Sect. 5.2.

In the subsystem, the Sender object is supposed to accept a value in the variable d as an argument of the operation send and send it over the « encrypted » Internet link to the Receiver object, which delivers the value as a return value of the operation receive. To associate the behavioral specifications in the statecharts to their context, we add the names of the relevant states in the activity diagram next to the statecharts. Note that the behavior of the sender could also be specified by a statechart consisting of only one state. The version given here is slightly more readable. According to the stereotype « critical » and the associated tag {secrecy}, the subsystem is supposed to preserve the secrecy of the variable d.

We show that this is actually the case. In fact, we show a result which is slightly stronger than the one stated above, where the adversary is allowed to have some additional initial knowledge, which will be useful in the following.

Proposition 5.1. *The subsystem* $\mathcal{C}$ *preserves the secrecy of the variable* d *from adversaries of type* $A =$ default *with specified previous knowledge* $\mathcal{K}_A^p$, *given inputs from* **Data** $\setminus \mathcal{K}_A^p$.

Note that this statement refers to an idealized model where the adversary is by definition unable to interfere with the protocol. Also, as mentioned above, we consider only fixed participants in this case, so that the intended protocol execution is in fact the only possible one. This is of course not realistic in general, but the aim is to exhibit conditions in the following under which it would be justified to use such an idealized model of a secure channel.

Integrity is not within the scope of the current considerations but holds for both d and d' since the adversary cannot actively interfere with the protocol. Since d' is intended to have the same value as d, secrecy of d' follows from secrecy of d and integrity of d' with respect to the value in d.

Now assume that we would like to replace the abstract requirement that the communication should happen over an encrypted link by a more concrete specification of the encryption mechanism. Thus we construct a refinement $\mathcal{C}'$ as in Fig. 5.2.

Since we only want to demonstrate the principle of developing a secure channel, we assume for simplicity that the sender and receiver already know each other's public keys. The protocol then exchanges a symmetric session key using those public keys, since encryption under symmetric keys is more efficient. Note that the protocol only serves as a simple example, not to propose a new protocol of practical value. We assume that the secret keys belonging to the public ones are kept secure. The session keys k_x, for $x \in \mathbb{N}$, are specified to be created freshly by the receiver before execution of the protocol, as stated by the tag {fresh}. As can be seen from the UML specification, the associated constraint as defined in Sect. 4.1.2 is actually fulfilled: The values k_x belong to the scope of Receiver within the subsystem specification SecureChannel, since expressions of the form k_x, for any subexpression x, only appear within the Receiver object and the associated statechart. For readability, in this chapter we just write k_ : **Data** to denote an array whose fields k_x have the type **Data**.

Recall that we leave out the explicit assignment of initial values to constant attributes and instead take these constants as attribute names, such as the keys in this example. As a convention, we distinguish these constant attributes by underlining the attribute type. Note that the keys and nonces, as different constant symbols in **Keys** $\cup$ **Data**, are mutually distinct by definition of the algebra of expressions in Sect. 3.3.3. Therefore, they are mutually independent in the sense of Definition 7.36 by Fact 7.38, and also independent of the other expressions in the diagram. We use the notation $var ::= exp$ to be able to write an expression exp more shortly as var, as explained in Sect. 3.2.4

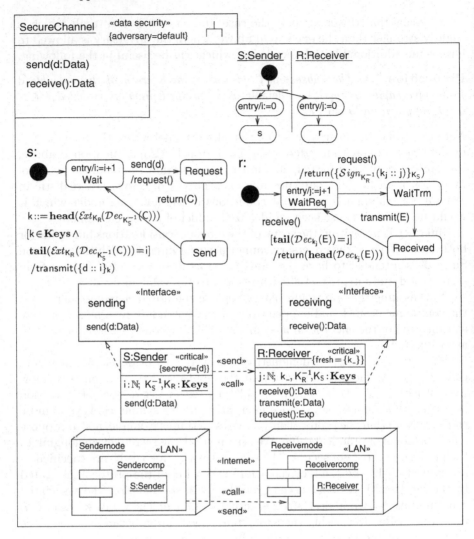

Fig. 5.2. Example subsystem: secure channel

The behavior of the sender thus includes retrieving the signed and encrypted symmetric session key k_j from the receiver, checking the signature, and encrypting the data under the symmetric key. Encryption is done together with a sequence number i, to avoid replay. We assume the natural numbers i, j to be in **Data** here and in the following: $\mathbb{N} \subseteq \mathbf{Data}$. The receiver first gives out the key k_j with a signature and also with a sequence number j, and later decrypts the received data, checking the sequence number.

The core message exchange between sender and receiver is thus as follows:

$$R \to S : \{Sign_{K_R^{-1}}(k_j :: j)\}_{K_S}$$
$$S \to R : \{d :: i\}_{k_j}.$$

We show that $\mathcal{C}'$ is a refinement of $\mathcal{C}$ in the sense of Definition 8.13.

Proposition 5.2. *The subsystem $\mathcal{C}'$ is a delayed black-box refinement of $\mathcal{C}$ in presence of adversaries of type $A =$ default with*

$$\mathcal{K}_A^p \cap (\{K_S^{-1}, K_R^{-1}\} \cup \{k_n, \{x :: n\}_{k_n} : x \in \mathbf{Exp} \land n \in \mathbb{N}\}) = \emptyset$$

and for which $Sign_{K_R^{-1}}(k' :: m) \in \mathcal{K}_A^p$ implies $k' = k_m$ for all $m \in \mathbb{N}$ and $k' \in \mathbf{Exp}$.

The condition in the statement of the above proposition means that the previous adversary knowledge $\mathcal{K}_A^p$ may not contain the secret keys K_S^{-1}, K_R^{-1} of the sender and the receiver, the secret session keys k_n, any encryptions of the form $\{x :: n\}_{k_n}$, and any signatures $Sign_{K_R^{-1}}(k' :: n)$ except for $k' = k_n$. Recall from Sect. 3.3.4 that $\mathcal{K}_A^p$ denotes the knowledge of the adversary before the start of the execution of the system, that is in this case, before the first iteration of the protocol. Thus the condition does not prevent the adversary from remembering information gained from early iterations of the protocol and use it in later iterations. The condition is thus not unrealistic, and it is in fact necessary because if the adversary knows the expression $\{x :: n\}_{k_n}$ before the execution of the protocol which may be different from the expression $\{y :: n\}_{k_n}$ which will be sent out by S in the nth round of the protocol, the adversary could substitute $\{y :: n\}_{k_n}$ with $\{x :: n\}_{k_n}$ without being noticed which would destroy the integrity of the communication channel and then $\mathcal{C}'$ would not be a refinement of $\mathcal{C}$. Note that the sequence number n is necessary to enable the receiver to check that the right session key is used for decryption in the condition $\mathbf{tail}(\mathcal{D}ec_{k_j}(E)) = j$, to prevent replay.

The analysis in the above proposition also covers the possibility that there may be parallel executions of other instances of Client and Server, because these can be simulated by the adversary. The result can be refined to establish a property of "forward security" in the sense that the compromise of a current session key does not necessarily expose future traffic, as defined in [And02]. We omit this here because we only want to demonstrate the basic technique using this example, but refer to Theorem 5.5 for such a result for a different protocol.

Note that $\mathcal{C}'$ is not an undelayed refinement of $\mathcal{C}$, because of the delay caused by the key exchange and possible additional delay caused by the adversary: In $\mathcal{C}$, the shortest output sequence containing a $\mathsf{return}_{\mathsf{receive}}(d)$, after some input $\mathsf{send}(d)$ is $(\emptyset, \emptyset, \emptyset, \{\mathsf{return}_{\mathsf{receive}}(d)\})$, namely in case the adversary does not delete any messages. In $\mathcal{C}'$, it is $(\emptyset, \emptyset, \emptyset, \emptyset, \emptyset, \{\mathsf{return}_{\mathsf{receive}}(d)\})$, because of the key exchange.

As an immediate conclusion of the above proposition, we derive the following result.

Proposition 5.3. *The subsystem* C' *preserves the secrecy of the variable* d *from adversaries of type* $A = $ default *with*

$$\mathcal{K}_A^p \cap (\{K_S^{-1}, K_R^{-1}\} \cup \{k_n, \{x :: n\}_{k_n} : x \in \mathbf{Exp} \wedge n \in \mathbb{N}\}) = \emptyset$$

and for which $Sign_{K_R^{-1}}(k' :: m) \in \mathcal{K}_A^p$ *implies* $k' = k_m$ *for all* $m \in \mathbb{N}$ *and* $k' \in \mathbf{Exp}$.

Thus the specification fulfills the constraints of the stereotype « data security » with respect to the adversary type stated above.

As for Proposition 5.2, this result can be refined to establish a version of "forward security".

5.2 A Variant of the Internet Protocol TLS

We analyze a variant of the handshake part of the Internet security protocol TLS[1] proposed in [APS99]. We uncover a flaw first published in [Jür01g], suggest a correction, and verify it.

The Handshake Protocol

The goal of the protocol whose core is given as a UML subsystem $\mathcal{T}$ in Fig. 5.3 is to establish a secure channel over an untrusted communication link between a client and a server. This channel is supposed to provide secrecy and server authenticity, as specified by the {secrecy} and {authenticity} tags.

We assume that the set of data values **Data** includes names C and S for each instance C : *Client* and S : *Server*. The protocol assumes that each client C is given the server name S_i before the ith execution round of the protocol part under consideration. The server is not given the client name in advace, since no client authenticity is to be provided by the protocol. In our model we restrict ourselves to considering the first I executions of the protocol, where I is an arbitrary but fixed natural number. Note that each C may be given a different sequence of server names. More precisely, these would have to be referred to as C.S_i. We omit the instance prefixing for readability where no confusion can arise. C and S are variables representing arbitrary names. In particular, both client and server can run the protocol with arbitrary servers and clients. Note also that the adversary controls the communication link between client and server. In our model, this is captured by enabling the adversary to read, delete, and insert messages at the corresponding link queue. Therefore, the adversary is able to insert any message communicated over the link in the adversary's current knowledge. In particular, the adversary may also perform the protocol with either the client or the server, by attempting to take on

---

[1] TLS (Transport Layer Security) is the current version of the Internet security protocol SSL (Secure Sockets Layer).

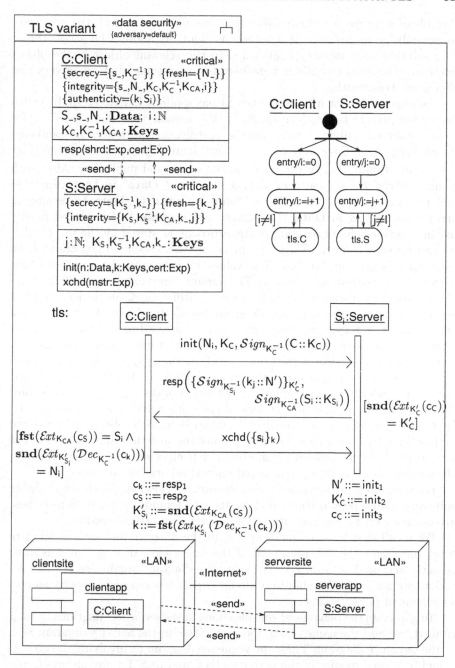

Fig. 5.3. Variant of the TLS handshake protocol

the role of a server or a client. Note that one may also specify the adversary to actually be an instance of a server or client, by adding the **access** threat to a suitable node stereotype attached to the relevant object in the object diagram. This is not consider here because we assume that all servers and clients are trustworthy.

We assume that each C (resp. each S) has a public key K_C (resp. K_S) with associated private key K_C^{-1} (resp. K_S^{-1}). We assume that there is a way for C to obtain the public key K_{CA} of the certification authority guaranteeing its integrity. Also, S securely obtains a certificate $Sign_{K_{CA}^{-1}}(S :: K_S)$ signed by the certification authority that contains its name and public key. Also, each client is given the sequence of secrets $s_1, \ldots, s_l \in \mathbf{Data}^s$ to be transmitted and the nonces $N_1, \ldots, N_l \in \mathbf{Data}$. Again we write $s_\_ : \mathbf{Data}$ to denote an array with fields s_i in **Data**. The nonces are specified to be created freshly by the receiver before execution of the protocol, as stated by the tag {fresh}. As can be seen from the UML specification, the associated constraint from Sect. 4.1.2 is actually fulfilled: The values N_i belong to the scope of Client within the subsystem specification **TLS variant**, since expressions of the form N_x, for any subexpression x, only appear within the Client object and the associated view of the sequence diagram. Similarly, the sequence of session keys $k_1, \ldots, k_l \in \mathbf{Keys}^s$ given to each server is specified to be fresh. Again, for readability, we leave out the explicit assignment of initial values to constant attributes, such as the keys, the nonces, and the values s_x and S_x here. Instead, we take these constants as attribute names. To indicate this, the relevant type names are underlined. Also, again, by definition of the algebra of expressions, the keys and nonces are independent of each other and other expressions by Fact 7.38. The subsystem specification given here could also be instantiated with other initial values for the keys, the nonces, and the values s_x and S_x, as long as the keys and nonces remain distinct from other values. In that sense, the specification can be viewed as parameterized over these values.

For readability we leave out a time-stamp, a session id, the choice of cipher suite and compression method, and the use of a temporary key by Ssince these are not relevant for the security requirements under consideration.

We recall that for each method msg in the diagram and each number n, msg_n represents the nth argument of the operation call msg that was most recently accepted according to the sequence diagram. Again, we use the notation $var ::= exp$ to be able to write an expression exp more shortly as var, as explained in Sect. 3.2.4.

To associate the behavioral specifications in the sequence diagrams to their context, we add the name of the relevant states in the activity diagram next to the sequence diagram. Thus, the sequence diagram tls involving the objects C and S_i is used to specify the activities tls.C and tls.S_i for any objects C and S_i. The sequence diagram is specified with respect to S_i, since this is where C sends its messages, depending on its attribute i. In contrast, the activity diagram is specified with respect to S, because all clients and servers are executed in parallel, independently of the value of i in any of the C. Note that it is well-defined to use a sequence diagram specifying S_i to specify an activity tls.S, because the object S_i in the sequence diagram does not use the parameter i.

The protocol proceeds as follows. We consider the ith execution round $C(i)$ of the client C and the jth execution round $S_i(j)$ of the server S_i and assume that $S_i(j) = S$. That is, in the current execution round i, the instance C aims to communicate with the instance S_i, which is in its jth execution round. The client C initiates the protocol by sending the message $\text{init}(N_i, K_C, Sign_{K_C^{-1}}(C :: K_C))$ to the server S. Suppose that the condition $[\mathbf{snd}(\mathcal{E}xt_{K_C'}(c_C))=K_C']$ holds, where $K_C' ::= \text{init}_2$ and $c_C ::= \text{init}_3$, that is, the key K_C contained in the signature matches the one transmitted in the clear. Then S sends the message $\text{resp}(\{Sign_{K_S^{-1}}(k_j :: N')\}_{K_C'}, Sign_{K_{CA}^{-1}}(S :: K_S))$ back to C, where $N' ::= \text{init}_1$. Now suppose that the condition

$$[\mathbf{fst}(\mathcal{E}xt_{K_{CA}}(c_S))=S \wedge \mathbf{snd}(\mathcal{E}xt_{K_{S_i}'}(\mathcal{D}ec_{K_C^{-1}}(c_k)))=N_i]$$

holds, where $c_S ::= \text{resp}_1$, $c_k ::= \text{resp}_2$, and $K_{S_i}' ::= \mathbf{snd}(\mathcal{E}xt_{K_{CA}}(c_S))$, that is, the certificate is actually for S and the correct nonce is returned. Then C sends $\text{xchd}(\{s_i\}_k)$ to S, where $k ::= \mathbf{fst}(\mathcal{E}xt_{K_{S_i}'}(\mathcal{D}ec_{K_C^{-1}}(c_k)))$. If any of the checks fail, the respective protocol participant stops the execution of the protocol.

In the traditional informal notation already used for example in [NS78], the protocol would be written as follows:

$$C \rightarrow S : N_i, K_C, Sign_{K_C^{-1}}(C :: K_C)$$
$$S \rightarrow C : \{Sign_{K_S^{-1}}(k_j :: N_i)\}_{K_C}, Sign_{K_{CA}^{-1}}(S :: K_S)$$
$$C \rightarrow S : \{s_i\}_{k_j}.$$

This notation may seem simpler than the sequence diagram in Fig. 5.3. However, it needs to be interpreted with care [Aba00]. For example, from the first line, we can conclude that C sends N_i, K_C, $Sign_{K_C^{-1}}(C :: K_C)$ to the network, with intended recipient S, and that S expects a message of the form N, K_1, $Sign_{K_3^{-1}}(X :: K_2)$, seemingly coming from C. If the message is sent over an untrusted network, we cannot conclude for example that $K_1 = K_C$. Therefore, one needs to make assumptions such as that S checks that the three occurrences of K_C do indeed coincide, that is, that $K_1 = K_2 = K_3$ holds. Unfortunately, misinterpretation of protocol specifications is a major source of security weaknesses in practice. Therefore, when using this notation, one should make sure that the above-mentioned assumptions are understood by the implementor of a protocol. Our aim here is to use the UML as a notation that is widely used among software developers beyond the community of security experts, without deviating from its standard definition any more than what may seem necessary. Since the UML sequence diagram semantics does not entail the above-mentioned assumptions, we include them explicitly by referring to sent and received values in different ways and including checks in the sequence diagram to ensure that they actually coincide.

The Flaw

When analyzing the specified protocol for the relevant security requirements using the automated analysis tools presented in Sect. 6.2.1, we observed the following attack.

Theorem 5.4. *For given* C *and* i, *the UML subsystem* $\mathcal{T}$ *given in Fig. 5.3 does not preserve the secrecy of* s_i *from adversaries of type* $A =$ default *with* $\{K_S, K_A, K_A^{-1}\} \subseteq \mathcal{K}_A^p$.

This means that the protocol does not provide its intended security requirement, secrecy of s_i, against a realistic adversary.

The message flow diagram corresponding to this man-in-the-middle attack follows.

$$C \xrightarrow{\quad N_i::K_C::Sign_{K_C^{-1}}(C::K_C) \quad} A \xrightarrow{\quad N_i::K_A::Sign_{K_A^{-1}}(C::K_A) \quad} S$$

$$C \xleftarrow{\quad \{Sign_{K_S^{-1}}(k_j::N_i)\}_{K_C}::Sign_{K_{CA}^{-1}}(S::K_S) \quad} A \xleftarrow{\quad \{Sign_{K_S^{-1}}(k_j::N_i)\}_{K_A}::Sign_{K_{CA}^{-1}}(S::K_S) \quad} S$$

$$C \xrightarrow{\quad \{s_i\}_{k_j} \quad} A \xrightarrow{\quad \{s_i\}_{k_j} \quad} S$$

The authors of [APS99] have been informed about the problem.

The Fix

We propose to change the protocol to get a specification $\mathcal{T}'$ by substituting $k_j :: N_i$ in the message resp by $k_j :: N_i :: K_C$ as in Fig. 5.4, and by including a check regarding this new message part at the client. Here, the public key K_C of C is included representatively for the identity of C. One could also use $k_j :: N_i :: C$ instead.

Again, in traditional informal notation, the modified protocol would be written as follows:

$$C \rightarrow S : N_i, K_C, Sign_{K_C^{-1}}(C :: K_C)$$
$$S \rightarrow C : \{Sign_{K_S^{-1}}(k_j :: N_i :: K_C)\}_{K_C}, Sign_{K_{CA}^{-1}}(S :: K_S)$$
$$C \rightarrow S : \{s_i\}_{k_j}.$$

We explain informally why this modification prevents the attack described in Theorem 5.4. Note that the certificate sent in the first message of the protocol is only a self-signed certificate, which does not provide full client authenticity. Therefore, the adversary can still send a certificate to the server claiming that the public key of the adversary in fact belongs to the client, as in the attack described above. However, when the adversary then forwards the

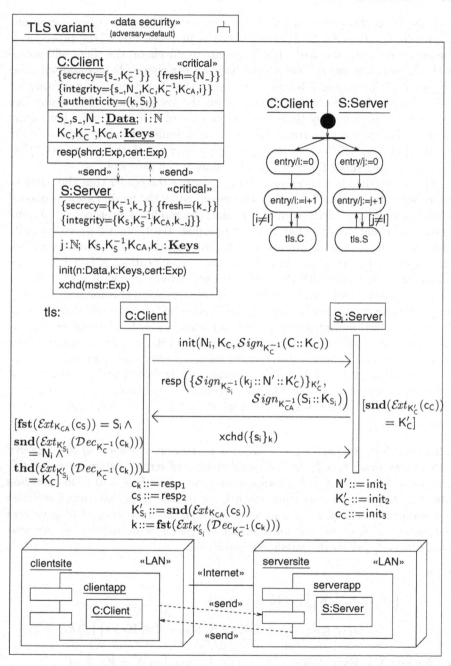

Fig. 5.4. Repaired variant of the TLS handshake protocol

response from the server to the client, the server signed certificate contains the public key received by the server in the first message of the protocol. If the adversary again forwards this certificate to the client, the client will notice that a false public key has been submitted on the client's behalf and will stop execution of the protocol because the check that has been newly introduced fails. Conversely, the client will only send the secret under the session key received if it is signed by the server concatenated with the public key of the client. This certificate, in turn, the server only sends out encrypted under the same public key, which the adversary cannot decrypt. Here it is essential that the session keys differ for different iterations of the protocol.

Of course, the above arguments may convince the reader that the particular attack exhibited in Theorem 5.4 is prevented by the modification proposed here, but they give little confidence that the modified protocol is immune against all other attacks that may be possible. We therefore prove formally that the protocol specification is secure with regards to our adversary model. More specifically, we show that the protocol specification in fact fulfills the constraints associated with the « data security » stereotype with respect to the adversary given below. We restrict outselves to proving this for the {secrecy} property. The properties {integrity} and {authenticity} can be established similarly. Note that the {integrity} goals formulated in Fig. 5.4, here meaning that the adversary should not be able to make the atttributes take on values previously known only to him, are straightforward to verify since they only concern attributes that in Fig. 5.4 remain constant, apart from i and j that are simply counted upwards. One could also formulate other integrity requirements, such as that the value C.k actually coincides with the key S.k$_j$, but we do not consider this here.

Theorem 5.5. *Suppose we are given a particular execution of the repaired* TLS *variant subsystem* T' *including all client and server instances, a client* C, *and a number* I *with* $S = S_I$. *Suppose that the server* S *is in its* J*th execution round in the current execution when* C *in its* I*th execution round initiates the protocol, that is,* C.i $= I$ *and* S.j $= J$. *Then this execution of* T' *preserves the secrecy of* C.s$_I$ *against adversaries of type* $A =$ default *whose previous knowledge* $\mathcal{K}_A^{\mathsf{p}}$ *fulfills the following conditions:*

- *we have*

$$\left(\{ \mathsf{C.s}_I, \mathsf{K}_\mathsf{C}^{-1}, \mathsf{K}_\mathsf{S}^{-1} \} \cup \{ \mathsf{S.k_j} : j \geq J \} \right.$$

$$\left. \cup \{ \{ Sign_{\mathsf{K}_\mathsf{S}^{-1}} (X :: \mathsf{C.N}_I :: \mathsf{K}_\mathsf{C}) \}_{\mathsf{K}_\mathsf{C}} : X \in \mathbf{Keys} \} \right) \cap \mathcal{K}_A^{\mathsf{p}} = \emptyset$$

- *for any* $X \in \mathbf{Exp}$, $Sign_{\mathsf{K}_\mathsf{C}^{-1}} (\mathsf{C} :: X) \in \mathcal{K}_A^{\mathsf{p}}$ *implies* $X = \mathsf{K}_\mathsf{C}$, *and*
- *for any* $X \in \mathbf{Exp}$, $Sign_{\mathsf{K}_\mathsf{CA}^{-1}} (\mathsf{S} :: X) \in \mathcal{K}_A^{\mathsf{p}}$ *implies* $X = \mathsf{K}_\mathsf{S}$.

The condition in the statement of this theorem means that the previous adversary knowledge $\mathcal{K}_A^{\mathsf{p}}$ may not contain the current secret C.s$_I$, the secret keys K_C^{-1}, K_S^{-1} of the sender and the receiver, the current and future session keys $S.k_j$, any encryptions of the form $\{Sign_{K_S^{-1}}(X :: C.N_I :: K_C)\}_{K_C}$, and any signatures $Sign_{K_C^{-1}}(C :: X)$ (except for $X = K_C$) and $Sign_{K_{CA}^{-1}}(S :: X)$ (except for $X = K_S$). This result covers the possibility that the adversary may gain information from previous or parallel executions of the protocol, possibly with other instances of Client or Server. With respect to parallel executions of other instances, the restrictions on the adversary knowledge allow the adversary to simulate other instances of the two classes, by giving the adversary access to their private keys and certificates. With respect to previous executions, one should note that the previous adversary knowledge $\mathcal{K}_A^p$ refers to the knowledge of the adversary before the *overall* execution of the system, not at the point of the system execution where $C.i = I$ and $S.j = J$ (see the definition in Sect. 3.3.4 and also the discussion and corollary below). In particular, the condition in the statement of the above theorem does not prevent the adversary from remembering information gained from earlier iterationsor the current iteration of the protocol and use it in later iterations. It does, however, assume that the adversary does not know the message $\{Sign_{K_S^{-1}}(k_j :: N_i :: K_C)\}_{K_C}$ of the server in the current protocol run *before* the current protocol. This assumption is in fact necessary, because otherwise the attack described in Theorem 5.4 would still work: The adversary would already have the certificate the client expects which includes the client's key K_C, and can in addition still get the current session key from the server as in the earlier attack by sending the message $N_i :: K_A :: Sign_{K_A^{-1}}(C :: K_A)$ containing the adversary's key K_A to the server.

Note also that since in the statement of the theorem we allow the keys $S.k_j$ for $j < J$ to be included in the previous adversary knowledge $\mathcal{K}_A^p$, the theorem establishes a form of "forward security" in the sense that the compromise of a current key does not necessarily expose future traffic. It is, however, not sufficient to only require that $S.k_J \notin \mathcal{K}_A^p$, because the adversary may initiate an intermediate interaction with S to increase its counter j.

The statement of the theorem concerns particular instances of Client and Server and particular execution rounds. It is formulated in a "rely-guarantee" way, stating that if the knowledge previously acquired by the adversary satisfies the conditions of the theorem, then this execution preserves secrecy. This approach allows one to consider security mechanisms such as security protocols in the system context. To do this, one needs to specify explicitly which values the remaining part of the system has to keep secret from the adversary for the protocol to function securely. For example, the theorem needs to assume that the certification authority does not issue any false certificates, which is the third pre-condition in the theorem.

Although the conditions in the statement of the theorem only concern the previous knowledge of the adversary before the *overall* execution of the system, it follows from the theorem that the adversary knowledge before each *iteration* of the system satisfies these conditions as well. That is, each iteration of the execution of the system preserves the conditions on the adversary knowledge: If the conditions on the adversary knowledge were to be violated in the course of the iterations before the one currently under consideration, the result of the theorem would not be valid, and this statement holds for each "current" iteration. Since the theorem above holds, this cannot be the case.

We have the following corollary to the above theorem, where we assume that the sets Client and Server of clients and servers are finite:

Corollary 5.6. *Any execution of $\mathcal{T}'$ over all clients and servers and all execution rounds preserves the secrecy of each* C.s$_I$, *for* C : Client *and* $1 \leq I \leq l$, *against adversaries of type* $A =$ default *whose previous knowledge* $\mathcal{K}_A^p$ *before the overall execution of* $\mathcal{T}'$ *fulfills the following conditions:*

- *we have*

$$\left(\{ \mathsf{K}_c^{-1}, \mathsf{K}_s^{-1}, c.s_i, s.k_j, \{ \mathcal{S}ign_{\mathsf{K}_s^{-1}}(X :: c.\mathsf{N}_i :: \mathsf{K}_c) \}_{\mathsf{K}_c} : \right.$$
$$\left. c : \mathsf{Client} \wedge s : \mathsf{Server} \wedge 1 \leq i \leq l \wedge 1 \leq j \wedge X \in \mathbf{Keys} \} \right) \cap \mathcal{K}_A^p = \emptyset,$$

- *for any* $X \in \mathbf{Exp}$ *and any* c : Client, $\mathcal{S}ign_{\mathsf{K}_c^{-1}}(c :: X) \in \mathcal{K}_A^p$ *implies* $X = \mathsf{K}_c$, *and*
- *for any* $X \in \mathbf{Exp}$ *and any* s : Server, $\mathcal{S}ign_{\mathsf{K}_{CA}^{-1}}(s :: X) \in \mathcal{K}_A^p$ *implies* $X = \mathsf{K}_s$.

The condition in the statement of this corollary generalizes that of Theorem 5.5 to arbitrary clients and servers. Note that the protocol rounds of each client and server do not have to correspond in any particular way. This means that any combination of clients c, servers s, secrets c.s$_i$, and session keys s.k$_j$ may occur. We only know that the same session key is not to be used repeatedly. In particular, the C.s$_I$ under consideration could be transmitted encrypted under s.k$_j$ for any server s and server round j. Thus we need to assume s.k$_j \notin \mathcal{K}_A^p$ for any s and j. Again note that $\mathcal{K}_A^p$ denotes the knowledge of the adversary *prior* to even the *first* execution round of the protocol. That the session keys are not leaked *during* any of the protocol runs between trustworthy participants then follows from our result.

5.3 Common Electronic Purse Specifications

In this section, we apply UMLsec to a security analysis of the Common Electronic Purse Specifications (CEPS) [CEP01]. CEPS are a candidate for a globally interoperable electronic purse standard supported by organizations representing 90 % of the world's electronic purse cards (including Visa International). It is thus likely to become an accepted standard [AJSW00], making its security an important goal.

Stored value smart cards, called "electronic purses", have been proposed to allow cash-free point-of-sale (POS) transactions offering more fraud protection than credit cards: Their built-in chip can perform cryptographic operations, which allow transaction-bound authentication. In contrast, credit card numbers are valid until the card is stopped, enabling misuse. The card contains an account balance that is adjusted when loading the card or purchasing goods.

Figure 5.5 gives an overview of the CEPS structure, following [CEP01]. The scheme participants are thus:

- the card issuer (issuing the cards),
- the funds issuer (processing the funds needed for a linked card load),
- the load acquirer operating a load device (where a card can be loaded),
- the merchant operating a POS device (where a card can be used to purchase a good),
- the card running a card application, and
- system operators for the processing of the transaction data.

Possible transactions are:

- Purchase (the cardholder may purchase a good using the card),
- Purchase Reversal (the merchant may reverse a purchase in case of a mistake),
- Incremental Purchase (purchases may be performed incrementally, for example for telephone calls),
- Cancel Last Purchase (the cardholder may cancel the last purchase),
- Currency Exchange (the cardholder may exchange currencies on the card),
- Load (the cardholder can load the card), and
- Unload (the card can be unloaded).

The general flow of resources through the system proceeds as follows: The cardholder loads his card with his money. During the post-transaction settle-

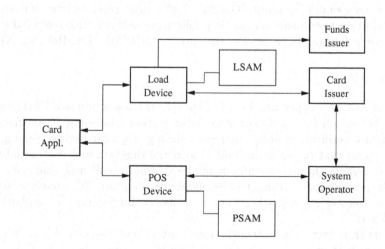

Fig. 5.5. Common Electronic Purse Specifications overview

ment process, the load acquirer sends the money to the relevant card issuer. The cardholder buys a good from a merchant using his card. In the settlement, the merchant receives the corresponding amount of money from the card issuer. Since the CEPS are designed to be a globally interoperable standard, this overall transaction process may involve not only untrustworthy cardholders, but also corrupt merchants and load acquirers. Since card issuers can take on the roles of load acquirers, the transactions may also involve competing card issuers that may not trust each other. In a global situation, there is often little hope to settle disputes using judicial means. It is therefore vital that the specifications are designed in a way that requires minimal trust relations between the transaction partners [CEP01].

Here we consider two central parts of the CEPS: the purchase transaction, an off-line protocol which allows the cardholder to use the electronic value on a card to pay for goods, and the load transaction, an on-line protocol which allows the cardholder to load electronic value on a card. In each case, we give a simplified account to keep the presentation readable. For example, we omit the request messages to the smart card that are only included in the protocol because current smart cards communicate only by answering requests.

5.3.1 Purchase Transaction

The participants involved in the off-line purchase transaction protocol are the customer's card and the merchant's POS device. Figure 5.6 gives an overview of a POS device, following [CEP01, Tech. Spec. p. 77]. The POS device contains a Purchase Security Application Module (PSAM) that is used to store and process data The PSAM, required to be tamper-resistant, could also be implemented on a smart card. After the protocol, the account balance in the customer's card is decremented, and the balance in the PSAM is incremented by the corresponding amount. The card issuer later receives transaction logs.

In addition to transactions using public terminals it is also intended to use CEPS cards for transactions over the Internet [CEP01, Bus. Req. ch. X].

Specification

In Fig. 5.7 we give a specification of the purchase transaction as a UML subsystem $\mathcal{P}$. For simplicity, we do not consider exception processing: if, for instance, a certificate verification fails, our model simply stops further processing.

We recall that for each method msg in the diagram and each number n, msg_n represents the nth argument of the operation call msg that was most recently accepted according to the sequence diagram. We continue to use the notation $var ::= exp$ where var is a shorthand for exp, as explained in Sect. 3.2.4.

Apart from incremental transactions that are not considered here, security functionality is provided only by the PSAM, and not the rest of the POS device. Thus our protocol participants are

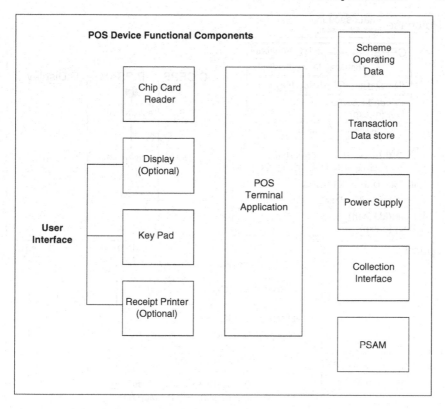

Fig. 5.6. POS device overview

- the CEP card C, with identity ID_C and public (resp. private) keys K_C (resp. K_C^{-1}), and
- the PSAM P, with identity ID_P and public (resp. private) keys K_P (resp. K_P^{-1}).

Both also have stored the public key K_{CA} of the certification authority before the transaction. In addition, we also model the display which is security-relevant in so far as the cardholder cannot communicate with his card directly.

Note that of course the protocol will be used with different cards during the lifetime of a PSAM. For simplicity, we omit this aspect. Card revocation is not considered here. Also, we assume that the sequence of transaction amounts M_{NT} indexed by the transaction number NT is given, as well as the sequence of session keys SK_{NT}. These keys are required to be fresh at the PSAM object, as indicated by the tag {fresh} defined in Sect. 4.1.2. In fact one can see from the specification that expressions of the form SK_x, for any subexpression x, appear only at the PSAM object and the associated view of the sequence diagram. Again, the keys, as different constant symbols in **Keys**, are mutually distinct and thus mutually independent. Again, we write $M_\_$ to denote an array whose

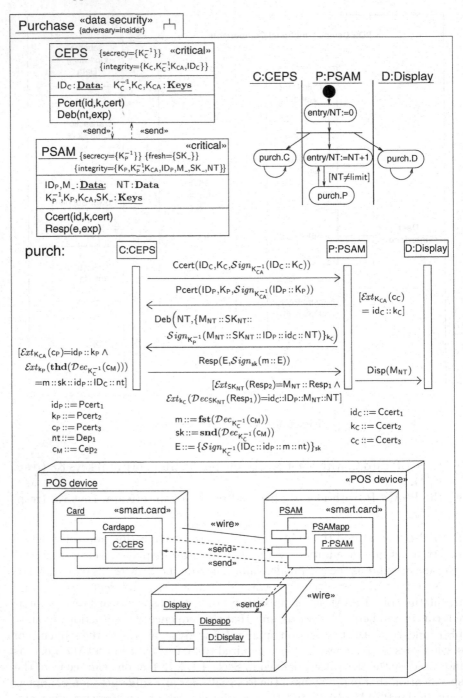

Fig. 5.7. Specification for the CEPS purchase transaction

fields M_x have the type **Data**. Also, again, constant attributes have their initial values as attribute names and the corresponding attribute types are underlined.

We leave as implicit the actual adjustment of the balance on the card, which includes checking that the balance is greater than the charged amount.

At the beginning of its execution in the POS device, the PSAM creates a transaction number NT with value 0. Before each protocol run, NT is incremented. If a certain limit is exceeded, the PSAM stops functioning, to avoid rolling over of NT to 0. Note that here we assume an additional operation, the $+$, to build up expressions.

The protocol between the card C, the PSAM P, and the display D is supposed to start after the card C is inserted into a POS device containing P and D and after the amount M is communicated to the PSAM by typing it into a terminal assumed to be secure.

Each protocol run consists of the parallel execution of the card's and the PSAM's part of the protocol. The card and PSAM begin the protocol by exchanging certificates ID_C, K_C, $Sign_{K_{CA}^{-1}}(ID_C :: K_C)$ (resp. ID_P, K_P, $Sign_{K_{CA}^{-1}}(ID_P :: K_P)$) containing their identifier ID_C (resp. ID_P) and their public key K_C (resp. K_P), together with the same information signed with the private key K_{CA}^{-1} of the certification authority. Both check the validity of the received certificate. That is, they check that the signature consists of the received identifier and public key, signed with the private key K_{CA}^{-1} of the certification authority, by verifying the signature with the public key K_{CA}.

Note that the card C "knows" that it has received a valid certificate, but does not know whether it has received the certificate for the PSAM P at the present physical location, because it has no information regarding the identity of P that ID_P itself could be verified against.

The PSAM then proceeds by sending the Debit-for-Purchase message containing the transaction number NT, and an encryption of the following data under the public key k_C received in the card's certificate: The concatenation of the price M_{NT} of the good to be purchased, a symmetric session key SK_{NT}, and the following data signed with the private key K_P^{-1}: the amount M_{NT}, the key SK_{NT}, P's identifier ID_P, the data id_C earlier received as C's identifier, and the transaction number NT. The card then checks the validity of the signature with the earlier received public key k_P against the received data amount m, the received key sk, the received identifier id_P, the own identifier ID_C, and the received transaction number nt. The card then returns, firstly, E, which consists of the values ID_C, id_P, m, and nt, signed with the private key K_C^{-1} and encrypted under the key sk, and, secondly, the values m and E signed with the key sk. The PSAM verifies that the second part of the received message is the concatenation of the amount M_{NT} sent out previously and the first part of the message, signed with the key SK_{NT} sent out earlier, and verifies that the first part of the message, after decryption with the key SK_{NT}, gives the signature of the concatenation of the values id_C, ID_P, M_{NT}, and NT. If all the verifications succeed, the protocol finishes, otherwise the execution of the protocol stops at the failed verification.

Security Threat Model

The CEPS require the smart card and the PSAM to be tamper-proof, but not the POS device [CEP01, Bus.req. p. 13, Funct. req. p. 20]. The purchase transaction is supposed to provide mutual authentication between the terminal and the card using a certificate issued by a certification authority and containing the card's or PSAM's public key.

The smart card is inserted into a POS device and can thus communicate with the PSAM. Since there is no direct communication between the cardholder and the card, the information displayed by the POS device regarding the transaction has to be trusted at the point of transaction. Security for the customer against fraud by the merchant is supposed to be provided by checking the card balance after the transaction and complaining to the merchant, and if necessary to the card issuer, in the case of incorrect processing. Similarly, security for the merchant against the customer is supposed to be provided by exchanging the purchased good only for a signed message from the card containing the transaction details, for which the merchant will receive the corresponding monetary amount from the issuer in the settlement process afterwards. More precisely, the merchant possessing the PSAM with identifier ID_P will, when presenting the signature $E = Sign_{K_C^{-1}}(ID_C :: ID_P :: M_{NT} :: NT)$, receive the monetary amount M_{NT} from the account of the cardholder of the card with identifier ID_C, once for each NT, provided K_C is the key for ID_C.

The idea is that risk of fraud is kept small since fraud should be either prevented or at least later detected in the settlement, and certificates of cards or PSAMs actively involved in fraud can be revoked using revocation lists whose treatment is omitted here. Note that some kinds of fraud can only be detected after a transaction. For example, the cardholder is unable to communicate with the card directly to authorize the transaction. Therefore, the POS device could simply charge a higher amount to the card than shown in its display.

Thus we have the following three security goals:

Cardholder security: The merchant can only claim the amount which is registered on the card after the transaction and thus can be checked with the cardholder's cardreader.

Merchant security: The merchant receives a valid signature in exchange for the sold good.

Card issuer security: The sum of the balances of all valid cards and all valid PSAMs remains unchanged by the transaction.

When investigating the threats, one needs to take into account that the protocol is also expected to be used over the Internet, and that the POS device in which the PSAM resides and which provides the communication link between the card and the PSAM is not considered to be within the security perimeter, as mentioned above.

The above discussion leads us to the following formalized security goals.

We call a key K_X *valid* for a card or PSAM with identifier ID_X if there exists $Sign_{K_{CA}^{-1}}(ID_X :: K_X)$ in a participant's knowledge.

Cardholder security: For all ID_C, ID_P, M_{NT}, NT, K_C^{-1} such that K_C is valid for ID_C, if P is in possession of $Sign_{K_C^{-1}}(ID_C :: ID_P :: M_{NT} :: NT)$ then C is in possession of $Sign_{K_P^{-1}}(M_{NT} :: SK_{NT} :: ID_P :: ID_C :: NT)$, for some SK_{NT} and K_P^{-1} such that the corresponding key K_P is valid for ID_P.

Merchant security: Each time D receives the value M_{NT}, P is in possession of $Sign_{K_{CA}^{-1}}(ID_C :: K_C)$ and $Sign_{K_C^{-1}}(ID_C :: ID_P :: M_{NT} :: NT)$ for some ID_C, K_C^{-1}, and a new value NT.

Card issuer security: After each completed purchase transaction, let S be the sum of all M_{NT} in the sequence consisting of the processed elements of the form $Sign_{K_C^{-1}}(ID_C :: ID_P :: M_{NT} :: NT)$ over all expressions ID_C, ID_P, and K_C^{-1}, such that the corresponding key K_C is valid for ID_C and where the NT are mutually distinct for fixed C. Also, let S' be the sum of all $M'_{NT'}$ in the sequence of processed $Sign_{K_{P'}^{-1}}(M'_{NT'} :: SK'_{NT'} :: ID_{C'} :: ID_{P'} :: NT')$, over all expressions $ID_{C'}$, $ID_{P'}$, and $K_{P'}^{-1}$, such that the corresponding key $K_{P'}$ is valid for $ID_{P'}$, and where the NT' are mutually distinct for fixed C'. Then S is no greater than S'.

Results

According to the assumptions of the CEPS, we consider a threat scenario where the attacker is able to access the POS device links, and can access other PSAMs over the Internet, but is not able to tamper with the smart cards. That is, we consider the *insider* attacker from Fig. 4.7.

Vulnerability

Under the current threat scenario, we find the following weakness with regards to the above goal of merchant security, arising from the fact that the POS device is not secured against a potential attacker that may try to betray the merchant, and that the CEPS are also to be used over the Internet. The attacker could for example be an employee, which is a realistic scenario. We first sketch the idea of the attack informally and then exhibit a corresponding attacker within our formal model.

The idea of the attack is simply that the attacker redirects the messages between the card C and the PSAM P to another PSAM P', for example with the goal of buying electronic content, and to let the cardholder pay for it. We assume that the attacker manages to have the amount payable to P' equal the amount payable to P. The attacker also sends the required message to the display which will then reassure the merchant that the required amount has been received. The attack has a good chance of going undetected: the cardholder will not notice anything suspicious, because the deducted amount is correct. Also, the card registers the identifier $id_{P'}$ rather than id_P, but the identifiers are non-self-explanatory data that the cardholder cannot be assumed to verify, and the card has no information about what the identity of P should be. Furthermore, the identifier id_C in the Deb message is as expected, since P' correctly assumes to be in a transaction with C. The merchant who owns P will notice only later a lacking amount of M_{NT}. Note that the PSAM P is not in any way involved in this attack.

The message flow diagram corresponding to this attack follows, where $E:=\{Sign_{K_C^{-1}}(ID_C :: ID_{P'} :: M_{NT} :: NT)\}_{sk}$.

$$C \xrightarrow{\quad Ccert(ID_C,K_C,Sign_{K_{CA}^{-1}}(ID_C::K_C)) \quad} A \xrightarrow{\quad Ccert(ID_C,K_C,Sign_{K_{CA}^{-1}}(ID_C::K_C)) \quad} P'$$

$$C \xleftarrow{\quad Pcert(ID_{P'},K_{P'},Sign_{K_{CA}^{-1}}(ID_{P'}::K_{P'})) \quad} A \xleftarrow{\quad Pcert(ID_{P'},K_{P'},Sign_{K_{CA}^{-1}}(ID_{P'}::K_{P'})) \quad} P'$$

$$A \xleftarrow{\quad Deb(NT,\{M_{NT}::SK_{NT}::Sign_{K_{P'}^{-1}}(M_{NT}::SK_{NT}::ID_{P'}::id_C::NT)\}_{k_C}) \quad} P'$$

$$C \xleftarrow{\quad Deb(NT,\{M_{NT}::SK_{NT}::Sign_{K_{P'}^{-1}}(M_{NT}::SK_{NT}::ID_{P'}::id_C::NT)\}_{k_C}) \quad} A$$

$$C \xrightarrow{\quad Resp(E,Sign_{sk}(m::E)) \quad} A \xrightarrow{\quad Resp(E,Sign_{sk}(m::E)) \quad} P'$$

$$A \xrightarrow{\quad Disp(M_{NT}) \quad} D$$

We now show that this attack is actually detected in our formal model, by exhibiting a suitable attacker.

Theorem 5.7. $\mathcal{P}$ *does not provide* merchant security *against* insider *adversaries with* $\{Sign_{K_{CA}^{-1}}(ID_{C'} :: K_{C'}), K_{C'}^{-1}\} \subseteq \mathcal{K}_A^p$.

This vulnerability has been first reported in [JW01b] and the CEPS security working group has been informed and acknowledged the observation [Hit01].

Note also that the attack is simplified if we assume that the attacker can also eavesdrop on the connection between the terminal where the amount M_{NT} is entered and the PSAM P. Then the attacker only has to intercept M_{NT}, redirect all messages from C to P' and back, and finally send $Disp(M_{NT})$ to the display. If in addition to this we assume that the cardholder coincides or collaborates with the attacker, the attacker could simply intercept and remove M_{NT} and send $\mathsf{Disp}(M_{NT})$ to the display, because then the cardholder receives the good without having to pay for it.

Proposed Solution

The problem can be solved by securing the communication link between the PSAM and display, for example by using a smart card with integrated display as the PSAM. One also needs to make sure that this PSAM cannot be replaced without being noticed. This modification leads to the specification $\mathcal{P}'$ with the modified deployment diagram given in Fig. 5.8, and an otherwise unchanged protocol specification.

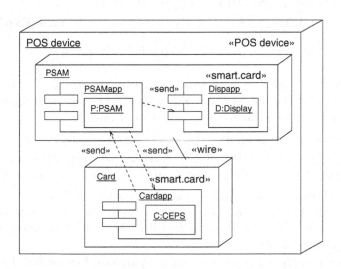

Fig. 5.8. Repaired part of CEPS purchase specification

We now discuss the security of the improved version of the protocol.

Firstly, we argue that the specification provides the security properties against *insider* adversaries ascribed to it according to its stereotypes following Sect. 4.1.2.

Proposition 5.8. $\mathcal{P}'$ *provides secrecy of* K_C^{-1}, K_P^{-1} *and integrity of* K_C^{-1}, K_C, K_{CA}, ID_C, K_P^{-1}, K_P, M_{NT}, SK_{NT}, NT *(meaning that the adversary should not be able to make the atttributes take on values previously known only to him) against* insider *adversaries with* $\mathcal{K}_A^p \cap \{K_C^{-1}, K_P^{-1}\} = \emptyset$.

Note that the proposition does not imply that C and P terminate the protocol with the same value for M_{NT}. In fact, this cannot be guaranteed, since a "redirection attack" similar to the above still applies. Since now the display can no longer be manipulated, it would be noticed immediately if the

PSAM received less money than expected, but the money could in principle still come from a different card than the one inserted into the POS device. The kinds of integrity property relevant here are considered below as "cardholder security" and "merchant security".

Note also that the secure definition of M_{NT}, which is outside the current specification, relies on a secure connection between the terminal where the amount is entered and the PSAM. Also, the creation of the session keys SK_{NT} is outside current scope. The values are simply assumed to be given.

We consider the formalized security goals from the above.

Theorem 5.9. *Consider adversaries of type* $A = $ insider *with*

$$\mathcal{K}_A^{p} \cap \Big(\{K_C^{-1}, K_P^{-1}, K_{CA}^{-1}\} \cup \{SK_{NT} : NT \in \mathbb{N}\}$$

$$\cup \{\mathcal{S}ign_{K_P^{-1}}(E) : E \in \mathbf{Exp}\} \cup \{\mathcal{S}ign_{K_C^{-1}}(E) : E \in \mathbf{Exp}\}$$

$$\cup \{\mathcal{S}ign_{SK_{NT}}(E) : E \in \mathbf{Exp} \wedge NT \in \mathbb{N}\} \Big) = \emptyset$$

and such that for each $X \in \mathbf{Exp}$ *with* $Sign_{K_{CA}^{-1}}(X :: K) \in \mathcal{K}_A^{p}$, $X = ID_C$ *implies* $K = K_C$ *and* $X = ID_P$ *implies* $K = K_P$. *The following security guarantees are provided by* $\mathcal{P}'$ *in the presence of adversaries of type* A:

Cardholder security: For all ID_C, ID_P, M_{NT}, NT, K_C^{-1} *such that* K_C *is valid for* ID_C, *if* P *is in possession of* $Sign_{K_C^{-1}}(ID_C :: ID_P :: M_{NT} :: NT)$ *then* C *is in possession of* $Sign_{K_P^{-1}}(M_{NT} :: SK_{NT} :: ID_P :: ID_C :: NT)$, *for some* SK_{NT} *and* K_P^{-1} *such that the corresponding key* K_P *is valid for* ID_P.

Merchant security: Each time D *receives the value* M_{NT}, P *is in possession of* $Sign_{K_{CA}^{-1}}(ID_C :: K_C)$ *and* $Sign_{K_C^{-1}}(ID_C :: ID_P :: M_{NT} :: NT)$ *for some* ID_C, K_C^{-1}, *and a new value* NT.

Card issuer security: After each completed purchase transaction, let S *be the sum of all* M_{NT} *in the sequence consisting of the processed elements of the form* $Sign_{K_C^{-1}}(ID_C :: ID_P :: M_{NT} :: NT)$ *over all expressions* ID_C, ID_P, *and* K_C^{-1}, *such that the corresponding key* K_C *is valid for* ID_C *and where the* NT *are mutually distinct for fixed* C. *Also, let* S' *be the sum of all* $M'_{NT'}$ *in the sequence of processed* $Sign_{K_{P'}^{-1}}(M'_{NT'} :: SK'_{NT'} :: ID_{C'} :: ID_{P'} :: NT')$ *over all expressions* $ID_{C'}$, $ID_{P'}$, *and* $K_{P'}^{-1}$, *such that the corresponding key* $K_{P'}$ *is valid for* $ID_{P'}$, *and where the* NT' *are mutually distinct for fixed* C'). *Then* S *is no greater than* S'.

Note that the card cannot verify that the identity ID_P corresponds to the actual PSAM with which it communicates. The certificate only proves that K_P is *a* valid public key that is linked to *some* identity ID_P. There is no information in ID_P that links it to the physical POS device containing the PSAM owning ID_P, such as the name of the shop, or its location. This information exists only at the card issuer and is not obtained during the transaction. Thus, the card "knows" it owes money to the PSAM P with which it communicates, but does not know whether P is registered as being in the physical location where the card currently is, and the card does not know what this physical location is. Including this information would probably improve the security of the protocol. For example, the attack described above could be detected by the cardholder immediately after the transaction with a portable cardreader, even if the POS device display is not within the security perimeter. It would, however, probably also incur higher organizational expenses. Even the validity of ID_P is not relevant to the cardholder in the case of a successful purchase. If ID_P is not a valid identity, the cardholder will have the purchased good anyway, but may not have to pay for it because in the settlement process there will not be a legitimate claimer of the money. However, the validity of ID_P gives the cardholder a better prospect of claiming back an amount which has been illegitimately charged to the card by a POS device, and therefore the certificate for the POS is not redundant.

5.3.2 Load Transaction

Load transactions in CEPS are on-line transactions using symmetric cryptography for authentication. We only consider unlinked load, where the cardholder pays cash into a, possibly unattended, loading machine and receives a corresponding credit on the card. Linked load, where funds are transferred for example from a bank account, the so-called funds issuer, is viewed as offering fewer possibilities for fraud, because funds are moved only within one financial institution [CEP01, Funct. Req. p. 12].

Figure 5.9 gives an overview over the components at the load acquirer, following [CEP01, Tech.Spec. p.19]. To perform a cash-based load transaction, the cardholder inserts his card into the card reader and the money into the cash slot of the load device. To load the cash on the card, he enters the PIN. Note again that the cardholder is not able to communicate with the card directly, but only through the display of the load device. A Load Secure Application Module (LSAM) is used to provide the necessary cryptographic and control processing. The LSAM may reside within the load device or at the load acquirer host. The load acquirer keeps a log of all transactions processed. Through the load host application, the LSAM communicates with the card issuer. Below, we analyze the load protocol between the card, the LSAM, and the card issuer that is executed after the cardholder inserts the cash.

Specification

We give a specification of the CEPS load transaction, slightly simplified by leaving out security-irrelevant details, but including exception processing.

The specification is given in form of the UML subsystem $\mathcal{L}$ in Fig. 5.12. For better readability, the enlarged class and statechart diagrams are also given in Fig. 5.10 to 5.14. The values exchanged in the protocol are listed in

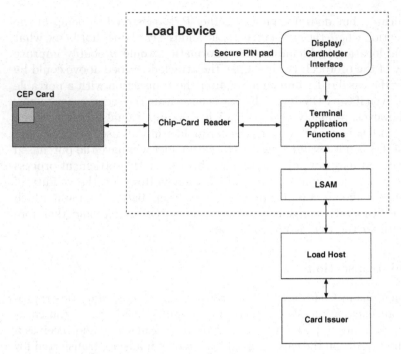

Fig. 5.9. Load acquirer components

Fig. 5.16. For illustration, we also give a sequence diagram in Fig. 5.15 for one scenario of the system behavior, namely the case where no exception occurs.

Again, we use the notation *var* ::= *exp* as a syntactic short-cut. Here *var* is a local variable not used for any other purpose and *exp* may not contain *var*. Before assigning a semantics to the diagram, the variable *var* should be replaced by the expression *exp* at each occurrence. Also, for increased readability, we use pattern matching: for example, (lda', m') ::= Init means that when deriving the formal semantics of the sequence diagram, one would have to replace lda' with $Init_1$ and m' with $Init_2$ in each case.

As with the purchase protocol, the link between the LSAM and the loading device, and the loading device itself, need to be secured. Otherwise an attacker could initiate the protocol without having inserted cash into the machine. For simplicity, we leave out the communication between the LSAM and loading device to determine the amount to be loaded, but assume that the amount is communicated to the LSAM in a secure way. Here, a CEP card name cep is called valid if the name is registered at the card issuer and not on the list of revoked cards.

For the participants of the protocol, we have the classes Card, LSAM, and Issuer. Also, each of the three classes has an associated class used for logging transaction data named CLog, LLog, and ILog, respectivly. The logging objects

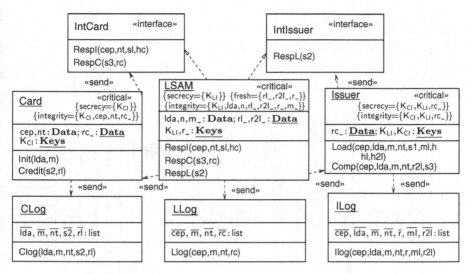

Fig. 5.10. Load transaction class diagram

simply take the arguments of their operations and update their attributes accordingly. Their behavior is for readability omitted in Fig. 5.12.

We assume a sequence of random values rc_{nt} to be given that is shared between the card **C** and its card issuer **I**. These random values are required to be fresh within the **Load** subsystem as indicated by the tag {**fresh**} attached to **Load** which was defined in Sect. 4.1.2. Note that when viewing the **Load** subsystem in isolation, the associated condition is vacuous: It just requires that any appearance of an expression rc_x in Load must be in Load. Using the {**fresh**} tag at a top-level subsystem is still meaningful, because one may want to include the subsystem in another subsystem also stereotyped « **data security** », which would extend the scope of the freshness constraint to the larger sub-

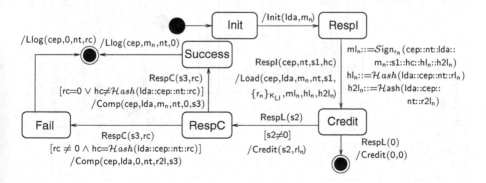

Fig. 5.11. Load transaction: load acquirer

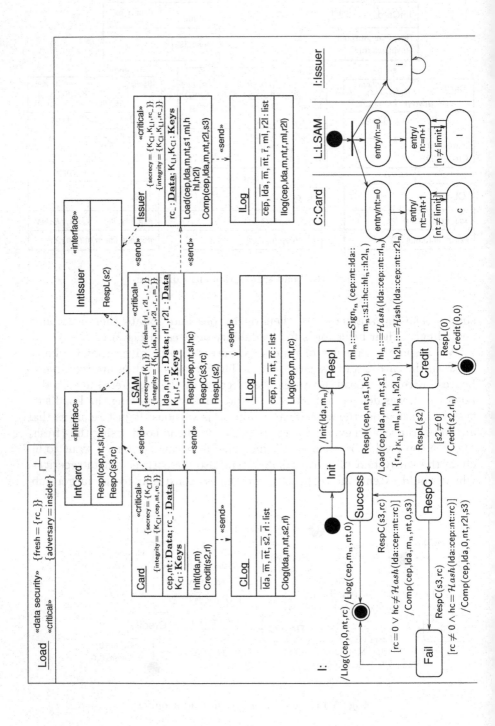

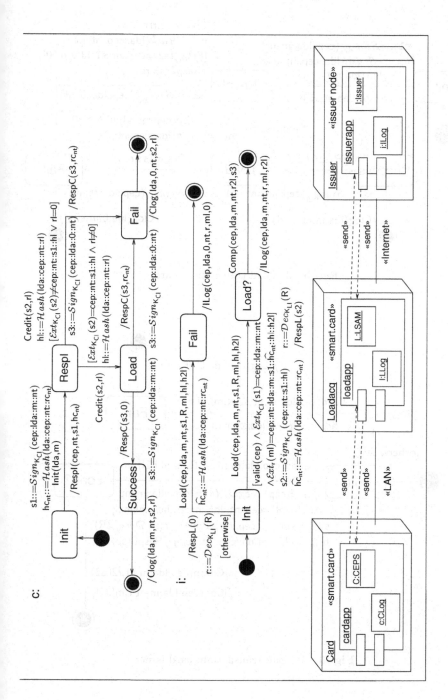

Fig. 5.12. Specification for load transaction

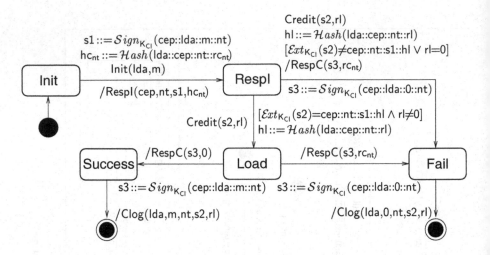

Fig. 5.13. Load transaction: card

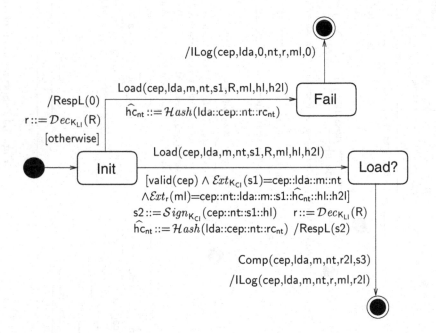

Fig. 5.14. Load transaction: card issuer

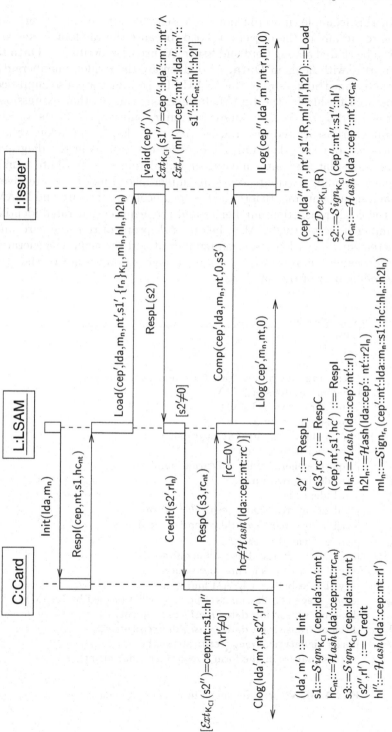

Fig. 5.15. Sequence diagram for load transaction

system. In this example, it would not make sense to attach the {fresh} tag with value rc_ to any of the objects in Load, because the random values are supposed to be shared among Card and Issuer. As usual, we write rc_ : **Data** to denote an array with fields in **Data**. Also given are the random numbers rl_n, $r2l_n$ and the symmetric keys r_n of the LSAM. These values are also supposed to be generated freshly by the LSAM. In fact, one can see that expressions of the form rl_x, $r2l_x$, r_x, for any subexpression x, only appear in the object and the statechart associated with LSAM. Again, the keys and random values are independent of each other and of the other expressions in the diagram. Also, again, constant attributes have their initial values as attribute names and the corresponding attribute types are underlined. Finally, we are given the transaction amounts m_n. Before the first protocol run, the card and LSAM initialize the card transaction number nt and the acquirer-generated identification number n, respectively. Also, before each protocol run, the card and LSAM increment the card transaction number nt and the acquirer-generated identification number n, repectively, as long as a given limit is not reached (to avoid the rolling over of the numbers).

Variable	Explanation
C	card
L	LSAM
I	card issuer
rc_{nt}	secret random values shared between card and issuer
rl_n, $r2l_n$	random numbers of LSAM
r_n	symmetric keys of LSAM
m_n	transaction amounts
m, rl, hl	m_n, rl_n, hl_n as received at card issuer
nt	card transaction number
n	acquirer-generated identification number
lda	load device identifier
cep	card identifier
s1	card signature: $Sign_{K_{CI}}(cep::lda::m::nt)$
hc_{nt}	card hash value: $Hash(lda::cep::nt::rc_{nt})$
$\widehat{hc}_{nt}$	hc_{nt} as created at issuer
rc, hc	rc_{nt}, hc_{nt} as received at load acquirer
K_{CI}	key shared between card and issuer
K_{LI}	key shared between LSAM and issuer
ml_n	$Sign_{r_n}(cep::nt::lda::m_n::s1::hc::hl_n::h2l_n)$ (signed by LSAM)
hl_n	hash of transaction data: $Hash(lda::cep::nt::rl)$
$h2l_n$	hash of transaction data: $Hash(lda::cep::nt::r2l)$
s2	issuer signature: $Sign_{K_{CI}}(cep::nt::s1::hl)$
s3	card signature of the form $Sign_{K_{CI}}(cep::lda::m::nt)$

Fig. 5.16. Values exchanged in the load specification

We give a textual explanation of the UML specification. The protocol between a card C, an LSAM L, and a card issuer I is supposed to start after the card C issued by I is inserted into a loading device containing L and the cardholder inserts the amount m_n of cash into the loading device.

The LSAM initiates the transaction after the CEP card is inserted into the load device, by sending the "Initialize for load" message Init with arguments the load device identifier Ida and the transaction amount m_n. This is the amount of cash paid into the load device by the cardholder that is supposed to be loaded onto the card. Whenever the card receives this message after being inserted into the load device, it sends back the "Initialize for load response" message RespI to the LSAM, with arguments the card identifier cep, the card's transaction number nt, the card signature s1, and the hash value hc_{nt}. s1 consists of the values cep, the received load acquirer identifier Ida' and amount m', and nt, all of which are signed with the key K_{CI} shared between the card C and the corresponding card issuer I. hc_{nt} is the hash of the values Ida, cep, nt, and rc_{nt}. rc_{nt} is a secret shared between the card and the issuer. The LSAM then sends to the issuer the "load request" message Load with arguments the received card identifier cep', Ida, m_n, the received transaction number nt' and card signature $s1'$, and the values $Enc(K_{LI}, r_n)$, ml_n, hl_n, and $h2l_n$. Here $Enc(K_{LI}, r_n)$ is the encryption of the key r_n under the key K_{LI} shared between the LSAM and the issuer. Also, $ml_n = \mathcal{S}ign_{r_n}(cep' :: nt' :: Ida :: m_n :: s1' :: hc' :: hl_n :: h2l_n)$ is the signature of the data cep', nt', Ida, m_n, $s1'$, hc', hl_n, and $h2l_n$ using the key r_n, where hc' is the message part hc_{nt} as received by the LSAM. hl_n is the hash of the values Ida, cep', nt', and rl_n, while $h2l_n$ is the hash of the values Ida, cep', nt', and $r2l_n$.

The issuer checks if the received card identifier cep'' is valid and verifies if the received signature $s1''$ is a valid signature generated from the values cep'', the received load device identifier Ida'', the received amount m'', and the received transaction number nt'' with the key K_{CI}. Technically, it is checked whether $\mathcal{E}xt_{K_{CI}}(s1'') = cep'' :: Ida'' :: m'' :: nt''$ holds. The issuer retrieves r' from the received ciphertext R, which is supposed to evaluate to $Enc(K_{LI}, r)$, using the key K_{LI} shared between the LSAM and the issuer. That is, we have $r' ::= \mathcal{D}ec_{K_{LI}}(R)$. He then checks if the received signature ml' is a valid signature of the values cep'', nt'', Ida'', m'', $s1''$, $\widehat{hc}_{nt}$, hl, and h2l using the key r, that is if $\mathcal{E}xt_r(ml) = cep :: nt :: Ida :: m :: s1 :: \widehat{hc}_{nt} :: hl :: h2l$. Here $\widehat{hc}_{nt}$ is the hash of the values Ida'', cep'', nt'', and rc_{nt}.

If all these checks succeed, the issuer sends the "respond to load" message RespL with argument s2 to the LSAM. s2 consists of the values cep'', nt'', $s1''$, and hl', signed with the key K_{CI}. Otherwise, the issuer sends RespL with argument 0 to the LSAM. He then sends the message Ilog with arguments cep'', Ida'', the amount 0 (since the load was unsuccessful), nt'', r', ml', and 0 (no r2l received from LSAM) to its logging object and finishes the protocol run.

If the LSAM receives an $s2' \neq 0$ as the argument of RespL, it sends the "credit for load" message Credit with arguments the received signature $s2'$ and the value rl to the card. If the LSAM receives a zero as the argument of RespL, it sends the "credit for load" message Credit with arguments $0, 0$ to the card and finishes the protocol run by returning the cash to the cardholder.

If the card receives the message Credit, it checks whether its first argument $s2'$ is the signature of the values cep, nt, s1, and hl'', which is defined to be the hash of the values lda', cep, nt, and the second argument rl' of Credit. Also, it checks whether $rl' \neq 0$. If either of the two checks fail, the card sends the "response to credit for load" message RespC with arguments s3 and rc_{nt} to the LSAM, where s3 consists of the values cep, lda', the amount 0, and nt, signed with the key K_{CI}. The card also sends the logging message Clog to the object CLog, with arguments lda', the amount 0, nt, $s2'$, and rk'. If both checks succeed, the card attempts to load itself with the amount m'. If it succeeds, it sends the message RespC with arguments s3 and 0, where s3 is defined to be the signature of the values cep, lda', m', and nt using the key K_{CI}. If it fails, it sends the message RespC with arguments s3 and rc_{nt}, where s3 is defined to be the signature of the values cep, lda', the amount 0, and nt using the key K_{CI}.

If the LSAM receives a message RespC with arguments $s3'$ and rc', assuming it has not finished already, it checks whether $rc' \neq 0$ and the hc' received in the first message from the card is the hash of the values lda, cep', nt', and rc'. If yes, that is, the load was unsuccessful, the LSAM sends the "transaction completion message" Comp with arguments cep', lda, the amount 0, nt', r2l, and $s3'$ to the issuer. Also, it sends the logging message Llog with arguments cep', the amount 0, nt', and rc to its logging object LLog. Then it finishes by returning the cash to the cardholder. If no, the LSAM sends the message Comp with arguments cep', lda, m_n, nt', 0 (no r2l), and $s3'$ to the issuer. Also, it sends Llog with arguments cep', m, nt', and 0 to LLog. Then it finishes without returning the cash to the cardholder.

If the issuer device receives the message Comp with arguments cep'', lda'', m'', nt'', r2l, and $s3''$ from the LSAM, assuming it has not finished already, it sends the message Ilog with arguments cep'', lda'', m'', nt'', r', ml', and r2l to the object ILog and finishes. In this case, either m'' is supposed to be the transaction amount and $r2l = 0$, or $m'' = 0$ and $r2l \neq 0$.

Security Threat Model

We consider the threat scenario for the load transaction. Again, the assumption is that the card, the LSAM, and the security module of the card issuer are tamper-resistant with respect to the adversary under consideration. In particular, the contained secret keys cannot be retrieved physically. The protocol can, for example, be attacked by attacking the communication links between the protocol participants. Also, one of the participants cardholder, load acquirer, or card issuer could exchange their respective device with one exhibiting different behavior. Again, since there is no direct communication between the cardholder and the card, security for the customer against fraud by the load acquirer is supposed to be provided by checking the card balance after the transaction and complaining to the load acquirer, and if necessary to the card issuer, in the case of incorrect processing.

Security for the load acquirer against the customer partly relies on the fact that the signed message from the load acquirer acknowledging receipt of the payment is sent to the card only after the cash is inserted into the loading device. However, since the load acquirer is obliged to return the cash in the case of a failure in the loading process, one needs to make sure in turn that the cash is returned only in exchange for a valid certificate from the card stating that the loading process has been aborted. Otherwise the cardholder could later claim not to have received the cash-back.

More precisely, the value ml_n "provides a guarantee that the load acquirer owes the transaction amount to the card issuer" for each new n, as required in [CEP01, Tech. Spec. 6.6.1.6]. This guarantee is negated if the load acquirer is in possession of the value rc_{nt} that is sent from the card to the LSAM in case the card wants to abort the loading protocol after the LSAM has released ml_n. A failed load is signaled by the LSAM to the issuer by sending the value $r2l_n$, which can be verified by the card issuer by computing the hash of $lda :: cep :: nt :: r2l_n$ and comparing it to the value $h2l_n$ received earlier from the LSAM. The load acquirer can verify that rc_{nt} is genuine by comparing the hash of $lda :: cep :: nt :: rc_{nt}$ with the value hc_{nt} received in the first message from the card, which is checked to be genuine by the card issuer, who receives it in the value ml_n. The value rl_n gives a guarantee by the LSAM to the card that the load can be completed and that the load acquirer will pay the transaction amount to the card issuer. The card can verify the validity of rl_n by computing the hash hl_n of $lda :: cep :: nt :: rl_n$ and verifying that the signature s2 forwarded by the LSAM from the card issuer was constructed from $cep :: nt :: s1 :: hl_n$. The signatures s1 and s3 from the card indicate, respectively, the card's intention to load the contained amount and the card's notification to have loaded the contained amount.

While it may seem reasonable that the cardholder trusts the card issuer, it may not be reasonable to expect that the load acquirer trusts the card issuer. The aim of the CEPS is to provide a globally interoperable system. Since many card issuers will also operate as load acquirers within their regional boundaries, this means that if cardholders load their cards elsewhere, these load acquirers are operated by competing card issuers. Competing card issuers may not trust each other, especially when jointly operating a relatively complex system that may provide temptation for fraud even at corporate level. This temptation is real: For example, according to [And01], the urban train operators in a major English metropolis attempted to cheat each other about passenger numbers on their respective parts of the urban train system to increase their own revenue at the expense of their competitors). The CEPS plainly contend that "electronic purse system participants must be assured that load/unload devices must not link to the system without security that protects all participants from fraud" [CEP01, Bus. req. p. 19]. However, the cardholder and the load acquirer may not trust each other, and the card issuer may not trust either the cardholder or the load acquirer. In particular, the issuer needs to have valid proof in case the cardholder or the load acquirer disputes a transaction in the post-transaction settlement process. Thus the security of the system relies crucially on the validity of the audit data.

Following the above discussion, we derive the following security conditions:

Cardholder security: If the card appears to have been loaded with a certain amount according to its logs, the cardholder can prove to the card issuer that there is a load acquirer who owes the amount to the card issuer.

Load acquirer security: A load acquirer has to pay an amount to the card issuer only if the load acquirer has received the amount in cash from the cardholder.

Card issuer security: The sum of the balances of the cardholder and the load acquirer remains unchanged by the transaction.

Note that the protocol does not ensure that if the cardholder inserts cash into the loading device, the card will be loaded – there is the usual risk that the machine simply retains the money without further action, or loads the card with a smaller amount than was inserted. In this case the cardholder can only make a complaint, if necessary through the card issuer in the post-transaction settlement scheme. The correct functioning of the settlement scheme relies on the fact that the cardholder should only be led to believe that a certain amount has been correctly loaded (for example, when checking the card with a portable cardreader) if the cardholder is later able to *prove* this using the card. Otherwise the load acquirer could first credit the card with the correct amount, but later in the settlement process claim that the cardholder tried to fake the transaction.

Results

We turn to the formalizations of the above security conditions.

We start with the condition providing security for the load acquirer. According to the CEPS, the value ml_n, together with the value rl_n sent in the CreditforLoad message to the card, is taken as a guarantee that the amount m specified in ml_n has to be paid by the specified load acquirer to the issuer of the specified card, unless it is negated with the value rc_{nt} [CEP01, Tech. Spec. 6.6.1.6]. The security condition is thus formalized as follows:

Load acquirer security: Suppose that the card issuer I possesses the value $ml_n = Sign_{r_n}(cep :: nt :: lda :: m_n :: s1 :: hc_{nt} :: hl_n :: h2l_n)$ and that the card C possesses rl_n, where $h_n = \mathcal{H}ash(lda :: cep :: nt :: rl_n)$. Then after execution of the protocol either of the following two conditions hold:

- a message $\mathsf{Llog}(\mathsf{cep}, \mathsf{lda}, \mathsf{m_n}, \mathsf{nt})$ has been sent to $\mathsf{I} : \mathsf{LLog}$ (which implies that L has received and retains $\mathsf{m_n}$ in cash) or
- a message $\mathsf{Llog}(\mathsf{cep}, \mathsf{lda}, 0, \mathsf{nt})$ has been sent to $\mathsf{I} : \mathsf{LLog}$ (that is, the load acquirer assumes that the load failed and returns the amount $\mathsf{m_n}$ to the cardholder) and the load acquirer L has received $\mathsf{rc_{nt}}$ with $\mathsf{hc_{nt}} = \mathcal{H}ash(\mathsf{lda} :: \mathsf{cep} :: \mathsf{nt} :: \mathsf{rc_{nt}})$ (thus negating $\mathsf{ml_n}$).

Vulnerabilities

When trying to prove the above condition, one comes across the following weaknesses which break *both* conditions required to hold for *load acquirer security*. We first explain the problem intuitively before we prove the corresponding result.

Firstly, the value $\mathsf{ml_n}$ is only protected with the key $\mathsf{r_n}$ which in turn is only protected with the key $\mathsf{K_{LI}}$ shared between the load acquirer and the card issuer. Further, the hash value $\mathsf{hl_n}$ does not depend on the amount m. Thus the card issuer can modify the amount $\mathsf{m_n}$ contained in $\mathsf{ml_n}$ to a greater amount $\tilde{\mathsf{m}}$. In more detail, having received $\{\mathsf{r_n}\}_{\mathsf{K_{LI}}}$ from the load acquirer, the issuer can replace the value $\mathsf{ml_n} = \mathcal{S}ign_{\mathsf{r_n}}(\mathsf{cep} :: \mathsf{nt} :: \mathsf{lda} :: \mathsf{m_n} :: \mathsf{s1} :: \mathsf{hc_{nt}} :: \mathsf{hl_n} :: \mathsf{h2l_n})$ received from the load acquirer by the value $\tilde{\mathsf{ml}} = \mathcal{S}ign_{\mathsf{r_n}}(\mathsf{cep} :: \mathsf{nt} :: \mathsf{lda} :: \tilde{\mathsf{m}} :: \mathsf{s1} :: \mathsf{hc_{nt}} :: \mathsf{hl_n} :: \mathsf{h2l_n})$. Consequently, the load acquirer only receives $\mathsf{m_n}$ in cash, but has to pay $\tilde{\mathsf{m}}$ to the card issuer.

Here we assume that the card issuer is in the judicially stronger position. For example, the load acquirer may have signed a contract to pay whichever amount m contained in such an $\mathsf{ml_n}$. In a different judicial situation, the *load acquirer* might instead betray the card issuer, by *claiming* that the card issuer modified $\mathsf{ml_n}$ to contain a greater amount m, and thus pay only the allegedly correct smaller amount m'. This is an example of the observation that security analysis of practical systems has to take into account the legislative situation [And01].

Secondly, there is a vulnerability against the load acquirer arising when the card sends an $\mathsf{rc_{nt}}$ to the load acquirer in the RespC message. The only way in which the load acquirer can verify the validity of this value is against the hash $\mathsf{hc_{nt}}$ sent from the card to the load acquirer in the RespI message. Since neither the secret $\mathsf{rc_{nt}}$ shared between the card and the issuer nor the hash $\mathsf{hc_{nt}}$ is protected by any signature, the load acquirer has no way to prove in the post-transaction settlement process that $\mathsf{rc_{nt}}$ is genuine, and that thus the cash has been returned to the cardholder: The card issuer can simply claim that the card did not send a value $\mathsf{rc_{nt}}$ to the load acquirer, but that the load acquirer invented $\mathsf{rc_{nt}}$ and computed $\mathsf{hc_{nt}}$ from it. Since the card issuer controls the settlement process, the load acquirer would have to pay (or go to court, with unclear prospects of success).

Theorem 5.10. $\mathcal{L}$ *does not provide* load acquirer security *against adversaries of type* insider *with* $\{\mathsf{cep}, \mathsf{lda}, \mathsf{m_n}\} \subseteq \mathcal{K}_A^\mathsf{p}$.

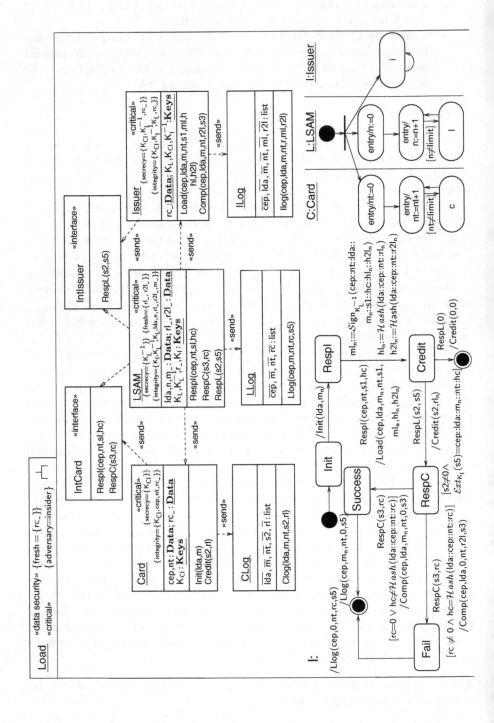

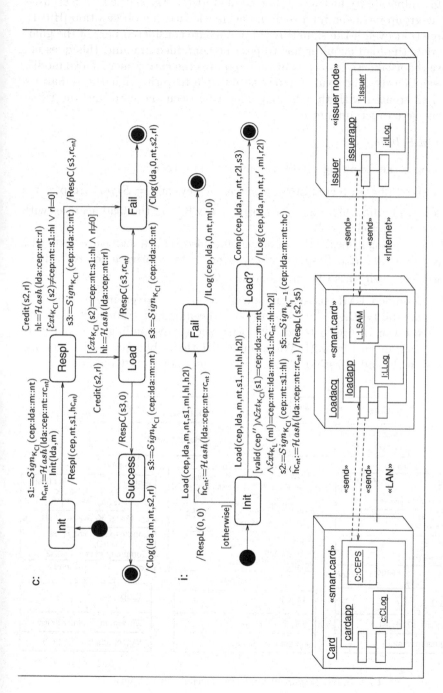

Fig. 5.17. Specification for repaired load transaction

This vulnerability has been reported in [Jür01e]. Again, the CEPS security working group has been informed and acknowledged the observation [Hit01].

Note that even if the signatures s1 and s3 are considered part of the guarantee that the load acquirer has to pay the contained amount, this does not remove the weakness entirely, but only requires the card issuer to also modify the issued cards. The load acquirer is not able to verify that the signatures s1 and s3 created with the key K_{CI} shared between the card and the issuer contain the correct amount m.

Proposed Solution

We propose the following modifications to the protocol:

- ml_n should be protected by an *asymmetric* key: $ml_n := \mathcal{S}ign_{K_L^{-1}}(cep' :: nt' :: lda :: m :: s1' :: hc' :: hl_n :: h2l_n)$ for a private key K_L^{-1} of the load acquirer with associated public key K_L, and
- in the message RespL, the issuer should also send a signature certifying the validity of hc_{nt}: $RespL(s2, \mathcal{S}ign_{K_I^{-1}}(hc_{nt}))$ for a private key K_I^{-1} of the card issuer with associated public key K_I.

The modified UML subsystem specification $\mathcal{L}'$ is given in Fig. 5.17. For better readability, the enlarged class and the modified statechart diagrams again are given in Fig. 5.18 to 5.20, with the corresponding exemplary sequence diagram in Fig. 5.21. We assume that the public keys have been exchanged in the initialization phase of the system not considered here.

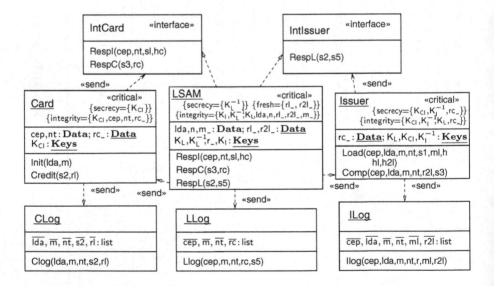

Fig. 5.18. Repaired load transaction class diagram

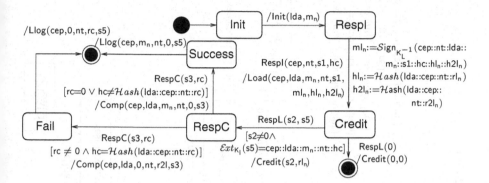

Fig. 5.19. Repaired load transaction: load acquirer

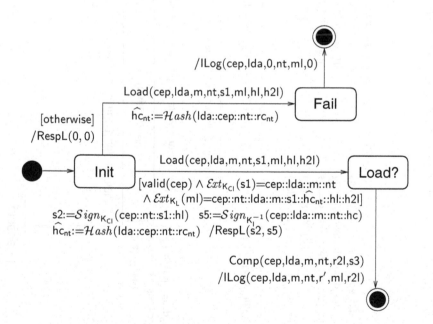

Fig. 5.20. Repaired load transaction: card issuer

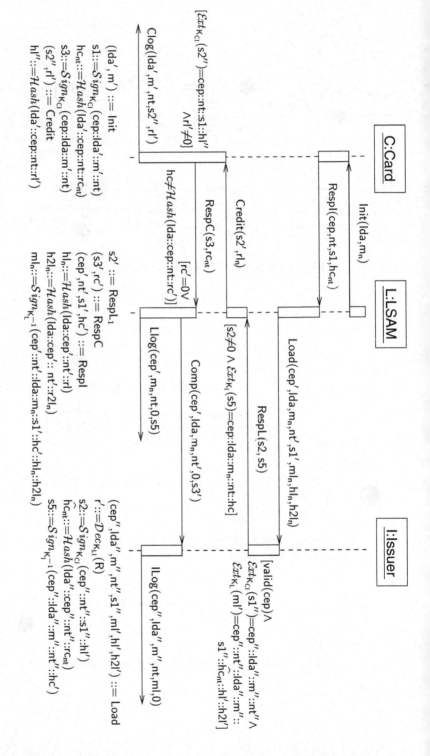

Fig. 5.21. Sequence diagram for repaired load transaction

We now discuss the security of the improved version of the protocol. Firstly, we argue that the specification is a well-defined UMLsec specification in the sense of Sect. 4.1.2.

Proposition 5.11. $\mathcal{L}'$ *provides secrecy of* $\mathsf{K_{CI}}, \mathsf{K_L^{-1}}, \mathsf{K_I^{-1}}$ *and integrity of* $\mathsf{K_{CI}}$, $\mathsf{K_L^{-1}}$, $\mathsf{K_I^{-1}}$, cep, nt, $\mathsf{rc_{nt}}$, lda, n, $\mathsf{rl_n}$, $\mathsf{r2l_n}$, $\mathsf{m_n}$ *(meaning that the adversary should not be able to make the atttributes take on values previously known only to him) against* insider *adversaries with* $\mathcal{K}_A^p \cap \{\mathsf{K_{CI}}, \mathsf{K_L^{-1}}, \mathsf{K_I^{-1}}\} = \emptyset$.

We now consider the formalizations of the above security goals with respect to the modified specification. They use the following two notational definitions.

- Let $\mathcal{K}$ be the joint knowledge set of all participants except L: any object in the classes Card or Issuer, any adversary (that is not able to penetrate the smart card on which L resides, according to the threat scenario), and any object in LSAM except L.
- Let $\mathcal{K}_L$ be the knowledge set of L.

Theorem 5.12. *In the presence of adversaries of type* $A =$ insider *with*

$$\mathcal{K}_A^p \cap \{\mathsf{K_{CI}}, \mathsf{K_L^{-1}}, \mathsf{K_I^{-1}}\} \cup \{\mathsf{rc_{nt}} : \mathsf{nt} \in \mathbb{N}\} \cup \{\mathsf{rl_n}, \mathsf{r2l_n} : n \in \mathbb{N}\} = \emptyset$$

the following security guarantees are provided by $\mathcal{L}'$:

Cardholder security: For any message $\mathsf{Clog(lda, m, nt, s2, rl)}$ *sent to* $\mathsf{c : CLog}$, *if* $\mathsf{m} \neq 0$ *(that is, the card seems to have been loaded with* m*) then* $\mathsf{rl} \neq 0$ *and*

$$\mathcal{E}xt_{\mathsf{K_{CI}}}(\mathsf{s2}) = \mathsf{cep} :: \mathsf{nt} :: \mathcal{S}ign_{\mathsf{K_{CI}}}(\mathsf{cep} :: \mathsf{lda} :: \mathsf{m} :: \mathsf{nt}) ::$$
$$\mathcal{H}ash(\mathsf{lda} :: \mathsf{cep} :: \mathsf{nt} :: \mathsf{rl})$$

holds (that is, the card issuer certifies rl *to be a valid proof for the transaction). For any two messages* $\mathsf{Clog(lda, m, nt, s2, rl)}$ *and* $\mathsf{Clog(lda', m', nt', s2', rl')}$ *sent to* $\mathsf{c : CLog}$, *we have* $\mathsf{nt} \neq \mathsf{nt'}$.

Load acquirer security: Suppose that we have $\mathsf{ml_n} \in \mathcal{K}$ *and* $\mathsf{rl_n} \in \mathcal{K}$ *where* $\mathsf{ml_n} = \mathcal{S}ign_{\mathsf{K_L^{-1}}}(\mathsf{cep} :: \mathsf{nt} :: \mathsf{lda} :: \mathsf{m_n} :: \mathsf{s1} :: y :: \mathsf{hl_n} :: \mathsf{h2l_n})$ *with* $\mathsf{hl_n} = \mathcal{H}ash(\mathsf{lda} :: \mathsf{cep} :: \mathsf{nt} :: \mathsf{rl_n})$ *and* $\mathsf{h2l_n} = \mathcal{H}ash(\mathsf{lda} :: \mathsf{cep} :: \mathsf{nt} :: \mathsf{r2l_n})$, *for some* cep, nt, s1, *and* y. *Then at the end of an execution of L either of the following two conditions hold:*

- *a message* $\mathsf{Llog(cep, lda, m_n, nt, x)}$ *has been sent to* $\mathsf{l : LLog}$ *(which implies that L has received and retains* $\mathsf{m_n}$ *in cash) or*
- *a message* $\mathsf{Llog(cep, lda, 0, nt, x)}$ *has been sent to* $\mathsf{l : LLog}$, *for some* x *(that is, the load acquirer assumes that the load failed and returns the amount* $\mathsf{m_n}$ *to the cardholder), and we have* $x' \in \mathcal{K}_L$ *and* $z \in \mathcal{K}$ *with* $z = \mathcal{S}ign_{\mathsf{K_I^{-1}}}(\mathsf{cep} :: \mathsf{lda} :: \mathsf{m_n} :: \mathsf{nt} :: y')$ *where* $y' = \mathcal{H}ash(\mathsf{lda} :: \mathsf{cep} :: \mathsf{nt} :: x')$ $= y$ *(that is, the load acquirer can prove that the load was aborted).*

Card issuer security: For each message $\mathsf{Clog}(\mathsf{lda}, \mathsf{m}, \mathsf{nt}, \mathsf{s2}, \mathsf{rl})$ *sent to* $\mathsf{c} : \mathsf{CLog}$, *if* $\mathsf{m} \neq 0$ *and*

$$\mathcal{E}xt_{\mathsf{K}_{\mathsf{CI}}}(\mathsf{s2}) = \mathsf{cep} :: \mathsf{nt} :: \mathcal{S}ign_{\mathsf{K}_{\mathsf{CI}}}(\mathsf{cep} :: \mathsf{lda} :: \mathsf{m} :: \mathsf{nt}) ::$$
$$\mathcal{H}ash(\mathsf{lda} :: \mathsf{cep} :: \mathsf{nt} :: \mathsf{rl})$$

holds for some lda, *then the card issuer has a valid signature* ml_n *corresponding to this transaction.*

We had to change the condition of *load acquirer security* slightly to accommodate the changes in the protocol. To see that it is formalized in an adequate way, note that a value $\mathsf{ml}_n = \mathcal{S}ign_{\mathsf{K}_{\mathsf{L}}^{-1}}(\mathsf{cep} :: \mathsf{nt} :: \mathsf{lda} :: \mathsf{m}_n :: \mathsf{s1} :: \mathsf{hc} :: \mathsf{hl}_n :: \mathsf{h2l}_n)$ is known outside L only after the load acquirer has received the amount m_n in cash. This follows from the facts that a protocol at L is started only after the cash is inserted, that ml_n is signed with the key $\mathsf{K}_{\mathsf{L}}^{-1}$, and that this key is only accessible to L by Proposition 5.11. Thus the critical question is whether the cash is returned to the cardholder after rl_n becomes known outside L. According to the specification of L this may happen only after a message of the form $\mathsf{Llog}(\mathsf{cep}, 0, \mathsf{nt}, \mathsf{rc})$ is sent to $\mathsf{l} : \mathsf{LLog}$.

5.4 Developing Secure Java Programs

Dynamic access control mechanisms such as those provided by Java since the JDK 1.2 Security Architecture [Gon99, Kar00] in the form of GuardedObjects can be difficult to administer since it is easy to forget an access check [Gon98, BV99]. If the appropriate access controls are not performed, the security of the entire system may be compromised. Additionally, access control may be granted indirectly and unintentionally by granting access to an object containing the signature key that enables access to another object. We show how to use UMLsec to address these problems by providing means of reasoning about the correct deployment of security mechanisms such as guarded objects.

After presenting some background on access control in Java in the following subsection, we outline the part of a design process relevant to enforcing access control in Java and give some results on verifying access control requirements. In Sect. 5.4.3 we illustrate our approach with the example of the development of a web-based financial application from formal specifications.

5.4.1 Access Control in Java

Authorization or *access control* is one of the cornerstones of computer security [SS94]. The objective is to determine whether the source of a request is *authorized* to be granted the request. Distributed systems offer additional challenges. The trusted computing bases (TCBs) may be in various locations and under different controls. Communication is in the presence of possible adversaries. Mobile code is employed that is possibly malicious. Further complications arise from the need for delegation, meaning that entities may act on behalf of other entities. Also, many security requirements are location-dependent. For example, a user may have more rights at the office terminal than when logging on from home.

In the JDK 1.0 Security Architecture, the challenges posed by mobile code were addressed by letting code from remote locations execute within a *sandbox* offering strong limitations on its execution. However, this model turned out to be too simplistic and restrictive.

From JDK 1.2, a more fine-grained security architecture is employed which offers a user-definable access control, and the sophisticated concept of guarded objects [Gon99, Kar00]. Permissions are granted to protection domains. A *protection domain* [SS75] is a set of entities accessible by a principal. In the JDK 1.2, protection domains consist of classes and objects. They are specified depending on the origin of the code, as given by a URL, and on the key with which the code may be signed. The system security policy set by the user or a system administrator is represented by a policy object instantiated from the class java.security.Policy. The security policy maps protection domains to sets of access permissions given to the code.

There is a hierarchy of typed and parameterized access permissions, of which the root class is java.security.Permission and other permissions are subclassed either from the root class or one of its subclasses. Permissions consist of a target and an action. For file access permissions in the class FilePermission, the targets can be directories or files, and the actions include read, write, execute, and delete.

An access permission is granted if all callers in the current thread history belong to domains that have been granted the said permission. The history of a thread includes all classes on the current stack and also transitively inherits all classes in its parent thread when the current thread is created.

The sophisticated JDK 1.2 access control mechanisms are not so easy to use. The granting of permissions depends on the execution context. Sometimes, access control decisions rely on multiple threads. A thread may involve several protection domains. Thus it is not always easy to see if a given class will be granted a certain permission.

This complexity is increased by the mentioned guarded objects [Gon99].

If the supplier of a resource is not in the same thread as the consumer, and the consumer thread cannot provide the access control context information, one can use a GuardedObject to protect access to the resource. The supplier of the resource creates an object representing the resource and a GuardedObject containing the resource object, and then hands the GuardedObject to the consumer. A specified Guard object incorporates checks that need to be met so that the resource object can be obtained. For this, the Guard interface contains the method checkGuard, taking an Object argument and performing the checks. To grant access the Guard objects simply returns, to deny access it throws a SecurityException. GuardedObjects are a quite powerful access control mechanism. However, their use can be difficult to administer [Gon98]. For example, guard objects may check the signature on a class file. This way, access to an object may be granted indirectly, and possibly unintentionally, by giving access to another object containing the signature key for which the corresponding signature provides access to the first object.

5.4.2 Design Process

We sketch the part of a design process for secure systems using UML that is concerned with access control enforcement using guarded objects:

(1) Formulate the permission sets for access control of sensitive objects.
(2) Use statecharts to specify Guard objects that enforce appropriate access control checks.
(3) Make sure that the Guard objects protect the sensitive objects sufficiently in that they only grant access implied by the security requirements (by making use of the tool support presented in Chap. 6.
(4) Ensure that the access control mechanisms are consistent with the functionality required by the system in that the objects that depend on guarded objects may perform their intended behavior, again by making use of the tool support.

Here the access control requirements in step (1) can be of the following form:

- origin of requesting object (based on URL)
- signature of requesting object
- external variables (such as time of day)

In Sect. 5.4.3 we discuss a specification following these steps. They enforce the following two requirements:

Security requirement: The access control requirements are strong enough to prevent unauthorized influence, given the threat scenario arising from the physical layer.
Functionality requirement: The access control requirements formulated are not overly restrictive, denying legitimate access from other components of the specification.

The functionality requirement is important since it is not always easy to see if stated security requirements are at all implementable. If their inconsistency is only noticed during implementation then, firstly, resources are wasted since work has to be redone. Secondly, most likely security will be degraded in order to reduce this extra work.

Before coming to the main example in the next subsection, we give a short example to point out that the kind of weaknesses in using the Java security access control mechanisms can be quite subtle, beyond just mistakenly sending out secret keys or forgetting to set access rules.

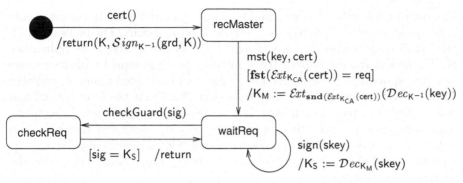

Fig. 5.22. Guard object example

Example

The statechart in Fig. 5.22 describes the behavior of a guard object grd enforcing a slightly more complicated access control policy.

To facilitate understanding, we give a typical message exchange of this access control mechanism to establish K_S in Fig. 5.23. In the envisioned situation, there is an object req used to grant to other objects the right to access a particular guarded object by signing the class files with a key K_S. There should be a possibility to update the key K_S: by substituting K_S with a different key K'_S it can be achieved that an object the class file of which is signed by K_S is no longer allowed access to the guarded object. Thus the object req needs to be able to submit the current signing key K_S to the guard object. For this, first a shared key K_M is established using the public key K of the guard object, which is used to encrypt the submitted key K_S. This is more secure and more efficient than directly using K, if K_S is updated rather frequently. The

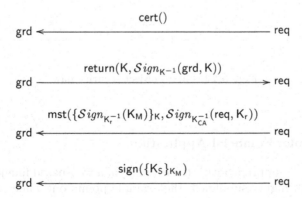

Fig. 5.23. Guard object message exchange

identity of req is taken as given and is bound to a public key in the certificate cert signed with the key K_{CA} of a certification authority. On request cert(), the guard object sends out a self-signed certificate certifying its public key K. The object req sends back the symmetric key K_M signed with its private key corresponding to the public key in cert and encrypted under K, together with the certificate cert. We recall from Sect. 3.3.3 that the functions fst and snd applied to a pair return their first and second components, respectively. The guard object can receive the signature key K_S encrypted under K_M and will then grant access to those objects in class files signed by K_S. We assume that the guard object is given the signature of the requesting object using the method checkGuard().

Note that here we do not focus on the exception processing mechanism. Thus a guard object that does not grant access simply does not return. Also, for simplicity we assume that the guard object receives the key sig with which the requesting applet was signed as the argument of the operation checkGuard, and that the execution context of the applet checks that it was actually signed with this key.

This access control mechanism, which for the sake of the example is derived from the protocol in Sect. 5.2, contains a flaw analogous to the one pointed out there: an adversary A intercepting the communication between req and grd, and modifying the exchanged values, can find out K_M and thus make grd accept a key K_S chosen by A. The critical part of the message exchange corresponding to this attack is given in Fig. 5.24. Here the intended access control policy is not enforced since the preservation of secrecy of the signing key K_S is violated in a subtle way. With our approach one can exhibit subtle flaws like this using the tool support provided for UMLsec.

$$\text{grd} \xrightarrow{\quad \text{return}(K, Sign_{K^{-1}}(\text{grd}, K)) \quad} A \xrightarrow{\quad \text{return}(K_A, Sign_{K_A^{-1}}(\text{grd}, K_A)) \quad} \text{req}$$

$$\text{grd} \xleftarrow{\quad \text{mst}(\{Sign_{K_r^{-1}}(K_M)\}_K, Sign_{K_{CA}^{-1}}(\text{req}, K_r)) \quad} A \xleftarrow{\quad \text{mst}(\{Sign_{K_r^{-1}}(K_M)\}_{K_A}, Sign_{K_{CA}^{-1}}(\text{req}, K_r)) \quad} \text{req}$$

Fig. 5.24. Guard object security flaw

5.4.3 Example: Financial Application

We illustrate our approach with the example of a web-based financial application. Although highly simplified, the example points out some typical issues when considering access control for web-based e-commerce applications: to have several entities, such as service providers and customers, interacting with

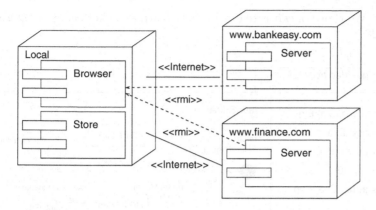

Fig. 5.25. Financial application specification: Architecture

each other while granting the other parties a limited amount of trust and by enforcing this using credentials. Since we would only like to illustrate the general idea, we only give parts of a system specification, rather than a complete UML subsystem. We show in UML diagrams how to employ GuardedObjects to enforce these security requirements. We argue that the specification given by the UML diagrams is secure in that it does not grant any access not implied by the security requirements. Again, this security analysis can be performed using the UMLsec tool support.

Two institutions offer services over the Internet to local users: an Internet bank, Bankeasy, and a financial advisor, Finance. The overall architecture of this system is given in Fig. 5.25, where « rmi » represents remote method invocations.

To make use of these services, a local client needs to grant the applets from the respective sites certain privileges:

(1) Applets that are signed by the bank can read and write the financial data stored in the local database, but only between 1 pm and 2 pm (when the user usually manages his or her bank account).
(2) Applets (for example, from the financial advisor) can access an excerpt of the local financial data to give the user advice on stock purchases. Since these applets also need access to the Internet to obtain stock information, but the financial information is not supposed to leave the local system, they have to be signed by a certification company, CertiFlow, certifying that they do not leak out information.
(3) Applets signed by the financial advisor may use the micropayment signature key of the local user (to purchase stock rate information on behalf of the user), but this access should only be granted five times a week.

Financial data sent over the Internet is encrypted to ensure integrity and confidentiality. Access to the local financial data is realized using Guarded-

Objects. We thus concentrate on the specification of the local system given in Fig. 5.26.

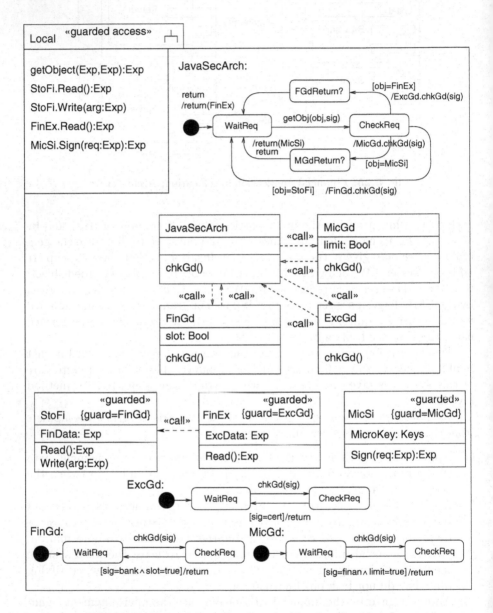

Fig. 5.26. Financial application specification: Local system

We only give a partial specification, containing the simplified relevant part of the Java Security Architecture which receives requests for object references and forwards them to the guard objects of the three guarded objects. We omit the behavior of the guarded objects, and also the activity diagram which would include their behavior, and the deployment diagram. The access controls are realized by the Guard objects FinGd, ExpGd, and MicGd, whose behavior is specified. We assume that the condition slot is fulfilled if and only if the time is between 1 pm and 2 pm, and that the condition limit is fulfilled if and only if the access to the micropayment key has been granted less than five times in the current calendar week. Here we assume that the execution context of an applet checks that the applet was actually signed by the authority *sig* whose name is given as the second argument to getObj, and again we do not model exception processing. In accordance with the UMLsec profile in Chap. 4, we assume that the names of the objects that are stereotyped « guarded » are not in $\mathcal{K}_A^p$ and thus not initially known to the adversary. In this way we model the passing of references in the Java 2 Security Architecture.

Now according to step (3) in Sect. 5.4.2, one may convince oneself that the guard objects sufficiently protect the guarded objects, as required by the access control requirements stated above. We omit the formal treatment. Note that one might also formalize these requirements using first-order logic and then use the UMLsec tool support to make sure that any access granted by one of the guard objects is legitimate in the sense that it may be derived from the original formalization in the logic. In this way our approach helps to bridge the gap between formal security policy models and system specifications.

Regarding step (4) in Sect. 5.4.2, one may also convince oneself that any legitimate access according to the above requirements is granted, again, using the tool support.

5.5 Further Applications

We give some examples for further applications of our Model-based Security Engineering approach.

5.5.1 Modeling and Verification of a Bank Application

In a project with a major German bank [GHJW03], we have applied our ideas about model-based development of security-critical systems to a web-based banking application, by making use of the CASE tool AUTOFOCUS [SH99], which has a UML-like notation.

The application can be used by clients to fill out and sign digital order forms. The main security requirements of this application are that the personal data in the forms must be kept confidential, and that orders cannot be submitted in the name of others.

For this purpose, when the user logs in, first an authentication protocol is run and an encrypted connection is established. The second part of the

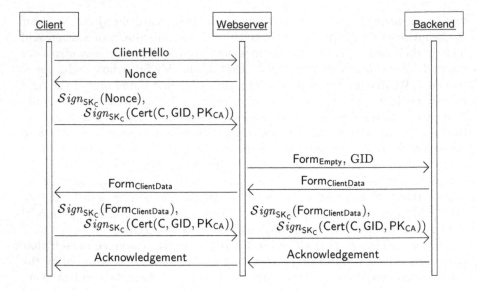

Fig. 5.27. Authentication protocol

transaction (filling out and digitally signing the order form) is carried out over this connection.

The authentication protocol is based on an underlying SSL connection layer which is initially established and which is supposed to provide a secure connection with regard to confidentiality and server authentication. The session key generated during the SSL handshake is used to encrypt the messages of the authentication protocol on the second layer. The protocol authenticates the client by making use of a cardreader and a smart card to compute digital signatures on the client's side. There is a need for a layered protocol here because the SSL client authentication feature cannot be used due to technical restrictions imposed by the architecture of the bank system (the web server does not support the forwarding of client certificates).

The complete protocol run is shown in Fig. 5.27. After the ClientHello message, a nonce (a randomly generated number) is sent by the web server. The client signs this nonce with his or her own private key and sends it together with his or her certificate back to the web server. The certificate contains the client's identity, a global identification number which references the client's data on the backend, and the client's public key. The web server checks the signature of the nonce and compares the received nonce with the one sent before. Furthermore a plausibility check of the global ID will be done and it will be saved for later purposes. The authentication is finished after the checks have been successful. The web server now sends the global ID and an empty form to the backend system, where it is filled with the client's data and sent back to the client. The global ID is also stored on the backend.

The client signs his or her data with his or her private key, thus creating an electronic signature. The backend checks the signature of the received data object and the certificate. The received global ID and the signed data object are compared with the ones stored. On success an order is generated and an acknowledgment is sent to the client. The end of connection signal can be caused by a timeout or a logout event.

In [GHJW03], the system architecture and the protocol are specified using the tool AUTOFOCUS in a notation which is very similar to UML deployment diagrams and UML statecharts (see there for the details). This model is then verified with regard to the relevant security requirements. For this purpose, the tool AUTOFOCUS generates an input file for the symbolic model checker SMV [McM93] which carries out the actual model checking process. Also, the required security properties are translated into the SMV language as well, and during the model checking process, SMV checks whether they are true with respect to the model (including both the modeled protocol and the adversary model). If SMV finds any flaw in the protocol, this counter-example is translated by the tool AUTOFOCUS into a notation similar to UML sequence diagrams, which helps to understand the way the protocol can be attacked. More details can be found in [GHJW03].

5.5.2 Biometric Authentication System

In the context of the Verisoft project [Ver03] funded by the German Federal Ministry of Research (BMBF), UMLsec is used for the development and security analysis of a smart-card-based biometric authentication system together with a major German telecommunications company. In this system, a biometric reference template stored on a smart card is compared with the data provided by the biometric sensor. If the two match, the user is authenticated. Because the communication links between sensor, host system and smart card are vulnerable, they have to be protected using a cryptographic protocol. Since the secure development of such a system is difficult, UMLsec is used to specify the system and then to perform an automatic security analysis using the tool support presented in Chap. 6.

While the system is still in development and the security analysis in progress at the time of writing, the UMLsec based approach has already made itself indispensable by detecting a security weakness which would have allowed an adversary to circumvent a misuse counter designed to prevent brute force attacks. The weakness has been removed and it is planned to implement the authentication system using code generation from the UMLsec specification.

5.5.3 Automotive Emergency Application

Also in the context of the Verisoft project mentioned above, an Automotive emergeny application is being developed together with a major German car manufacturer which in the case of an accident should automatically contact a central server over a wireless network. Since the data that is communicated may include information related to the cause of the accident raising questions of liability, the communication has to be secured against adversaries trying to manipulate this data or trying to breach its confidentiality. Therefore, we also use UMLsec in this context to help constructing a reliable system.

5.5.4 German Electronic Health Card

At the time of writing, the German Federal Ministry of Health and Social Security (BMGS) is currently developing an Electronic Health Card (Gesundheitskarte) [eHe03]. It is supposed to be issued until 2006 to all people insured by the public health insurance system, which is the vast majority of the 80 million Germans. It will be designed to support, besides administrative functions such as the handling of electronic prescriptions, also the storage of health data. Therefore it is implemented on a smart card that can perform cryptographic authentication, encryption and signatures. Part of the card is planned to be interoperable on a European level. Evidently, data integrity and protection is vital for such a system. Because of its sheer size and complexity and the tight time-frame, designing such a system securely is a very ambitious task. We currently try to assist this endeavor by performing a UMLsec based security analysis of the available specifications.

5.5.5 Electronic Purse for the Oktoberfest

In a further industrial application of the UMLsec methodology, we are currently investigating an electronic purse system in development for the Oktoberfest in Munich, one of the largest festivals in the world. While similar in its goals to the CEPS presented in Sect. 5.3, it is implemented in a proprietary design. As an additional challenge for its security, the communication between smart card and card reader is supposed to be wireless, facilitating attempts to attack this communication channel. A security analysis of the security-critical parts of the system using UMLsec and its tool support is in progress.

5.5.6 Electronic Signature Architecture in Insurance Companies

A large German insurance company is currently investigating the possibilities of using electronic signature pads to allow a completely paperless signing and processing of contracts by its clients and within the company. Here, UMLsec is used to describe possible technical and architectural variants of such a system and to perform a security analysis and risk assessment using the UMLsec tools. Based on these results, a decision will be reached if and how such a system should be implemented.

5.6 Notes

The material from Sections 5.1 and 5.2 has been presented, in a different formal model, in [Jür01g]. Related work for Sect. 5.1 includes [AFG02]. The work shows how to translate a specification language related to the pi-calculus but including secure channel abstractions into a lower-level language that includes cryptographic primitives. Communication on secure channels is thus mapped to encrypted communication on public channels. Correctness results for this translation imply that it is safe to reason on the more abstract level. An example for research related to Sect. 5.2 is the verification of the TLS protocol using the interactive theorem prover Isabelle [NPW02] in [Pau98a]. One should emphasize, however, that the protocol investigated in Sect. 5.2 is a *variant* of TLS proposed in [APS99]. To our knowlegde, this variant has not been otherwise formally analyzed.

Part of the research in Sect. 5.3 was reported in [JW01b, Jür01e, Jür04c], where [JW01b] uses the AUTOFOCUS CASE tool [HMR⁺98] which uses a notation very similar to UML. This work was extended in [JW01a] beyond specification-based analysis to security testing of the CEPS by automatically deriving test-sequences from the specification. More on this can be found in Sect. 6.4.1. Related to Sect. 5.3, information on smart cards is gathered in [RE00]. An overview of electronic payment systems is given in [AJSW00]. Smart card protocols have been investigated using formal logic in [ABKL93]. Smart card payment systems are analyzed using formal methods in [And99, SCW00].

The approach in Sect. 5.4 has been discussed in [Jür01h]. In a similar vain, [Jür02e] shows how to use UMLsec for developing secure CORBA applications. Related to the research in Sect. 5.4, Java 2 security and in particular the advanced topics of signed, sealed, and guarded objects is explained in [Gon99]. There has also been some work giving formal reference models for Java 2 access control mechanisms, thus clarifying possible ambiguities in the informal accounts and enabling proof of compiler conformance to the specification [KG98, WF98, Kar00] (but without considering signed, sealed, or guarded objects). To our knowledge, the secure use of signed, sealed, or guarded objects in JDK 1.2 has so far not otherwise been considered in a formally based approach.

5.7 Discussion

We gave examples of secure systems development using UMLsec. We exemplified stepwise formal development of a security-critical system by considering a secure channel design. We uncovered a flaw in a variant of the handshake protocol of the Internet protocol TLS proposed in [APS99], suggested a correction, and verified the corrected protocol. We examined the Common Electronic Purse Specifications, discovered flaws in the two central parts of the specifications, proposed corrections, and gave a verification. We demonstrated how to use UMLsec for formal development of security-critical Java systems.

These case studies demonstrate the adequacy of the UMLsec definition for modeling and verifying secure systems. With the CEP specifications in particular, we presented an industrial application of realistic size and complexity to demonstrate that the use of UMLsec is not restricted to the kind of compact core cryptographic protocols often considered in the academic formal methods in security literature.

Necessarily, this complexity is reflected in the CEP specifications in so far as it is relevant to the security analysis, for example with respect to the cryptographic data included in the diagrams. One should note, however, that the use of a graphical specification language such as UML helps mastering this complexity. Although a two-page UML diagram with lots of cryptographic expressions may look daunting at first sight, it is considerably more quickly accessible than the 500 pages of textual specifications in [CEP01], and even more so when compared to what a logical formula equivalent to the UML model would look like. Using a graphical specification language has the advantage of providing a quick overview of the physical and logical structure of the system that is modeled, while all the needed technical details are there as well. That security practitioners are already starting to realize this can be inferred from the fact that many industrial specifications today already make use of UML like notations, although still in an often fragmentary and not fully coherent way. It should be hoped that the level of precision and detail can be raised by providing a general framework which provides a payoff for the increased effort, in particular by providing the kind of tool support for automated security analysis which we present in Chap. 6.

In all, our experience with using UMLsec in industrial application projects indicates that its use has the potential for significantly improving the security of systems in development or already existing.

Part III

Tool Support

6

Tool support for UMLsec

For the ideas that were presented in the previous chapters to be of benefit in practice, it is important to have advanced tool support to assist in using them. In this chapter, we present the necessary background and some results achieved so far toward developing tool support for UMLsec. The developed tools can be used to check the constraints associated with UMLsec stereotypes mechanically, based on XMI output of the diagrams from the UML drawing tool in use. We also explain a framework for implementing verification routines for the constraints associated with the UMLsec stereotypes. The goal is that advanced users of the UMLsec approach should be able to use this framework to implement verification routines for the constraints of self-defined stereotypes.

Furthermore, we present research on linking the UMLsec approach with the automated analysis of security-critical data arising at runtime. Specifically, we present research on the construction of a tool which automatically checks the SAP R/3 configuration for security policy rules formulated as UML specifications. Because of its modular architecture and its standardized interfaces, the tool can be adapted to check security constraints in other kinds of application software, such as firewalls or other access control configurations.

Finally, we present some approaches for linking UML models to implementations. The aim is to ensure that the benefits gained from the model-based approach on the level of the system model actually carry over to the implemented system, as one would hope.

6.1 Extending UML CASE Tools with Analysis Tools

We present some background useful for constructing tool support for XMI-based analysis of UML models. In the first subsection, we explain how the syntax of UML diagrams is defined on a technical level using the Meta-Object Facility (MOF) and how the data contained in UML diagrams can be saved using the XML Metadata Interchange (XMI) format. In the second subsection, we explain how one can conveniently access the information stored in an XMI file.

6.1.1 Meta-Object Facility (MOF)

Early tool support for processing UML models had to rely on storage formats of the various UML tools which made exchange and reuse of the models and tools impossible. Having chosen a UML tool, the developer was tied to using it through the whole project. Applying emerging technologies to the UML modeling on the industrial level was virtually impossible. To suggest any custom UML processing, one would have to develop a complete UML editor and persuade the developers to use it.

The development of XML as a universal data storage format changed this situation. In the year 2000, the Object Management Group (OMG) issued the first specification for the XML Metadata Interchange (XMI) language [XMI02] which became a standard for exchanging UML models between tools. The XMI language again is compliant with MOF [MOF02]. MOF is a standard defining an abstract language and a framework for specifying, constructing and managing modeling languages, also called meta-models, such as UML and CWM (Common Warehouse Model). It allows software systems to be modeled particularly flexibly in an approach based on several layers of information. The differenz meta-levels are displayed in Fig. 6.1.

Initially it was developed to define CORBA-based services for managing meta-information. Currently, its applications include the definition of modeling languages such as UML and CWM.

We explain the different MOF layers at the hand of an example in Fig. 6.2. The lowest level M0 deals with the data instances, for example "Bob Marley", "Kingston". The level M1 describes data models, in software development this corresponds to the UML model of the application. An example for this layer is a *Person* with attribute *City*. The next abstraction level M2 is the modeling language itself. There exist different modeling languages for different application domains, and the last abstraction level M3 is the common environment

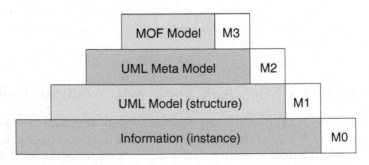

Fig. 6.1. MOF framework: meta-levels

M3	Meta-Meta-model	MetaClass, MetaAssociation – MOF Model
M2	Meta-model	Class, Attribute, Dependency – UML (as a language), CWM
M1	Model	Person, City – UML Model
M0	Data	Bob Marley, Kingston – Running program

Fig. 6.2. MOF framework: example

for defining these modeling languages, standardized by the MOF. The MOF makes use of the following three concepts:

MOF objects define object types for the target model. The information associated with an MOF object includes a *name*, a set of *attributes*, a set of *operations*, a set of *association references*, and a set of *supertypes* it inherits. The MOF object is a *container* for its component features, namely its its *attributes*, *operations*, and *association references*. It may also contain MOF definitions of *data types* and *exceptions*.

MOF associations define links between two MOF objects. These links are always binary and directed. A link is a *container* for two *association ends*, each representing one object which the link is connected to.

MOF packages group related MOF elements for reuse and modularization. An MOF package is defined by a *name*, a list of *imports* consisting of other MOF packages whose components may be reused, a list of *supertypes* which defines a set of other MOF packages whose components form a part of the package, and a set of contained elements including other objects, associations, and packages.

The MOF also defines the following secondary elements:

- Data types can be used to define *constructed* and *reference* data types.
- Constants define compile-time constant expressions.
- Exceptions can be raised by object operations.
- Constraints can be attached to other MOF elements. Constraint semantics and verification are not part of the MOF specification, and therefore they can be defined with any language.

The MOF is related to two other standards:

XML Metadata Interchange (XMI) is a mapping from MOF to XML. It can be used to automatically produce an XML interchange format for any language described with MOF. For example, to produce a standardized UML interchange format, we need to define the UML language using MOF, and use the XMI mapping rules to derive DTDs and XML Schemas for UML serialization. The MOF itself is defined using MOF, and therefore XMI can be applied not only for meta-model instances, but for meta-models themselves: They are also instances of a meta-model, which is a MOF model.

The Java Metadata Interface (JMI) standard defines a MOF-to-Java mapping, similarly to the MOF-to-XML mapping provided by XMI. It is used to derive Java interfaces tailored for accessing instances of a particular meta-model. As MOF itself is MOF-compliant, it can be used to access meta-models as well. The standard also defines a set of *reflective* interfaces that can be used similarly to the meta-model-specific API without prior knowledge of the meta-model.

Today, many UML editors support model interchange in the XMI format. Together with the wide support for the XML language, including a broad range of libraries, editors, and accompanying technologies, this enables development of lightweight UML processing tools.

6.1.2 XML-Based Data-Binding with MDR

There exist at least three technologies for processing XMI files:

- Common high-level languages with appropriate libraries for parsing XML files (such as Java, C++, and Perl).
- Specialized XML parsing and transformation languages (such as XPath and XSLT).
- XMI data-binding, where a framework extracts the data from an XMI file, which can then be accessed for example through a Java method.

The first two methods, although flexible, require some effort related to parsing the XMI file. This suggests trying to use XMI data-binding for our purposes. There exist libraries supporting data-binding for the more general case of XML, such as the widely used Castor library [Cas03]. However, there exist XMI-specific data-binding libraries which directly provide a representation of an XMI file on the abstraction level of a UML model. This allows the developer to operate directly with UML concepts, such as classes, statecharts, and stereotypes. For UMLsec tool support, we use the MDR (Meta-Data Repository) library which is part of the Netbeans project [Net03] and also used by the freely available UML modeling tool Poseidon 1.6 Community Edition [Gen03]. Another such library is the Novosoft NSUML project [NSU03].

The MDR library implements an MOF repository with support for XMI and JMI standards. Figure 6.3 illustrates how the repository is used for working with UML models.

In step 1, the XMI description of the modeling language is used to customize the MDR for working with a particular model type, which is UML in this case. The XMI description of UML 1.5 is published by the Object Management Group (OMG). A storage customized for the given model type is

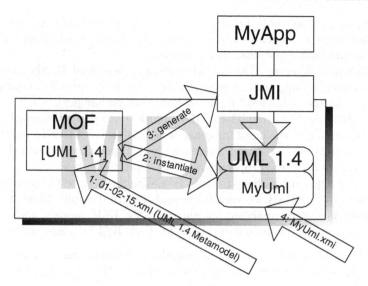

Fig. 6.3. Using the MDR library

created in step 2. Additionally, based on the XMI specification of the modeling language, the MDR library creates the JMI implementation for accessing the model in step 3. This allows the application to manipulate the model directly on the conceptual level of UML. In step 4, the UML model is loaded into the repository. Now it can be accessed through the supplied JMI interfaces from a Java application. The model can be read, modified, and later saved in an XMI file again.

Because of the additional abstraction level implemented by the MDR library, using it in the UMLsec tool is hoped to facilitate upgrading to upcoming UML versions, and promises a high-standard compatibility.

6.2 Automated Tools for UMLsec

This section presents research on tool support for the automated analysis of UMLsec models with regard to security requirements currently under development at TU Munich and available at [JSA+04].

6.2.1 Tool Functionality

There are several possible degrees of functionality in the verification of UMLsec models, depending on which of the stereotypes in Sect. 4.1.2 should be verified:

Static features: The tool should be able to verify security properties included as stereotypes in the structure and deployment diagrams, such as « secure links » and « secure dependency ».

Simple dynamic features: The model behavior, described by the statechart and sequence diagrams, is analyzed to verify basic security requirement, defined on the behavioral level (such as « fair exchange »).

Complex dynamic features: The UMLsec model describing dynamic behavior is translated into the input language of an analysis tool (such as a temporal logic formula in the case of a model-checker). It can thus be verified against even subtle dynamic properties, such as « data security ».

External application binding It would be desirable to have the possibility to connect to the UMLsec tool framework external applications that may provide data to be analyzed together with the UML models, such as security permissions from configurations for SAP R/3 business applications.

The following aspects have to be considered when trying to construct tool support for secure systems development with UML following the UMLsec approach.

To be able to apply verification tools, such as model-checkers or automated theorem provers, one needs a front-end which automatically produces a semantic model and includes the relevant formalized security requirements, when given a UMLsec model. This avoids requiring the software developers themselves to perform this formalization, which usually needs a high level of specialized training in formal methods. UMLsec supports this approach by offering predefined security primitives with a strictly defined semantics, which can be applied by a developer who may not be expert in security by including the relevant stereotypes in the UML model. These primitives are translated into the targeted formal language, protecting from potential errors in manual formalization of the security properties. See Chap. 7 for a definition of the formal language used for UMLsec and the formalization of the security primitives and Chap. 8 for the formal semantics of the (restricted and simplified) fragment of UML used. Since security requirements are usually defined relative to an adversary, to analyze whether the UML specification fulfills a security requirement, the tool support has to automatically include the adversary model arising from the physical view contained in the UML specification.

The architecture and basic functionality of the UMLsec analysis suite are illustrated in Fig. 6.4. The overall architecture is divided between the UML drawing tool in use and the analysis suite. This way the analysis suite can be offered as a web application, where the users use their drawing tools to construct the UML model which is then uploaded to the analysis suite. Additionally, a locally installable version is available (as a prototype at the time of writing). Plugins for various UML drawing tools are also planned.

The usage of the analysis suite as illustrated in Fig. 6.4 proceeds as follows. The developer creates a model and stores it in the UML 1.5/XMI 1.2 file format. The file is imported by the UMLsec tool into the internal MDR

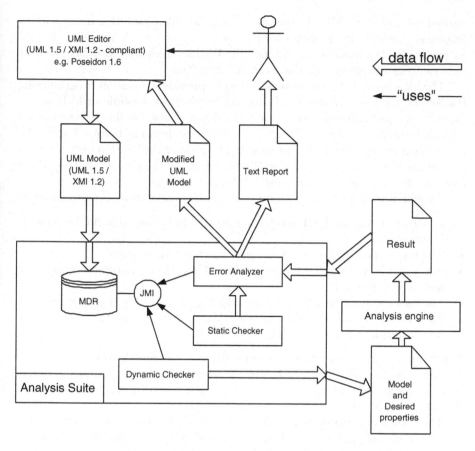

Fig. 6.4. UML tools suite

repository. The tool accesses the model through the JMI interfaces generated by the MDR library. The static checker parses the model, verifies its static features, and delivers the results to the error analyzer. The dynamic checker translates the relevant fragments of the UML model into the model-checker input language. The model-checker is spawned by the UML suite as an external process. Its results, and a counter-example in case a problem was found, are delivered back to the error analyzer. The error analyzer uses the information received from both the static checker and dynamic checker to produce a text report for the developer describing the problems found, and a modified UML model, where the found errors are visualized and, as far as possible, corrected.

6.2.2 Implementation Details

We now explain a framework for implementing verification routines for the constraints associated with the UMLsec stereotypes. The goal is that advanced users of the UMLsec approach should be able to use this framework to implement verification routines for the constraints of self-defined stereotypes. In particular, the framework includes the UMLsec tool web interface, so that new routines are also accessible over this interface.

The idea behind the framework is thus to provide a common programming framework for the developers of different verification modules which in the following we just call *tools*. Thus a tool developer should be able to concentrate on the verification logic and not be required to become involved with the input/output interface. Different tools implementing verification logic modules can be independently developed and integrated. At the time of writing, there exist verification modules for most UMLsec stereotypes.

An added tool implementation needs to obey the following assumptions:

- It is given a default UML model to operate on. It may load further models if necessary.
- The tool exposes a set of commands which it can execute.
- Every single command is not interactive. They receive parameters, execute, and deliver feedback.
- The tool can have an internal state which is preserved between commands.
- Each time the tool is called with a UML model, it may give back a text report and also a UML model.

These assumptions were made in order for the framework to cover as much common functionality as possible while not becoming overly complicated. Experience indicates that the assumptions are not too restrictive, given the architecture in Fig. 6.4.

The tool architecture in Fig. 6.5 then allows the development of the verification logic independently of the input and output media with minimum

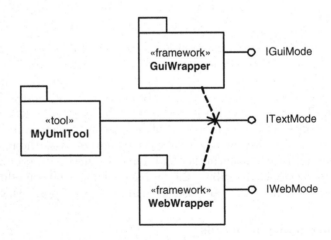

Fig. 6.5. Tool interfaces

effort. Each tool is required to implement the ITextMode interface which exposes tool functionality in text mode, with a string array as input and text as output. The framework provides default wrappers for the graphical user interface (GUI) GuiWrapper and the web mode WebWrapper. These wrappers enable use of the tool without modifications in the GUI application which is part of the framework, or through a web interface by rendering the output text on the respective media. However, each tool may itself implement the IGuiMode and/or IWebMode to fully exploit the functionality of the corresponding media, for example to fully use GUI mode capabilities to display graphical information.

At the time of writing, the UMLsec tools are working with the UML 1.5 version, which can be stored in an XMI 1.2 format [XMI02] by a number of UML design tools.[1] In the next few subsections, we will shortly present some examples for existing analysis plugins for the UMLsec tool framework. In each, we have to omit the technical details but refer to the corresponding articles that are listed in Sect. 6.5. Other examples for plugins include:

- a test-sequence generation for subsystems, sequence diagrams, activity diagrams, and statechart diagrams and
- a checker for the static security constraints in UMLsec.

6.2.3 Model-Checking UMLsec Specifications

We start with an analysis plug-in that utilizes the model-checker Spin [Hol03] to automatically verify UMLsec models making use of cryptography for the security requirements from Chap. 4 such as « data security ». This verification is done with respect to the formal semantics presented in Chap. 8, and using an adversary model arising from the physical security specification given in the deployment diagram contained in the subsystem.

To check the constraint associated with « data security » attached to a subsystem, we collect the security-relevant information from the class, statechart, and deployment diagrams contained in the subsystem, such as the values of the {secrecy} tags, which should remain secret. The behavior of the adversary is modeled by a separate Spin process which is derived from the definition associated with the deployment diagram using the threat sets from Chap. 4. Then, for example, the security requirement expressed by the stereotype « secrecy » is translated into a so-called *never claim* construct in the Spin code that says that the adversary should never get to know the secret values. It defines a process which runs in parallel with the rest of the Spin model and monitors this property. As part of the verification process, Spin produces a trail file, which records the sequence of actions of the potential attack. This information can be used by the system developer to improve the protocol.

---

[1] An upgrade to UML 2.0 is in development.

6.2.4 Automated Theorem Proving

We present a plugin for verifying UMLsec models that utilizes an automated theorem prover (atp) for first-order predicate logic to verify security properties of UMLsec models which make use of cryptography. Compared with the model-checking plugin, its advantage is a higher performance. The disadvantage is that it is less easy to extract an attack trail for insecure specifications, so the two plugins complement each other well.

The plugin translates a UML sequence diagram and an adversary model automatically to first-order logic. That way, it constructs an upper bound for the set of knowledge the adversary can gain which is represented by the predicate knows. The resulting first-order logic formula written in the well-known TPTP notation [SS01] can then be processed by atp's such as e-SETHEO [MIL+97, SW00, Sch01], SPASS [WBH+02], Waldmeister [HBVL97], and Vampire [RV01]. From the first-order logic formulas generated from the UML specification and the adversary model, the atp then tries to deduce whether the security requirements may be violated. For example, if the value secret is supposed to remain secret, the atp tries to deduce known(secret) from the protocol formulas. If this is possible, it means that there may be the possibility for an attack. If not, the value remains secret.

Since the adversary knowledge set is approximated from above, the analysis is rather efficient. Note that it is a safe approximation in the sense that one will find all possible attacks, but one may also encounter "false positives", although this rarely occurs.

6.2.5 Prolog-Based Attack Generation

Since the first-order logic formulas mentioned above are in fact Horn formulas, one can also evaluate them using Prolog. The difference to a verification using atp's is that Prolog uses a search algorithm over the valuations of the variables, while the atp's perform abstract derivations. Similarly to the model-checking approach, the Prolog-based analysis has the disadvantage of being less performant. However, it has the advantage that for insecure specifications, attack models can be generated automatically.

6.3 Linking Models to Runtime Data: SAP R/3 Permissions

This section presents research on linking the UMLsec approach with the automated analysis of security-critical data arising at runtime.

Specifically, it presents research on the construction of a tool which automatically checks the SAP R/3 configuration for security policy rules, such as separation of duty [HJ03a]. The permissions are given as input in an XML format through an interface from the SAP R/3 system, the rules are formulated as UML specifications in a standard UML CASE tool and output as XMI as part of the UMLsec framework explained in the previous section, and the tool checks the permissions against the rules using an analyzer written in Prolog. Because of its modular architecture and its standardized interfaces, the tool can be adapted to check security constraints in other kinds of application software, such as firewall, or other access control configurations.

Configuring user security permissions in standard business applications, such as SAP R/3 systems, is difficult and error-prone. There are many examples of wrongly configured systems that are open to misuse by unauthorized parties. To cmanually heck permission files of a realistic size in a medium to large organization – which can consist of up to 60,000 entries – can be a daunting task.

The management and configuration of security-related resources in standard business applications are important tasks. Potential threats include public disclosure of confidential information but also direct financial loss. In up to half the number of overall cases, the incidents are caused from within the company [Ric03]. This demonstrates the importance of properly configuring security permissions in business applications. It is important to realize that the existence of security mechanisms itself does not provide any level of security if they are not properly configured.

That this is actually the case is often clear to see. This applies especially to the financial sector, where user permissions have to satisfy more complex correctness conditions. One example is the rule of "separation of duty", meaning that a certain transaction should only be performed jointly among two distinct employees, for example, granting a large loan. Difficulties arise firstly from the inherent dynamics of permission assignment in real-life applications, for example due to temporary delegation of permissions (for example, to vacation substitutes). Secondly, they arise from the sheer size of data that has to be analyzed. In the situation of a large German bank, which the current work had motivated, it consists of about 60,000 data entries. A manual analysis of the security-critical configurations through system administrators on a daily basis is thus practically impossible, and might result in security weaknesses in practice. This observation motivated the current research which has been initialized in a discussion with the above bank and its security consulting partner. This resulted in a tool which automatically checks SAP R/3 configurations for security policy rules, such as separation of duty. This allows the user of the tool to construct a link between general information of the system, such as business processes specified in UML diagrams, to security-critical run time information. This is very useful from a security viewpoint, since security is an overall requirement which needs to take into consideration all aspects of a system in an integrated way to avoid potential weaknesses at the interfaces between different system parts.

The tool is part of the UMLsec framework explained in Sect. 6.2. The permissions are given as input in an XML format through an interface from the SAP R/3 system, the rules are formulated as UML specifications in a standard

UML CASE tool and output as XMI, and the tool checks the permissions against the rules using an analyzer written in Prolog. Because of its modular architecture and its standardized interfaces, the tool can be adapted to check security constraints in other kinds of application software, such as firewalls or other access control configurations. In this section, we explain the design of this tool.

6.3.1 Automated Analysis of Security Rules

The Goals

The tool is supposed to take a detailed description of the relevant data structure of the business application, the business data, and some rules written by the administrator. Using this information, the tool checks whether the rules hold for the given configuration. Violation of rules is included in the generated security report. The tool should accomplish the following specific tasks:

- It should read the configuration from the business application.
- It should automatically generate a report of possible weaknesses.
- It should provide a flexible configuration of the report's data.
- It should be easily configurable for different business applications.
- It should be able to check large-scale databases.
- The checking should be based on freely configurable rules.

Two other goals are particularly important to enable use of the tool beyond the specific task of checking SAP permissions of the SAP installation at hand: it has to be easy to integrate the tool with different business applications, and the rules that have to be checked need to be very flexible. To make the tool as flexible as possible and also as easy to use as one could, a modular design is of great importance.

Architecture

The tool mainly consists of three parts displayed in Fig. 6.6. They store the information describing the relevant data structure of the business application, define the rules, and evaluate the rules. An additional part is needed to import the data from the business application, such as the SAP system. This can be the user data and some structural information about transactions.

The complete separation of the tool and the business application provides additional security and privacy. Firstly, by separating the tool from the business application, there is no way the tool could add any weaknesses to this security-critical part of the company's IT system. Secondly, in this way it can be made sure that only the information needed for the analysis is exported to the tool, which prevents andy unnecessary exposure of confidential data. The information itself is completely stored in XML. The business application's data has to be exported to XML files. ing The data structure of the

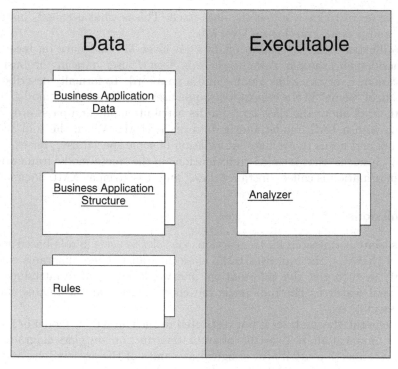

Fig. 6.6. Overview of the tool's architecture

business application is defined by UML class diagrams. Any case tool capable of saving XMI data according to the tool's schema files can thus be used to do the modeling. Rules are stored in XML as well. With all this information, the tool can check the rules and create the report.

As an option, the report can use templates to generate the layout that the user wants. To adapt the level of information to the given needs, every rule has a "level of verbosity". Then the rule is only evaluated if the report's desired "level of verbosity" is higher than the rule's level.

The Business Application as a Model

Throughout the description of the analyzer there will be several types of information that fit into different layers on OMG's meta-model framework explained in Sect. 6.1. In this framework there are UML models on layer 1 (M1) and application data on layer 0 (M0).

According to this separation of "model" and "information" the analyzer needs two distinct types of data. First it needs "metadata" which is the description of the data structure of the business application itself and is given as a UML model of the application. This is what is sometimes called the "structure of the business" application and it is on level M1. On the other hand, the analyzer needs to know about the data itself. This is what is called "instance data" and it is information on level M0.

To illustrate the separation of data on layer M1 and data on layer M0 we consider an example. Assume there is "some" user data in the business application. Every user has a name and a password. To formally describe the meaning of "some" in the expression "some user data" there is a "model" that tells the tool about the class user and its attribute name and password. This is done with a UML model and is data on level M1. When the tool checks the rules and needs to evaluate information of some special user, for example "John", it needs what is called "information" in the "meta-model framework". This information is called "instance data" and it is given as XML documents.

Permissions

To associate permissions for transactions via roles to users in role-based access control (RBAC), the tool uses UML class diagrams. These diagrams can be directly used to give this information, and we do not need to introduce any additional features. The tool reads the class diagram and evaluates classes and associations.

In general, the analyzer is not restricted to such an RBAC model or to any specific model at all. It is capable of evaluating rules on any class diagram that has the connection attributes assigned as names of the associations and the direction of associations defined by the navigable flag. The analyzer evaluates the model as a graph with classes as nodes and associations as edges, where edges are directed. As we will see later, for the evaluation of rules, we need to require that there must be a path between the two classes involved in that rule, and there must be instance data so that the connecting attributes of each class match.

To explain this in more detail, we consider the example in Fig. 6.7: the class diagram assigning permissions to users consists of the classes user, role, transaction, and permission, with attributes as in Fig. 6.7. There is an association role_id between user and role, an association role_id between role and transaction, and an association transaction_id between transaction and permission. The analyzer uses this model to automatically find a user's permissions.

Note that when assigning a permission p to a user u via a role r, and the user u also happens to have another role r', then it is not admissible to conclude that any user u' with the role r' should also be granted the permission p. In that sense, assigning permissions to users via roles is "unidirectional". In the class diagrams defining permissions, this is specified by using the "navigable" flag of UML class diagrams. This flag is an attribute of an association's endpoint. If this flag is set to "true" at the endpoint of a class c, signified by an arrow at that side of the association, our rule-analyzer may associate information from the other end of the association with c. If it is set to "false", this information may not be evaluated. In this way our tool may gather the permissions with respect to transactions granted to a given user by

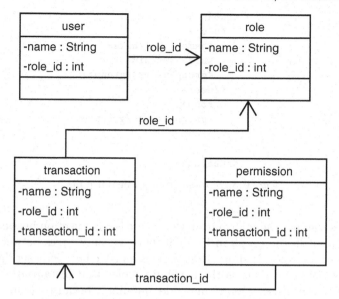

Fig. 6.7. Simple role-based access control

traversing the class diagram along the associations in the navigable directions permitting a "flow of information". Thus the tool "collects" all users that have a given role, but does not recursively collect all users that have any of the roles that a given user has, as explained above.

6.3.2 Instance Data

Besides the structural data elements explained above, we need so-called "instance data". Here an instance may, for example, be a real user of the system. This information is important for most of the rules one would like to evaluate. It is read by the analyzer from additional XML files containing a tag for every class, and within that tag another tag for each attribute. An example is given in Fig. 6.8. The analyzer is able to generate the XML Schema file for a UML model specified by the user, because the contents of the instance file depend on the model of the business application. With the generated XML Schema file the analyzer is able to validate the input file.

Rules

As defined in the previous section, the business application data structure is represented by a class diagram, that is a directed graph together with the data from the business application. These two pieces make up a rather complex graph whose structure can be seen in Fig. 6.9 as an example. One can see that for every user in the business application data structure, a node is added. The

```
<rubacon>
    <name>john</name>
    <uid>500</uid>
    <group>users</group>
  <group>
    <group>users</group>
  </group>
  ...
<rubacon>
```

Fig. 6.8. Snippet from an instance file

model gives the tool the information that there is a connection between "user" and "role", but in the graph in Fig. 6.9 there are only edges between certain users and certain roles. It shows that there is an edge between user "john" and role "users", because there is the attribute "role" that instantiates it. There is no edge between user "john" and role "admins", because "john" does not have "admins" in his roles. This is the graph that the analyzer uses to analyze the rules.

Rules in this instance consist of the following elements, as displayed in Fig. 6.10:

- a name (used as a reference in the security report)
- the type of the rule, which can be either of PROHIBITION or PRECON-DITION (meaning that the condition given in the sub-rule defined below should either not be fulfilled, or be fulfilled)
- a message (printed in the report if the rule fails)
- a priority level (to build a hierarchy of importance, so that less important rules can be turned off easily – typical values may include DEBUG, INFO, WARNING, ERROR, FATAL, or a numeric value)

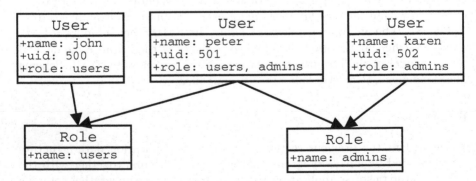

Fig. 6.9. The graph after model and information are inserted

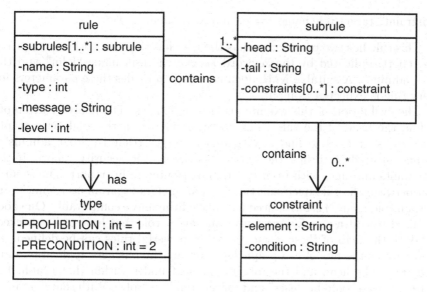

Fig. 6.10. Class diagram showing the structure of rules

- a sub-rule, which defines a path in the analyzer's graph and a set of constraints, as defined below

A sub-rule has the following elements:

- the head, which is the starting point of the path in the analyzer's graph defined by the sub-rule
- the target, which is the target of that path
- a list of constraints, which defines conditions that the path has to satisfy

Here a constraint consists of the following elements:

- element, the node that has to be checked
- condition, to be checked on that node

We consider the following example. If it has to be ensured that a certain user, say "john", does not have the role "admins" assigned, the following parameters would be set for the rule:

name: check user roles
type: PROHIBITION
message: check user for given roles
priority: ERROR=4

In this example, we have a single sub-rule:

head: user
target: role
constraint: head.user.name == param.user.name

constraint: target.role.name == param.role.name

This rule has two parameters that the user has to provide when generating the report, indicated by the keyword *param*: the user-name "john" and the role "admins". A suitable XML document that provides these parameters for every rule is expected as input.

The evaluation of this example rule is as follows. The analyzer attempts to find the head of the rule (that is, "user: john") in the analyzer's graph. Afterwards, it tries to find a path to the target (that is, "role: admins"). If that succeeds it prints the given message in the security report, if the user wants messages with priority ERROR printed in his report. The separation between the rule itself and the two parameters ("param.user.name" and "param.role.name") is introduced to make editing more comfortable: One does not need to edit a rule for every user and every role that have to be checked.

With the help of these elements rather powerful rules can be defined. To the analyzer the model is a graph representing the business application data structure. The head and the target represent nodes within that graph. For example, head could be "user" and target could be "role". With that definition there should exist a path between head and target. If it does not, the rule fails. If that path exists, the analyzer will try to fill that path with valid data from the given instance data. This means that for a valid connection from head to target, every association along that path is instantiated with a discrete entry from the business application's data. If there is no valid instantiation, the rule fails. If there is one, the constraints are checked. Every instantiated element will be examined, and if one of the conditions fails, the rule fails. Otherwise, it succeeds.

To make the rules more expressive, a rule can consist of several sub-rules, where a sub-rule does not have the additional name, type, message, and level attributes. In this way the analyzer is powerful enough to check rules such as separation of duty, for example by using the sub-rules:

- check for distinct role A,
- check for distinct role B, and
- ensure that no user has both of them.

For a rule to succeed, each of the sub-rules has to succeed.

The additional information is needed to configure the analyzer properly, and to customize the report. The name of the rule is used to output which rules failed. The type is given to distinguish between preconditions and prohibitions, meaning that either the success or failure of that rule is reported. So it is conveniently possible to define states that must be fulfilled for every configuration and to define states that may not appear within a configuration. For example, it may be vital for a system to have the password set for the superuser account. Conversely, for separation of duty, it would be forbidden for the same user to have two exclusive roles. A message is printed if a precondition fails or if a prohibition succeeds. The message attribute simply gives the text that is written to the report if a message is printed. A template system prints out the messages with any of the instance's attributes in a freely configurable manner. So it is possible to insert values from the violating instance into the message, for example as "there is no password for user Joe". Only with such a feature do the messages become readable and thus the tool easily usable by a human user.

The level attribute gives a "level of verbosity" to a rule. So the user can have the tool evaluate some rules only. Level 1 means that, the rule is relatively unimportant. An increasing number will show increasing importance for the rule. The analyzer evaluates only the rules with a level higher than that given as "level of verbosity" to that report.

6.3.3 Evaluating Rules

We use Prolog for the evaluation of the rules, which allows a rather elegant treatment as it is designed for evaluating logical statements. In our experience, it is also sufficiently efficient for a real-life application.

If one translates structural elements to "Atomic Prolog Terms" and the analyzer rules to "Non-Atomic Terms", one can ask the Prolog interpreter for the instances of the Prolog rules. The advantage of using Prolog is that we can concentrate on the essential problems specific to the analyzer without having to solve the hard problems of finding the instances along the paths.

Evaluating Separation of Duty in SAP Systems

We use an example configuration from [Sch03b] to explain how separation of duty in SAP systems can be evaluated by the analyzer. First of all, the structure of the business application needs to be defined. For simplicity it will be assumed that the structure looks like the one presented in Figure 6.7. It certainly is just a very small part of the SAP security concept but as an example, it will be sufficient. As displayed in Fig. 6.11, there are three

User	Role	Transaction	Permission
Karen	employee (in charge of service)	Create purchase	Is allowed to create some purchase in SAP.
Susan	employee (in charge of service, senior in rank to Karen)	Commit purchase	Is allowed to release purchase created by Karen.
John	employee purchasing agent	Place orders	Is allowed to place orders with some delivery agent.

Fig. 6.11. Small separation of duty example

employees: Karen, Susan and John. Karen and Susan are just employees in any department, and John is a purchasing agent at the company. To have separation of duty, Karen may create a purchase and Susan may release that purchase to John. John may order the desired goods from some supplier firm. With this in place the Prolog rules would be very straightforward:

```
user(Karen, 1)
role(create-purchase, 1)
  ...
```

To have separation of duty in place there are two exclusive roles, which may not be assigned to the same user: "create-purchase" and "release-purchase". John just places the orders, he does not do any supervision here. The first sub-rule must have the head "user" and the target "role". The second sub-rule must have the same head and target but it needs a condition:

```
rule1.user.name == rule2.user.name
```

The type of this rule is PROHIBITION, the other attributes do not matter for this example. What does the tool do now? It has created the predicates and inserted the users and the role from the instance files. Afterwards it searches the paths for the rule. The path from user to rule is quite obvious, so the "connecting" predicate is created: at

```
user_role(name, role_id, rname)
  :- user(name, role_id),
     role(rname, role_id).
```

With that predicate the rule can be evaluated to:

```
user_role_rule(name,
               role_id1, role_id2)
  :- user_role(name1, role_id1, X),
     user_role(name2, role_id2, Y),
     name1 = name2.
```

Now Prolog can be asked for:

```
user_role_rule(X,
               'create-purchase',
               'release-purchase').
```

and it calculates the correct answer. In the example in Fig. 6.11 there is no solution to the predicate, because there is only Karen for role "create-purchase" and Susan for role "release-purchase", and user Karen is not equal to user Susan.

Although this example is very simple, it serves as a demonstration of how the analyzer can be used. In a real application, the path from user to role might contain several nodes or one might not know the roles that have to be exclusive, just the permissions, so one could exclude permissions contained in roles with several hundreds of entries each. In cases were a role contains several hundreds of permissions, it is not obvious whether separation of duty is in place.

SAP Transactions

Another example of the use of the analyzer to improve security is when the transactions are also part of the data structure. Because of the design of the SAP system, there are no security checks performed when a transaction calls another one. By this transitivity, it is very difficult in large systems to see who can execute a transaction. The permission to execute a transaction includes the permission to execute every transaction called by the first one and there does not seem to be a possibility to disable this feature. Thus creating a transaction in SAP is a permission that gives access to everything. One should notice that an employee who is allowed to create a transaction and execute it can execute any transaction by calling it from his or her self-created one.

If access needs to be restricted to some transactions, it is therefore not sufficient to ensure that the permission is given only in the roles associated with that transaction, and that only the users allowed to execute that transaction are assigned those roles. It has to be ensured furthermore that there is no transaction calling the restricted one, because SAP would not perform security checks there and one would not prevent execution of the restricted transaction.

To do so, one may model the transactions with their sub-transactions as part of the analyzer's model. Then the tool creates rules to check whether permissions grant any user additional rights that are not part of his or her role. It is usually not advisable to report every transaction that can be executed without explicit permission. Because of the error-prone design, there will be a lot of transactions that are meant to be called implicitly. One should however at least check the potentially dangerous transactions, such as the ones for changing permissions and roles.

Use Case for Checking SAP Permissions

Figure 6.12 presents a sample "use case" for checking the permissions on a running SAP system. The SAP database is used to generate the information necessary for the analyzer. An employee creates a UML model describing the SAP system. We use the CASE tool Poseidon for UML to do so. These two documents describe the business application. With these documents in place one can create the rules. For creating the rules there is a GUI but the XML files necessary can be edited manually, too.

When all the documents are prepared, the analyzer can check the rules automatically. After the analyzer has finished the checks, the user can read the security report and start reconfiguring the business application in order to fulfil all the conditions contained in his rule set.

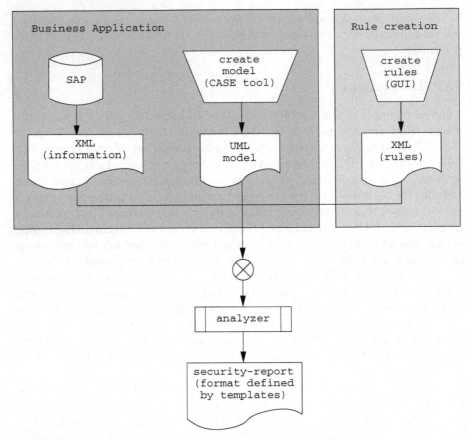

Fig. 6.12. Sample configuration for using the analyzer

The security report is formatted as defined by the templates that are part of the analyzer. The analyzer writes a freely configurable HTML file for review with a web browser.

Further Applications

The analyzer can be used not only to check SAP systems, but also to check most configurations of large-scale applications. The modular architecture makes it easy to adapt to a new application. One needs to define the application's structure in UML, then the instance data must be converted to proper XML files, corresponding to the XML Schema provided by the tool's schema generator. Afterwards, the rules have to be defined. Then the GUI can be used, or the XML files can be written manually or generated by any tool fitting the needs of the application. Finally the report can be generated by the analyzer.

In further work, other plugins have been developed for the UMLsec tool which allow consistency checks to be performed between business process models specified in UML and permission configuration data. For example, one can ensure that only the minimally necessary permissions for a given business process have been assigned to the users, as required by the *least privilege* security principle from Sect. 4.2.

6.4 Linking Models to Code

As noted for example in [Fow04], of ultimate benefit in software development are not "pretty pictures", but the running implementation of a system. In this section, we present some approaches for linking UML models to implementations. The aim is to ensure that the benefits gained from the model-based approach on the level of the system model, namely such as increased confidence in satisfaction of critical requirements, actually carries over to the implemented system, as one would hope.

6.4.1 Test-Sequence Generation

In this section we briefly refer to research on model-based testing of security-critical systems using UML-like notations. Details have to be omitted for space reasons but can be found in [JW01a, JW02, WJ02].

In specification-based testing, test sequences are generated from an abstract system specification to provide confidence in the correctness of an implementation. The traditional approach in this direction, namely that of conformance testing, establishes that an implementation conforms to its specification. However, a complete test coverage is often infeasible, resulting in a need for test-case selection. For security-critical systems, finding tests likely to detect possible vulnerabilities is particularly difficult, as they usually involve subtle and complex execution scenarios and the consideration of domain-specific concepts such as cryptography and random numbers.

The cited research aimes at generating test sequences for transaction systems from a formal security model supported by the CASE tool AUTOFOCUS which has a UML-like notation. To test an implementation for vulnerabilities, we compute test sequences from the security model covering possible violations of the security requirements. The test sequences are determined with respect to the system's required security properties, using mutations of the system specification and attack scenarios. To be able to apply them to an existing implementation, the abstract test sequences are concretized.

The motivation for specification-based testing is that, in general, the implementation of a system is very complex. To allow proofs of security properties, abstraction techniques are used: in models of cryptographic transactions, messages, keys, and random numbers are usually represented by abstract data entities which can be arguments to abstract operations such as encryption or hashing, and part of the actual messages exchanged may have been left out. Besides, where the security model is developed independently of the implementation, it cannot be concluded from the correctness of a security model that the implementation is secure.

Confidence in the correctness of an implementation can be gained by extensive testing. Testing for security holes is usually restricted to penetration testing: A so-called "tiger team" of experts manually tries to break the system or tools such as SATAN are used to search for known vulnerabilities. This approach is not satisfactory as it depends largely on the skill of the employed tiger team or the knowledge encoded into the tool, which does not consider application-specific security requirements.

[JW01a, JW02, WJ02] show how to complement this approach by generating test sequences from a security specification. The aim is to find those test sequences that are most likely to detect possible vulnerabilities. For this purpose, one adapts methods from classical specification-based testing to the application domain of security-critical systems. Specifically, domain-specific concepts such as cryptography, knowledge of or access to secrets, and threat scenarios are included. Test sequences likely to detect vulnerabilities are computed using mutations of the specification that lead to violation of the security requirements. Further, it is shown how to translate the abstract test sequences derived from the security model to concrete test sequences that can be applied to an existing implementation.

Vulnerability Coverage Using Mutations

As it is not feasible to exhaustively test every behavior of a security-critical system, first appropriate test-case specifications have to be selected. For security testing, the aim is to cover a large number of possible vulnerabilities.

One can use structural coverage criteria such as state or transition coverage on the models [OXL99] and restrict them to those that are marked "critical", but this has the drawback that it does not take into account the security requirements.

The difficulty with defining coverage criteria related to the security requirements is that they are mostly universal properties. Therefore, a security requirement Φ_i can only be used to verify the model, not the implementation. If a trace fulfilling $\neg\Phi_i$ is found, the model violates the security requirement and must be corrected. Otherwise, Φ_i by itself cannot be used to select relevant traces, as *all* traces satisfy Φ_i.

In this case, mutation testing and fault injection techniques [Off95, VM98] prove to be promising approaches. In mutation testing, errors are introduced into a program, and the quality of a test suite is measured by its ability to distinguish the modified program from the original program. Fault injection works in a similar way, but is often also used for reliability evaluation: to determine if a program tolerates a perturbation of the code or data states.

We introduce errors into the specification of the security-related behavior, generate the threat scenarios, and determine if and how the introduced errors can lead to security violations. The introduced errors can correspond to errors in the implementation or to attacks leading to such errors, for example subjecting a smart card to environmental stress.

A mutation function ε can be based on general possible mutations for expressions and operands. For security testing, ε should be based on common programming errors likely to lead to vulnerabilities, such as missing plausibility checks or wrong use of identities [AKS96]. In addition, in our model cryptography must be taken into account, leading to mutations corresponding to confusion of keys or secrets, or to missing or wrongly implemented verification of authentication codes.

Concretization of Abstract Tests

The abstract test sequences computed from the formal security specification still have to be translated to byte sequences as the concrete test data that can be used to test the actual implementation.

In many cases, concretization can be achieved using straightforward mappings between abstract and concrete test data [DBG01], and executing the test using a test driver that passes the inputs to the component to be tested and verifies if the outputs are as expected. However, testing security-critical systems involves additional complications, mainly because of non-determinism, for example arising from randomly generated keys and nonces, and the use of cryptographic primitives:

- In formal specifications, cryptographic primitives are usually modeled symbolically, rather than as sequences of bytes, to make verification feasible (see [AR00a, AJ01] for a justification of this approach in general). The test driver has to map these symbols to sequences of bytes in a consistent way. Conversely, sequences of bytes created and output by the tested component must be stored by the test driver and used in place of the relevant symbols in the test data of the remainder of the execution. For example, these could be random values such as nonces or session keys.
- Sometimes, values are abstracted away in formal specifications to simplify verification because they are seen to be independent of a security property at hand. These have to be included in the concrete test data in a consistent way.
- If encryption is used, the test driver must know the corresponding keys and encryption algorithms to be able to compute the encrypted input data and verify encrypted output data.
- Hash values or message authentication codes contained in the output data can only be verified when the complete data that was hashed is available to the test driver.

6.4.2 Code Generation and Code Analysis

There are other ways to link models to code besides test-sequence generation, as we briefly point out.

Code generation can be used to directly generate code from a UML model. Where this is possible, there is usually no need for conformance testing. Testing for security properties may, however, still be useful to detect weaknesses not apparent on the design level.

So far, code generation is mainly used in a fragmentary way. A main application is, for example, to generate class definitions from class diagrams. More extensive support for code generation, such as code generation from statecharts, is being developed. However, it will remain to be seen to what extent the use of UML as a visual programming language will be established. When writing visual programs for complete systems questions of scalability may become more apparent than when writing abstract specifications of parts of a system. For this reason, test-sequence generation may still be useful in the foreseeable future.

Code analysis: The same concepts and definitions used in the previous chapters to analyze UML models for security requirements can also be used to analyze suitable abstractions of programs. For example, there exist static analysis tools which extract a state machine model from source code and allow our security analysis algorithms to be used after a suitable adaptation.

6.5 Notes

The general material from Sections 6.1 and 6.2 is based on [JS04c, JS04b]. The model-checking UMLsec plugin in presented in [JS04a]. The first-order logic analysis plugins are explained in [Jür04g, Jür04c]. The UMLsec tool framework altogether is demonstrated in [Jür04k]. Part of the implementation effort has been performed in the context of about 20 Master's and Bachelor theses and advanced study projects. The construction of this tool has profited from experience in the development of the industrial-strength computer aided software engineering tool AUTOFOCUS at the TU Munich [HMR+98, RJW+03].

The literature on how to use XMI to provide tool support for UML includes [Ste01b, Ste03a], including an example using the Edinburgh Concurrency Workbench for analyzing UML models. Some new developments on diagram interchange for UML are explained in [BJMF02]. There are several existing tools for automatic verification of UML models described in the literature. The HUGO Project [SKM01] checks the behavior described by a UML Collaboration diagram against a transitional system comprising several communicating objects. The functionality of each object is specified by a UML Statechart diagram. The vUML Tool [LP99] analyzes the behavior of a set of interacting objects, defined in a similar way. The tool can verify various properties of the system, including deadlock freeness and liveliness, and find problems like entering a forbidden state or sending a message to a terminated object. Both tools do not have any special features for describing the security features of the system being modeled. [CRS04] presents a tool which extracts execution sequences from UML statecharts given as XMI and simulates them by translation to the Abstract State Machine programming system AsmGofer. Although there is an increasing amount of research on advanced tool support for UML, it seems that little work has been done to provide advanced tool support, such as model-checkers or automated theorem provers, for verifying particular properties included as stereotypes in application-specific UML extensions.

The research in Sect. 6.3 has been presented in [HJ03a]. Related approaches to analyzing security configurations include for example the "Configuration Review Test" [Pol92]. There seems to be no implementation of these tests that uses rules for this purpose. Existing tools for this approach check some conditions of specific applications, mostly operating systems. These tools are designed to check for certain security weaknesses, common to a number of systems. Other approaches using logic programming for access control analysis include [BdVS02]. [RS01] uses SQL to administer permissions for distributed data. [GHR03] uses a model-checker to analyze Linux configurations. [BP04] uses the predicative specification of user rights within an object oriented use case driven development process. The specification of methods is extended by a permission section which describes the right of some actor to call the method of an object. A representation function is introduced that describes how actors are represented in the system.

The work in Sect. 6.4.1 was presented in [JW01a, JW02, WJ02]. Work related to it includes extensive research into specification-based testing, such as [DF93, PS97, HNS97]. Dushina et al explain concretization in their Genevieve framework [DBG01]. The AVA approach [VM98] focusses on identifying critical statements rather than finding test sequences, for which random distributions are used.

With respect to code analysis against abstract security properties such as secrecy and authentication, relatively little work has been done yet. For example, most work in verifying security protocols so far has concentrated on the specification, rather than the implementation level. Research in code verification that might be fruitfully used in this direction includes [MH98, AGMO04, CCG+03, NPW02].

6.6 Discussion

After explaining the necessary background, we presented tool support for the automated analysis of UMLsec models with regard to security requirements. It includes analysis plugins based for example on model-checkers, automated theorem provers, and verification engines realized in Prolog. The UMLsec analysis suite also includes a framework for implementing verification routines for the constraints associated with the UMLsec stereotypes. On the one hand, the existing analysis routines allow the UMLsec user an easy and automated security analysis of his system just by applying the predefined stereotypes, without requiring the user to formalize these requirements first. On the other hand, advanced users of the UMLsec approach are able to use this framework to implement verification routines for the constraints of self-defined stereotypes and to include them into the UMLsec tool.

We also presented research on linking the UMLsec approach with the automated analysis of security-critical data arising at runtime. The example presented here is a tool which automatically checks the SAP R/3 configuration for security policy rules. Because of its modular architecture and its standardized interfaces, it should be possible to adapt it to check security constraints in other kinds of application software, such as firewalls or other access control configurations. Although there already exist commercial tools for analyzing SAP data, the work presented here offers a greater range of properties to be checked, and also offers the new possibility to enhance the security analysis by linking it with other information, such as security-critical business process specifications formulated in UML diagrams, in an integrated setting within the UMLsec framework.

Finally, we briefly referred to some approaches for linking UML models to implementations to make sure that the implementation is actually secure, and not just the model. There are three approaches to achieve this, namely model-based test-sequence generation, code generation, and code analysis.

7

A Formal Foundation

In this chapter, we present the foundation used in Chap. 8 to define a formal model for a part of UML to enable advanced tool support.

We introduce the notion of UML Machines. They give a mathematically rigorous framework for the approach to secure software engineering explained in the previous chapters. While having a sound mathematical foundation, their notation is rather flexible and allows capturing complex concepts straightforwardly. In particular, they let us model interaction with the environment of a system. We also define *UML Machine Systems (UMSs)* that allow one to build up UML Machine specifications in a modular way and to treat external influences on the system beyond the planned interaction, such as attacks on insecure communication links. We define notions of refinement and rely-guarantee specifications for UML Machines and prove that rely-guarantee specifications are preserved under refinement. Finally, we explain how we use UML Machine Systems to specify security-critical systems, that may employ cryptographic operations. We also give definitions for secrecy, integrity, authenticity, freshness, and secure information flow, together with equivalent internal characterizations which allow easier verification. These security properties are shown to be preserved under refinement, avoiding the so-called *refinement problem.* Because of the modular way UML Machines are defined, they give a formal framework for formally analyzing security-critical systems in their own right, independently of the UML notation.

The proofs for statements in this chapter are given in Appendix C.

7.1 UML Machines

Our choice of the formalism of UML Machines is motivated by our goal to use them to formulate our security modeling concepts in a mathematically precise way. In particular, they provide a foundation for security modeling with UML. We will also explain how this formalism can be used as a foundation for advanced tool support. UML Machines are transition systems the states of which are algebraic structures, and which have built-in communication mechanisms similar to the corresponding mechanisms in UML. Inspired in their presentation by Abstract State Machines [Gur95], the role of UML Machines is thus to provide the framework for formulating the concepts we use, which are close in spirit to the models of data-flow, such as [Bro86, Abr90].

We will use UML Machines to specify components of a system that interact by exchanging messages from a given set **Events** which are dispatched from (resp. received in) multi-set buffers called *output queues* (resp. *input queues*)[1]. The idea is that a UML Machine may interact with its environment by adding values to its output queue and by retrieving the values from its input queue.

We assume a set of *variables*. *Terms* are defined as usual by starting with variable names and applying function names recursively:

- A variable is a term.
- If f is a function name of arity $r \geq 0$ and $t_1, \ldots, t_r$ are terms, then $f(t_1, \ldots, t_r)$ is a term.

Definition 7.1. *Given a set F of function names containing at least the nullary function names true, false, and undef, a state A consists of:*

- *a set X (its base set) and*
- *interpretations of the function names in F on X: an r-ary function name f is interpreted as a function $f : X^r \to X$. We assume that true, false, and undef are interpreted as mutually distinct elements of X.*

F is called the vocabulary *of A and is denoted as* **Voc** A.

As usual, a set can be interpreted as a function taking values in $\{true, false\}$. Also, one often notationally identifies an algebra with its base set, for example by writing $x \in A$ instead of $x \in X$ in the above situation. Similarly, we only distinguish between a function name and its interpretation when necessary to avoid misunderstanding. We write **Bool** for the set $\{true, false\}$. A *variable assignment* over a state S is a function from a set of variables to the base set of S. It is extended to evaluations of terms in the usual way using the interpretation of function names.

Definition 7.2. *A UML Machine $A = (\textbf{Voc}\, A, \textbf{Init}\, A, \textbf{Rule}\, A)$ consists of*

- *a set* **Voc** A *of function names that contain at least the set names* inQu$_A$ *and* outQu$_A$,
- *an initial state* **Init** A *of vocabulary* **Voc** A, *and*
- *a transition rule* **Rule** A *which can be of the form as defined inductively in Fig. 7.1.*

The set names inQu$_A$, outQu$_A$ model the input buffer and the output buffer of the UML Machine A that may change them only by deleting elements from

---

[1] Here we follow the UML terminology which is confusing in so far as input/output queues are not queues, but multi-sets.

$$R ::= \textbf{skip}$$

$$f(\bar{s}) := t$$

$\textbf{if } g \textbf{ then } R \textbf{ else } S$

$\textbf{do} - \textbf{in} - \textbf{parallel} \ \ R_1 \ \ \ldots \ \ R_k \ \textbf{ enddo}$

$\textbf{choose } v \textbf{ with } g(v) \textbf{ do } R(v)$

$\textbf{seq } R_1 \ \ldots \ R_n \textbf{ endseq}$

$\textbf{forall } v \textbf{ with } g(v) \textbf{ do } R(v)$

$\textbf{iterate}(R)$

$\textbf{loop } v \textbf{ through list } X \ \ R(v)$

$\textbf{loop } v \textbf{ through set } X \ \ R(v)$

$\textbf{while } g \textbf{ do } R$

$\textbf{case } v \textbf{ of}$

$\qquad v \in X_1 : \textbf{do } R_1$

$\qquad \ldots$

$\qquad v \in X_n : \textbf{do } R_n$

$\qquad \textbf{else } S$

Fig. 7.1. UML Machine rules

inQu_A and by adding elements to outQu_A. We assume that at the initial state **Init** A of the UML Machine, they always have the value $\emptyset$.

Below we give an informal semantics for the transition rules; the formal semantics can be found in Appendix B. A UML Machine A is executed by iteratively firing the transition rule **Rule** A, starting from the initial state **Init** A. Thereby, its current state is *updated*; that is, the interpretations of its functions are redefined in terms of the previous interpretations. This way, the UML Machine changes between different states. By Definitions 7.1 and 7.2, each state consists of a base set and interpretations of the function names in F, which includes the names inQu_A and outQu_A.

Skip rule: **skip** is a rule. It causes no change.

Update: Given terms $s_1, \ldots, s_r$ and t, we have an *update rule* $f(s_1, \ldots, s_r) := t$. Suppose that at the point of execution of a given instance of this rule, the terms $s_1, \ldots, s_r, t$ evaluate to the values $\hat{s_1}, \ldots, \hat{s_r}, \hat{t}$ in the base set of a UML Machine A, respectively. Then the execution of this rule updates the interpretation of the r-ary function name f at the r-tuple $(\hat{s_1}, \ldots, \hat{s_r})$ of values of A to map to $\hat{t}$. Thus an update rule updates the function at a single position; all other interpretations are left unchanged.

Conditional: If g is a closed formula of first-order predicate logic and R, S are rules then

$\textbf{if } g$

then R
else S

is a rule. If g holds, the rule R is executed, otherwise S. If S is equal
to **skip** then **else skip** can be omitted, provided indentation is used to
prevent confusion.

Blocks: If $R_1, \ldots, R_k$ are rules, then

do − in − parallel
    R_1
    $\ldots$
    R_k
enddo

is a rule. To fire this rule, $R_1, \ldots, R_k$ are executed simultaneously, if
they are mutually consistent. Consistency means that updates concerning
the same function name define the same value: for any two update rules
$f(\bar{s}) := t$ and $f(\bar{s}) := t'$, we have $t = t'$. In case of inconsistency, the execution of the UML Machine stops. Note that this *parallel composition* is
truly parallel, rather than a non-deterministic interleaving. For example,

$$\textbf{do − in − parallel} \quad x := y \;\; y := x \;\; \textbf{enddo}$$

swaps x and y.

Choose: If v is a variable, $g(v)$ is a logical formula with one free variable, v,
and $R(v)$ is a rule, then

choose v **with** $g(v)$ **do**
    $R(v)$

is a rule that chooses an element a of the base set of A such that $g(a)$ holds
and executes $R(a)$. In case such an a does not exist, the rule is interpreted
as **skip**.

Sequential composition: If $R_1, \ldots, R_n$ are rules, then

seq
    R_1
    $\ldots$
    R_n
endseq

is a rule, meaning that $R_1, \ldots, R_n$ are executed sequentially. If no confusion can arise, the shorter notation $R_1; \;\ldots; \; R_n$ may be used.

Forall: If v is a variable, $g(v)$ is a first-order formula with one free variable,
v, and $R(v)$ is a rule, then

forall v **with** $g(v)$ **do**
    $R(v)$

is a rule, which is fired by executing $R(a)$ for all elements a in the base set of A such that $g(a)$ holds before they are executed in parallel, if they are mutually consistent. Otherwise, the execution of the UML Machine stops.

Iteration: If R is a rule then

iterate(R)

is a rule that iteratively executes the rule R until executing R gives no change or causes the execution to stop.

Note that the **do − in − parallel** rule may be expressed in terms of the **forall** rule, as in the Abstract State Machine setting [Gur97].

For convenience, we define some more transition rules which may be defined in terms of the ones above:

Loop through list: If v is a variable, X is a finite sequence of values in A, and $R(v)$ is a rule, then

loop v **through list** X
$\quad R(v)$

is a rule that iteratively chooses all elements $x \in X$ if $X \neq \emptyset$, according to the content and order of X before executing the rule, and executes $R(x)$. The rule acts as **skip** if $X = []$.

Loop through set: If v is a variable, X is a multi-set name, and $R(v)$ is a rule, then

loop v **through set** X
$\quad R(v)$

is a rule that iteratively chooses all multi-set elements $x \in X$ as X was before executing the rule, with the correct multiplicities and in a non-deterministic order, and executes $R(x)$. The rule does nothing if $X = \emptyset$. This rule is used instead of **loop** v **through list** X $R(v)$ in situations where the order of the chosen elements does not matter, to avoid over-specification at the level of abstract modeling.

While: If g is a closed first-order formula and R is a rule then

while g **do**
$\quad R$

is a rule. The rule R is executed while g holds.

Case distinction: If v is a variable, $X_1, \ldots, X_n$ are mutually disjoint subsets of the base set of A, and $R_1, \ldots, R_n$ are rules, then the following is a rule:

case v **of**
$\quad v \in X_1 : \textbf{do } R_1$
$\quad \ldots$
$\quad v \in X_n : \textbf{do } R_n$
$\quad \textbf{else } S$

The rule is executed by evaluating v and executing one of the rules $R_1, \ldots, R_n$ depending on the value of v. $v \in \{x_i\} : \mathbf{do}\ R_i$ may be abbreviated to $x_i : \mathbf{do}\ R_i$.

We define the following syntactic shortcuts, where A is a UML Machine and X is a multiset, and $\equiv$ is syntactic equality between transition rules.

$$\mathsf{tooutQu}_A(X) \equiv \mathsf{outQu}_A := \mathsf{outQu}_A \uplus X$$
$$\mathsf{toinQu}_A(X) \equiv \mathsf{inQu}_A := \mathsf{inQu}_A \uplus X$$

A run $r \in \mathbf{Run}\,A$ of a UML Machine A is a finite or infinite sequence $S_0, S_1, \ldots$ of states such that the following conditions are satisfied:

- S_0 is the initial state $\mathbf{Init}\,A$.
- For each $n \in \mathbb{N}$, if S_n is the last element of the sequence r then
    - any consistent application of the transition rule $\mathbf{Rule}\,A$ at state S_n leaves the state S_n unchanged, or
    - there exists an inconsistent application of $\mathbf{Rule}\,A$ at state S_n.
- For each $n \in \mathbb{N}$, if S_n is not the last element of the sequence r, then there exists a consistent application of $\mathbf{Rule}\,A$ in S_n which S_{n+1} is the result of, and we have $k > n$ such that $S_k \neq S_n$.

Thus the definition of runs models termination by a finite sequence; runs can only be infinite if the state keeps on changing.

The idea of this definition is that the hypothetical "machine" which executes the UML Machine models chooses an update set non-deterministically. If it turns out to be inconsistent, the machine cannot proceed and the run stops. Choosing the update set is an internal action of the hypothetical execution machine which cannot be observed by the environment.[2]

Note that due to the non-determinism introduced for example by the **choose with do** rule, there may be a non-singleton *set* of runs of a UML Machine A. In particular, some of the branches of the **choose with do** rule may lead to an inconsistent application of a rule, while others may lead to a consistent rule application. In such a situation, there are runs that terminate at that **choose with do** rule while others continue with the consistent rule application.

We define two UML Machines A and B to be *equivalent* if $\mathbf{Voc}\,A = \mathbf{Voc}\,B$ and $\mathbf{Run}\,A = \mathbf{Run}\,B$.

---

[2] For readers familiar with process algebras this is, for example, just like the unobservable τ action in the process algebra CCS [Mil89]. Intuitively, in CCS notation, the situation of having both consistent and inconsistent update sets at a point would thus look like $\tau + p$ where after firing τ, the machine gets stuck, while after choosing p, the execution may continue.

One may observe the input/output behavior of a UML Machine as follows. Given a UML Machine A, tuples $\mathbf{i}$ and $\mathbf{o}$ of input and output names, and a sequence $\mathbf{I}$ of $\mathbf{i}$-indexed multi-set tuples, consider the UML Machine $\mathbf{Behav_{i,o}}(A(\mathbf{I}))$ with

- the vocabulary $\mathbf{Voc}\,(\mathbf{Behav_{i,o}}(A(\mathbf{I}))) = \mathbf{Voc}\,A \cup \mathrm{outlist}(A)$, assuming $\mathrm{outlist}(A) \notin \mathbf{Voc}\,A$, if necessary by renaming,
- the initial state $\mathbf{Init}\,(\mathbf{Behav_{i,o}}(A(\mathbf{I})))$ defined as $\mathbf{Init}\,A$ and such that $\mathrm{outlist}(A) = [\,]$, and
- the transition rule $\mathbf{Rule}\,(\mathbf{Behav_{i,o}}(A(\mathbf{I})))$ as given in Fig. 7.2.

$\mathbf{Rule}\,(\mathbf{Behav_{i,o}}(A(\mathbf{I})))$:
$\mathbf{loop}\ I\ \mathbf{through\ list}\ \mathbf{I}$
$\quad \mathrm{toinQu}_A(I_{\mathrm{inQu}_A});$
$\quad \mathbf{forall}\ f\ \mathbf{with}\ f \in \mathbf{i}\ \mathbf{do}$
$\qquad f := I_f$
$\quad \mathbf{Rule}\,A;$
$\quad \mathbf{forall}\ f\ \mathbf{with}\ f \in \mathbf{o} \cup \{\mathrm{outQu}_A\}\ \mathbf{do}$
$\qquad \mathrm{outlist}(A)_f := \mathrm{outlist}(A)_f.f;$
$\quad \mathrm{outQu}_A := \emptyset$

Fig. 7.2. Behavior of UML Machine

Here $f := I_f$ means that the input name f is assigned the f-component of the $\mathbf{i}$-indexed tuple I of input multi-sets. $\mathrm{outlist}(A)_f := \mathrm{outlist}(A)_f.f$ means to append the current value of the name f to the f-component of the sequence $\mathrm{outlist}(A)$. After completion of any possible run of this rule starting from an initial state where $\mathrm{outlist}(A)$ evaluates to the empty list $[\,]$, $\mathrm{outlist}(A)$ contains a sequence of $\mathbf{o}$-indexed tuples of multi-sets of values. Intuitively, this is the set of possible sequences of multi-set tuples of output values in the output names in $\mathbf{o}$ by iteratively adding each multi-set in $\mathbf{I}_{\mathrm{inQu}_A}$ to inQu_A and assigning each multi-set in $\mathbf{I}_f$ to f for $f \neq \mathrm{inQu}_A$, then calling A, and recording the multi-set of output values from outQu_A and the values of the output names in $\mathrm{outlist}(A)$.

Definition 7.3. *Given a a UML Machine A and tuples $\mathbf{i}$ and $\mathbf{o}$ of input and output names, the $(\mathbf{i}, \mathbf{o})$-input/output behavior of A is a function $[\![A]\!]_{\mathbf{i},\mathbf{o}}()$ from finite sequences of multi-sets of values to sets of sequences of multi-sets of values obtained by defining $[\![A]\!]_{\mathbf{i},\mathbf{o}}(\mathbf{I})$ to consist of the possible contents of $\mathrm{outlist}(A)$ for each run of $\mathbf{Behav_{i,o}}(A(\mathbf{I}))$. For $\mathbf{i} = \mathbf{o} = \emptyset$, we simply write $[\![A]\!]()$ and call it the input/output behavior of A.*

Example

As an example consider the UML Machine *Sndr* with

- vocabulary **Voc** $Sndr = \{$currState, inQu$_{Sndr}$, outQu$_{Sndr}\}$, where currState is a set name,
- the initial state **Init** $Sndr$ defined by currState $=$ inQu$_{Sndr}$ $=$ outQu$_{Sndr}$ $=$ $\emptyset$, and
- whose transition rule **Rule** $Sndr$ is given in Fig. 7.3.

Rule $Sndr$:
case currState **of**
    $Wait$: **do**
        choose e **with** $e \in$ inQu$_{Sndr}$ **do**
            do − **in** − **parallel**
                inQu$_{Sndr}$:= inQu$_{Sndr} \setminus \{\!| e |\!\}$
                if $e = send$ **then** currState := $Send$
        enddo
    $Send$: **do**
        do − **in** − **parallel**
            currState := $Wait$
            tooutQu$_{Sndr}(\{\!| transmit |\!\})$
    enddo

Fig. 7.3. Example UML Machine

The resulting input/output behavior can be characterized as follows.

Fact 7.4. *For each sequence* $(I_1, \ldots, I_n)$, $[\![Sndr]\!](I_1, \ldots, I_n)$ *consists of those sequences* $(O_1, \ldots, O_n)$ *that fulfill the following conditions, for each* $i \in \{1, \ldots, n\}$:

- $O_i \subseteq \{\!| transmit |\!\}$ *(that is, each* O_i *is either empty or contains the single element transmit).*
- $\sharp(O_1 \uplus \ldots \uplus O_i) \leq \sharp(I_1 \uplus \ldots \uplus I_{i-1}) \setminus \{\!| send |\!\}$ *(there must be at most as many transmit outputs as there are send inputs).*[3]
- *The conditions that*

$$\sharp(I_j \uplus \ldots \uplus I_{i-1}) - \sharp((I_j \uplus \ldots \uplus I_{i-1}) \setminus \{\!| send |\!\}) < i - j - 2 * \sharp(O_j \uplus \ldots \uplus O_{i-1})$$

for each $j < i$ *and that* $\sharp(O_1 \uplus \ldots \uplus O_{i-1}) < \sharp(I_1 \uplus \ldots \uplus I_{i-1}) \setminus \{\!| send |\!\}$ *imply* $\sharp O_i > 0$.

The last point means that an output of *transmit* is produced at time i, which means $\sharp O_i > 0$, provided that not all inputs of *send* that have previously been received have already prompted outputs, formalized as $\sharp(O_1 \uplus \ldots \uplus O_{i-1}) < \sharp(I_1 \uplus \ldots \uplus I_{i-1}) \setminus \{\!| send |\!\}$, and provided any other input received has already been consumed. The last condition can indeed be formalized as

---

[3] The definitions of $\sharp$ and $\setminus$ can be found in Sect. 3.3.1.

$$\sharp(I_j \uplus \ldots \uplus I_{i-1}) - \sharp((I_j \uplus \ldots \uplus I_{i-1}) \backslash \{\!\!\{ send \}\!\!\}) < i - j - 2 * \sharp(O_j \uplus \ldots \uplus O_{i-1})$$

as in the statement of Fact 7.4, because each processing of a *send* input takes two cycles, and during the remaining number of cycles, the system must have processed other inputs, provided there were any inputs at all. Note that in this example, it is not the case that $send \in I_i$ implies $transmit \in O_{n+1}$, because there may be another message received in I_i which is processed at step n instead of the *send* and which does not produce an output. A similar effect occurs within the UML semantics, where there is also no fixed order of dequeuing elements from the input queues prescribed by the UML definition, as explained in Chap. 8.

7.2 UML Machine Systems

We would like to build up UML Machine specifications in a modular way, by letting a set of UML Machines together with a set of communication links connecting them form a new UML Machine. To achieve this, we firstly define the notion of an *UML Machine System (UMS)*. It allows a rather flexible treatment using a scheduler for the UML Machines contained. Our explicit way of modeling the communication links and the messages exchanged over them allows modeling exterior influence on the communication within a system, such as attacks on insecure connections. Also, UMSs give a natural foundation for UML subsystems, as explained in Sect. 8.1.7.

To define the concept of *UML Machine Systems*, we first define the set **Events** from the previous section, containing the communication events, in more detail. We assume a set **MsgNm** of *message names* consisting of finite lists $n_1 :: n_2 :: \ldots :: n_k$ of names, where $k \geq 2$ and

- $n_1, \ldots, n_{k-2} \in$ **UMNames**, for a set **UMNames** of UML Machine names, are UMSs (when $k \geq 3$),
- $n_{k-1} \in$ **UMNames** is a UML Machine, and
- $n_k \in$ **locMsgNm** for a given set **locMsgNm** of local message names.

Here $n_1 :: n_2 :: \ldots :: n_{k-1}$ is called the *address* of the message with name $n_1 :: n_2 :: \ldots :: n_k$. We assume that **MsgNm**∪**locMsgNm** is partitioned into sets of operation names **Op**, signal names **Sig**, and return message names **Ret**, such that $n_1 :: n_2 :: \ldots :: n_k \in$ **Op** (resp. **Sig** resp. **Ret**) if and only if $n_k \in$ **Op** (resp. **Sig** resp. **Ret**). For each operation name $op \in$ **Op** ∩ **locMsgNm** there is a corresponding return message name $\text{return}_{op} \in$ **Ret** ∩ **locMsgNm**. Messages with names in **Op** are called *synchronous*, meaning that the sender of the message passes the thread of control to the receiver and receives it back together with the return message. Those in **Sig** are called *asynchronous*, meaning that the thread of control is split in two, one each for the sender and the receiver. These kinds of messages are motivated by the analogous concepts in UML, as defined in Chap. 8.

We then define the set **Events** of events to consist of terms of the form $msg^{sdr}(exp_1, \ldots, exp_n)$, for an arbitrary number n, where:

- $msg \in \mathbf{MsgNm}$ is an n-ary message name,
- $sdr = []$ if $msg \in \mathbf{Sig} \cup \mathbf{Ret}$ and otherwise sdr is a message address as defined above, and
- $exp_1, \ldots, exp_n \in \mathbf{Exp}$ are expressions, the *parameters*, or *arguments* of the event, for a given set of expressions **Exp**.

Thus an element of **Events** is a message with arguments, and a sender address in the case of a synchronous message. The latter is necessary for handling synchronous messages, for which return values have to be sent back to the sender. If the superscript sdr is equal to the empty list $[]$, it may be omitted. We define $\mathbf{Args}(m) \stackrel{\text{def}}{=} (exp_1, \ldots, exp_n)$ to be the sequence of the arguments of $m = msg^{sdr}(exp_1, \ldots, exp_n)$, $\mathbf{msgnm}(m) \stackrel{\text{def}}{=} msg$ to be the name of its message, and $\mathbf{sndr}(m) = sdr$ to be its sender. We write $\mathbf{head}(msg^{sdr}(exp_1, \ldots, exp_n))$ for $\mathbf{head}(msg)$, which is the first part of the address of msg (for example, the UMS which contains the UML Machine that is the recipient of msg). Similarly, we define $\mathbf{tail}(msg^{sdr}(exp_1, \ldots, exp_n))$ for $\mathbf{tail}(msg)^{sdr}(exp_1, \ldots, exp_n)$, which is the message with the remainder of the address. The definitions are used to "unpack" the address of a message when executing a UMS.

Definition 7.5. *A* UML Machine System (UMS) $\mathcal{A} = (\mathsf{Name}_{\mathcal{A}}, \mathsf{Comp}_{\mathcal{A}}, \mathsf{Sched}_{\mathcal{A}}, \mathsf{Links}_{\mathcal{A}}, \mathsf{Msgs}_{\mathcal{A}})$ *is given by the following data:*

- *A name* $\mathsf{Name}_{\mathcal{A}} \in \mathbf{UMNames}$ *from a fixed set of* UML Machine names **UMNames**.
- *A finite set* $\mathsf{Comp}_{\mathcal{A}} \subseteq \mathbf{UMNames}$ *of* components. *Each component* $\mathcal{C} \in \mathsf{Comp}_{\mathcal{A}}$ *has associated finite sets* $\mathsf{Act}_{\mathcal{C}}^{\mathcal{A}}$ *of activities and* $\mathsf{Att}_{\mathcal{C}}^{\mathcal{A}}$ *of local attributes. Each activity in* $\mathsf{Act}_{\mathcal{C}}^{\mathcal{A}}$ *has an associated UML Machine, possibly associated with a UMS from which it arises as defined in Fig. 7.4.*
- *A UML Machine* $\mathsf{Sched}_{\mathcal{A}}$, *the scheduler.*
- *A set* $\mathsf{Links}_{\mathcal{A}}$ *of links* $l = \{C, D\} \subseteq \mathsf{Comp}_{\mathcal{A}}$.
- *A set* $\mathsf{Msgs}_{\mathcal{A}} \subseteq \mathbf{MsgNm}$ *of names of messages that the UMS is ready to receive.*

Each activity UML Machine A of a component $\mathcal{C}$ is assumed to have the attributes of $\mathcal{C}$ as names, and also a flag finished$_A$. *Similarly, the scheduler UML Machine* $\mathsf{Sched}_{\mathcal{A}}$ *has a flag* finished$_{\mathsf{Sched}_{\mathcal{A}}}$. *The activities of a component $\mathcal{C}$ are required to have disjoint vocabularies except for the input and output queues* $\mathsf{inQu}_{\mathcal{C}}$ *and* $\mathsf{outQu}_{\mathcal{C}}$ *and the attributes. The scheduler may call each activity A as a subroutine and may read each flag* finished$_A$. *Otherwise, the components and the scheduler are required to have disjoint vocabularies.*

The intuition is that a UMS models a computer system that is divided into a set of components that may communicate by sending messages through bi-directional communication links. $\{C, D\} \in \mathsf{Links}_{\mathcal{A}}$ means that there is a *communication link* between the components C and D, where we may have $C = D$. The behavior of each component is specified using activities that are coordinated using the scheduler that calls the respective UML Machines, and which have access to the input and output queues and local attributes of the component. These UML Machines specifying the activities may themselves arise from UMSs as defined below. In that case, each UMS $\mathcal{A}$ specifying an activity of a component C has its own link set $\mathsf{Links}_{\mathcal{A}}$, rather than sharing the links with the UMSs specifying other activities of C. This feature can be exploited to include mobility aspects [JK03], which is, however, beyond scope here. Note that the disjointness constraints on the vocabularies in the above definition are not a restriction but may be achieved by renaming.

The execution of a UMS $\mathcal{A}$ is the joint execution of the UML Machines giving the component activities of the UMS, scheduled by the UML Machine giving the scheduler. It is modeled as a UML Machine **Exec** $\mathcal{A}$ with

- the vocabulary **Voc** (**Exec** $\mathcal{A}$) which is the union of the vocabularies of the UML Machines modeling the activities in $\mathsf{Act}_C^{\mathcal{A}}$ and of the scheduler UML Machine $\mathsf{Sched}_{\mathcal{A}}$, with the set $\{\mathsf{linkQu}_{\mathcal{A}}(l) : l \in \mathsf{Links}_{\mathcal{A}}\}$ of link queue names and which additionally contains the name $\mathsf{finished}_{\mathbf{Exec}\,\mathcal{A}}$,
- the initial state **Init** (**Exec** $\mathcal{A}$) defined as the initial states of the UML Machines modeling the activities in $\mathsf{Act}_C^{\mathcal{A}}$ and of the scheduler UML Machine $\mathsf{Sched}_{\mathcal{A}}$ and where all input, output and link queues evaluate to $\emptyset$ and all finished flags evaluate to *false*, and
- the transition rule **Rule** (**Exec** $\mathcal{A}$) given in Fig. 7.4.

In Fig. 7.4, we use the following syntactic shortcut, where $\mathcal{A}$ is a UMS, $l\mathsf{Links}_{\mathcal{A}}$ a link of $\mathcal{A}$ and X is a multiset:

$$\mathsf{tolinkQu}_{\mathcal{A},l}(X) \equiv \mathsf{linkQu}_{\mathcal{A}}(l) := \mathsf{linkQu}_{\mathcal{A}}(l) \uplus X$$

The rule processes each incoming message, provided it is in the set of messages accepted by $\mathcal{A}$. In the case of an operation call, one needs to keep track of the message sender by adjusting the sender name attached to the message name. The message is then forwarded to the relevant component of $\mathcal{A}$. Then, similarly, the messages sent over links within $\mathcal{A}$ are processed and the scheduler is called, which in turn may call the UML Machines in $\mathsf{Comp}_{\mathcal{A}}$. Thus the definition **Exec** $\mathcal{A}$ is recursive; it is well-defined because by construction a UMS cannot be contained in itself. Finally, the output messages from the components in $\mathcal{A}$ are processed. Again, in the case of operation calls the sender names are adjusted. Note that if the name $\mathcal{A}$ itself appears in the list of UML Machine names determining the sender (resp. receiver) of a message while this message is actually within $\mathcal{A}$, this signifies that the message comes from (resp. goes to) an UML Machine outside $\mathcal{A}$.

Precisely, a message $n_1 :: n_2 :: \ldots :: n_k$ sent by a UMS which is part of the system n is delivered as follows:

Rule Exec $\mathcal{A}$:

loop e **through set** $\{e \in \text{inQu}_{\mathcal{C}} : \textbf{msgnm}(e) \in \text{Msgs}_{\mathcal{A}} \wedge \textbf{head}(e) \in \text{Comp}_{\mathcal{A}} \}$

    if msgnm$(e) \in$ **Op then** $e' := \textbf{msgnm}(e)^{\mathcal{A}.\textbf{sndr}(e)}(\textbf{Args}(e))$

        else $e' := e;$

    toinQu$_{\textbf{Exec head}(e)}(\{\!\{ \textbf{tail}(e') \}\!\});$

inQu$_{\mathcal{C}} := \emptyset;$

loop e **through set** $\{e \in \biguplus_{l \in \text{Links}_{\mathcal{A}}} \text{linkQu}_{\textbf{Exec} \,\mathcal{A}}(l) : \textbf{head}(e) \in \text{Comp}_{\mathcal{A}} \}$

    toinQu$_{\textbf{Exec head}(e)}(\{\!\{ \textbf{tail}(e) \}\!\});$

forall l **with** $l \in \text{Links}_{\mathcal{A}}$ **do**

    linkQu$_{\mathcal{A}}(l) := \emptyset;$

Rule Sched$_{\mathcal{A}};$

finished$_{\textbf{Exec}\,\mathcal{A}} :=$ finished$_{\text{Sched}_{\mathcal{A}}};$

forall S **with** $S \in \text{Comp}_{\mathcal{A}}$ **do**

    loop e **through set** outQu$_{\textbf{Exec}\,S}$

        if msgnm$(e) \in$ **Op then** $e' := \textbf{msgnm}(e)^{S.\textbf{sndr}(e)}(\textbf{Args}(e))$

        else $e' := e;$

        if head$(e) = \mathcal{A}$ **then** tooutQu$_{\mathcal{C}}(\{\!\{ \textbf{tail}(e') \}\!\})$

        else if $\{S, \textbf{head}(e)\} \in \text{Links}_{\mathcal{A}}$ **then** tolinkQu$_{\textbf{Exec}\,\mathcal{A},\{S,\textbf{head}(e)\}}(\{\!\{ e' \}\!\});$

    outQu$_{\textbf{Exec}\,S} := \emptyset$

Fig. 7.4. Behavior of UMS

- If $n_1 = n$ then the system n sends out the tail $n_2 :: \ldots :: n_k$ of the message within the UML Machine containing n.
- If n_1 is a part of n, then the tail $n_2 :: \ldots :: n_k$ of the message is delivered to n_1.

Note that the definition of **Rule Exec** $\mathcal{A}$ is complicated by the handling of synchronous messages $op \in$ **Op** and their returns, introduced since these are offered by UML. To use UML Machines just with asynchronous messages $sig \in$ **Sig**, which will be our main usage, the simpler definition in Fig. 7.5 suffices. Here $links_S \overset{\text{def}}{=} \{\{A, B\} \in \text{Links}_{\mathcal{A}} : A = S\}$ is the set of links connected to S. It is a straightforward formal exercise to show that, if all messages are asynchronous, the rule in Fig. 7.5 indeed defines a UML Machine equivalent to the on defined in Fig. 7.4.

An example for a scheduler Sched$_{\mathcal{A}}$ is the one given in Fig. 7.6 that, given n activities as UML Machines $A_1, \ldots, A_n$, simply executes them in parallel. Each of these UML Machines may in turn be defined as the behavior **Exec** $\mathcal{A}$ of a UMS $\mathcal{A}$, as defined above.

7.3 Refinement

A useful paradigm of system development is that of *stepwise refinement* [Dij68, Wir71]. One starts with an abstract specification and refines it in several steps

Rule Exec $\mathcal{A}$:
forall S **with** $S \in \mathsf{Comp}_\mathcal{A}$ **do**
$\qquad \mathsf{toinQu}_{\mathbf{Exec}\,S}\Big(\{\!\!\{\mathbf{tail}(e) : e \in (\mathsf{inQu}_\mathcal{C} \setminus \mathsf{Msgs}_\mathcal{A}) \uplus$
$\qquad\qquad\qquad\qquad\qquad \biguplus_{l \in links\,S} \mathsf{linkQu}_{\mathbf{Exec}\,\mathcal{A}}(l) \wedge \mathbf{head}(e) = S\}\!\!\}\Big)\,;$
$\mathsf{inQu}_\mathcal{C} := \emptyset;$
forall l **with** $l \in \mathsf{Links}_\mathcal{A}$ **do**
$\qquad \mathsf{linkQu}_\mathcal{A}(l) := \emptyset;$
Rule $\mathsf{Sched}_\mathcal{A};$
$\mathsf{finished}_{\mathbf{Exec}\,\mathcal{A}} := \mathsf{finished}_{\mathsf{Sched}_\mathcal{A}};$
forall l **with** $l \in \mathsf{Links}_\mathcal{A}$ **do**
$\qquad \mathsf{linkQu}_{\mathbf{Exec}\,\mathcal{A}}(l) := \{\!\!\{e \in \mathsf{outQu}_{\mathbf{Exec}\,S} : S \in \mathsf{Comp}_\mathcal{A} \wedge l = \{\mathbf{head}(e), S\}\}\!\!\}\,;$
$\mathsf{tooutQu}_\mathcal{C}\big(\biguplus_{S \in \mathsf{Comp}_\mathcal{A}} \{\!\!\{\mathbf{tail}(e) : e \in \mathsf{outQu}_{\mathbf{Exec}\,S} \wedge \mathbf{head}(e) = \mathbf{Exec}\,\mathcal{A}\}\!\!\}\big);$
forall S **with** $S \in \mathsf{Comp}_\mathcal{A}$ **do**
$\qquad \mathsf{outQu}_{\mathbf{Exec}\,S} := \emptyset$

Fig. 7.5. Behavior of UMS (only asynchronous messages)

$\qquad$ **Rule** $\mathsf{Sched}_\mathcal{A}$:
$\qquad\qquad$ **do $-$ in $-$ parallel**
$\qquad\qquad\qquad$ **Rule** A_1
$\qquad\qquad\qquad\qquad \cdots$
$\qquad\qquad\qquad$ **Rule** A_n
$\qquad\qquad$ **enddo**;
$\qquad\qquad \mathsf{finished}_{\mathsf{Sched}_\mathcal{A}} := \mathsf{finished}_{\mathbf{Exec}\,A_1} \wedge \ldots \wedge \mathsf{finished}_{\mathbf{Exec}\,A_n}$

Fig. 7.6. Simple scheduler

to a concrete specification which can then easily be implemented. For more discussion on the role of refinement in system development see Sect. 8.2.1.

We use *underspecification* to postpone design decisions to a later stage of system development, for example by making use of the **choose** rule defined in Sect. 7.1. Correspondingly, we will define a notion of *refinement* that allows us to proceed from abstract to more concrete specifications in a well-defined way. It is inspired by a definition given in [BS01] in the setting of stream-processing functions, as well as the related notion of *interface refinement*, which is more flexible. We will also define a notion of *delayed refinement*, which is a relaxation of refinement by allowing delays to be inserted. It allows a more flexible treatment, while still offering convenient structural properties. Our use of refinement is demonstrated in the case-study in Sect. 5.1.

First we give some preliminary definitions for delayed refinement. The following definition is influenced by the treatment in [AL93].

Definition 7.6. *Two sequences s, t of event multi-sets are* stutter-equivalent *if $\tilde{s} = \tilde{t}$, where for a sequence s of event multi-sets, $\tilde{s}$ is the sequence obtained from s by leaving out all empty multi-sets.*

For sets S, T of sequences of event multi-sets we write $S \subseteq T$ if for each multi-set $s \in S$ there is a multi-set $t \in T$ such that s and t are stutter-equivalent. Two sets S, T of sequences of event multi-sets are stutter-equivalent if $S \subseteq T$ and $T \subseteq S$.

Thus, two sets of sequences of event multi-sets are equivalent if they are the same up to inclusion of empty event multi-sets into the sequences.

For a set S of finite sequences of event multi-sets and a set $\mathcal{E}$ of events, we define

$$S \curvearrowright \mathcal{E} \stackrel{\text{def}}{=} \{(M_1 \backslash \mathcal{E}, \ldots, M_i \backslash \mathcal{E}) : (M_1, \ldots, M_i) \in S\}.$$

This is simply a generalization of the filter operator $\backslash$ from Sect. 3.3.1 to sequences of event multi-sets: all events except those in $\mathcal{E}$ are filtered out. It is needed to make the following definition relative to a set $\mathcal{E} \subseteq \mathbf{Events}$.

Definition 7.7 (Behavioral refinement of UML Machines).
Suppose we are given UML Machines A, A', tuples $\mathbf{i}$ and $\mathbf{o}$ of input and output names, and a set $\mathcal{E} \subseteq \mathbf{Events}$.

We say that A' $\mathcal{E}$-$(\mathbf{i}, \mathbf{o})$-refines A if for each sequence $I_1, \ldots, I_n$ of event multi-set tuples with $\bigcup_i \lfloor I_i \rfloor \subseteq \mathcal{E}$, we have

$$[\![A']\!]_{\mathbf{i},\mathbf{o}}(I_1, \ldots, I_n) \curvearrowright \mathcal{E} \subseteq [\![A]\!]_{\mathbf{i},\mathbf{o}}(I_1, \ldots, I_n) \curvearrowright \mathcal{E}.$$

We say that A' delayed $\mathcal{E}$-refines A if for each sequence $I_1, \ldots, I_n$ of event multi-sets with $\bigcup_i \lfloor I_i \rfloor \subseteq \mathcal{E}$ there exists a number $m \geq n$ such that for every extension $I_1, \ldots, I_m$ of the sequence $I_1, \ldots, I_n$, we have

$$[\![A']\!]_{\mathbf{i},\mathbf{o}}(I_1, \ldots, I_m) \curvearrowright \mathcal{E} \subseteq [\![A]\!]_{\mathbf{i},\mathbf{o}}(I_1, \ldots, I_n) \curvearrowright \mathcal{E}.$$

For $\mathcal{E} = \mathbf{Events}$ and $\mathbf{i} = \mathbf{o} = \emptyset$, we say A' (delayed) refines A if A' (delayed) $\mathcal{E}$-$(\mathbf{i}, \mathbf{o})$-refines A.

One can thus use the set of events $\mathcal{E}$ in order to hide the events not contained in it with respect to the refinement. This is inspired by the corresponding operators in CSP [Hoa85] and CCS [Mil89] although not precisely the same. It gives us more flexibility, as required by a practically applicable notion of refinement, by allowing the events outside $\mathcal{E}$ to change arbitrarily.

Example

Let $R(0), R(1)$ be any two rules. The UML Machine B with the rule **Rule** $B = R(1)$ refines the UML Machine A with the following rule **Rule** A, assuming that they have the same initial state:

choose b **with** $b \in \{0, 1\}$ **do**
    $R(b)$

This notion of refinement enjoys the usual structural properties one would expect from a refinement relation.

Fact 7.8. *(Delayed) $\mathcal{E}$-$(\mathbf{i}, \mathbf{o})$-refinement of UML Machines is a preorder for each set of events $\mathcal{E} \subseteq$ **Events** and tuples $\mathbf{i}$ and $\mathbf{o}$ of input and output names.*

We extend the definition of refinement to UMSs. Here we are interested in a kind of *white-box* refinement that preserves the system structure, such as the links between components and the scheduler. In that respect, this notion of refinement is stricter than the "black-box" refinement between UML Machines **Exec** $\mathcal{A}$ generated from UMSs $\mathcal{A}$, as we will show in Fact 7.10, but is nevertheless useful in certain situations. We do not consider hiding in refinement, as in the case of refinement of UML Machines. Variations are, however, possible and may be useful in a given situation.

Definition 7.9 (Behavioral refinement of UMSs). *A UMS $\mathcal{A}' = (\mathsf{Comp}_{\mathcal{A}'}, \mathsf{Sched}_{\mathcal{A}'}, \mathsf{Links}_{\mathcal{A}'}, \mathsf{Msgs}_{\mathcal{A}'})$ is a (delayed) $(\mathbf{i}, \mathbf{o})$-refinement of a UMS $\mathcal{A} = (\mathsf{Comp}_{\mathcal{A}}, \mathsf{Sched}_{\mathcal{A}}, \mathsf{Links}_{\mathcal{A}}, \mathsf{Msgs}_{\mathcal{A}})$ if $\mathsf{Msgs}_{\mathcal{A}} \subseteq \mathsf{Msgs}_{\mathcal{A}'}$ and if for each $C \in \mathsf{Comp}_{\mathcal{A}}$ there are bijections $b : \mathsf{Comp}_{\mathcal{A}} \to \mathsf{Comp}_{\mathcal{A}'}$ and $b_C : \mathsf{Act}_C^{\mathcal{A}} \to \mathsf{Act}_{b(C)}^{\mathcal{A}'}$ such that*

- *for each component $C \in \mathsf{Comp}_{\mathcal{A}}$ and activity $A \in \mathsf{Act}_C^{\mathcal{A}}$, the UML Machine of $b_C(A)$ is a (delayed) $(\mathbf{i}, \mathbf{o})$-refinement of the A Machine where $\mathbf{i} = \mathsf{Att}_C^{\mathcal{A}}$ and $\mathbf{o} = \mathbf{i} \cup \{\mathsf{finished}_A\}$, and*
- *$\mathsf{Sched}_{\mathcal{A}} = \mathsf{Sched}_{\mathcal{A}'}$ and $\mathsf{Links}_{\mathcal{A}} = \mathsf{Links}_{\mathcal{A}'}$, each up to renaming of components using the bijections b, b_C.*

We show that refinement of UMSs behaves well with respect to defining their behavior using UML Machines. Here we only state this and the following results for undelayed refinement. They also hold for delayed refinement, under a suitable *delay-invariance* assumption on the UML Machines, but we do not need this here.

Fact 7.10. *If the UMS $\mathcal{A}'$ is a refinement of the UMS $\mathcal{A}$ then the UML Machine* **Exec** $\mathcal{A}'$ *is a refinement of the UML Machine* **Exec** $\mathcal{A}$.

If for UMSs $\mathcal{A}$ and $\mathcal{A}'$, the UML Machine **Exec** $\mathcal{A}'$ is a refinement of the UML Machine **Exec** $\mathcal{A}$, we also say that the UMS $\mathcal{A}'$ is a *black-box refinement* of the UMS $\mathcal{A}$. Next, the structural properties of UML Machine refinement carry over to the UMS case.

Fact 7.11. *Refinement of UMSs is a preorder.*

We show that refinement of UMSs is preserved by substitution and is thus a precongruence with respect to composition by system formation. A *parameterized UMS $\mathcal{A}(\mathcal{Y}_1, \ldots, \mathcal{Y}_n)$* is a UMS specification where n of the component activities are replaced by variables $\mathcal{Y}_1, \ldots, \mathcal{Y}_n$. For UML Machines $A_1, \ldots, A_n$, we define that $\mathcal{A}(A_1, \ldots, A_n)$ is the UMS obtained by substituting in $\mathcal{A}$ the UML Machine A_i for $\mathcal{Y}_i$, for each i.

Fact 7.12. *Suppose we are given a parameterized UMS $A(\mathcal{Y}_1, \ldots, \mathcal{Y}_n)$, where the activity variable $\mathcal{Y}_i$ belongs to the component C_i, for each $i = 1, \ldots, n$, and that we are given UMSs A_i and A_i' for each i.*

*If for each $i = 1, \ldots, n$, **Exec** A_i' is a $(\mathbf{i}_i, \mathbf{o}_i)$-refinement of **Exec** A_i where $\mathbf{i}_i = \text{Att}_{C_i}^A$ and $\mathbf{o}_i = \mathbf{i}_i \cup \{\text{finished}_{\textbf{Exec }A_i}\}$ then $A(\textbf{Exec } A_1', \ldots,$ **Exec** $A_n')$ is a refinement of $A(\textbf{Exec } A_1, \ldots, \textbf{Exec } A_n)$.*

We can summarize the above facts in the following theorem.

Theorem 7.13. *Refinement of UMSs is a precongruence with respect to composition by system formation using parameterized UMSs.*

Next, we define what it means for two UMSs to be exchangeable, with respect to their observable behavior.

Definition 7.14 (Behavioral equivalence). *Two UMSs A and A' are (delayed) equivalent if A is a (delayed) refinement of A' and A' is a (delayed) refinement of A.*

We can then extend the above theorem to this definition.

Corollary 7.15. *Equivalence of UMSs is a congruence with respect to composition by system formation.*

We provide a more flexible concept of refinement.

Definition 7.16 (Interface refinement). *Given UMSs A and A' and a parameterized UMS $\mathcal{I}(\mathcal{Y})$, A' is a (delayed) $\mathcal{I}$-interface refinement of A if A' is a (delayed) refinement of $\mathcal{I}(A)$.*

This kind of refinement is again a preorder in a certain sense.

Theorem 7.17. *Each UMS A is a $\mathcal{I}d$-interface refinement of itself, where $\mathcal{I}d(\mathcal{Y}) \stackrel{\text{def}}{=} \mathcal{Y}$.*

For all UMSs A, A', and A'' such that A' is a $\mathcal{I}$-interface refinement of A and A'' is a $\mathcal{I}'$-interface refinement of A', A'' is a $\mathcal{I}' \circ \mathcal{I}$-interface refinement of A, where $\mathcal{I}' \circ \mathcal{I}(\mathcal{Y}) \stackrel{\text{def}}{=} \mathcal{I}'(\mathcal{I}(\mathcal{Y}))$.

7.4 Rely-Guarantee Specifications

To reason about system specifications in a modular way, one may usefully employ *rely-guarantee* specifications (also called *assume/guarantee*). The following definition follows a corresponding notion in [BS01].

Definition 7.18. *Given a UML Machine A and sets R, G of sequences of event multi-sets, we say that A fulfills the rely-guarantee specification (R, G) if for any $(I_1, \ldots, I_n) \in R$, we have $[\![A]\!](I_1, \ldots, I_n) \subseteq G$. A rely-guarantee specification (R, G), where R is the set of all sequences of event multi-sets accepted by A, is also called a trace property.*

We say that a set S of sequences of event multi-sets are *stutter-closed* if it contains every sequence of events that is stutter-equivalent to a sequence in S.

Theorem 7.19. *Suppose that the UML Machine A fulfills the rely-guarantee specification (R, G) where $R \frown \mathcal{E} = R$ and $G \frown \mathcal{E} = G$, and suppose $E = \{\mathbf{I} : \mathbf{I} \frown \mathcal{E} = \mathbf{I}\}$.*

If the UML Machine A' $\mathcal{E}$-refines A and A' fulfills the rely-guarantee specification (R, E) then A' fulfills the rely-guarantee specification (R, G).

If the UML Machine A' delayed $\mathcal{E}$-refines A, G is stutter-closed, and A' fulfills the rely-guarantee specification (R, E), then A' fulfills the rely-guarantee specification (R, G).

In particular, the above theorem implies that (delayed) refinement preserves (stutter-closed) trace properties. Note that we do not require R to be stutter-closed; intuitively, the reason is that the above statement holds for each fixed sequence of input event multi-sets.

7.5 Reasoning About Security Properties

We now use the notions from Sect. 3.3.3 in the context of security analysis using UML machines. The notion of UMSs allows a rather natural modeling of potential adversary behavior. We can model specific types of adversaries that can attack different parts of the system in a specified way. For example, an attacker of type *insider* may be able to intercept the communication links in a company-wide local area network. We model the actual behavior of the adversary by defining a class of UML Machines that can access the communication links of the system in a specified way. To evaluate the security of the system with respect to the given type of adversary, we consider the joint execution of the system with any UML Machine in this class. This way of reasoning allows an intuitive formulation of many security properties. Since the actual verification is rather indirect this way, we also give alternative intrinsic ways of defining security properties below, which are more manageable, and show that they are equivalent to the earlier ones.

Security evaluation of specifications is done with respect to a given type $\mathcal{A}$ of adversary. The capabilities of an adversary of a given type are captured as follows.

Firstly, given a UMS $\mathcal{A}$ we recursively define the set $cps_{\mathcal{A}}$ of contained components:

- for a UML Machine A not associated with a UMS, we define $cps_A \stackrel{\text{def}}{=} \emptyset$ and
- for a UML Machine A associated with a UMS $\mathcal{B}$, we define $cps_A \stackrel{\text{def}}{=} \mathsf{Comp}_{\mathcal{B}} \cup \bigcup_{\mathcal{C} \in \mathsf{Comp}_{\mathcal{B}}} \bigcup_{A \in \mathsf{Act}_{\mathcal{C}}^{\mathcal{B}}} cps_A$.

Similarly, for a UMS $\mathcal{A}$ we define the set $lks_\mathcal{A}$ of contained links:

- for a UML Machine A not associated with a UMS, we define $lks_A \stackrel{\text{def}}{=} \emptyset$ and
- for a UML Machine A associated with a UMS $\mathcal{B}$, we define $lks_A \stackrel{\text{def}}{=} \text{Links}_\mathcal{B} \cup \bigcup_{C \in \text{Comp}_\mathcal{B}} \bigcup_{A \in \text{Act}_C^g} cps_A$.

To capture the capabilities of an attacker, we assume that, given a UMS $\mathcal{A}$, we have a function $\text{threats}_A^\mathcal{A}(x)$ that takes an activity or link $x \in cps_\mathcal{A} \cup lks_\mathcal{A}$ and a type of adversary A and returns a set of strings $\text{threats}_A^\mathcal{A}(x) \subseteq \{\text{delete}, \text{read}, \text{insert}, \text{access}\}$ under the following conditions:

- for $x \in cps_\mathcal{A}$, we have $\text{threats}_A^\mathcal{A}(x) \subseteq \{\text{access}\}$,
- for $x \in lks_\mathcal{A}$, we have $\text{threats}_A^\mathcal{A}(x) \subseteq \{\text{delete}, \text{read}, \text{insert}\}$, and
- for $l \in lks_\mathcal{A}$ with $i \in l$ and $\text{threats}_A^\mathcal{A}(i) = \{\text{access}\}$, the equation $\text{threats}_A^\mathcal{A}(l) = \{\text{delete}, \text{read}, \text{insert}\}$ holds.

The idea is that $\text{threats}_A^\mathcal{A}(x)$ specifies the *threat scenario* against a component or link x in the UMS $\mathcal{A}$ that is associated with an adversary type A. On the one hand, the threat scenario determines which data the adversary can obtain by *accessing* components; on the other hand, it determines which actions the adversary is permitted by the threat scenario to apply to the links concerned. See Chap. 4 for examples of functions $\text{threats}()$.

Then each function $\text{threats}()$ gives rise to the set $\mathcal{K}_A^a \subseteq \mathbf{Exp}$ of *accessible knowledge* which contains knowledge that may arise from accessing components and is defined to consist of all expressions $E \in \mathbf{Exp}$ appearing as initial values of attributes in the specification for any $i \in cps_\mathcal{A}$ with $\text{access} \in \text{threats}_A^\mathcal{A}(i)$.

Next, for an adversary type A, one has to specify a subalgebra $\mathcal{K}_A^p \subseteq \mathbf{Exp}$ of *previous knowledge* of adversaries of type A. Then we define the set $\mathcal{K}_A^0 \subseteq \mathbf{Exp}$ of the *initial knowledge* of any adversary of type A to be the $\mathbf{Exp}$-subalgebra generated by $\mathcal{K}_A^a \cup \mathcal{K}_A^p$. Thus it is closed under application of the algebra operations.

We now define the set $\text{Advers}_\mathcal{A}(A)$ of *adversaries* of type A against a UMS $\mathcal{A}$.

Definition 7.20. *An adversary $adv \in \text{Advers}_\mathcal{A}(A)$ of type A with previous knowledge $\mathcal{K}_A^p \subseteq \mathbf{Exp}$ against the a UMS $\mathcal{A}$ is a UML Machine such that*

- knows $\in \mathbf{Voc}\, adv$ *for a set name* knows *and* $\mathbf{Voc}\, adv \cap \mathbf{Voc}\, \mathcal{A} = \{\text{linkQu}_\mathcal{A}(l) : \neg \text{threats}_A^\mathcal{A}(l) \subseteq \{\text{access}\}\}$,
- *at the initial state* $\mathbf{Init}\, adv$ *we have* knows $= \mathcal{K}_A^0$ *as defined above, and*
- *the transition rule* $\mathbf{Rule}\, adv$ *fulfills the following three conditions, where f denotes the value of the name f before, and $adv(f)$ the value after executing* $\mathbf{Rule}\, adv$:
  - $adv(\text{knows}) = \langle \text{knows} \cup \{E \in \mathbf{Args}(e) : e \in \bigcup_{\text{read} \in \text{threats}_A^\mathcal{A}(l)} \text{linkQu}_\mathcal{A}(l)\rangle$, *where $\langle S \rangle$ is the $\mathbf{Exp}$-subalgebra generated of a set $S \subseteq \mathbf{Exp}$, as defined in Sect. 3.3.3*

- $adv(\text{linkQu}_{\mathcal{A}}(l)) \subseteq adv(\text{knows})$ or $\text{linkQu}_{\mathcal{A}}(l) \subseteq adv(\text{linkQu}_{\mathcal{A}}(l)) \subseteq$ $\text{linkQu}_{\mathcal{A}}(l) \cup adv(\text{knows})$
- $\text{delete} \notin \text{threats}_{\mathcal{A}}^{\mathcal{A}}(l)$ $implies$ $\text{linkQu}_{\mathcal{A}}(l) \subseteq adv(\text{linkQu}_{\mathcal{A}}(l))$
- $\text{insert} \notin \text{threats}_{\mathcal{A}}^{\mathcal{A}}(l)$ $implies$ $adv(\text{linkQu}_{\mathcal{A}}(l)) = \text{linkQu}_{\mathcal{A}}(l)$ or $adv(\text{linkQu}_{\mathcal{A}}(l)) = \emptyset$

The intuition behind this definition is that an adversary may initially know only the data contained in $\mathcal{K}_{\mathcal{A}}^0$, arising from previous knowledge and the data gained from accessing unprotected system parts. The adversary may apply only those actions to the link queues which arise from the threats() sets defined above. The definition accommodates the fact that an adversary A able to remove all values sent over the link l, formalized as $\text{delete}_l \in \text{threats}_{\mathcal{A}}^{\mathcal{A}}(l)$, may not be able to selectively remove a value e with known meaning from l. For example, the messages sent over the Internet within a virtual private network are encrypted. Thus, an adversary who is unable to break the encryption may be able to delete all messages indiscriminately, but not a single message whose meaning would be known to the adversary.

The execution $\mathcal{A}_{adv}$ of $\mathcal{A}$ in the presence of the attacker $adv \in \text{Advers}_A(A)$ of type A is modeled by a UML Machine $\mathcal{A}_{adv}$ such that

- $\mathbf{Voc}\,\mathcal{A}_{adv} = \mathbf{Voc}\,\mathcal{A} \cup \mathbf{Voc}\,adv$,
- the initial state $\mathbf{Init}\,\mathcal{A}_{adv}$ is defined as $\mathbf{Init}\,\mathcal{A}$, and in addition knows $= \mathcal{K}_{\mathcal{A}}^0$, and
- the transition rule $\mathbf{Rule}\,\mathcal{A}_{adv}$ is defined as the sequential composition

$$\mathbf{Rule}\,\mathcal{A}_{adv} \overset{\text{def}}{=} \mathbf{Rule}\,\mathbf{Exec}\,\mathcal{A};\ \ \mathbf{Rule}\,adv.$$

Suppose we are given a UMS $\mathcal{A}$ and an adversary $adv \in \text{Advers}_A(A)$ of type A. For any execution $\mathbf{e} \in \mathbf{Run}\,\mathcal{A}_{adv}$ of length $n \in \mathbb{N}$, as defined in Sect. 7.1, we define the knowledge set $\mathcal{K}_{adv}^{\mathbf{e}}(\mathcal{A})$ of expressions known to adv after execution of $\mathbf{e}$:

- $\mathcal{K}_{adv}^{[]}(\mathcal{A})$ is the set $\mathcal{K}_{\mathcal{A}}^0$ of initial knowledge defined above.
- $\mathcal{K}_{adv}^{\mathbf{e}::e}(\mathcal{A}) = \langle \mathcal{K}_{adv}^{\mathbf{e}}(\mathcal{A}) \cup \bigcup_{\text{read} \in \text{threats}_{\mathcal{A}}^{\mathcal{A}}(l)} link_{\mathcal{A}}^{e}(l) \rangle$ where $link_{\mathcal{A}}^{e}(l)$ is the set of elements in the multi-set $\text{linkQu}_{\mathcal{A}}(l)$ in state e.

We have the following characterizations of the adversary's capabilities.

Fact 7.21. *Suppose we are given a UMS $\mathcal{A}$, an adversary $adv \in \text{Advers}_A(A)$ of type A, and an execution $\mathbf{e} \in \mathbf{Run}\,\mathcal{A}_{adv}$. Then after execution of $\mathbf{e}$, knows evaluates to $\mathcal{K}_{adv}^{\mathbf{e}}(\mathcal{A})$.*

We consider the overall *adversary knowledge*, which is simpler to handle and often sufficient. The overall knowledge of expressions known to *any* adversary adv of type A after n iterations of $\mathbf{Rule}\,\mathcal{A}_{adv}$ is $\mathcal{K}_{A}^{n}(\mathcal{A}) \overset{\text{def}}{=} \bigcup_{adv,\mathbf{e}} \mathcal{K}_{adv}^{\mathbf{e}}(\mathcal{A})$, where $adv \in \text{Advers}_A(A)$ ranges over all adversaries of type A and $\mathbf{e}$ over all executions of $\mathcal{A}_{adv}$ of length n. We write $\mathcal{K}_A(\mathcal{A}) \overset{\text{def}}{=} \bigcup_{n \in \mathbb{N}} \mathcal{K}_{A}^{n}(\mathcal{A})$.

Note that the definition of $\mathcal{K}_A^n(\mathcal{A})$ does not depend on any particular adversary, only on the adversary type A. This allows one to give equivalent intrinsic definitions for the security properties considered in the following subsections, which simplifies reasoning.

Fact 7.22. *Given a UMS $\mathcal{A}$ and an adversary $adv \in \mathsf{Advers}_A(A)$ of type A, the set knows of $\mathcal{A}_{adv}$ evaluates to a subset of $\mathcal{K}_A(\mathcal{A})$, at any point.*

This means that, during the execution of $\mathcal{A}_{adv}$, an adversary of type A will get to know, and thus can add to a link only expressions in $\mathcal{K}_{adv}^e(\mathcal{A})$.

Suppose we are given a UMS $\mathcal{A}$ with a name v and an adversary $adv \in \mathsf{Advers}_A(A)$ of type A. For any execution $\mathbf{e} \in \mathbf{Run}\,\mathcal{A}_{adv}$ of length $n \in \mathbb{N}$ of $\mathcal{A}_{adv}$, we define the *influence set* $\mathcal{I}_{adv}^e(\mathcal{A}, v)$ of expressions that may be written to v after execution of $\mathbf{e}$:

- $\mathcal{I}_{adv}^{[\,]}(\mathcal{A}, v) \overset{\text{def}}{=} \emptyset$.
- $\mathcal{I}_{adv}^{\mathbf{e}::e}(\mathcal{A}, v)$ is the union of $\mathcal{I}_{adv}^e(\mathcal{A}, v)$ and the value to which v evaluates at state e.

We consider the overall influence set, which is simpler to handle and often sufficient. The overall influence of any adversary adv of type A on a variable v after n iterations of $\mathbf{Rule}\,\mathcal{A}_{adv}$ is $\mathcal{I}_A^n(\mathcal{A}, v) \overset{\text{def}}{=} \bigcup_{adv, \mathbf{e}} \mathcal{I}_{adv}^{\mathbf{e}}(\mathcal{A}, v)$, where $adv \in \mathsf{Advers}_A(A)$ ranges over all adversaries of type A and $\mathbf{e} \in \mathbf{Run}\,\mathcal{A}_{adv}$ over all executions of $\mathcal{A}_{adv}$ of length n. We write $\mathcal{I}_A(\mathcal{A}, v) \overset{\text{def}}{=} \bigcup_{n \in \mathbb{N}} \mathcal{I}_A^n(\mathcal{A}, v)$.

Fact 7.23. *Given a UMS $\mathcal{A}$ with a name v and an adversary $adv \in \mathsf{Advers}_A(A)$ of type A, then during any run $\mathbf{e} \in \mathbf{Run}\,\mathcal{A}_{adv}$, the name v evaluates to an element of $\mathcal{I}_A(\mathcal{A}, v)$, at any point.*

This means that, during the execution of $\mathcal{A}_{adv}$, an adversary adv of type A can only cause $\mathcal{A}$ to write to v expressions in $\mathcal{I}_A(\mathcal{A}, v)$.

7.5.1 Refinement

When refining specifications, the concrete specification must have all relevant properties of the initial specification. This is indeed the case for system properties that can be expressed as properties on traces, if one takes refinement to be reverse inclusion on trace sets: A system A refines a system B is the trace set of B is contained in the trace set of A. A classical example is the Alpern–Schneider framework of safety and liveness properties [AS85].

However, many security properties proposed in the literature are properties on trace sets rather than traces and give rise to the refinement problem, which means that these properties are not preserved under many standard definitions of refinement. For non-interference this is pointed out in [McL94, McL96]; a similar situation arises when using these notions of refinement with equivalence-based notions of secrecy explained for example in [Aba00]).

For such properties, developing secure systems in a stepwise manner requires one to redo security proofs at each refinement step. More worryingly, since an implementation is necessarily a refinement of its specification, an implementation of a secure specification may not be secure. Thus the results of verifying such properties on the level of specifications need to be applied with care, as pointed out in [RS98].

We show that our security notions, which follow a standard approach, are preserved by the standard refinement operators defined in Sect. 7.3. To understand the cause of the refinement problem and how to fix it, we first give some background information on non-determinism and refinement.

In the specification of systems one may employ non-determinism in different ways, including the following:

Underspecification: to simplify design or verification of systems. Certain details may be left open in the early phases of system development or when verifying system properties, to simplify matters or because they may not be known. An example could be the particular scheduler used to resolve concurrency.

Unpredictability: to provide security. For example, keys or nonces are chosen in a way that should make them unguessable.

While the first kind of non-determinism is merely a tool during the development or verification, the second is a vital part of the functionality of a system. When one identifies the two kinds of non-determinism one faces the refinement problem mentioned above.

We separate the two kinds of non-determinism in the following way. The non-determinism of functional importance for the system is *only* modeled by specific mechanisms. For example, key generation is modeled by having separate sets of private keys for the different actors. Thus the security of a system does *not* rely on non-deterministic choice in the formal model.

It is quite common with the formal modeling of security to provide special primitives for operations such as key generation, encryption, etc. However, security properties for non-deterministic specifications often also use the non-deterministic choice operators to provide unpredictability. Our security property rules this out.

We note that our notion of white-box refinement of UMSs is preserved by adding the adversary model, as defined above. To formulate this, we first define a security-aware version of black-box refinement of UMSs.

Definition 7.24. *The UMS $\mathcal{B}$ is a (delayed) $(\mathbf{i}, \mathbf{o})$-black-box refinement in presence of adversaries of type A of the UMS $\mathcal{A}$ if for every adversary $adv' \in$* Advers$_{\mathcal{B}}(A)$ *there exists an adversary $adv \in$* Advers$_{\mathcal{A}}(A)$ *such that the UML Machine* **Exec** $\mathcal{B}_{adv'}$ *is a (delayed) $(\mathbf{i}, \mathbf{o} \cup \{\mathsf{knows}\})$-refinement of the UML Machine* **Exec** $\mathcal{A}_{adv}$*.*

We can then formulate the result.

Fact 7.25. *Suppose we are given UMSs $\mathcal{A}$ and $\mathcal{B}$ such that $\mathcal{B}$ is a refinement of $\mathcal{A}$, and an adversary type A, such that the accessible knowledge for A in $\mathcal{B}$ is no larger than that in $\mathcal{A}$. Then the UMS $\mathcal{B}$ is a black-box refinement in presence of adversaries of type A of the UMS $\mathcal{A}$.*

7.5.2 Secrecy

One possibility to specify security requirements is to define an idealized UMS where the required security property evidently holds, for example, because all links and components are secure according to the kind of adversary under consideration. Then one proves that the analyzed UMS is behaviorally equivalent to the idealized one, using Definition 7.14. An example for this approach is given in Sect. 5.1.

In the following subsections, we consider ways of specifying important security properties, which do not require one to explicitly construct such an idealized system.

First, we consider a secrecy property following the standard approach of [DY83] that is defined in an intuitive way by incorporating the attacker model, and we give an equivalent internal characterization of the property which allows easier verification. The secrecy property considered here relies on the idea that a system specification preserves the secrecy of a piece of data d if the system never sends out any information from which d could be derived, even in interaction with an adversary.

Definition 7.26. *Given a UMS $\mathcal{A}$, we say that an adversary of type A may eventually find out an expression $E \in \mathbf{Exp}$ from $\mathcal{A}$ given inputs in $\mathcal{E} \subseteq \mathbf{Events}$ if there exists an adversary $adv \in \mathsf{Advers}_\mathcal{A}(A)$, an input sequence $\mathbf{I}$ whose multi-sets only contain elements in $\mathcal{E}$, and a sequence $s \in [\![\mathcal{A}_{adv}]\!]_{\emptyset,\{\mathsf{knows}\}}(\mathbf{I})$ such that one of the knowledge sets in s contains E. Otherwise we say that $\mathcal{A}$ preserves the secrecy of E from adversaries of type A given inputs in $\mathcal{E}$.*

Given a variable v, we say that $\mathcal{A}$ preserves the secrecy of the variable v from adversaries of type A given inputs in $\mathcal{E} \subseteq \mathbf{Events}$ if for every expression E which is a value of the variable v at any point, $\mathcal{A}$ preserves the secrecy of E from adversaries of type A given inputs in $\mathcal{E}$.

We say that $\mathcal{A}$ preserves the secrecy of E from adversaries of type A if $\mathcal{A}$ preserves the secrecy of E from adversaries of type A given inputs in **Events**.

Note that, alternatively, one could formulate this definition using the concept of a "most general adversary" defined in Sect. 3.3.4 which non-deterministically behaves like any possible adversary of the given type.

Examples

- The UML Machine that sends the expression $\{m\}_K :: K \in \mathbf{Exp}$ over an Internet link does not preserve the secrecy of m or K against attackers eavesdropping on the Internet, but the UML Machine that sends $\{m\}_K$ and then terminates does, assuming that it preserves the secrecy of K against attackers eavesdropping on the Internet.

- The UML Machine $\mathcal{A}$ that receives a key K encrypted with its public key $K_{\mathcal{A}}$ over a communication link and sends back $\{m\}_K$ over the link does not preserve the secrecy of m against attackers eavesdropping on and inserting messages on the link, because such an adversary can insert $\{K_0\}_{K_{\mathcal{A}}}$ for a key K_0 known to him into the communication to $\mathcal{A}$ and then decrypt the message $\{m\}_{K_0}$ received back. $\mathcal{A}$ does preserve the secrecy of m against attackers that cannot insert messages on the link.

More substantial examples can be found in Chap. 5. We give an intrinsic characterization of preservation of secrecy in terms of knowledge sets, which makes it easier to verify.

Theorem 7.27 (Secrecy Characterization). *A UMS $\mathcal{A}$ preserves the secrecy of E against adversaries of type A if and only if $E \notin \mathcal{K}_A(\mathcal{A})$.*

There is a similar characterization of preservation of secrecy given inputs in $\mathcal{E}$, which, however, we will not need in the following.

This theorem is especially useful if one can give an upper bound for $\mathcal{K}_A(\mathcal{A})$, which is often possible when the security-relevant part of the specification of $\mathcal{A}$ is given as a sequence of commands of the form *await event e – check condition g – output event e'*. For example, this is the case when using UML sequence or statechart diagrams together with their UML Machine semantics defined in Chap. 8.

We now consider in how far this secrecy property is preserved by refinement in our setting. First, we consider white-box refinement of UMSs.

Theorem 7.28 (Secrecy Preservation by White-Box Refinement). *If the UMS $\mathcal{A}$ preserves the secrecy of E from adversaries of type A and the UMS $\mathcal{B}$ (delayed) refines $\mathcal{A}$, such that the accessible knowledge for A in $\mathcal{B}$ is no larger than that in $\mathcal{A}$, then $\mathcal{B}$ preserves the secrecy of E from adversaries of type A given inputs in $\mathcal{E}$.*

This result also carries over to black-box refinement of UMSs.

Theorem 7.29 (Secrecy Preservation by Black-Box Refinement). *If the UMS $\mathcal{A}$ preserves the secrecy of E from adversaries of type A and the UMS $\mathcal{B}$ is a black-box refinement in presence of adversaries of type A of the UMS $\mathcal{A}$ then $\mathcal{B}$ preserves the secrecy of E from adversaries of type A.*

Intuitively, these results hold because the definition of preservation of secrecy refers to the *existence* of an output sequence revealing E, and the possibility of this existence is decreased by refinement.

7.5.3 Integrity

We now formalize that definition that a system preserves the integrity of a variable if there is no adversary such that at some point during the execution of the system in presence of the adversary, the variable has a value different from the ones it should have.

Definition 7.30. *Suppose we are given a variable v in a UMS $\mathcal{A}$ and a set $E \subseteq$ **Exp** of acceptable expressions. We say that an adversary of type A may eventually violate integrity of the variable v in $\mathcal{A}$ with respect to E, given inputs in $\mathcal{E} \subseteq$ **Events**, if there exists $adv \in$ Advers$_A(A)$ and an input sequence $\mathbf{i}$ whose multi-sets only contain elements in $\mathcal{E}$, such that at some point of the execution of $\mathcal{A}_{adv}$ on the inputs $\mathbf{i}$, v takes on a value not contained in E. Otherwise we say that $\mathcal{A}$ preserve the integrity of v with respect to E from adversaries of type A given inputs in $\mathcal{E}$. If $E = $ **Exp** $\setminus \mathcal{K}^0$, we simply say that $\mathcal{A}$ preserves the integrity of v from adversaries of type A.*

The idea of this definition is that $\mathcal{A}$ preserves the integrity of v if no adversary can make v take on a value different from the ones it is supposed to have, in interaction with $\mathcal{A}$. Intuitively, it is the "opposite" of secrecy, in the sense that secrecy prevents the flow of information from protected sources to untrusted recipients, while integrity prevents the flow of information in the other direction. Again, it is a relatively simple definition, which may, however, not prevent implicit flows of information. Examples for this security property are given in Chap. 5.

For simplified verification, we give a sufficient condition for preservation of integrity in terms of influence sets.

Theorem 7.31 (Integrity Characterization). *Each UMS $\mathcal{A}$ preserves the integrity of a variable v with respect to a set $E \subseteq$ **Exp** of acceptable expressions against adversaries of type A if $\mathcal{I}_A(\mathcal{A}, v) \subseteq E$.*

To derive a preservation result for integrity, we need to refine with respect to the variable that is supposed to be protected.

Theorem 7.32 (Integrity Preservation). *Suppose we are given UMSs $\mathcal{A}$ and $\mathcal{B}$. Suppose that $\mathcal{A}$ preserves the integrity of v with respect to a set $E \subseteq$ **Exp** of acceptable expressions from adversaries of type A given inputs in $\mathcal{E}$ and that the UMS $\mathcal{B}$ is a $(\emptyset, \{v\})$-black-box refinement in presence of adversaries of type A of the UMS $\mathcal{A}$. Then $\mathcal{B}$ preserves the integrity of v with respect to E from adversaries of type A given inputs in $\mathcal{E}$.*

A similar result can be achieved for white-box refinement. Intuitively, these results hold because the definition of preservation of integrity refers to the *existence* of an execution corrupting v, and the possibility of this existence is decreased by refinement.

7.5.4 Authenticity

We now formalize our notion of *message authenticity*, which is supposed to secure the information on the message origin.

Definition 7.33. *Suppose we are given variables v and o in a UMS $\mathcal{A}$, where o is supposed to store the origin of the message stored in v. We say that $\mathcal{A}$ provides (message) authenticity of v with respect to its origin o from adversaries of type A given inputs in $\mathcal{E} \subseteq$ Events if for all $adv \in \mathsf{Advers}_A(A)$ and each input sequence $\mathbf{i}$ whose multi-sets only contain elements in $\mathcal{E}$, at any point of the execution of $\mathcal{A}_{adv}$ on the inputs $\mathbf{i}$, v takes on a value which appeared first within the execution in outQu_o, of all output queues and link queues in $\mathcal{A}$.*

The idea of this definition is that $\mathcal{A}$ provides authenticity of v with respect to its origin o if no adversary can make v take on a value not originating from o, in interaction with $\mathcal{A}$. Examples can be found in Chap. 5.

We can derive a preservation result for authenticity similar to that for integrity.

Theorem 7.34 (Authenticity Preservation). *Suppose we are given UMSs $\mathcal{A}$ and $\mathcal{B}$. Suppose that $\mathcal{A}$ provides authenticity of v with respect to its origin o from adversaries of type A given inputs in $\mathcal{E}$ and that the UMS $\mathcal{B}$ is a $(\emptyset, \{v, o\})$-white-box refinement of the UMS $\mathcal{A}$, such that the accessible knowledge for A in $\mathcal{B}$ is no larger than that in $\mathcal{A}$. Then $\mathcal{B}$ provides authenticity of v with respect to its origin o from adversaries of type A given inputs in $\mathcal{E}$.*

A similar result holds for black-box refinement. We recall that message authenticity is closely related to data integrity, as discussed in Sect. 3.3.5.

7.5.5 Freshness

We define freshness of data for UMSs.

Definition 7.35. *An atomic value $d \in$ Data $\cup$ Keys in a UMS $\mathcal{A}$ is fresh within a component $\mathcal{D}$ contained in $\mathcal{A}$ if the value d appears in the specification $\mathcal{A}$ only within the specification of $\mathcal{D}$. In this case, we also say that the scope of d is contained in $\mathcal{D}$.*

See Chap. 5 for examples of this security requirement. To support this definition, we note that our formal model captures the fact that security-critical data such as keys and nonces are usually assumed to be independent; that is, that no equations should hold between them from which an adversary could derive information, such as $K = K' + 1$ for two different keys $K, K' \in$ **Keys**. This follows from the fact that the algebra of expressions is the quotient of a free algebra under the equations given in Sect. 3.3.3, in particular, only equations that follow from these equations hold in **Exp**. We will make this more precise.

Definition 7.36. *An expression $E \in$ **Exp** is independent of a set of expressions $\mathcal{E} \subseteq$ **Exp** if E is not an element of the subalgebra of **Exp** generated by $\mathcal{E}$.*

We establish some simple facts about this definition with regard to *atomic* expressions, which we call those in **Data** $\cup$ **Var** $\cup$ **Keys**. For this, we first need an additional definition regarding such expressions.

Definition 7.37. *An expression $E \in$ **Data** $\cup$ **Var** $\cup$ **Keys** is a subexpression of an expression $E' \in$ **Exp** if for each term t' over the operations in **Exp** that evaluates to E' when interpreted in **Exp**, the unique term $t \in$ **Data** $\cup$ **Var** $\cup$ **Keys** which evaluates to E in **Exp** is a subterm of t'.*

For example, $E \in$ **Data** is a subexpression of $\{E\}_K$: Any term t' which evaluates to $\{E\}_K$ has E as a subterm, because none of the equations which define **Exp** in Sect. 3.3.3 would eliminate E from $\{E\}_K$. $E \in$ **Data** is not a subexpression of **head**$(E' :: E)$ for $E' \in$ **Data** with $E' \neq E$, since **head**$(E' :: E) = E'$ by definition in **Exp**, and E is not a subterm of E' since both are atomic and $E' \neq E$.

Fact 7.38. *For any expression $E \in$ **Data** $\cup$ **Var** $\cup$ **Keys** and any set of expressions $\mathcal{E}$, E is independent of $\mathcal{E}$ if there exists no expression $E' \in \mathcal{E}$ such that E is a subexpression of E'.*

Note that the converse does not hold: For example, $E \in$ **Data** is independent of and also a subexpression of $\{E\}_K$.

Fact 7.39. *For any expression $E \in$ **Data** $\cup$ **Var** $\cup$ **Keys** and any set of expressions $\mathcal{E} \subseteq$ **Data** $\cup$ **Var** $\cup$ **Keys**, E is independent of $\mathcal{E}$ if and only if $E \notin \mathcal{E}$.*

Thus it is sufficient to require of fresh values that they do not appear in the UMS specification $\mathcal{A}$ outside their scope $\mathcal{D}$, as in Definition 7.35, because by Fact 7.39, they are then independent of all atomic values outside of $\mathcal{D}$ in $\mathcal{A}$.

Note also that a value d that is fresh within a component $\mathcal{D}$ in the UMS $\mathcal{A}$ appears as a subexpression in the trace of messages exchanged within $\mathcal{A}$ only *after* it has been sent out by $\mathcal{D}$ as a message argument:

Fact 7.40. *Suppose we are given an atomic value $d \in$ **Data** $\cup$ **Keys** in a UMS $\mathcal{A}$ which is fresh within a component $\mathcal{D}$ contained in $\mathcal{A}$, an adversary type A which does not have access to $\mathcal{D}$ and does not have d in its set $\mathcal{K}_A^p$ of previous knowledge, and an adversary adv of type A. Then during any run $\mathbf{e} \in \mathbf{Run} \mathcal{A}_{adv}$, if at any state S in $\mathbf{e}$ an output or link queue outside $\mathcal{D}$ contains d as a subexpressions, then there exists a state S' preceding S in $\mathbf{e}$ where outQu$_\mathcal{D}$ contains d as a subexpressions.*

Here the restriction on the adversary is necessary: if the adversary had access to the component containing the fresh value, or would know the fresh value from the start, he could inject it into a link queue outside this component before it is sent out by the component.

7.5.6 Secure Information Flow

We explain an alternative way of specifying secrecy- and integrity-like requirements, which gives protection also against partial flow of information, but can
be more difficult to deal with, especially when dealing with encryption.

Given a set of message names $H \subseteq \mathbf{MsgNm}$ and a sequence $\mathbf{m}$ of event
multi-sets, we write:

- $\mathbf{m}^H$ for the sequence of event multi-sets derived from those in $\mathbf{m}$ by deleting all events the message names of which are *not* in H, and
- $\mathbf{m}_H$ for the sequence of event multi-sets derived from those in $\mathbf{m}$ by deleting all events the message names of which *are* in H.

Definition 7.41. *Given a UML Machine A and a set of high message names*
$H \subseteq \mathbf{MsgNm}$, we say that:

- *A prevents down-flow with respect to H if for any two sequences $\mathbf{i}, \mathbf{j}$ of*
  event multi-sets and any two output sequences $\mathbf{o} \in [\![A]\!](\mathbf{i})$ and $\mathbf{p} \in [\![A]\!](\mathbf{j})$,
  $\mathbf{i}_H = \mathbf{j}_H$ implies $\mathbf{o}_H = \mathbf{p}_H$, and
- *A prevents up-flow with respect to H if for any two sequences $\mathbf{i}, \mathbf{j}$ of event*
  multi-sets and any two output sequences $\mathbf{o} \in [\![A]\!](\mathbf{i})$ and $\mathbf{p} \in [\![A]\!](\mathbf{j})$, $\mathbf{i}^H =
  $\mathbf{j}^H$ implies $\mathbf{o}^H = \mathbf{p}^H$.

Intuitively, to prevent down-flow means that outputting a *non-high* (or
low) message does not depend on *high* inputs. This can be seen as a secrecy requirement for messages marked as high. Conversely, to prevent up-flow means
that outputting a *high* value does not depend on *low* inputs. This can be seen
as an integrity requirement for messages marked as high. Examples for the
use of this security requirement can be found in Sect. 4.1.2.

This notion of *secure information flow* is a generalization of the original notion of non-interference for deterministic systems in [GM82] to non-
deterministic systems. Many such generalizations have been proposed in the
literature; the current one is motivated by the fact that it should be preserved
under refinement. Essentially, a UML Machine prevents down-flow if and only
if each refinement to a deterministic UML Machine satisfies non-interference.
Recall that we use non-determinism for underspecification, rather than for a
functional kind of non-determinism that should still exist on the implementation level. Thus a non-deterministic specification of a system that may output
any value to the untrusted environment is not seen to prevent down-flow,
because a legal implementation of it may output *low* messages that depend
on *high* inputs. If instead one wanted to model "functional" (or *possibilistic*)
non-determinism, the current definition might turn out to be rather strong.

We show that this formulation of secure information flow is also preserved
under refinement. This, again, is possible since non-determinism is supposed
to represent underspecification, while security-providing non-determinism is
modeled through the generation of random values (such as keys). Note that
computers currently in use are in fact deterministic, apart from special components that produce such random values.

Theorem 7.42 (Secure Information Flow Preservation). *Suppose that the UML Machine A prevents down-flow (resp. up-flow) with respect to the set $H \subseteq \mathbf{MsgNm}$ and that the UML Machine B refines A. Then B prevents down-flow (resp. up-flow) with respect to H.*

Note that secure information flow is not preserved under *delayed* refinement, since an introduced time delay may be used to leak information.

7.6 Notes

UML Machines have been introduced, under a different name, in [Jür02a, Jür02d]. The idea of defining UML Machines with input and output queues is similar to that of Algebraic State Machines [BW00, Jür03a] which are in turn based on a mathematical foundation of reactive systems and software engineering methods proposed in [Bro00, Bro01, BS01]. In particular, the notions of refinement and rely-guarantee specifications defined here are inspired by those in [Bro97, Bro98]. More on refinement of state machines can be found in [PR94, Rum96].

A notion of "interacting ASMs" similar to UML Machines has been introduced in [MIB98, Sch98], but without the possibility to construct ASM specifications in the same way as using UML Machine Systems.

Security notions were introduced into our formal framework in [Jür03a]. The preservation of secrecy by refinement was proved, in a similar formal model, in [Jür01g]. Preservation of secrecy and secure information flow by composition was proved in [Jür00, Jür01b]. This had to be omitted here.

There has been extensive related research in using formal models to verify secure systems. An overview of some approaches is given in Chap. 9. Here we just mention some results related to the ones presented in this chapter. [Sch96] gives a confidentiality property preserved under refinement. However, cryptographic primitives are not considered and it is pointed out that their treatment may be less straightforward. [HPS01] gives a necessary and sufficient condition for a notion of confidentiality to be preserved under refinement in a probabilistic extension of CSP. [SHP02] considers compositionality. For a discussion on the refinement of secure information flow properties, see [GCS91, Mea92, McL94, McL96]. [RWW94] avoids the "refinement problem" by giving a security property that requires systems to appear deterministic to the untrusted environment. Special refinement operators that preserve information flow security are considered for example in [Man01]. Compositionality is considered in [Man02].

The problem of how far formal models of cryptography are faithful to computational models is considered in [AJ01]. Similar investigations regarding failure probabilities in the setting of safety-critical systems are presented in [Jür01a].

7.7 Discussion

We introduced formal models, *UML Machines* and *UML Machine Systems*, to model the interaction between a system and its environment and to construct specifications in a modular way. In Chap. 8, they will be used to define a formal semantics for a simplified fragment of UML. This semantics in turn is the basis for the analysis routines in the UMLsec tool support presented in Chap. 6, which allows us to reach general insights about the properties checked by the tool, such as preservation under refinement. Also, we defined notions of refinement and rely-guarantee specifications for UML Machines, allowing stepwise and modular development, as demonstrated in Chap. 5. Rely-guarantee specifications were showed to be preserved under refinement.

We explained how we use UML Machines to specify security-critical systems, exploiting the fact that UML Machine Systems are designed to allow the treatment of external influences on the system beyond the planned interaction. This allows a rather natural modeling of potential adversary behavior that specifies which parts of the system are assumed to be accessible to an adversary in which way. The adversary behavior is again modeled by a class of UML Machines with the specified capabilities. This gives us an evaluation of the system's security in a natural way, by considering the joint execution of the system with any UML Machine in this class. Security properties can thus be formalized intuitively. To support verification, we gave alternative ways of defining these security properties that do not refer to particular adversaries and proved them to be equivalent to the earlier formulations.

We addressed a formerly open problem in the formal development of security-critical systems, namely the so-called *refinement problem*: we showed security properties to be preserved under refinement in our formal framework. Thus one can use stepwise development of security-critical systems without having to redo security proofs at each refinement step. Also, this result may increase the confidence that an implementation conforming to a verified specification, which is necessarily a refinement of it, is also secure. The security properties and the refinement relation are defined in a standard way, avoiding definitions specially tailored to avoid the refinement problem.

8

Formal Systems Development with UML

We use UML Machines and UML Machine Systems to give a formal semantics for a simplified part of UML to enable advanced tool support for UMLsec. It allows one to use subsystems in a specific way to group together several kinds of diagrams, giving a formal semantics of a simplified version of UML subsystems and their interactions. Objects, or system components, can communicate by exchanging messages with parameters, which can be used in the subsequent execution. The behavior of actions and activities can be modeled explicitly. Since our semantics builds on UML Machine Systems, it allows us to make use of the treatment of security-critical systems in Chap. 7 to evaluate UML specifications for security aspects. We give consistency conditions for different diagrams in a UML specification. We define notions of refinement and behavioral equivalence, and investigate structural properties, such as substitutivity. Finally we consider rely-guarantee properties for UML specifications and their structural properties.

The proofs for the statements in this chapter are given in Appendix C.

8.1 Formal Semantics for a Fragment of UML

The semantics of UML is given only in prose form [UML03], leaving room for ambiguities. This is a problem especially when providing tool support or trying to establish behavioral properties of UML specifications. To *reason* about system behavior in a precise way, however, we need a precise semantics for the behavioral model elements of UML.

There has been a considerable amount of work to generally provide a formal semantics for UML, see Sect. 8.3 for a partial overview. To use UML for critical systems development, we need a semantics that, more specifically, supports different views of a system on the syntax level, including its logical structure, its physical environment including attack scenarios, and its behavior. At the same time, the semantics should be sufficiently simple to allow its use for mechanical reasoning.

We provide a formal semantics for a simplified part of UML that allows one to use a restricted version of UML subsystems to group together several diagrams. It is formulated using UML Machines. The statecharts semantics builds on part of the statechart semantics from [BCR00]. The formal semantics for subsystems incorporates the formal semantics of the diagrams contained in a subsystem. Actions and internal activities are modeled explicitly, rather than treating them as atomic given events. They are executed explicitly, for example, by assigning new values to attributes. In particular, objects, or system components, can communicate by exchanging messages with parameters, which can be used in the subsequent execution. We show how to *compose* our subsystems by including them in other subsystems. To our knowledge, this is the first published formal semantics of UML subsystems, the contained diagrams, and their interactions. Our aim is to provide a sound foundation for the tool support presented in Chap. 6.

Note that we only consider a simplified fragment of the UML syntax. In particular, the notion of subsystem considered here is restricted, for example, in the kinds and numbers of diagrams that may be contained. Also, following [KW01, p. 15], we do not model the creation and deletion of objects explicitly. A sufficient number of required objects are assumed to exist at the start of the execution. The activation of objects is controlled by the activity diagram in the subsystem. An object that reaches a final state within its top state is terminated, and may be reactivated. Note that is has been argued that the explicit modeling of the creation and destruction of objects could lead to unbounded behaviors that would be impossible to verify automatically for example with a model-checker [LP99]. Furthermore, in our approach, we identify the objects in the runtime system with UML objects. We thus aim to provide an executable semantics for UML models to allow simulation. We feel that, although non-executable specifications also have their value, simulatability of a model can be of value for use in industrial practice, because it may assist understanding. See [Rum02] for a supporting discussion. Also, our main goal for providing a formal semantics is the use for security analysis of UML models, and some of the security properties considered later refer to an execution trace of the model. However, code generation of the models is not our goal here and we do not aim to propose a visual programming language.

One should also note that the semantics does not attempt to support simultaneous modeling of several overlapping aspects of the system behavior in different parts of the UML model. That is, in our approach, at any one time the behavior of a given thread of an object is represented by only one diagram. For example, our semantics enforces that different statecharts contained in a UML specification are always mapped to disjoint state sets of distinct sub-state machines of the overall semantics. This way our approach sidesteps questions that would arise from having different parts of a UML specification model the same part of the system behavior, which are interesting but beyond the scope of the current treatment.

However, the semantics provides a possibility to check whether such overlapping aspects are consistent: by creating two separate models which are identical apart from the non-overlapping parts and then establishing whether they are behaviorally equivalent using the corresponding definition in Sect. 8.2.1.

There are further simplifications whose explanation requires more detailed knowledge of the diagrams and which therefore will be explained in detail in the respective sections. The simplifications were done because of space restrictions and to increase readability. The semantics can be extended with other parts of the notation that have to be omitted here. Note that, since UML is a rather large and complex notation, a full formalization of *all* of the notation may be neither desirable not feasible. Since our main motivation is to provide sophisticated tool support using automated theorem provers and model-checkers to automatically analyze the specifications for security requirements, we also have to take into account the efficiency of the analysis, which is greatly improved when having a reasonably simple notation. Thus, we concentrate on those features of the UML notation which are really needed for our purposes. Developers who may already know UML could be taught relatively easily to use only a fragment of UML, rather than having to be taught a completely different notation. Our approach is in accordance with the view seeing UML as a "family of languages" [Coo00], each for a specific purpose, such as tool supported validation, but sharing a common core. To demonstrate that our choice of a subset of UML is reasonable for our present needs and our semantics of sufficient interest, we presented several case studies in Chap. 5 which only make use of those parts of UML whose semantics is defined here. Some of these originate from an industrial context and are therefore realistic in size and complexity. Thus they may demonstrate that the fragment of UML used in our work seems to be sufficient for our needs.

Since our semantics uses UML Machines and UML Machine Systems defined in Chap. 7, it allows us to make use of the treatment of security-critical systems there. In particular, UML specifications can be evaluated using the attacker model from Sect. 7.5, which incorporates the possible attacker behaviors, to find vulnerabilities. Thus our semantics defines a solid foundation for the automatic analysis presented in Chap. 6 of the constraints for the UMLsec stereotypes defined in Chap. 4. For the trivial kind of adversary who is not able to access any part of the system, our approach gives us the usual simplified UML semantics without security considerations.

Diagrams

Our formal semantics includes simplified versions of the following kinds of diagrams: static structure diagrams (which are class or object diagrams that may also contain subsystems), statechart diagrams, sequence diagrams, activity diagrams, deployment diagrams, and subsystems.

The semantics for statecharts presented here is based on part of [BCR00], which, however, had to be extended to incorporate features such as explicit modeling of the passing of messages with their arguments between different objects or components, and use of the arguments in the subsequent execution.

Consistency

We give some conditions for *consistency* between different kinds of diagram in a UML specification, such as static versus behavioral diagrams.

Refinement

In UML, *refinement* denotes a certain kind of dependency relation between model elements [UML03, p. 2-18]. There is no constraint on the semantic relationship between the model elements, also not in the heuristics for state machine refinement on [UML03, p. 2-172]. When trying to establish system properties, behavioral conformance of refinement can help to save effort: Properties may be easier to establish at a more abstract level, and preservation by refinement means that this is in fact sufficient.

We aim for a trade-off between flexibility of a refinement relation and the gain from establishing that a specification refines another by considering two kinds of refinement for UML specifications. The first of these, *property refinement*, provides full behavioral conformance, and thus preserves all safety properties. The second, *interface refinement*, allows some degree of control over the extent to which the structure and behavior of the system is preserved. Both were inspired by notions of refinement in [BS01]. For both kinds of refinement, we define a relaxation, called *delayed refinement*, that allows time delays to be introduced during refinement.

Equivalence

We define a notion of behavioral equivalence between UML specifications. This can be used for example to verify the consistency of two of our kinds of subsystem specifications that are supposed to describe the same behavior, one of which uses statecharts to specify object behavior, and the other sequence diagrams.

Rely-Guarantee Specifications

Finally, we consider rely-guarantee specifications, following the definitions in Sect. 7.4, in the setting of UML and prove some results regarding them.

8.1.1 General Concepts

Note that there are some aspects that are omitted in the following simply because they are not used in the sequel, such as associations in class diagrams, and which one should be able to add in easily. Generally, for our present needs it is sufficient to remain on the instance level, as for other non-functional requirements [Wat02, sl. 4]. In fact, emphasizing the type rather than the instance level can lead to security problems, as pointed out in [LGS01] for CORBASec.

For our intended use in security analysis, we only need the abstract syntax of the static modeling elements given below, while for the behavioral diagrams, we need an execution semantics. The abstract syntax of the structural diagrams is needed to define the formal semantics of subsystems containing them, because the execution semantics depends on it.

The UML specification document [UML03] gives the abstract syntax of the UML notation using a fragment of the UML notation. The logical cycle arising from this could be avoided by giving a separate definition of the abstract syntax of that fragment. For simplicity, we define the abstract syntax of the fragment of UML we use entirely in basic set-theoretical terms.

In our approach, we view an object or component as an entity characterized by a unique name. It may have associated information such as its attributes and their values which may change during its execution, for example specified as a statechart. Thus we identify the objects or components in the runtime system with UML objects or components. Thereby, we aim to provide an executable semantics for a simplified kind of UML models. Note that in more general use of UML, the relation between UML objects and system objects may not be functional in either direction.

Objects, or system components, can communicate by exchanging messages. These consist of the message name and possibly arguments to the message, which are assumed to be elements of a set **Exp**. Message names may be prefixed with object or subsystem instance names, analogous to the names of UML Machines or UMLSs as defined in Sect. 7.1.

Messages can be synchronous or asynchronous. The sender of a synchronous message passes the thread of control to the receiver and receives it back together with the return message. When sending asynchronous messages, the thread of control is split in two, one each for the sender and the receiver, unless they already had separate threads of control. Exchanging a synchronous (resp. asynchronous) message is called "calling an operation" (resp. "sending a signal"). Accordingly, in Sect. 7.2 we partitioned the set of message names **MsgNm** into sets of operation names **Op**, signal names **Sig**, and return message names **Ret**.

Note that the UML specification in some parts makes a distinction between the term "Stimulus" and the term "Message", which is "a specification of a Stimulus" [UML03, 3.63.1]. However, in other places distinction is again removed or blurred:

- Firstly, in the case of the usage of "message name": According to [UML03, 3.72.2.5], a message name is "the name of the Operation to be applied to the receiver, or the Signal that is sent to the receiver".
- Secondly, the glossary defines:

- receive (a message): The handling of a stimulus passed from a sender instance.
- send (a message): The passing of a stimulus from a sender instance to a receiver instance.

To avoid confusion, we do not use the term "Stimulus" at all, but use the term "message" (or "message instance" for emphasis) to denote the actual message that is exchanged (as in Sect. 7.2), and "message specification" for the specification of a message.

An event is "the specification of a significant occurrence that has a location in time and space" [UML03, p. Glos.-7]. Here we consider the events arising from the reception of an operation call or a signal. Accordingly, in Sect. 7.1 we defined the set **Events** to consist of messages $msg^{snd}(exp_1, \ldots, exp_n)$ for $msg \in$ **MsgNm**, $snd = n_1 :: \ldots :: n_k$ with $n_1, \ldots, n_k \in$ **UMNames**, and $exp_i \in$ **Exp**. In our model, every object or subsystem instance O has associated multi-sets inQu_O and outQu_O (event queues). As explained in detail in Sect. 7.2, our formal semantics using UMLSs models sending a message $msg = op(exp_1, \ldots, exp_n) \in$ **Events** from an object or subsystem instance S to an object or subsystem instance R as follows:

(1) S places the message instance $R.msg$ into its multi-set outQu_S.
(2) The "virtual machine" **Exec** A for a UMS A defined in Sect. 7.2 distributes the message instances from output queues to the intended input queues, while removing the message head. In particular, $R.msg$ is removed from outQu_S and msg added to inQu_R.
(3) R removes msg from its input queue and processes its content.

In the case of operation calls, we also need to keep track of the sender to allow sending return signals. As defined in Sect. 7.2, this is done by associating the sender name as a superscript of the name of a message instance.

This way of modeling communication allows for a relatively flexible treatment. For example, we can modify the behavior of the scheduler to take account of knowledge of the underlying communication layer, such as regarding security or performance issues.

Note that messages with the same name and possibly the same arguments can appear several times at different places in a UML specification. As mentioned above, our semantics does not attempt to support overlapping model parts. Whenever two such messages are sent during a given model execution, they are interpreted as two different message instances created by distinct system events, namely the corresponding method called by the calling objects. They are later also consumed by distinct system events: the events in the UML sense at the called objects. Thus, whenever a message instance is sent in a UML model, our semantics models this by adding a new element to the outQu multi-set, as explained above. This directly implies that, conversely, for any element of an input or output queue, there is a unique occurrence of this message instance in the UML model from which it originates. Thus, in our approach, at each point of a given execution of a system, the same message instance in the running system is only represented once in the UML diagrams, and hence only once in our semantics. More concretely, each time an expression call(msg) or send(msg) appears as an action in a statechart diagram, or a message msg appears at a connection in a sequence diagram that is "executed", it is interpreted as a different message instance, which may happen to have the same name and the same arguments as a previous message instance. Thus, this message instance is newly added to the output queue using the macro tooutQu(), as we will define in Sects. 8.1.3 and 8.1.4. Since these are the only ways message instances are introduced during the execution of a model, this ensures that a message instance appears only once in the semantics, by definition.[1] This observation is presented in more detail in Fact 8.1.

The mechanism for handing on the message instances explained above is performed locally at the subsystems and objects. Where it will be sent depends on its place and on the relative addressing of the recipient. For example, assume we have subsystem instances S (resp. S') each with objects S and R. Then the object $S.S$ (resp. $S'.S$) may each be specified to send the message instance $R.msg$. For example, this could be done in two different statecharts contained in S (resp. S'). Then the message instance msg sent by $S.S$ will be delivered to $S.R$, while the message instance msg sent by $S'.S$ will be delivered to $S'.R$.

We model a synchronous operation call by sending two asynchronous signals – the message and its return value. By imposing restrictions on statecharts and sequence diagrams in the respective sections, we can model the passing of control implicitly. The semantics does keep track of the sender of a synchronous operation, so that the return message can be delivered.

Note that an object may receive several synchronous messages calling the same operation op before sending back a corresponding return value. To enable sending back the return value to the sender, the statechart and sequence diagram semantics include last-in–first-out buffers containing the names of the senders of the message calls, assuming that the calls and their returns are "well-bracketed" in a sense detailed below. On the level of the semantics using UMSs, the sender names are attached to the messages sent, as defined in Sect. 7.2. When return messages are sent out, the recipients of these messages are taken from that buffer.

The situation when an object's statechart invokes another object's operation, with the called object calling others and so on until this leads back to the same thread of the first object instance, is called an *invocation cycle*. Such as cycle is not permitted, an attempt to execute it will result in deadlock, similar to the treatment in [HG97]. This restriction seems to be inherent

---

[1] This might be compared to abstraction in the lambda-calculus, where one may have two appearances of the same variable on the syntax level, which, however, evaluate to different entities on the semantics level.

in the current UML run-to-completion semantics, as pointed out in [TS02]. Instead, one may call another thread of the first object, or another instance of the relevant class, with the needed data. Details and discussions are given in Sects. 8.1.3 and 8.1.4.

Note also that there is only one input buffer and one output buffer for a given object or component. This buffer may be accessed in various ways – for example, concurrent substates of a statechart diagram read from the same input buffer and write to the same output buffer. That this happens consistently is ensured by the semantics. For example, the execution of the internal activities of concurrent substates is defined interleavingly in Fig. 8.2.

The UML semantics includes some semantic variation points to allow adjusting the semantics to a given application domain. For example, the order of dequeuing events at an object or component is not defined. Similarly, in the case of statechart diagrams, the order in which enabled transitions are executed is left open, except that transitions with innermost source states have highest priority (see Sect. 8.1.3 for an explanation of these concepts). In both cases, we use the non-deterministic choice operator of UML Machines to determine the order. The intention here is to not prejudice any view over what the UML specification document prescribes. By using the non-deterministic choice operator, it is made sure that in our use of the formal semantics for formulating our concepts regarding security, we do not make use of any additional properties in our semantics that are not specified in the UML specification document regarding this issue, such as a partial specification of order. Otherwise, this might lead to problems when using our ideas with a different semantics. When implementing this semantics in the form of a tool, either this non-determinism could be preserved by giving a probabilistic interpretation, in order to keep designers using the tool from making use of any specified order. Alternatively, one could refine the non-deterministic choice operator by an operator determining any kind of choice based on the situation at hand. Thus, by using the non-deterministic choice to determine the order, we are covering all possibilities of choosing an order, so that the results based on our definitions will automatically cover all such more detailed elaborations.

Note also that we follow the UML specification in that we do not make any fairness assumptions on the input queue of an object. Thus dispatching an event can be delayed indefinitely provided the event queue contains more than one event at each point during the execution. This could be changed easily, for example, by taking the event queue to be a list.

Objects may have *attributes*, which are variables that are local to the object and whose names are given in the set **Attribute** $\subseteq$ **Var** $\cup$ **Keys** $\cup$ **Data**. Here the names in **Keys** $\cup$ **Data** denote constant attributes with the same value. We will not consider situations where changing attributes may lead to unexpected side-effects, such as changes to object references. We assume that attribute names are only used for attributes and that the attributes of an object can only be changed by the object itself. They can only indirectly be changed by other objects, namely through sending messages. This is important not only for a clean software engineering, but also from the point of view of security, as explained in Sect. 3.1.

Each element in **Var** has an associated UML Machine variable with the same name which represents it on the semantics level, by storing assigned values. Initially, all variables are set to the value *undef*.

An *action* is "the specification of an executable statement that forms an abstraction of a computational procedure. An action typically results in a change in the state of the system" [UML03, p. Glos.-2]. We consider the actions *sending a message* to an object or component and *modifying the value of an attribute*. Thus actions and events are related in that the execution of an action at one object may or may not cause the occurrence of an event at another object. We write **Action** for the set of actions which are expressions of the following forms:

Call action: $\mathsf{call}(op(a_1, \ldots, a_n))$ for an n-ary operation $op \in \mathbf{Op}$ and expressions $a_i \in \mathbf{Exp}$, called the *arguments* of op.

Send action: $\mathsf{send}(sig(a_1, \ldots, a_n))$ for an n-ary signal $sig \in \mathbf{Sig}$ and argument $a_i \in \mathbf{Exp}$.

Return action: $\mathsf{send}(\mathsf{return}_{op}(a))$ for an operation $op \in \mathbf{Op}$ with return value $a \in \mathbf{Exp}$.

Assignment: $att := exp$ where $att \in \mathbf{Attribute}$ is an attribute and exp is a term evaluating to an expression in **Exp**.

Void action: *nil*.

Before we define the semantics of these actions in terms a UML Machine, we need an additional binary function $\mathsf{sender}\_()$ in its vocabulary. Given a parameter S, such as the state in a statechart diagram, and a synchronous operation op, the function $\mathsf{sender}_S(op)$ returns the list of previous senders of op which are needed when sending back return messages. The parameter S allows parallel processing of several operations with the same name. We define the following syntactic shortcut for sending back return messages, where A is a UML Machine, $op \in \mathbf{Op}$, and S is a parameter.

$$\mathsf{retMsg}_{A,S}(op) \equiv \mathbf{if}\ \mathsf{sender}(S, op) \neq [\,]\ \mathbf{then}$$
$$\mathsf{tooutQu}_A(\{\!|\, \mathbf{head}(\mathsf{sender}(S, op)).\mathsf{return}_{op}(args) \,|\!\}\,);$$
$$\mathsf{sender}(S, op) := \mathbf{tail}(\mathsf{sender}(S, op))$$

Then for any action a executed at an object or component O and for a parameter S, we define the expression $\mathbf{ActionRule}_S(a)$, where $op \in \mathbf{Op}$ and $msg \in \mathbf{Sig}$:

Call action: $\mathbf{ActionRule}_S(\mathsf{call}(op(args))) \equiv \mathsf{tooutQu}_O(\{\!|\, op^{[]}(args) \,|\!\}\,)$
Send action: $\mathbf{ActionRule}_S(\mathsf{send}(msg(args))) \equiv \mathsf{tooutQu}_O(\{\!|\, msg^{[]}(args) \,|\!\}\,)$
Return action: $\mathbf{ActionRule}_S(\mathsf{send}(\mathsf{return}_{op}(args))) \equiv \mathsf{retMsg}_{O,S}(op)$
Assignment: $\mathbf{ActionRule}_S(att := exp) \equiv att := exp$
Void action: $\mathbf{ActionRule}_S(nil) \equiv \mathbf{skip}$

Note that in our usage of these rules to define a formal semantics for a simplified fragment of UML statecharts and sequence diagrams below, the assumption is that whenever a rule $\mathbf{ActionRule}_S(a)$ for a *call* or *send* action a is fired during a single execution of a given UML specification, a new message is created and added to the relevant output queue. Note that messages with the same name and the same arguments may already be in use during this execution. This is also realized by the rules defined above. Note also that these rules are the only way that messages are created in the execution of a UML specification. Thus, during a single execution of a particular specification, each message is only created once, and only at one particular location of the specification. Note also that in the definition of a behavior of UMSs in terms of UML Machines, no messages are newly created or duplicated, but only transferred between different input, output, and link queues. The only other place a message is referred to in a UML specification is the event in the statechart or sequence diagram of its recipient where it is consumed. Again, in each given execution of a specification, there can be at most one such event, because when a message is consumed, it is removed from the queues of a specification. This is a restriction in so far as diagrams cannot be used in a way that permits "overlapping" in time. More details about this are given in Fact 8.1. It is a simplification for us in that related questions of consistency within a single specification are avoided.

We fix a set **Activity** of *activity names* such that each activity has an associated UML Machine representing the activities in a UML specification. Each such UML Machine A has a Boolean finished$_A \in out$ as one of its output values, which is set to *true* by A when it is finished. These UML Machines may themselves be given as the formal semantics of UML diagrams defined in the following sections. They may also be defined directly using UML Machine rules, for example, an assignment to an attribute. We assume that there is an activity $Nil \in$ **Activity** representing absence of activity, whose UML Machine has the following rule:

Rule Exec *Nil* :
  finished$_{Nil}$:= *true*

We assume a set **Stereotypes** of *stereotype* names to be given, as well as a function mapping each stereotype to its set of associated tags and its constraint. In a UML diagram, stereotypes are written in double angle brackets « ». For examples see Chap. 4 where we present the stereotypes used for the extension UMLsec of UML for secure systems development.

The set of *Boolean expressions* **BoolExp** is the set of first-order logical formulas with equality statements between elements of **Exp** as atomic formulas. They are used for example as guards in UML diagrams.

In the following sections, we will define the abstract syntax of the various UML diagrams considered here using mathematical notation, and then give a precise semantics of the modeled system behavior for each of the diagram kinds using UML Machines. In Sect. 8.1.7, we explain how to use the different kinds of diagram in the context of a UML system specification, and we put the formal semantics of the various diagram types together to form one formal semantics for a UML system specification.

8.1.2 Class Diagrams

We define the abstract syntax for class and object diagrams.

A message specification $O = (oname, args, otype)$ is given by:

- an operation or signal name $oname \in \mathbf{Op} \cup \mathbf{Sig}$,
- a set $args$ of $arguments$ of the form $A = (argname, argtype)$ where $argname$ is the argument name and $argtype$ its type, and
- the type $otype$ of the return value.

Note that the set of arguments may be empty, and that the return type may be the empty type $\emptyset$ denoting absence of a return value. We assume the "default" types $\mathbf{Exp}$ for arguments and $\emptyset$ for return values, which may be omitted to increase readability.

An $object$ $O = (oname, cname, stereo, aspec, mspec, int)$ is given by:

- an object name $oname$,
- a class name $cname$,
- a set $stereo \subseteq \mathbf{Stereotypes}$ of stereotypes,
- a set of $attribute$ $specifications$ $aspec$ of the form $A = (aname, gtype)$ where $aname \in \mathbf{Attribute}$ is the attribute name and $gtype$ the attribute type,
- a set of message specifications $mspec$, and
- a set of $interfaces$ int of the form $I = (iname, mspec)$ where $iname$ is the interface name and $mspec$ a set of message specifications, such that messages with the same name in different interfaces have the same type.

A $class$ is, formally, an "object" (as defined above) $C = (oname, cname, stereo, aspec, mspec, int)$ where $oname$ is the empty string.

A $dependency$ is a tuple $(dep, indep, int, stereo)$ consisting of:

- the names dep of the dependent and $indep$ of the independent class, signifying that dep depends on $indep$,
- an interface name int (the interface of the class $indep$ through which instances of dep accesses instances of $indep$; if the access is direct this field contains the name of the independent class), and
- a stereotype $stereo \in \{\langle\!\langle\, call\,\rangle\!\rangle, \langle\!\langle\, send\,\rangle\!\rangle\}$.

A class diagram $D = (\mathsf{Classes}(D), \mathsf{Dep}(D))$ is given by a set $\mathsf{Classes}(D)$ of classes and a set $\mathsf{Dep}(D)$ of dependencies.[2] We require that the names of the classes are mutually distinct.

---

[2] Again, we omit modeling elements such as associations, specific notation for $active$ $objects$, other stereotypes, and other modeling elements only because they are not used in the following. They can be added without complication.

An object diagram $O = (\mathsf{Objects}(D), \mathsf{Dep}(D))$ is given by a set $\mathsf{Objects}(D)$ of objects and a set $\mathsf{Dep}(D)$ of dependencies, such that object specifications from the same class coincide up to the object name, and the names of different objects are mutually distinct. Note that on the level of abstract syntax, it is sufficient to specify dependencies between classes rather than objects, although on the level of concrete syntax of object diagrams, dependencies are drawn between objects.

Note that in UML, class (resp. object) diagrams may contain subsystems (resp. subsystem instances) rather than classes (resp. objects). To avoid confusion, we use the term *static structure diagram* as defined in Sect. 8.1.7 in this case, following a suggestion in [UML03, p. 3-34].

8.1.3 Statechart Diagrams

Usually statecharts are used to describe the behavior of classes of objects rather than single objects, for simplicity. Note that this has to be handled with care because often subclassing does not preserve behavior, so that a statechart may not actually give the behavior of an object of the class it is associated with, if the object is in a subclass with different behavior. When assigning a meaning to a UML specification, one eventually has to associate statecharts with objects, because objects, rather than classes, execute the behavior modeled by statecharts. To simplify the treatment, in the following we assume that this step to the instance level has already been made, and associate statecharts with objects already. From the perspective of our usage of UML, this suggests itself also because the difficulties that we will focus on (such as security properties of a system) are typically not closely related to the fact that there are a high number of objects in a given class. Rather, they are related to the behavior of a few objects or components that has to be analyzed rather carefully. This is similar to the situation with other non-functional requirements, which are usually analyzed on the instance level [Wat02]. Therefore, it seems to make sense to explicitly model these instances, and thus to remain on the instance level, for our purposes. We thus let the user of our approach determine how far objects in the same class are supposed to have the same behavior. Note that statecharts may also define other model elements, rather than complete object behavior. For example, we will later use statecharts to define activities.

We extend a part of the formal semantics for statecharts from [BCR00] in the following respects:

- Events can carry *parameters*. This is also one of the major differences from Harel's statecharts [UML03, p. 2-174].
- We incorporate a dispatching mechanism for events and the handling of actions.

To keep the treatment accessible, we give the formal semantics for statecharts that are simplified as follows, which is sufficient for our present needs:

- Events cannot be deferred.
- There are no history states.
- Transitions may not cross boundaries within or across composite states. Transitions from composite states must be completion transitions.
- Invocation cycles, as defined in Sect. 8.1.1, are not permitted, and an attempt to execute any will result in deadlock, as explained in Sect. 8.1.1 and similar to the treatment in [HG97]. More details are given below.

Also, fork-join and junction pseudostates, and submachine, stub, and synch states, can be defined using the constructs treated here. We therefore omit their treatment, as well as that of time and change events.

Abstract Syntax of Statechart Diagrams

We define the abstract syntax of statechart diagrams.

A *statechart diagram* $D = (\mathsf{Object}_D, \mathsf{States}_D, \mathsf{Top}_D, \mathsf{Transitions}_D)$ is given by an object name Object_D, a finite set of *states* States_D, the top state $\mathsf{Top}_D \in \mathsf{States}_D$, and a set $\mathsf{Transitions}_D$ of transitions, defined in the following. We use Object_D to provide the *context* of a statechart diagram which links a state machine to another model element. This is usually not part of the concrete statechart syntax but needed when giving a formal semantics to complete specifications as in Sect. 8.1.7.

States_D is a set that is disjointly partitioned into the sets $\mathsf{Initial}_D$ of initial states in D, Final_D of final states, Simple_D of simple states, Conc_D of concurrent states, and Sequ_D of sequential states in D, together with the following data for each $S \in \mathsf{States}_D$:

- a string $\mathsf{name}(S)$ of characters called the *name* of the state,
- an action $\mathsf{entry}(S) \in \mathbf{Action}$ called the *entry action*,
- a set of states $\mathsf{state}(S) \subseteq \mathsf{States}_D$, the set of *substates* of S,
- an activity $\mathsf{internal}(S) \in \mathbf{Activity}$ called the internal activity (or do-activity) of the state, and
- an action $\mathsf{exit}(S) \in \mathbf{Action}$ called the exit action,

under the following conditions:

- We have $\mathsf{Top}_D \in \mathsf{Conc}_D \cup \mathsf{Sequ}_D$.
- For every $S \in \mathsf{Sequ}_D$ there exists exactly one $T \in \mathsf{state}(S) \cap \mathsf{Initial}_D$ (which we write as $\mathsf{init}(S)$).
- $S \in \mathsf{Simple}_D \cup \mathsf{Final}_D \cup \mathsf{Initial}_D$ implies $\mathsf{state}(S) = \emptyset$ and $S \in \mathsf{Conc}_D$ implies that $\mathsf{state}(S)$ has at least cardinality 2.
- $T \in \mathsf{Conc}_D$ and $S \in \mathsf{state}(T)$ implies $S \in \mathsf{Conc}_D \cup \mathsf{Sequ}_D$.
- For all $S, T \in \mathsf{States}_D$, $\mathsf{state}(S) \cap \mathsf{state}(T) \neq \emptyset$ implies $S = T$.
- For $S \in \mathsf{Initial}_D \cup \mathsf{Final}_D \cup \{\mathsf{Top}_D\}$, we have $\mathsf{entry}(S) = nil$, $\mathsf{internal}(S) = Nil$, and $\mathsf{exit}(S) = nil$.

- Let the relation $\prec$ on states $S \in \mathsf{States}_D$ be defined by $S \prec T$ if there exist states $S_1, \ldots, S_n$ with $n \geq 1$ such that $S_1 = S$, $S_n = T$, and $S_i \in \mathsf{state}(S_{i+1})$ for $i < n$. Then $\prec$ is acyclic (in particular irreflexive), and fulfills the condition that for all $S, T, U \in \mathsf{States}_D$ with $S \prec T$ and $S \prec U$ we have $T \prec U$ or $U \prec T$. Top_D is the largest element in States_D with respect to $\prec$.

Intuitively, therefore, a state $S \in \mathsf{States}_D$ in a statechart D may be an initial, final, simple, concurrent, or sequential state. A state has a name. Unless it is initial or final, it may have entry and exit actions executed when entering and exiting it, and an internal activity executed while the state is active. Concurrent and sequential states have substates, which in the case of concurrent states are again concurrent or sequential states (and the sets of substates are mutually disjoint). The substate relation fulfills certain saneness conditions that follow directly from the definition of statecharts at the concrete syntax level. An example is the non-existence of substate cycles. Note that the name of the state has no semantic significance. It may be omitted, then $\mathsf{name}(S)$ is the empty string. We allow the same internal activity to be used in different states. It is initialized whenever such a state is entered and is executed at each current state of which it is the internal activity, until it finishes. For technical reasons, there exists a "top" state which includes all other states as substates, possibly in a nested way. At the beginning, the initial state which is a direct substate of the top state is entered.

$\mathsf{Transitions}_D$ is a set with subset $\mathsf{Internal}_D \subseteq \mathsf{Transitions}_D$ such that for $t \in \mathsf{Transitions}_D$, we have the following data:

- a state $\mathsf{source}(t) \in \mathsf{States}_D$, the source state of t,
- an event $\mathsf{trigger}(t) \in \mathbf{Events}$, the triggering event of t,
- a Boolean expression $\mathsf{guard}(t) \in \mathbf{BoolExp}$ called the *guard* of t,
- an action $\mathsf{effect}(t) \in \mathbf{Action}$ (to be performed when firing t), and
- a state $\mathsf{target}(t) \in \mathsf{States}_D$, the target state of t

under the following conditions for each $t \in \mathsf{Transitions}_D$:

- $\mathsf{source}(t) \notin \mathsf{Final}_D \cup \{\mathsf{Top}_D\}$ (final states and the top state have no outgoing transitions).
- $\mathsf{target}(t) \notin \mathsf{Initial}_D \cup \{\mathsf{Top}_D\}$ (initial states and the top state have no incoming transitions).
- $\mathsf{source}(s) = \mathsf{source}(t) \in \mathsf{Initial}_D$ implies $s = t$ for any $s, t \in \mathsf{Transitions}_D$.
- $\mathsf{source}(t) \in \mathsf{Initial}_D$ implies $\mathsf{trigger}(t) = \mathsf{ComplEv}$ and $\mathsf{guard}(t) \equiv true$ (where $\equiv$ denotes syntactic equality).
- For any $S \in \mathsf{States}_D$, $\mathsf{source}(t) \in \mathsf{state}(S)$ implies $S \in \mathsf{Sequ}_D$ and $\mathsf{target}(t) \in \mathsf{state}(S)$.
- $\mathsf{trigger}(t)$ must be of the form $op(exp_1, \ldots, exp_n) \in \mathbf{Events}$ where exp_1, $\ldots$, $exp_n \in \mathbf{Var}$ are *variables* (called *parameters*), which must be mutually distinct.
- If $t \in \mathsf{Internal}_D$ then $\mathsf{source}(t) = \mathsf{target}(t)$.

- Multiple completion transitions leaving the same state must have mutually exclusive guard conditions. For $s, t \in$ Transitions$_D$ such that source$(s) =$ source(t) and trigger$(s) =$ trigger$(t) =$ ComplEv, the condition guard$(s) \wedge$ guard(t) evaluates to *false* for any variable valuations [UML03, p. 2-159].

The intuition is that transitions describe how to proceed from one state of an object (the source state of the transition) to another (the target state). Firing a transition is caused by its triggering event. This is an event whose message has mutually distinct variables as arguments. The transition is only fired if its guard is currently fulfilled. In that case, the effect of the transition is also executed. There are some consistency restrictions on the abstract syntax: final states and the top state have no outgoing transition, and initial states and the top state no incoming transition. An initial state has only one outgoing transition, which is a completion transition the guard of which is the constant true. A state with outgoing transition can be a substate only of a sequential state, which also contains the target state of that transition. For internal transitions the source and target states coincide. Multiple completion transitions leaving the same state must have mutually exclusive guard conditions.

As in [BCR00], we assume a special *completion event* ComplEv $\in$ **Events**, with no parameters. A transition t with trigger$(t) =$ ComplEv is called a *completion transition*. The trigger ComplEv is not written explicitly in the diagram.

A guard consisting of the expression *true* may be omitted in the diagram, as well as any occurrence of the action *nil* (in both states and transitions) or the internal activity *Nil*. If $t \in$ Internal$_D$ then t is called an *internal* transition, otherwise it is called *external*.[3]

To model the passing of control, we assume that return messages return$_{op}$ are given explicitly in the diagrams and that the following conditions are fulfilled:

- A target state S' of a transition whose action op is a synchronous call operation has no internal activities and exactly one outgoing transition, and this transition carries the corresponding return event *return$_{op}$*, and no guards or actions, as follows:

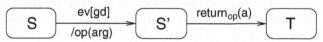

- For any transition t with effect$(t) =$ return$_{op}$ for some op $\in$ **Op**, we have internal(target(t)) $= Nil$ and trigger$(s) \neq$ ComplEv for any transition s with source$(s) =$ target(t).

The first condition ensures that, within a concurrent substate, an object that makes a synchronous operation call hands over the control thread and waits

---

[3] Note that there can be external transitions with the same source and target states and that these are different from internal transitions, because triggering the latter does not involve executing entry or exit actions of the corresponding state.

until the return message arrives. The second condition ensures that, within a concurrent substate, an object gives *back* the thread of control when passing back the return message of a synchronous operation call. Note that both conditions apply to each concurrent substate of a statechart separately. For example, this means that after sending a synchronous message, and while waiting for the return message, an object may be specified to accept an other message, through a different concurrent substate. For an example see Fig. 8.1 and the explanation there. If confusion is impossible, the subscript op on return messages may be omitted in the diagram.

Since the standard UML statecharts definition does not treat recursive calls properly, as pointed out in [TS02], we do not permit recursive calls, similar to the treatment in [HG97].

Nevertheless, for the assignment of return values, one may use the notation:

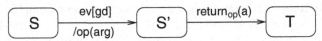

as a shortcut for

Here ev is an event, gd a guard, and S' is a simple state with no other incoming or outgoing transitions, and no entry nor exit actions, nor internal activities. We emphasize that we treat this simply as a syntactic shortcut.

As a further syntactic shortcut, one may use pattern matching with constants as arguments in the event specifications for increased readability. These event specifications should be replaced by events with variables as arguments and the relevant guard conditions before assigning the formal semantics.

Behavioral Semantics

We give a formal semantics of statechart diagrams using UML Machines. It is based on part of [BCR00], which, however, had to be extended to incorporate features such as explicit modeling of the passing of messages with their arguments between different objects or components, and use of the arguments in the subsequent execution.

The central part of the UML statechart semantics is the run-to-completion step, which means that events are processed one at a time, and that the current event is completely executed before the next event is dispatched. Any dispatched event that does not trigger any transition is lost.

We explain how our statechart semantics, for multi-threaded objects, treats the fact that an object may receive several synchronous messages calling the same operation op before sending back a corresponding return value, in different concurrent substates. To enable sending back the return value to the sender, each state S containing substates that accept op has an associated

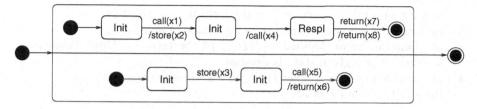

Fig. 8.1. Example: parallel invocations

last-in–first-out buffer sender(S, op) containing the names of the senders of the
message calls. See the vocabulary of $[\![D]\!]^{SC}$ defined below. This buffer is updated by the macro execEv(t, e) given below. When return messages are sent
out from within S, the recipients of these messages are taken from that buffer,
as defined in **ActionRule**$_S$(send(return$_{\mathsf{op}}(args)$)) below. Thus the assumption
is that, within a state S, a return message for op corresponds to the last call of
op received beforehand. Also, we assume that return messages are sent while
the execution is still in a (direct) substate of S. Otherwise, the return message
is lost, to avoid confusion with return messages from concurrent substates. A
simple example of such a situation is given in Fig. 8.1. A typical execution
of this statechart would be, firstly, to wait for reception of the synchronous
operation call with argument x1, handled by the first of the two concurrent
substates. Then, it would call itself first with the asynchronous message store
with argument x2 and then with the operation call with argument x4. This is
both done by the first substate, while the reception is handled by the second
substate. Then, it would send the return value x6 back to itself and finally the
return value x8 back to the sender of the first call message.

Note that we do not consider call-backs within *one* state, rather than across
several concurrent substates. We refer to the comment in [HG97, p. 39]: "When
the client's statechart invokes another object's operation, its execution freezes
in midtransition, and the thread of control is passed to the called object.
Clearly, this might continue, with the called object calling others, and so on.
However, a cycle of invocations that leads back to the same object instance is
illegal, and an attempt to execute it will abort." In fact, recursive call-backs
within one thread cannot be handled properly within the current official UML
statechart run-to-completion semantics, as pointed out in [TS02].

We fix a statechart diagram D together with a set Att$_D \subseteq$ **Attribute** of
used attributes and give its behavioral semantics as a UML Machine $[\![D]\!]^{SC}$
with name $O \stackrel{\text{def}}{=}$ Name$_{\mathcal{A}} =$ Object$_D$ and the following functions:

- the set name currState (storing the set of currently active states),
- the multi-set names inQu$_O$, outQu$_O$ (the input and output queues),
- the function name sender(S, op) mapping each concurrent or sequential
  state $S \in$ Conc$_D \cup$ Sequ$_D$ and each synchronous operation name $op \in$ **Op**

to a list of sender names each of the form $n_1 :: \ldots :: n_k$ where $n_1, \ldots, n_{k-1}$ are names of subsystems and n_k is the name of an object,

- the function name finished : $\{[\![D]\!]^{SC}\} \cup$ States$_D \to$ **Bool** (indicating whether D or a given state is finished),
- all variable names in trigger(t) for all $t \in$ Transitions$_D$, and
- the attribute names in Att$_D$.

Recall from the definition of UML Machines in Sect. 7.1 that whenever several UML Machines are executed in parallel (for example, those arising from different statecharts), they may generally share only input and output queues and their finished flag, if necessary by suitable renaming. The only exception occurs in the semantics for subsystems in Sect. 8.1.7 where different UML Machines modeling activities of the same object may share input and output queues and attributes. Therefore, to improve readability, we refrain from explicitly parameterizing names such as currState and Completed (see below), for example, although they are associated with a specific statechart diagram. On the other hand, each value finished$_S$ for a state $S \in$ States$_D$ of D is shared between the UML Machine $[\![D]\!]^{SC}$ modeling D and the UML Machine modeling the internal activity of S (if any exists), by assumption on activities, as explained in Sect. 8.1.1.

The Boolean finished$_S$ may be set to *true* by the rule **Exec** internal(S) of an internal activity at state S to indicate that the activity has finished. In particular, the UML Machine $[\![D]\!]^{SC}$ sets finished$_{[\![D]\!]^{sc}}$ to *true* at the end of its execution.

For each state $S \in$ States$_D \setminus \{\text{Top}_D\}$, we write upState($S$) for the unique state of which S is a direct substate.

At the initial state of the UML Machine $[\![D]\!]^{SC}$, we define:

- inQu$_O$ and outQu$_O$ to be equal to $\emptyset$,
- currState $\overset{\text{def}}{=} \{\text{Top}_D\} \cup (\text{Initial}_D \cap \text{state}(\text{Top}_D))$,
- finished$_{[\![D]\!]^{sc}}$ and finished$_A$ for any internal activity A to be equal to *false*, and
- sender$_S$(op) $\overset{\text{def}}{=} []$ for each state S and operation name $op \in$ **Op**.

The UML Machine $[\![D]\!]^{SC}$ has the rule **Exec** D given in Fig. 8.2 using macros defined in the rest of the subsection. It selects the event to be executed next, where priority is given to the completion event, and executes it. Then, it executes the rules for the internal activities in a random order.

The idea behind the statechart rule in Fig. 8.2 is the following. Firstly, it is checked whether all active states are final and direct substates of the top state, in which case the execution of the statechart is finished, which is indicated by setting finished$_{[\![D]\!]^{sc}} := true$. Otherwise, an event is executed. If there is a state that is *completed*, and thus contained in the set Completed defined below, the completion event is executed. Otherwise, an event e is dispatched from the input queue, provided it is non-empty, which is executed. After the event

Rule Exec D :
if currState $\subseteq$ Final$_D$ $\cap$ state(Top$_D$) **then** finished$_{\llbracket D \rrbracket^{SC}}$:= *true*
else

       if Completed $\neq \emptyset$ **then** eventExecution(ComplEv)
          else

                choose e **with** $e \in$ inQu$_O$ **do**
                    inQu$_O$:= inQu$_O$ \ $\{\!\!\{\, e \,\}\!\!\}$;
                    eventExecution(e);
     loop S **through set** currState
       Exec (internal(S))

Fig. 8.2. Statechart rule

execution, a further iteration of the internal activities of the active states is performed.[4]

Thus our semantics is "based on the premise that a single run-to-completion step applies to the entire state machine and includes the concurrent steps taken by concurrent regions in the active state configuration" [UML03, p. 2-162].

Here we make use of the *macro* Completed. With *macro* we mean a name that is just introduced for presentation purposes. It is not a function updated by $\llbracket D \rrbracket^{SC}$, but instead its definition is included in the rule at each of its occurrences when executing $\llbracket D \rrbracket^{SC}$. This remark also applies to the other macros used in the following. Completed is defined to be syntactically equal to the following expression:

Completed $\equiv$
$\{S \in$ currState $: \exists t \in$ Transitions$_D$.(source(t) $= S \wedge$ trigger(t) $=$ ComplEv)$\wedge$
             ($S \in$ Initial$_D$
             $\vee$ finished$_{\text{internal}(S)}$
             $\vee$ ($S \in$ Sequ$_D \cup$ Conc$_D \wedge$ state(S) $\cap$ currState $\subseteq$ Final$_D$))$\}$

eventExecution(e), for an event e, is defined to be syntactically equal to the expression given in Fig. 8.3.

Note that at any given point in time, an event may fire several transitions in different concurrent regions. The rule **loop** T **through set** FirableTrans(e) in the eventExecution(e) rule ensures that this is done consistently by sequentializing it.

The set FirableTrans(e) is defined as follows. For any transition t we define enabled(t, ComplEv) $\stackrel{\text{def}}{=}$ *true* if the following conditions are fulfilled (otherwise it is false):

- trigger(t) $=$ ComplEv,

---

[4] Recall that internal activities are themselves modeled as UML Machines, which means that executing **Exec** internal(S) for a state S does not *restart* the activity internal(S), but only executes a further cycle of that activity.

eventExecution(e) $\equiv$
    loop T **through set** FirableTrans(e)
      choose t **with** $t \in T$ **do**
        if $t \in$ Internal$_D$ **then** execEv(t, e)
        else
            exitState(source(t));
            execEv(t, e);
            enterState(target(t))

Fig. 8.3. Event execution rule

- guard(t) is *true*, and
- source(t) $\in$ currState $\cap$ Completed.

For any transition t and any event $e \neq$ ComplEv we define enabled(t, e) $\overset{\text{def}}{=}$ *true* if the following conditions are fulfilled (otherwise it is false):

- the operation or signal names of **trigger**(t) and e coincide: **msgnm**(trigger(t)) = **msgnm**(e),
- guard(t) evaluates to *true* when its variables are substituted with the arguments of e, and
- source(t) $\in$ currState.

Let FirableStates(e) be the set of $\prec$-minimal elements in the following set:

$$\{S \in \text{States}_D : \exists t.\text{enabled}(t, e) \land \text{source}(t) = S\}.$$

Then we define the set of sets of enabled transitions with the same, innermost state:

$$\text{FirableTrans}(e) \overset{\text{def}}{=} \{\{t \in \text{Transitions}_D : \text{enabled}(t, e) \land \text{source}(t) = S\} :$$
$$S \in \text{FirableStates}(e)\}$$

We define the macro exitState(S) for a state S in Fig. 8.4.

exitState(S) $\equiv$
    if state(S) $\cap$ currState $\neq \emptyset$
      then
        loop T **through set** state(S) $\cap$ currState
          exitState(T)
      else
        currState := currState $\setminus \{S\}$;
        ActionRule$_S$(exit(S))

Fig. 8.4. Exit state rule

The intuition behind this rule is the following. First the substates of the state S to be exited are exited recursively. Then S is exited by removing it from the set of current states and by firing its exit rule.

The macro $\mathsf{execEv}(t, e)$, for a transition t and an event e, is defined in Fig. 8.5. In $\mathbf{Args}(\mathsf{trigger}(t)) := \mathbf{Args}(e)$, each of the variables in $\mathsf{trigger}(t)$ is assigned the respective input value in $\mathbf{Args}(e)$.

$\mathsf{execEv}(t, e) \equiv$
  $\quad \mathbf{Args}(\mathsf{trigger}(t)) := \mathbf{Args}(e);$
  $\quad \textbf{if } \mathsf{msgnm}(e) \in \mathbf{Op} \textbf{ then}$
  $\qquad \mathsf{sender}(\mathsf{upState}(\mathsf{source}(t)), \mathbf{msgnm}(e)) :=$
  $\qquad\qquad\qquad \mathbf{sndr}(e).\mathsf{sender}(\mathsf{upState}(\mathsf{source}(t)), \mathbf{msgnm}(e));$
  $\quad \mathbf{ActionRule}_{\mathsf{upState}(\mathsf{source}(t))}(\mathsf{effect}(t))$

Fig. 8.5. Execute event rule

We define the macro $\mathsf{enterState}(S)$ for a state S in Fig. 8.6. The idea here is the following. First S is added to the set of current states, its entry action is executed, and its internal activity is initialized. $\mathsf{sender}(S, op)$ is initialized to the empty list for each operation op. If S is a sequential state, its initial state is entered. Otherwise, that is, if S is a concurrent state or if its set of substates is empty, its substates are entered recursively.

$\mathsf{enterState}(S) \equiv$
  $\quad \mathsf{currState} := \mathsf{currState} \cup \{S\};$
  $\quad \mathbf{ActionRule}_{\mathsf{upState}(S)}(\mathsf{entry}(S));$
  $\quad \textbf{forall } op \textbf{ with } op \in \mathbf{Op} \textbf{ do}$
  $\qquad \mathsf{sender}(S, op) = [];$
  $\quad \textbf{if } S \in \mathsf{Sequ} \textbf{ then } \mathsf{enterState}(\mathsf{init}(S))$
  $\quad \textbf{else loop } T \textbf{ through set } \mathsf{state}(S)$
  $\qquad \mathsf{enterState}(T)$

Fig. 8.6. Enter state rule

Example

The interpretation $[\![Sndr]\!]^{SC}$ defined above of the statechart $Sndr$ given in Fig. 8.7 which describes the behavior of the object $Sndr$ is equivalent, in the sense of Sect. 7.1, to the UML Machine $[\![Sndr]\!]^{SC}$ whose rule is given in Fig. 8.8. The execution of a simplified version of this UML Machine is explained in Fact 7.4. Further examples are given in Chap. 5.

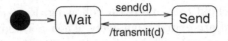

Fig. 8.7. Example: sender statechart

8.1.4 Sequence Diagrams

We emphasize again that we give a formal semantics only for a simplified fragment of sequence diagrams, for reasons explained in Sect. 8.1, which, however, is sufficient for our present needs. Recall that in our approach, we view an object as an entity characterized by a unique name. We thus identify the objects in the runtime system with UML objects. Also, recall that at each point of a given execution of a system, the same message instance in the running system is only represented once in the UML diagrams.

Following [UML03] we assume that no two events happen exactly at the same time. This implies that some behavior that could be viewed as concurrent may be sequentialized, for example, if two subsequent messages involve completely distinct components as senders and receivers. Note that this design decision in [UML03] is not a restriction in practice. In particular, in the example mentioned, the formal semantics given below allows the two messages to be sent in an arbitrary order. For simplicity, we omit the possibility to specify time information in sequence diagrams.

Furthermore, UML sequence diagrams in their full generality allow one to use *branching lifelines* to specify conditional branching. It has been argued,

case currState **of**
  $\{\mathsf{Top}_{Sndr}, \mathsf{Initial}_{Sndr}\}$: **do** currState := $\{\mathsf{Top}_{Sndr}, \mathit{Wait}\}$
  $\{\mathsf{Top}_{Sndr}, \mathit{Wait}\}$: **do**
    choose e **with** $e \in \mathsf{inQu}_{Sndr}$ **do**
      do − in − parallel
        $\mathsf{inQu}_{Sndr} := \mathsf{inQu}_{Sndr} \setminus \{\!\!\{ e \}\!\!\}$
        if msgnm$(e) = send$ **then**
          do − in − parallel
            currState := $\{\mathsf{Top}_{Sndr}, \mathit{Send}\}$
            $d := \mathbf{Args}(e)$
          enddo
      enddo
  enddo
  $\{\mathsf{Top}_{Sndr}, \mathit{Send}\}$: **do**
    do − in − parallel
      currState := $\{\mathsf{Top}_{Sndr}, \mathit{Wait}\}$
      $\mathsf{tooutQu}_{Sndr}(\{\!\!\{\mathit{transmit}(d)\}\!\!\})$
    enddo

Fig. 8.8. Example interpretation

however, that branching lifelines can become confusing when the system under consideration has a significant amount of conditional branching [Fow04]. Thus, in our approach we do not consider branching lifelines in sequence diagrams, but use statecharts when necessary to model conditional behavior. Similarly, we do not use sequence diagrams, but instead statecharts, if we want to describe concurrent behavior within a given component. Sequence diagrams are mainly used to describe behavior *exemplarily*. When needed, it would be possible to extend our sequence diagram semantics with branching lifelines, or with the possibility to model sequence diagrams with partially overlapping behavior.

Under the above assumptions, all connections in a sequence diagram can be ordered strictly by their occurrence, that is, by their horizontal position in the sequence diagram. This relies on the above assumption that for physical reasons, two events do not happen exactly at the same time, and that therefore only one event is specified to happen at any point in time.

Recall also that following [KW01, p. 15], we do not model the creation and deletion of objects explicitly. In particular, we do not have creation or deletion messages in sequence diagrams.

Note also in our intended application domain of security-critical systems that sequence diagrams have to be used carefully [Aba00]: precisely, a message msg on a connection from an object O to an object P, where O and P are connected by an untrusted network, means that:

- O sends msg to the network with intended recipient P, and
- if P receives a message msg' with the same message name as msg, it will proceed with its protocol part using the arguments of msg'.

There is no guarantee that P will ever receive a message with the same name as msg, or that msg' contains the same arguments as msg. Therefore we treat the sent and received arguments as potentially different entities in the sequence diagram. We do this below by using, for each object O, each message msg accepted by O, and each number n up to the number of arguments of msg, a local variable $O.msg_n$ of O that denotes the nth argument of the most recent instance of the message msg that is supposed to be received by the object O according to the sequence diagram. As usual, the prefix O may be omitted if no confusion will arise. These variables may have different values from those intended by the protocol, depending on a possible adversary. Also, an object has no information about the sender of a message. So at any point during the execution of the sequence diagram, the object may actually receive the expected message, which may or may not come from the expected sender, from inside or outside the sequence diagram. See Sect. 5.2 for a discussion of these issues in the specific situation of modeling security protocols.

An example of a sequence diagram is given in Fig. 3.4, which is discussed in more detail in Sect. 5.2. To increase readability, we use the notation $var ::= exp$ as a syntactic shortcut. Here var is a local variable not used for any other purpose and *exp* may not contain *var* . Before assigning a semantics to the diagram, the variable *var* is replaced by the expression *exp* at each occurrence.

Abstract Syntax of Sequence Diagrams

A sequence diagram $D = (\mathsf{Obj}(D), \mathsf{Cncts}(D))$ is given by:

- a set $\mathsf{Obj}(D)$ of pairs (O, C) where O is an object of class C whose inter-action with other objects is described in D, and
- a finite sequence $\mathsf{Cncts}(D)$ consisting of elements of the form $l = (\mathsf{source}(l), \mathsf{guard}(l), \mathsf{msg}(l), \mathsf{target}(l))$ (so-called *connections*) where
  - $\mathsf{source}(l)$ is the source object of the connection,
  - $\mathsf{guard}(l) \in \mathbf{BoolExp}$ is a Boolean expression that is the guard of the connection,
  - $\mathsf{msg}(l) \in \mathbf{Events}$ is the message of the connection, and
  - $\mathsf{target}(l) \in \mathsf{Obj}(D)$ is the target object of the connection,

such that for each $l \in \mathsf{Cncts}(D)$, we have $\mathsf{source}(l) \in \mathsf{Obj}(D)$ or $\mathsf{target}(l) \in \mathsf{Obj}(D)$, or both. A guard syntactically equal to *true* may be omitted in the diagram.

Note that our semantics for sequence diagrams given below supports the joint use of different sequence diagrams D, D' where $\mathsf{Obj}(D) \cap \mathsf{Obj}(D') \neq \emptyset$ provided that the parts of D and D' referring to the same object O relate to different parts of the possible behavior of O separated in time or depending on mutually exclusive preconditions. Different aspects of parts of its behavior that may not overlap over a period in time. That is, at any one time the behavior of a given thread of an object is represented by only one diagram.

To model the passing of control, we assume that return messages return_{op} are given explicitly in the diagrams and that the following condition is fulfilled for each sequence l of connections at nodes in $\mathsf{Cncts}(D)$: The number of return messages return_{op} for an operation *op* sent from an object O is at any time bounded by the number of calls of *op* received up to that time. That is, no return_{op} message is sent without previously receiving a corresponding op call.

If confusion is impossible, the subscript *op* on return messages may be omitted in the diagram.

Behavioral Semantics

We present the formal semantics for sequence diagram behavior. It supports explicit modeling of the passing of messages with their arguments between different objects or components, and further use of the arguments in the subsequent execution. For example, the guards of the transitions may refer to the input arguments and the attributes may be assigned values received as input.

In the semantics defined below, the sequence l of connections in a sequence diagram is split into "views" l_O for each of the involved objects O, consisting of the connections going out from or coming into O, as defined more precisely below. For each such view, we define a UML Machine modeling the behavior of O as defined by the sequence diagram.

As with statecharts, we model the order of dequeuing events from the event queue using the non-deterministic choice operator of UML Machines, to cover the different possibilities of this semantic variation point. A motivation for this treatment is given in Sect. 8.1.3.

As in the case of statecharts, we also have to account for the possibility that an object may receive several synchronous message instances calling the same operation op before sending back a corresponding return value. To enable sending back the return value to the sender, each UML Machine representing an object O in the sequence diagram that accepts op has an associated last-in–first-out buffer $\mathsf{sender}_{Top}(op)$ containing the names of the senders of the message calls, as defined for UML Machines in Sect. 7.1. This may be shortened to $\mathsf{sender}(op)$ because a sequence diagram has only one control state Top.

When return messages are sent out from O, the recipients of these messages are taken from that buffer, according to the definition of the macro $\mathbf{ActionRule}_{Top}(\mathsf{return}_{op}(args))$ in Sect. 8.1.1. The condition on the return messages in the above subsection on the abstract syntax ensures that the buffer is not empty at that point. Thus the assumption is that a return message from O for op corresponds to the last call of op received by O beforehand.

Note that there is only one input buffer and one output buffer for a given object or component, even if it occurs in several sequence diagrams. How to nevertheless consistently model the joint use of several behavioral diagrams within one subsystem is explained in Sect. 8.1.7.

We fix a sequence diagram D and an object $O \in \mathsf{Obj}(D)$. We give the behavior of O as defined in D as a UML Machine $[\![D.O]\!]^{SD}$.

We assume that for each object O, each message msg accepted by O, and each number n up to the number of arguments of msg, the set $\mathbf{Var}$ of variables contains an element $O.msg_n$ that will store the nth argument of the most recent instance of the message msg that is supposed to be received by the object O according to the sequence diagram. We define $O.msg = [O.msg_1, \ldots, O.msg_k]$, where the operation msg is assumed to have k arguments.

The signature of $[\![D.O]\!]^{SD}$ has the following function names:

- the multi-set names inQu_O, outQu_O (the input and output queues),
- the name $\mathsf{finished}_{[\![D.O]\!]^{SD}} \in \mathbf{Bool}$ (indicating whether $[\![D.O]\!]^{SD}$ is finished),
- a name cncts (the subsequence of $\mathsf{Cncts}(D)$ consisting of the connections relevant to O that are still to be processed),
- the function name $\mathsf{sender}(op)$, as shorthand for $\mathsf{sender}_{Top}(op)$ since a sequence diagram has only one control state Top, mapping each synchronous operation name $op \in \mathbf{Op}$ to a list of sender names each of the form

$n_1 :: \ldots :: n_k$ where $n_1, \ldots, n_{k-1}$ are the names of subsystems and n_k is the name of an object, and

- the names $O.msg_n$.

Sending a synchronous message $op \in \mathbf{Op}$, asynchronous message $msg \in \mathbf{Sig}$, or return message return_{op} is modeled as the actions $a = \mathsf{call}(op)$, $a = \mathsf{send}(sig)$, and $a = \mathsf{send}(\mathsf{return}_{op})$, respectively, with the UML machine rules $\mathbf{ActionRule}_{Top}(a)$ defined in Sect. 8.1.1. For sequence diagrams, we write this shorter as $\mathbf{ActionRuleSD}(op)$, $\mathbf{ActionRuleSD}(sig)$, or $\mathbf{ActionRuleSD}(\mathsf{return}_{op})$, respectively.

Given a sequence of connections l and an object O, we define l_O to be the subsequence l of those elements l with $\mathsf{source}(l) = O$ or $\mathsf{target}(l) = O$, called the object O's *view* of the connections.

At the initial state of the UML Machine $[\![D.O]\!]^{SD}$, we define:

- inQu_O and outQu_O to be equal to $\emptyset$,
- $\mathsf{cncts} \stackrel{\text{def}}{=} \mathsf{Cncts}(D)|_O$, and
- $\mathsf{finished} := \textit{false}$.

The rule of the UML Machine $[\![D.O]\!]^{SD}$ is given in Fig. 8.9.

Thus the sequence cncts of connections with source or target O is processed from the beginning to the end. If the connection c under consideration has O as its source and the guard of c evaluates to true, the message of c is sent out, and, unless c has O also as its target, the next connection is examined. If the guard of c evaluates to false, the execution of the sequence diagram does not proceed. If the connection c under consideration has O as its target, an event with the same message name as the message of c is chosen and dispatched from the input queue (if existent), and its arguments are stored in

---

Rule Exec $D.O$:
if cncts $= [\,]$ **then** finished$_{D.O} := \textit{true}$
else
    if source(**head**(cncts)) $= O \wedge$ guard(**head**(cncts))
        then
            ActionRuleSD(msg(**head**(cncts)));
            if target(**head**(cncts)) $\neq O$ **then** cncts $:=$ **tail**(cncts);
    if target(**head**(cncts)) $= O$ **then**
        choose e **with** $e \in$ inQu$_O$
                    $\wedge$**msgnm**(msg(**head**(cncts))) $=$ **msgnm**(e) **do**
        inQu$_O := $ inQu$_O \setminus \{\!\!\{ e \}\!\!\}$;
        O.msg(**head**(cncts)) $:=$ **Args**(e);
        if msgnm(e) $\in$ **Op then**
            sender(**msgnm**(e)) $:=$ **sndr**(e).sender(**msgnm**(e));
        cncts $:=$ **tail**(cncts)

Fig. 8.9. UML Machine rule for sequence diagram

the variable O.msg($\mathbf{head}$(cncts)). If the specified system executes as planned there will be such a message in our input queue put there by another object in the diagram under consideration, that is the one put there by the object from whose point of view c is an outgoing message. If such an event does not currently exist, the input queue is checked at each iteration round until it does exist. When the sequence cncts is reduced to the empty list, finished$_{D.O}$ is set to *true* and no further processing is done.

Note that it is not checked whether an object actually uses up all the contents of its input queue. Also, this semantics automatically enforces the (realistic) assumption that the behavior of an object after reception of a message does not depend on the identity of the sender of this message. In particular, at any point during the execution of the sequence diagram, the object may actually receive the expected message, which, however, may or may not originate from the expected sender, which may or may not be part of the sequence diagram.

8.1.5 Activity Diagrams

In our treatment, the only actions admitted in activity diagrams are assignments, since messages are processed by the activities in the activity diagram.

As in the statechart case, fork-join and junction pseudostates, and submachine, stub, and synch states, can be reduced to the constructs treated here. Note that this, in particular, requires that the activity diagrams are well-structured in the sense that they can be viewed as statecharts, following what the UML 1.x definition requires on [UML03, p. 2-178]. Note, however, that the UML definition document is not entirely consistent with regard to this point. In particular, some additional features of activity diagrams mentioned in the UML definition may contradict its requirement that activity diagrams should be a special kind of statechart, such as multiple parallel invocations of the same activity. In our simplified account of activity diagrams, we do not consider such features. Despite the different notation, the same well-formedness rules on states as in state-machines then apply [UML03, p. 2-178]. Since we only consider a simplified fragment of statecharts, we thus also only consider a simplified fragment of activity diagrams, which is sufficient for our needs. We do not consider the additional concept of object flow states, since we will not need it.

Thus the abstract syntax of activity diagrams is defined as follows, which is a simplification of the abstract syntax of statecharts from Sect. 8.1.3.

An *activity diagram* $D = (\mathsf{States}_D, \mathsf{Top}_D, \mathsf{Transitions}_D)$ is given as a finite set of *states* States_D, the top state $\mathsf{Top}_D \in \mathsf{States}_D$, and a set $\mathsf{Transitions}_D$ of transitions, defined in the following.

States_D is a set that is disjointly partitioned into the sets $\mathsf{Initial}_D$, Final_D, Simple_D, Conc_D, Sequ_D, together with the following data for each $S \in \mathsf{States}_D$:

- a string name(S) of characters called the *name* of the state,

Rule Exec D :

if currState $\subseteq$ Final$_D$ $\cap$ state(Top$_D$) **then** finished$_{\llbracket D \rrbracket^{SC}}$:= *true*
    loop S **through set** currState
        Exec internal(S)

Fig. 8.10. Activity diagram rule

- an action entry(S) $\in$ **Action** called the *entry action*,
- a set of states state(S) $\subseteq$ States$_D$, the set of *substates* of S,
- an activity internal(S) $\in$ **Activity** called the internal activity (or *do-activity*) of the state,
- an action exit(S) $\in$ **Action** called the exit action, and
- the name swim(S) of the swimlane containing S,

under the conditions given in Sect. 8.1.3 and the condition that access to attributes applies only to attributes of the object in the relevant swimlane.

Transitions$_D$ is a set with subset Internal$_D$ $\subseteq$ Transitions$_D$ such that for $t \in$ Transitions$_D$ we have the following data:

- a state source(t) $\in$ States$_D$, the source state of t,
- a Boolean expression guard(t) $\in$ **BoolExp** called the *guard* of t, and
- a state target(t) $\in$ States$_D$, the target state of t

under the conditions given in Sect. 8.1.3. Transitions in activity diagrams do not have events or actions. They are triggered by completion events.

Then following the statechart semantics in Sect. 8.1.3, an activity diagram D with a set Att$_D$ $\subseteq$ **Attribute** of attributes, used by the activities in D, and a set S of swimlanes representing objects or components are modeled by a UML Machine $\llbracket D \rrbracket^{AD}$. It is defined as $\llbracket D \rrbracket^{SC}$, except that there is no access to the input and output queues, which happens on the activity level. For completeness, the simplified rules are repeated below.

An internal activity S in an activity diagram can for example be given as D for a statechart D, or $D.O$ for a sequence diagram D and specified object O. Here Object$_D$ or O is the name of the object or component swim(S)

eventExecution(e) $\equiv$
    loop T **through set** FirableTrans(e)
        choose t **with** $t \in T$ **do**
            if $t \in$ Internal$_D$ **then** execEv(t, e)
            else
                exitState(source(t));
                enterState(target(t))

Fig. 8.11. Activity diagram Event execution rule

labeling the swimlane containing S. For more details on how this could be done and on the restrictions we impose to achieve this, see Sect. 8.1.7. In this way our statechart semantics deals with the fact that activity diagrams can contain several objects or components in different swimlanes. In each case, the rule **Exec** D or **Exec** $D.O$ is executed. By general assumption on the joint execution of UML Machines made in Sect. 7.1, these generally have their own namespaces, except for those variables in their input and output signatures. Thus different UML Machines modeling activities of the same object may share input and output queues and attributes.

We give the rules for the activity diagram semantics, a simplified version of those for the statecharts explained in Sect. 8.1.3. The UML Machine $[\![D]\!]^{AD}$ has the rule **Exec** D given in Fig. 8.10. Completed is defined as in Sect. 8.1.3. eventExecution(e), for an event e, is defined to be syntactically equal to the expression in Fig. 8.11. exitState(S) is defined as in Sect. 8.1.3. We define the macro enterState(S) for a state S in Fig. 8.12.

$$
\begin{aligned}
&\text{enterState}(S) \equiv \\
&\quad \text{currState} := \text{currState} \cup \{S\} \\
&\quad \textbf{ActionRuleSC}_{\text{upState}(S)}(\text{entry}(S)) \\
&\quad \textbf{if } S \in \text{Sequ } \textbf{then } \text{enterState}(\text{init}(S)) \\
&\quad \textbf{else loop } T \textbf{ through set } \text{state}(S) \\
&\qquad \text{enterState}(T)
\end{aligned}
$$

Fig. 8.12. Activity diagram Enter state rule

8.1.6 Deployment Diagrams

We give the abstract syntax of deployment models. A *node* $N = (loc, comp)$ is given by:

- the name *loc* of its location and
- a set of contained *components*[5] *comp* of the form $C = (name, int, cont)$ where *name* is the component name, *int* a possibly empty set of interfaces, and *cont* the set of subsystem instance and object names contained in the component.

A *deployment diagram* $D = (\text{Nodes}(D), \text{Links}(D), \text{Dep}(D))$ is given by:

- a set $\text{Nodes}(D)$ of nodes,
- a set $\text{Links}(D)$ of *links* of the form $l = (\text{nds}(l), \text{ster}(l))$ where $\text{nds}(l) \subseteq \text{Nodes}(D)$ is a two-element set of nodes being linked and where $\text{ster}(l) \subseteq$ **Stereotypes** is a set of stereotypes, and

---

[5] With components we mean component *instances*. We do not consider component or node *types* which are optionally allowed by the UML syntax specification.

- a set $\mathsf{Dep}(D)$ of *dependencies* of the form $(clt, spl, int, stereo)$ where clt and spl are component names (the client and supplier of the dependency), int is the interface of spl accessed by the dependency (with $int = spl$ if the access is direct), and $stereo \subseteq \mathbf{Stereotypes}$ is a set of stereotypes. We assume that for every dependency $D = (C, S, I, s)$ there is exactly one link $L_D = (N, s')$ such that $N = \{C, S\}$ for the set of linked nodes.

8.1.7 Subsystems

In the UML definition document, there is relatively little restriction on the kinds of diagrams a subsystem may contain and on the relation the diagrams should have to each other. Therefore, giving a formal semantics for this unrestricted use of UML subsystems, which assigns a formal meaning to the diagrams contained in a subsystem as well, would amount to giving a formal semantics to all of UML. For reasons explained in the introduction to this chapter, this is not attempted in the present work. In particular, the notion of subsystem considered here is restricted, for example in the kinds and numbers of diagrams that may be contained. To demonstrate that our use of UML subsystems is reasonable and our semantics of sufficient interest, we present several non-trivial case studies in Chap. 5.

Thus in our treatment, a system part C given by a subsystem instance S may contain sub-parts $C_1, \ldots, C_n$, given in a so-called *static structure diagram*, as defined below. Note that [UML03] uses the name *static structure diagram* at the instance level although in the implemented system, objects may be created at runtime. The diagram S contains an activity diagram that describes the activities performed by the sub-parts: each swimlane in the activity diagram gives the behavior of the sub-part C_i whose name labels the swimlane, which may be an object or may itself contain other system parts. Each activity in the activity diagram may be specified either itself as a subsystem instance. Its behavior may also be described directly as a UML Machine rule, such as an assignment to an attribute. Alternatively, it can be defined using a set of statecharts or sequence diagrams, for example, if the swimlane describes an object.

Each statechart describes the behavior of one activity, following the semantics in Sect. 8.1.3. The name of the activity is written next to the statechart. This way, we capture the *context* of the statechart, for which the UML specification currently does not offer a special notation [UML03, 3.74.2].[6]

Alternatively, the sequence diagrams describe the behavior of a set of activities that interact during their execution, as explained in Sect. 8.1.4. To achieve this, the sequence diagram is split up into different *views* of the objects or components described in it, as explained in Sect. 8.1.4. Each such view may then describe an activity in the swimlane of the relevant object or component. Again the context of the sequence diagram is written next to

---

[6] This may change with UML 2.0.

the diagram, such that the name of a corresponding activity in the activity diagram is the name written next to the sequence diagram followed by the name of the object or system part carrying out the activity.

Two activities in the activity diagram in a subsystem may not at the same time refer to the same sequence diagrams or statecharts *and* the same object, to avoid overlapping specifications. This is explained in more detail and defined precisely further below.

Recall that in our approach, we view an object or component as an entity characterized by a unique name, which may have associated information such as its attributes and their values which may change during its execution, which may be specified as a statechart. Thus we identify the objects or components in the runtime system with UML objects or components.

In modeling non-atomic activities using statecharts we follow [UML03, 2.13.2.7] which requires that at a subactivity state "an associated subactivity graph is executed". Since UML 1.x activity diagrams are special kinds of state machines, we are more general by allowing the use of statecharts, but one can of course restrict oneself to activity diagrams.

We will explain the idea behind this way of modeling activities. Firstly, note that we take activity diagrams to be special kinds of statecharts, in accordance with the UML 1.x specification, as defined in Sect. 8.1.5. Also, one may observe that within a statechart one may view the sequential substates of a given state S to form a statechart themselves: one that describes a certain activity performed at state S, provided that the statechart is well-structured as the ones we consider here are. Thus, conversely, one may use statecharts to define the activities in activity diagrams in a rather natural way: when giving a meaning to an activity diagram, seen as a statechart C, the activities of which are defined using statecharts, one essentially inserts the statecharts as substates of the states in the statechart C. Intuitively, then, the statecharts defining the activities appearing in the swimlane belonging to an object or component C could be put together to give a larger statechart describing the behavior of C. Since from a sequence diagram, the formal semantics given in Sect. 8.1.4 derives a state machine for each of the involved objects, corresponding to the object's *view* of the sequence diagram, one may also use sequence diagrams to describe activities.

As mentioned above, our way of modeling activities supports the joint use of different sequence diagrams D, D' where $\mathsf{Obj}(D) \cap \mathsf{Obj}(D')$ is nonempty provided that the parts of D and D' referring to the same object O relate to different parts of the possible behavior of O separated in time or depending on mutually exclusive preconditions. By using the different views of sequence diagrams to specify different activities, the assumptions on our semantics enforce that at any one time the behavior of a given thread of an object is represented by only one diagram. To see this, note that for any two different activities belonging to the swimlane of a given object one of the following conditions holds:

- either they belong to different concurrent subpaths of the path of activities in that swimlane (which means that they are associated with different threads of that object),
- or they belong to different subpaths depending on a conditional, such that in any given execution, at most one of the paths is executed,
- or they belong to the same subpath but are separated by at least one transition, meaning that one of the two is executed only after the other has finished.

Note that we do not currently make any restrictions that would prevent a designer from creating a model that may not be particularly intuitive or useful. For example, the following situations might occur. Suppose we are given a sequence diagram D containing objects O, P, and Q. Suppose there is an activity $s.O$ in the activity diagram, but no activity $s.P$. Then, in our formal model, the sequence diagram is translated to three UML machines modeling the behavior of O, P, and Q, and the first of them, but not the second, is executed when executing the system. What this means for the overall behavior of the system depends on the sequence diagram. It may mean that object O waits for a message from P indefinitely. Suppose now that, instead, the activities $s.O$, $s.P$, and $s.Q$ all occur in the activity diagram, but in such a way that they are not concurrent. Then the three UML Machines are executed, but not concurrently. Again what this means for the overall behavior of the system depends on the sequence diagram. It may mean that object O waits for a message from P or Q indefinitely and that these are never executed, and that therefore the activity modeled by O never finishes.

Although according to the UML specification statecharts can be used to describe the behavior of various kinds of model elements, such as activities, they are often used to describe the complete behavior of the objects in a given class. This can also be achieved with our approach: One can use an activity diagram which for each of the objects involved contains exactly one activity, the behavior of which is given by a statechart, and where these activities are synchronized in parallel using synchronization bars.

Furthermore, a subsystem instance contains a deployment diagram specifying the physical layer of the system. This information is exploited when analyzing UML specifications under security aspects, as explained in Chap. 4. A subsystem instance may specify a set of accepted messages, and may also offer interfaces.

Abstract Syntax

A *subsystem (instance)*[7] $S = ($name(S), Msgs(S), Ints(S), Ssd(S), Dd(S), Ad(S), Sc(S), Sd$(S))$ is given by:

- the name name(S) of the system part modeled by the subsystem,

---

[7] By *subsystem* in the following we always mean subsystem *instance*.

- a (possibly empty) set $\mathsf{Msgs}(\mathcal{S}) \subseteq \mathbf{MsgNm}$ of names of offered operations and accepted signals,
- a (possibly empty) set $\mathsf{Ints}(\mathcal{S})$ of subsystem interfaces,
- a static structure diagram $\mathsf{Ssd}(\mathcal{S})$ (defined below),
- a deployment diagram $\mathsf{Dd}(\mathcal{S})$,
- an activity diagram $\mathsf{Ad}(\mathcal{S})$, and
- for each of the activities in $\mathsf{Ad}(\mathcal{S})$, a corresponding interactive UML Machine $act \in \mathbf{Activity}$ specifying the behavior of objects appearing in $\mathsf{Ssd}(\mathcal{S})$ by defining the activities in the activity diagram. They may be given directly as UML Machine rules, or as UML machines arising as the formal semantics from the following kinds of diagrams: a (possibly empty) set $\mathsf{Sc}(\mathcal{S})$ of statechart diagrams, a (possibly empty) set of sequence diagrams $\mathsf{Sd}(\mathcal{S})$, and the subsystems in $\mathsf{Ssd}(\mathcal{S})$. Each diagram $D \in \mathsf{Sc}(\mathcal{S}) \cup \mathsf{Sd}(\mathcal{S})$ has an associated name $\mathsf{context}(D)$, which in the concrete syntax is written next to it.

Note that a subsystem is only well-defined if it satisfies the consisteny conditions listed below.

A *static structure diagram* [UML03, p. 3-34] $D = (\mathsf{SuSys}(D), \mathsf{Dep}(D))$ is given by a set $\mathsf{SuSys}(D)$ consisting of objects or subsystem instances, and a set $\mathsf{Dep}(D)$ of dependencies $(dep, indep, int, stereo)$ defined in Sect. 8.1.2, except that dep and $indep$ may now be subsystems, rather than objects. We require that the names of the subsystems or objects are mutually distinct. Note that in UML, static structure diagrams are called class or object diagrams even though they may contain not just class or objects, but also subsystems. In our usage here, we follow a suggestion on [UML03, p. 3-34].

Consistency Between UML Diagrams

A subsystem $\mathcal{S}$ is called *consistent* if the following conditions are fulfilled.

Activities

For every activity $act \in \mathbf{Activity}$ in a swimlane labeled O in the activity diagram exactly one of the following holds:

- There is a subsystem $\mathcal{S} \in \mathsf{SuSys}(\mathsf{Ssd}(\mathcal{S}))$ with $\mathsf{name}(\mathcal{S}) = act$.
- There is a statechart $D \in \mathsf{Sc}(\mathcal{S})$ with $O = \mathsf{Object}_D$ and $\mathsf{context}(D) = act$.
- We have $act = D.O$ where $D \in \mathsf{Sd}(\mathcal{S})$ is a sequence diagram with $O \in \mathsf{Obj}(D)$ and $\mathsf{context}(D) = act$.
- The activity is defined directly as a UML Machine which accesses only the input and output queues and attributes in its own swimlane, as required in the definition of UMSs in Chap. 7.

Note that, in particular, several activities can be modeled by statecharts. The above condition ensures that an activity is not modeled in more than one way and enforces that at any one time the behavior of a given thread of an object is represented by only one diagram. However, activities in the same swimlane may access the same attributes of the object specified by the swimlane.

Names of Behavioral Diagrams

For any two diagrams $D, D' \in \mathsf{Sc}(\mathcal{S}) \cup \mathsf{Sd}(\mathcal{S})$, the condition $\mathsf{context}(D) = \mathsf{context}(D')$ implies $D = D'$.

Object Communication

Each object modeled by a swimlane in $\mathcal{S}$ must appear exactly once in the deployment diagram.

Each subsystem in the deployment diagram and each object in the deployment diagram must appear in the static structure diagram. For any « call » or « send » dependency between subsystems or objects in the static structure diagram there must be the same dependency between the components containing the corresponding subsystems or objects in the deployment diagram.

For each statechart diagram $S \in \mathsf{Sc}(\mathcal{S})$ the following conditions must hold:

- For each call action $\mathsf{call}(obj.e)$ (resp. send action $\mathsf{send}(obj.e)$) in S, for an object name obj, the object diagram C in S must have a « call » (resp. « send ») dependency from the object Object_S to the object obj or one of its interfaces supplying the operation $\mathbf{msgnm}(e)$ (resp. able to receive the signal $\mathbf{msgnm}(e)$). The types of the message specifications in the class diagrams and those of the values in the statechart diagrams must match.
- For each assignment action $att := exp$ in S, att is contained in the set of attributes of Object_S given in C.

Similarly, for each sequence diagram $S \in \mathsf{Sd}(\mathcal{S})$ the following condition must hold: for each call action $\mathsf{call}(obj.e)$ (resp. send action $\mathsf{send}(obj.e)$) sent out from an object $O \in \mathsf{Obj}(D)$ in S, for an object name obj, the object diagram C in S must have a « call » (resp. « send ») dependency from the object O to the object obj or one of its interfaces supplying the operation $\mathbf{msgnm}(e)$ (resp. able to receive the signal $\mathbf{msgnm}(e)$). The types of the message specifications in the class diagrams and those of the values in the sequence diagram must match.

Scope of Data

We define the notion of *scope* of a piece of data within a subsystem which is needed to lift the definition of freshness of data in Sect. 7.5.5 to UML specifications.

The idea is that the scope of a piece of data or key $d \in \mathbf{Data} \cup \mathbf{Keys}$ within a subsystem diagram $\mathcal{S}$ is part of to an object or subsystem instance C contained in $\mathcal{S}$ if d is initially under the control of C. More precisely, the scope of d is contained in C in $\mathcal{S}$if d occurs within $\mathcal{S}$ at most in:

- the object or subsystem instance representing C in the static structure diagram contained in S,
- the swimlanes belonging to C in the activity diagram contained in S,
- the statechart diagrams contained in S that model parts of the behavior of C, or
- C's view l_C of the sequence of connections l in the sequence diagram contained in S, as defined in Sect. 8.1.4.

Behavioral Semantics of Subsystems

The different subsystems and objects have their own input and output queues. Recall that there is only one input buffer and one output buffer for a given object or component. This buffer may be accessed in various ways – for example, concurrent substates of a statechart diagram read from the same input buffer and write to the same output buffer. That this happens consistently is ensured by the semantics.

The run-to-completion step for each subsystem is performed in parallel, each with its own dispatcher only dispatching events prefixed by the subsystem name. This joint run-to-completion step is composed sequentially with the execution of the scheduler that takes the events from the output queues of the client subsystems requesting a service from another object and distributes them to the input queues of the server subsystems requested to provide the service. For the formal semantics of this we use the corresponding concepts for UMSs defined for this purpose in Sect. 7.2.

Recall that following [KW01, p. 15], we do not model the creation and deletion of objects explicitly. A sufficient number of required objects is assumed to exist at the start of the execution. The activation of objects is controled by the activity diagram in the subsystem. An object that reaches a final state within its top state is terminated and may be reactivated.

We give the formal behavioral interpretation for subsystems.

Suppose we are given a consistent subsystem S. The behavioral interpretation of S is defined to be the UMS $[\![S]\!]$ = (name(S), Comp, Sched, Links, Msgs) where:

- the set Comp $\subseteq$ **UMNames** of UMS components is the set consisting of the names of the components in the deployment diagram Dd(S), where for each $N \in$ Comp, its set Act$_N$ of activities consists of the activities appearing in the activity diagram Ad(S), and its set of attributes Att$_N$ is the union of the sets of attributes of its activities,
- Sched is the UML Machine $[\![Ad(S)]\!]^{AD}$ modeling the activity diagram Ad(S),
- Links is the set consisting of the links $l \in$ Links(Dd(S)) in the deployment diagram Dd(S) and a link l_{ST} for any two (possibly coinciding) subsystems or objects S, T residing on the same node in Dd(S), and
- Msgs is the set Msgs(S) of messages accepted by the subsystem S.

By the assumption regarding activity diagrams in the section on consistency between UML diagrams above, activities can thus be defined as subsystems, statecharts, or object views of sequence diagrams contained in the subsystem $\mathcal{S}$, or can be defined directly as a UML Machine.

As usual, we assume that the names of the UML Machines involved in the above definition are renamed to avoid unwanted name-clashes, except for the input and output queues. For the attributes referred to in any statecharts above, we require more specifically that they are renamed by prefixing the attribute name with the name of the object it belongs to. This way, different statecharts modeling activities of the same object can all access its attributes. Note that no conflicts arise from the shared access to attributes even by concurrent activities, because according to the activity diagram semantics defined in Sect. 8.1.5, they are executed by interleaving them.

We discuss an important property of our semantics.

Fact 8.1. *During each given execution of a UML specification, each occurrence of a message is created at at most one location in the specification.*

In particular, each occurrence of a *call* or *send* action in a statechart or a message sent out in a sequence diagram adds a new occurrence of the corresponding message to the communication queues of the UMS modeling the UML specification, rather than refer to an existing one. This follows from the definition of the rules **ActionRuleSC**$_S(a)$ for a *call* or *send* action a and **ActionRuleSD**(msg) for a message msg. Also, each occurrence of a message is consumed at at most one location in the specification.

In that sense, a message cannot be referred to more than once. This feature of our semantics is a restriction in so far as diagrams cannot be used in a way that permits "overlapping" in time. This way, related consistency problems within a single specification can be avoided.

8.2 Development with UML

Iterative development and modularity are two important concepts in system development. We consider the corresponding technical tools, refinement and rely-guarantee specifications, in the context of UML.

8.2.1 Refinement

System development is about turning an idea of what a system should accomplish into a product implementing the idea. This may be achieved by constructing a first abstract system specification satisfying the given requirements and by applying a number of successive transformations that add more detail while preserving the relevant requirements. This has been followed in the approach of *stepwise development* [Dij68, Wir71], also called the *top-down* approach. One advantage of this approach is that mistakes may be detected rather early in the development cycle, which may lead to considerable savings: Late correction of requirements errors costs up to 200 times as much as early correction [Boe81].

Changes to the system specification during the development process are supported by *refinements*. A *refinement* relates two descriptions of the same thing at two levels of detail, of which the more concrete one realizes the more abstract one. Thus we have the corresponding notion of *stepwise refinement*: a complex problem is decomposed into smaller subproblems and thereby simplified. Subproblems are refined step by step and integrated to solve the original problem.

In practice, one often has to modify a part of a system to account for changes in the environment of this part or in the requirements on it: *iterative development* is an "incremental production of a series of prototypes, which eventually evolve into the final implementation" [Boo91].

In the latter case, refinement is usually not assumed to provide full behavioral conformance [HG97, p. 40] or even to preserve the exact structure of the refined subsystem. This applies in particular to the kinds of refinement proposed in the context of UML:

- In UML, *refinement* denotes a certain kind of dependency relation[8] between model elements [UML03]. There is no constraint on the semantic relationship between the model elements. Examples of refinements in this general sense are state machine refinement and substitution. [UML03] gives also some heuristics on how state machines can be refined. Refining state machines corresponds to specializing the model elements whose behavior the state machines model.
- There is a related kind of dependency called realization which specifies a relationship between a specification model element and a model element that implements it. The implementation model element is required to support all of the operations or received signals that the specification model declares. Again there is no other constraint on the semantic relationship between the model elements.

On the other hand, in situations requiring high confidence that certain properties of a system are fulfilled, behavioral conformance of refinement can help to save effort to gain this confidence by theorem proving, model checking, simulation, testing, etc.. For example, this is the case when there are stringent requirements on the security or safety of a system. The reasons are the following:

(1) It is often easier to verify system properties at a rather high degree of abstraction.
(2) If one has to make changes to the specification during the development process, without any behavioral conformance one would have to redo all the verification work which has been done earlier in the process.

---

[8] More precisely, it is a kind of abstraction.

Thus, formal methods research has traditionally focussed on refinements that do preserve behavioral properties, for example in [Mil71, Hoa72, Jon72, Jon87, AL91]. In the context of object subtyping, this has been advocated for example in [LW94].

There seems to be a tension between flexibility of a refinement relation and the gain from establishing that a specification refines another: The trivial refinement relation that declares any system to be a refinement of any other system can be applied quite widely but is not very useful. Our focus is on the development of systems satisfying critical requirements, such as security requirements. We thus try to find the right trade-off by giving several kinds of refinement. Some of them strictly preserve the behavior of the system. Others allow for a modification in the behavior which is controlled in a way that allows one to reuse established knowledge on critical properties of the system. Of these, the more liberal kinds of refinement are especially useful in the early parts of system development, when the system is still subject to much change, and from one iteration in an iterative development process to the next. The stricter kinds are more useful in the later parts, when some properties have already been established that should be preserved, and within one iteration in an iterative process.

We introduce several kinds of refinement by referring to the corresponding definitions in Chap. 7 through the formal semantics defined in previous sections.

The strictest kind of refinement is called *behavioral refinement*. This is essentially refinement by reverse subset inclusion of the sets of inputs and outputs. With variations on what part of the system behavior is included, there are *black-box refinement* and *white-box refinement*. This kind of refinement reduces the possible behaviors of the overall system and preserves all trace properties, such as safety properties [AS85]. It also has pleasant structural properties, and preserves security requirements as explained in Sect. 7.5.1.

Definition 8.2 (Black-box refinement). *Suppose we are given UML subsystems S, S', tuples $\mathbf{i}$ and $\mathbf{o}$ of input and output names, and a set $\mathcal{E} \subseteq$* **Events**. *We say that S' is a (delayed) $\mathcal{E}$-$(\mathbf{i}, \mathbf{o})$-black-box refinement of S if the derived UML Machine* **Exec** *$[\![S']\!]$ is a (delayed) $\mathcal{E}$-$(\mathbf{i}, \mathbf{o})$-refinement of the UML Machine* **Exec** *$[\![S]\!]$.*

For example, given a set $\mathcal{M} \subseteq$ **MsgNm** of message names, one may consider $\mathcal{E}$-black-box refinements where $\mathcal{E} \stackrel{\text{def}}{=} \{e \in$ **Events** $:$ **msgnm**$(e) \in \mathcal{M}\}$. One can thus use the set of message names $\mathcal{M}$ in order to hide the events with different message names with respect to the refinement.

Fact 8.3. *(Delayed) $\mathcal{E}$-$(\mathbf{i}, \mathbf{o})$-black-box refinement of UML subsystems is a preorder for each set of events $\mathcal{E} \subseteq$* **Events** *and tuples $\mathbf{i}$ and $\mathbf{o}$ of input and output names.*

The next kind of refinement, *white-box refinement*, preserves the system structure, such as the links between components, and considers the behavior of the components in a UML subsystem. In contrast, the black-box refinement defined above only considers externally visible behavior.

Definition 8.4 (White-box refinement). *The UML subsystem S' is a (delayed) $(\mathbf{i}, \mathbf{o})$-white-box refinement of the UML subsystem S if the derived UMS $[\![S']\!]$ is a (delayed) $(\mathbf{i}, \mathbf{o})$-white-box refinement of the UMS $[\![S]\!]$.*

We show that white-box refinement is stronger than black-box refinement.

Fact 8.5. *If the UML subsystem S' is a white-box refinement of the UML subsystem S then S' is also a black-box refinement of S.*

The following result can be derived from the corresponding result on UMSs in Theorem 7.13.

Theorem 8.6. *White-box refinement of UML subsystems is a precongruence with respect to composition by subsystem formation.*

Definition 8.7 (White-box equivalence). *Two subsystem specifications S and S' are (delayed) white-box equivalent if S is a (delayed) white-box refinement of S' and S' is a (delayed) white-box refinement of S.*

White-box equivalence can be used for example to verify consistency of two subsystem specifications that are supposed to describe the same behavior, for instance, one of which uses statecharts to specify object behavior, and the other a sequence diagram.

Corollary 8.8. *White-box equivalence of UML subsystems is a congruence with respect to composition by subsystem formation.*

In practice, one often needs more flexible refinements that allow one to modify the subsystem's interface. *Interface refinement* is a looser kind of refinement which allows a change in the external interface of the part of the system under refinement. To exhibit the extent to which behavioral properties are preserved under the refinement, interface refinement is parameterized by system parts relating a system to its refinement.

Definition 8.9 (Interface Refinement). *Given UML subsystems S and S' and a parameterized UML subsystem $\mathcal{I}(\mathcal{Y})$, S' is a (delayed) $\mathcal{I}$-interface refinement of S if S' is a (delayed) white-box refinement of $\mathcal{I}(S)$.*

This definition allows one to handle the trade-off between the generality of a refinement relation and the degree to which it preserves system properties in a very flexible way. It is motivated by the observation that, in practice, subsystems are often reused as part of their refinements. A well-known example is the *wrapper facade* pattern where subsystems are refined by encapsulating them in other subsystems [SSRB00].

Theorem 8.10. *Each UML subsystem S is a $\mathcal{I}d$-interface refinement of itself, where $\mathcal{I}d(\mathcal{Y}) \stackrel{\text{def}}{=} \mathcal{Y}$.*

For all UML subsystems S, S', and S'' such that S' is a $\mathcal{I}$-interface refinement of S and S'' is a $\mathcal{I}'$-interface refinement of S', S'' is a $\mathcal{I}' \circ \mathcal{I}$-interface refinement of S, where $\mathcal{I}' \circ \mathcal{I}(\mathcal{Y}) \stackrel{\text{def}}{=} \mathcal{I}'(\mathcal{I}(\mathcal{Y}))$.

A more liberal kind of refinement is that of a *pattern-based transformation*. Patterns [GHJV95] encapsulate the design knowledge of software engineers in the form of recurring design problems. Here the developer may construct a refinement by applying a predefined transformation together with results on the preservation of behavior provided by this transformation, which may be either defined for this purpose or reused from other work. This kind of refinement is the most application-dependent. We consider it in the context of secure systems development in Sect. 4.3.

An extended example of the application of refinement is given in Sect. 5.1.

8.2.2 Rely-Guarantee Specifications

To reason about system specifications in a modular way, one may usefully employ rely-guarantee specifications. The following definitions are again adapted from Chap. 7.

Definition 8.11. *Given a UML subsystem S and sets R, G of sequences of event multi-sets, we say that S fulfills the rely-guarantee specification (R, G) if the derived UML Machine* **Exec** $[\![S]\!]$ *fulfills (R, G).*

Theorem 8.12. *Suppose that the UML subsystem S fulfills the rely-guarantee specification (R, G) and that $R \frown \mathcal{E} = R$ and $S \frown \mathcal{E} = S$.*

If the UML subsystem S' $\mathcal{E}$-black-box refines S then S' fulfills the rely-guarantee specification (R, G).

If the UML subsystem S' delayed $\mathcal{E}$-black-box refines A and G is stutter-closed then S' fulfills the rely-guarantee specification (R, G).

In particular, white-box refinement of UMSs preserves rely-guarantee specifications by Fact 8.5.

8.2.3 Reasoning About Security Properties in UML

We define a notion of black-box refinement that is relative to types of adversaries, using the corresponding Definition 7.24 for UMSs.

Definition 8.13. *The UML subsystem $\mathcal{T}$ is a (delayed) black-box refinement in presence of adversaries of type A of the UML subsystem S if the UMS $[\![\mathcal{T}]\!]$ is a (delayed) black-box refinement in presence of adversaries of type A of the UMS $[\![S]\!]$.*

Again, the refinement relation is preserved by including the adversary model.

Fact 8.14. *Suppose we are given UML subsystems S and T such that T is a refinement of S, and an adversary type A, such that the accessible knowledge for A in B is no larger than that in $\mathcal{A}$. Then the UMS B is a black-box refinement in presence of adversaries of type A of the UMS $\mathcal{A}$.*

We also define the security properties on the level of UML subsystems.

Definition 8.15. *We say that a UML subsystem S preserves the secrecy of an expression $E \in \mathbf{Exp}$ (resp. of a variable v) from adversaries of type A given inputs in $\mathcal{E}$ if the UMS $[\![S]\!]$ does.*

S preserves the integrity of a variable v with respect to the set E of acceptable expressions from adversaries of type A given inputs in $\mathcal{E}$ if $[\![S]\!]$ does.

S provides (message) authenticity of a variable v with respect to its origin o from adversaries of type A given inputs in $\mathcal{E} \subseteq \mathbf{Events}$ if $[\![S]\!]$ does.

An atomic value $d \in \mathbf{Data} \cup \mathbf{Keys}$ in S is fresh within a component $\mathcal{D}$ contained in S if the scope of d, as defined in Sect. 8.1.7, is contained in $\mathcal{D}$.

S prevents down-flow (resp. up-flow) with respect to H if all UML Machines in $[\![S]\!]$ do.

We then have the following results similar to those in Sect. 7.5.

Theorem 8.16. *Suppose we are given UML subsystems S and T.*

If the UML subsystem S preserves the secrecy of E from adversaries of type A and T is a black-box refinement in presence of adversaries of type A, or T (delayed) refines S given adversaries of type A such that the accessible knowledge for A in B is no larger than that in $\mathcal{A}$, then T preserves the secrecy.

If S preserves the integrity of v with respect to a set $E \subseteq \mathbf{Exp}$ of acceptable expressions from adversaries of type A given inputs in $\mathcal{E}$ and T $(\emptyset, \{v\})$-black-box refines S then T preserves the integrity of v.

If S provides authenticity of v with respect to its origin o from adversaries of type A given inputs in $\mathcal{E}$ and T is a $(\emptyset, \{v, o\})$-black-box refinement of S such that the accessible knowledge for A in B is no larger than that in $\mathcal{A}$, then T B provides authenticity.

If S prevents down-flow (resp. up-flow) with respect to the set $H \subseteq$ $\mathbf{MsgNm}$ and T white-box refines S then T prevents down-flow (resp. up-flow) with respect to H.

8.3 Notes

The UML semantics in this chapter has been presented in [Jür02a, Jür02d]. There has been a considerable amount of related work on a formal semantics for various parts of UML. Our approach here differs from most other work on UML semantics since usually diagrams are considered in isolation: For security analysis, they have to be considered together. In fact, the formal semantics for subsystems including certain kinds of diagrams and their interactions seems to be the only one published so far.

We can only mention some representative examples for related work. An overview on formal approaches to systems analysis using UML is given in [Whi00]. [FELR98, EFLR99] discuss some fundamental issues concerning a formal foundation for UML. [KER99, RW99, RACH00] point out some related problems. [BHH+97, BGH+97, BGH+98] uses a framework based on stream-processing functions to define a semantics for UML. [SW97] gives a formal definition of UML's package concept. [Kna99] gives a formal semantics for UML interactions. [GPP98, EHHS00] employ graph transformations for defining UML semantics. [LP99] gives a formalization of UML state machines. [RACH00, RCA00] give an approach using algebraic specification. [MS00] translates UML class diagrams to B abstract machines. [ML02] defines transformation rules for OCL constraints into the formal method B. [BD00] gives a translation of statecharts into the process algebra CSP. [BCR00, BCR04] uses ASMs for UML statecharts. [Cav00] also contains a formal semantics for other kinds of diagrams. [ÖP00] considers interacting UML subsystems, but without giving a formal semantics. [Ste01a] give a semantics for use case diagrams based on transition systems. A combined formal semantics for UML statecharts and class diagrams has been given in [RCA01]. [Mer02, SKM01] gives a semantics for statecharts and show exemplarily how to check whether a set of statecharts satisfies a collaboration. [RFBLO01] constructs a UML virtual machine. [Krü02] gives a formal foundation for services in UML and UML-RT. [DGH02] defines a translation of UML statecharts to UPPAAL timed automata. [ZG02] defines an extension of OCL with temporal logic. [vdB02] gives a structured operational semantics for UML-statecharts. [Jan02] proposes a probabilistic version of UML statecharts. [WS02] gives results on compile-time scope resolution for statechart transitions. [VP03] applies an approach for automated formal verification of model transformations to a transformation from UML statecharts to Petri nets. [BG03] examines UML actions and activities. There has also been a significant amount of work on the semantics for formalisms related to UML, including work regarding Message Sequence Charts in [Krü00].

Refinements have been investigated in the object-oriented setting, for example in [DB00, DS00a], where the introduced structural refinement has a similar motivation to our interface refinement; for an overview see [DB01]. A further discussion on refinement in UML can be found in [HK98]. [Weh02] investigates behavioural subtypes in UML using refinement. [Stö03] considers assertion, negation, and refinement in UML interaction specifications. [BB03] defines a formal notion of refinement of UML diagrams.

8.4 Discussion

We defined a formal semantics for a simplified part of UML using UML Machines and UML Machine Systems. It gives a precise meaning to groups of diagrams of various kinds gathered in a special kind of UML subsystems. Actions and internal activities are modeled explicitly, rather than treating them as atomic given events. In particular, objects, and more generally system components, can communicate by exchanging messages with parameters, which can be used in the subsequent execution. The formal semantics presented in this chapter gives the basis for the tool support for security analysis of UML specifications presented in Chap. 6. This allows us to reach general insights about the properties checked by the tool, such as preservation under refinement.

We gave supplementary results for formal UML development, such as consistency conditions for different diagrams in a UML specification, and notions of refinement, behavioral equivalence, and rely-guarantee specifications, which enjoy nice structural properties, such as substitutivity. The formal semantics delivers the required mathematical foundation to reason about subtle behavioral properties such as security requirements. Since our semantics builds on UML Machine Systems, it allows us to make use of the treatment of security-critical systems in Sect. 7.5 to evaluate UML specifications for security in the following chapters. In all, due to their flexibility, expressiveness, and preciseness, UML Machines appear to be an adequate tool to handle the complexities both in defining a semantics for part of UML, and in dealing with subtle behavioral security properties.

While we considered only a core fragment of the UML syntax, we believe that extending the work to include other aspects is possible. Note, however, that this may cause an increase in complexity and therefore possibly a performance penalty when performing tool supported checks on the UML models, apart from the fact that "richer" UML models are not necessarily easier to understand. Since the UML definition itself is inconsistent in several ways, it is not possible to define a consistent semantics for *all* of UML as it is presently defined. Our choice of a core UML notation is based on experiences from several industrial application projects. This way we made sure that it is sufficiently expressive for our purpose to develop security-critical systems, which can also be seen from the case studies in Chap. 5.

Part IV

Epilogue

9

Further Material

In this chapter, we give a short overview of material related to the content of this book. We start by listing some more material within the UMLsec approach that had to be omitted for space reasons and then give an overview of other approaches.

9.1 More on the UMLsec Approach

The following further material related to UMLsec has to be omitted here:

- [Jür03b, Jür04h] gives more detail on specification-based testing for critical systems with UML.
- [Jür02e] uses UMLsec to provide formally based development methods for CORBA-based applications.
- [Jür02b, Jür03c, Jür03d, Jür04b, Jür03b, Jür04a, Jür04h] demonstrate how to generalize the approach presented here to develop systems with other criticality requirements, such as safety-critical, performance-critical, or real-time systems, using an appropriate extension of UML.
- [Jür02g] presents applications of UMLsec in the telemedicine application domain, [JG03] in the automotive domain, and [JK03] considers secure mobile systems.
- [JPW02] gives more results about using security patterns in model-based development in the context of UMLsec.
- [JPW03, PJWB03, BBH$^+$03, Jür04j] propose some development methods for security-critical systems using UMLsec.
- [Jür03a] explores the notion of algebraic state machines similar to the UML Machines considered here, and applications to security.
- [JH03, HJ03b] show how to combine the use of UMLsec with model-based risk assessment.

9.2 Other Approaches to Security Engineering

We give an overview of other approaches to security engineering using formal methods or UML. Here we only give a general overview of topics relevant to the main focus of the UMLsec approach; more specific references are given in the notes sections of the preceding chapters.

9.2.1 Software Engineering and Security

Compared to research done using formal methods reviewed below, less work has been done more generally using software engineering techniques for computer security. Examples include [Eck95, EM97, DFS98], for an overview of the topic see [DS00b]. [And94] suggests using software engineering techniques to ensure security. In practice, penetration tests are commonly used to assess the security of a system [Wei95]. [FH97] defines role-based access control rights from object-oriented use cases, and [Fer98] presents a holistic view on Internet security engineering. Work on security patterns includes [FP01, Sch03a]. The security of object-oriented systems has been considered for example in [JKS95, SBCJ97]. The Tropos Requirements Engineering methodology is extended to cover security aspects in [GMM03, MGM03].

There is an increasing interest in the topic of software engineering and security. In Germany, this is exemplified by the recent foundation of a related national working group [Jür03f].

9.2.2 Other Approaches Using UML

After the research on model-based security engineering using UML presented in this book started in [Jür01i], and after some earlier work on role-based access control such as [FH97], there exist now several lines of research toward using UML for security systems development. They seem to differ from the one presented here that they usually aim to cover a less comprehensive set of security requirements, mostly focussing on role-based access control requirements. Also, most of them do not attempt to perform an analysis of the security requirements based on a formal semantics of a simplified fragment of UML.

[HF97] extends use cases and interaction diagrams to support distributed system architecture requirements. [FH97] proposes a method determining role-based access rights. Use cases are extended with rights specifications and the rights of a role are derived from the use cases. The method thus enforces the design principle of least privilege. Work on security patterns using UML includes [Fer99, FP01].

Some other approaches have been discussed at recent workshops on the topic [JCF+02, JFS04, JRFF03]:

- [GFR02] demonstrates how to use UML for aspect-oriented development of security-critical systems. Design-level aspects are used to encapsulate security concerns that can be woven into the models. In [GFR03], authentication mechanism models are considered in an abstract aspect model and more detailed models are created from these. The models can be composed with primary decomposition models, allowing system architects to analyze different mechanisms to realize a particular concern, such as authentication. [RFLG03] proposes to use aspect-oriented modeling for addressing access control concerns. Functionality that addresses a pervasive access control concern is defined in an aspect. The remaining functionality is specified in a so-called primary model. Composing access control aspects with a primary model then gives a system model that addresses access control concerns. [RLKF03, KRFL04] uses a variant of UML to model Role Based Access Control and Mandatory Access Control and to compose access control policy frameworks.
- [HdBLS02] uses UML for the risk assessment of an e-commerce system within the CORAS framework for model-based risk assessment [DRR⁺02, FKG⁺02, AdBD⁺02]. This framework is characterized by an integration of aspects from partly complementary risk assessment methods. It incorporates guidelines and methodology for the use of UML to support and direct the risk assessment methodology as well as a risk management process based on standards such as AS/NZS 4360 and ISO/IEC 17799. It uses a risk documentation framework based on RM-ODP together with an integrated risk management and system development process based on UP and offers a platform for tool inclusion based on XML. [HH03b] presents SecurityAssessmentUML, a UML profile for model-based security assessments, as well as a security assessment process and its associated documentation framework. The main objective is to support documentation of output based on risk identification and risk analysis in a security assessment. The profile supports specification of concrete scenarios demonstrating how attacks may occur, as well as a combination of fault trees and activity diagrams for analyzing the frequency of risks.
- [FMMMP02] uses UML for the design of secure databases. It proposes an extension of the use case and class models of UML using their standard extension mechanisms designing secure databases. It uses an OCL-based language for specifying security constraints called OSCL. The paper demonstrates how to use the methodology to classify information into different sensibility levels and to specify which user roles will be able to access the information.
- [KPP02, BKL02] demonstrate how to deal with access control policies in UML. The specification of access control policies is integrated into UML. A graph-based formal semantics for the UML access control specification permits one to reason about the coherence of the access control specification.

[Blo02] uses UML for modeling security-critical systems in the health sector. [LBD02, BDL03] show how UML can be used to specify access control in an application and how one can then generate access control mechanisms from the specifications. The approach is based on role-based access control and gives additional support for specifying authorization constraints.

[HH03a] provides support for the use of UML with secrecy annotations so that the code produced from the UML models can be be validated by the Java information flow (Jif) language-based checker.

[AW03] suggests a method for specifying access control policies with UML use cases and proposes a methodology to resolve some issues of consistency and completeness of access control specifications.

Internationally, several research projects exist now on the topic of secure systems development with UML, including the European working groups CORAS [Stø01], NEPTUNE [NEP01], and DEGAS [DEG01], as well as one German project [Arc01].

9.2.3 Formal Methods Applied to Security

There has been extensive research in using formal models to verify secure systems. The main areas of formal methods application in this domain include secure information flow and security protocols. Because of the amount of material in this area, it is virtually impossible to present a complete overview, and this is not attempted here.

[Lam73] drew attention to covert channels; this initiated early influential work on secure information flow in [GM82, GM84]. An overview of secure information flow and other formal security models can be found in [McL94]. More recent approaches to secure information flow include [FG95, FG97, Ald01, BFPR02, MS03, DHS03]. Other approaches were mentioned in Sect. 7.6.

Many references attribute the approach for using formal methods to analyze abstract models of cryptographic protocols as influenced by the early reference [DY83]. Overviews of applications of formal methods to security protocols can be found in [Mea95, GSG99, Aba00, Mea00, SC01] and [RSG+01, Chap. 9]. See there for those references that we have to omit here.

Roughly, one can try to classify the different approaches into the following categories:

Intensional methods model the behavior of the protocol participants together with an attacker who can perform well-defined actions such as eavesdropping, storing, deleting, and inserting messages at a communication link, but is usually assumed not to be able to break cryptographic mechanisms. In these approaches, one often starts with the specification of the protocol, which is usually relatively straightforward. The security requirements are formulated by referring to this specification. It is then established whether the possible behaviors of the model give rise to violations of security goals. Towards this, one can use different techniques.

- State-space search is an approach for constructing and analyzing all possible attack scenarios used for example in model checking. Examples include [MCF87, Kem89, Mea96, FGG97, MMS97, GL97, Eck98, JW01b, GOR02, BMV03, KW04]. The process algebra CSP has been employed for example in [Low96, LR97, RSG+01], and the process algebra CCS for example in [DFG00, FGM03] There exist specification languages tailored to security protocols, including [Low98, BMM99], which translate abstract protocol models to low-level specifications that can then be verified.
- Proof-construction methods are used to establish the absence of attacks relevant to the adversary model by mathematical proof, which may be mechanically assisted or even automatic. Examples include [Sch96, Sch97, Sch99b, TFHG99, Wei99, Gut00, BDNN01, NNS02, BBD+03, Her03, Bla04]. [AG99] introduces the spi calculus. An inductive method of proving protocols correct using the mechanical proof assistant Isabelle [NPW02] is explained for example in [Pau98b]. [KAH99, Hei01] use the Software Cost Reduction toolset. There has been some work using ASMs reported in [BR97, BR98]. In [Lot00], threat scenarios are used to formally develop secure systems using the stream-based specification language FOCUS [BS01]. [PW00] considers reactive systems that are secure in a cryptographic sense.

Extensional methods focus more on the security requirements, rather than the protocol specification. They often use specialized logics to model and analyze security protocols, often by modeling the changing knowledge and beliefs of the protocol participants during the execution of the protocol. Formulating security properties is often intuitive and elegant, while specifying the protocol may be more indirect than with intensional methods. The most famous example is probably the BAN logic, named after its inventors Michael Burrows, Martín Abadi, and Roger Needham [BAN89]. In the BAN logic, one can formulate statements such as "P sees X" (meaning that P has received X), "P believes X" (P is led to believe that X is true), "X is fresh", "K is a good key for communication between P and Q", and so on. One can use logical inferences to construct the set of statements which hold about a protocol according to the logic. For example, if P receives X encrypted under the key K, and also believes that K is a good key for communication with Q, then P believes that Q said X. In particular, one can verify that a certain security property, formalized as a BAN logic statement, holds for the protocol according to the logic. There exist several extensions to the BAN logic, including [GNY90, SvO94, KN98]. An overview can be found in [SC01].

A formal approach close to UMLsec is that using the computer-aided software engineering (CASE) tool AUTOFOCUS [BHP+97, HMR+98, SH99, RJW+03].[1]

Similar to the UMLsec approach presented in this book, cryptographic systems can be specified with diagrams similar to UML sequence diagrams and

---

[1] A German introduction is contained in [BS03].

statecharts and examined for security weaknesses using the model-checker SMV included in AUTOFOCUS [JW01b, WW01]. Additionally, the specifications can be simulated or tested. In a particular application [VWW02], a secure electronic purse application for personal digital assistants (PDAs) has been developed using the AUTOFOCUS approach following a development process based on the Common Criteria [CC01]. [vOL02] uses AUTOFOCUS to perform formal security analyses using Isabelle [NPW02] in a state machine model.

Related to the work using AUTOFOCUS is research using the formal method FOCUS involving stream-processing functions, on which AUTOFOCUS is based. [Lot97] uses threat scenarios to develop secure systems. [Jür01g] extends FOCUS by cryptographic operations including symmetric and asymmetric encryption and signing. [Jür01b] examines composability of secrecy. [Jür00] considers secure information flow.

Unfortunately, due to a perceived high cost in personnel training and use, formal methods have not yet been employed very widely in industrial development [Hoa96, Hei99, Sch00, AR00b, KK04].

9.2.4 Other Non-functional Requirements

[LLK$^+$02] proposes a basis for partially automated risk analysis in early development phases with UML. [PMP01, BDCL$^+$01, HG02, HTB03] propose to use UML for safety-critical or dependable systems development. [Pat02] presents a methodology to extend the OMG General Resource Modeling sub-profile to model component faults in a UML design. [Pet02] proposes a strategy for a development of critical control systems using UML. [FHH$^+$03, Sel03] discusses the use of modeling techniques in critical systems design. [CLM$^+$03, LMM03, vKSZ03] report on the usage of UML for real-time systems. [XLL03, JHK03] deals with software performance prediction and Quality of Service aspects based on UML models.

10

Outlook

The method for model-based development of security-critical systems proposed here has been successfully applied in industrial projects involving German government agencies and major banks, insurance companies, smart card and car manufacturers, and other companies. The experiences made indicate that the approach is adequate for use in practice, after relatively little training, when compared to some of the heavy-weight formal methods approaches. As a first introductory book in the young field of model-based security engineering, this book had to try to strike a balance between readers interested in just using UMLsec as secure software engineers, and those wanting themselves as researchers to contribute to the further development of the field, or wanting to try to generalize these ideas to other application domains. Considering thus that a significant part of the material presented here is not mandatory for normal users of UMLsec and the associated tool support, we have made the experience that on the basis of the material in this book, usage of UMLsec can in fact be rather easily taught to developers in industrial practice. A beginning has already been made in an ongoing series of tutorials on model-based security engineering using UMLsec [Jür04b].

Given the current state of computer security in practice, with many vulnerabilities reported continually, it is a promising idea to apply model-based development to security-critical systems, since it enables developers who are not experts in security to make use of security engineering knowledge encapsulated in a widely used design notation. Since there are many highly subtle security requirements which can hardly be verified with the "naked eye", even security experts may profit from this approach. Although the approach explained here puts some emphasis on the weaknesses arising from the design level, it can also be used for analyzing code for security weaknesses, as indicated in Sect. 6.4. It can also be combined with the analysis of data arising during the execution of a system, such as security configurations, as demonstrated in Sect. 6.3. The UMLsec approach even generalizes to other application domains such as dependability, as mentioned in Sect. 9.1.

Although we only used a core of UML and in a more disciplined way than in average current industrial usage of UML in order to allow use of advanced tool support, the industrial case studies presented in Chap. 5 indicate that our usage of UML is sufficient for our needs. Since UML is widely taught, even a more focused and disciplined use of UML is easier to learn and use than a completely different notation. When analyzing a system for security requirements, there may already be a specification in UML or enough knowledge in UML available to enable constructing one without too much further training, reducing costs. In particular, this approach is supported by tools for automated analysis of UMLsec models presented in Sect. 6.2. This should assist in transferring ideas and results from model-based security engineering to industrial practice, in a way that complements the usual methods of quality assurance by testing. Thus one can avoid mistakes that are difficult to find by testing alone, such as breaches of subtle security requirements, as well as the disadvantages of the "penetrate-and-patch" approach. Since preventing security flaws early in the system life-cycle can significantly reduce costs, there is a potential for developing securer systems in a cost-efficient way.

Part V

Appendices

Appendices

A

Towards UML 2.0

At the time of writing, the next major version of the Unified Modeling Language, UML 2.0, is being finalized. In this chapter, we shortly sketch how to accommodate the changes from the current version, UML 1.5, with respect to the approach proposed in this book. A good introduction to UML 2.0 and a list of the changes between the different UML versions is contained in [Fow04].

Most changes do not have a significant impact on our approach: For example, *object diagrams*, which already exist in UML 1.5, are in UML 2.0 more explicitly defined. In UML 1.5, packages can be contained in class diagrams, while in UML 2.0 such diagrams are now independently named as *package diagrams*. The UML 1.5 collaboration diagrams are called *communication diagrams* in UML 2.0. The UML 2.0 *interaction overview diagrams* are a new kind of diagram integrating activity and sequence diagrams. – While in UML 1.5, the activities in activity diagrams can already be defined using other diagrams, such as sequence diagrams, this link can be made more explicitly in UML 2.0 by actually including the sequence diagrams in the respective activity states. *Timing diagrams* are a kind of diagram which is entirely new to UML with version 2.0. These diagrams, which will be familiar to many hardware engineers from electronic engineering, do not seem to be particularly specific to secure software engineering.

Composite structure diagrams have been included in UML 2.0 from the real-time UML-RT extension. They contain *parts* represented by rectangles that may be connected by *connectors* drawn as lines between parts. These diagrams are useful for specifying component structures and hierarchies within components. In that, they are similar to the static structure diagrams of UML 1.5, which can contain subsystems that may themselves in turn contain static structure diagrams, and to component models, which can be part of deployment diagrams. Thus, stereotypes such as « secrecy », « integrity », « authenticity », and « high » defined for dependencies in static structure diagrams and deployment diagrams can also be applied to the connectors in composite structure diagrams. Also, parts can be marked as « critical », such as class models or subsystems in static structure diagrams. Although the

UMLsec notation can be extended quite nicely to UML 2.0 composite structure diagrams, one should note that this information can already be expressed in UML 1.5 static structure and deployment diagrams, so using UML 1.5 is not a restriction in this respect. Note that while deployment diagrams and component diagrams are integrated in UML 1.5, they are written in different diagrams in UML 2.0.

UML 2.0 also adds quite a few new model elements for existing diagram types. These include state machine extensions, gates in interaction diagrams, and power types in class diagrams. They are not very particular to secure software engineering but are also not in conflict with the UMLsec notation and can be used within the context of the approach presented in this book without any problems. Similarly, some existing model elements have been changed, but most of these do not appear in our treatment in this book at all. In particular, we do not make use of any UML 1.5 model elements that have been dropped in UML 2.0. In UML 2.0 sequence diagrams, *interaction frames* extend the guards used in UML 1.5 sequence diagrams to specify conditional behavior. Again, this extension can be used with UMLsec as well, although it remains to be seen in which situations the added expressivity outweighs the increase of complexity in the notation. Stereotypes are in UML 2.0 more tightly defined than before and exclude a previous usage as a kind of keywords, but include the usage of stereotypes in UMLsec. Activity diagrams are defined more liberally in UML 2.0 than before: While UML 1.x views activity diagrams formally as a special case of statechart diagram, this imposes some constraints on the structure of a diagram that are removed in UML 2.0, for example that forks and joins have to match. To accommodate this liberalization, the semantics is now formulated in a Petri-net style by referring to token flows. Swimlanes can be multidimensional in UML 2.0 and are called partitions.

B

The Semantics of UML Machine Rules

We give a formal definition for the semantics of UML Machine rules. It is inspired by those for Abstract State Machines in [SSB01, BS00].

Definition B.1 (Update). *An* update *for a UML Machine A is a triple (f, $a_1, \ldots, a_n$), b), where f is an n-ary function name, and $a_1, \ldots, a_n$ and b are elements of the base set of A.*

Thus an update specifies that the interpretation of the function f in A has to be changed at the arguments $a_1, \ldots, a_n$ to the value b. An update set is a set of updates.

For two update sets U, V, we define the update set $U; V$ (U followed by V) as follows: $U; V \overset{\text{def}}{=} \{(f, a, b) \in U : \neg \exists c.(f, a, c) \in V\} \cup V$.

A transition rule of a UML Machine produces, in any given state, an update set for each variable assignment. Recursive calls to other rules are allowed; thus it is possible that a rule has no well-defined semantics at all. For the calculus that defines the semantics of transition rules in Fig. B.1 we need some further technical definitions.

Given a UML Machine A, a term t over **Voc** A, a state S of A and a variable assignment ζ which assigns the variables in t to elements of the base set X of A, we write $[\![t]\!]_\zeta^S$ for the interpretation of t over X in state S which extends ζ.

We write $\zeta[x \mapsto a]$ for the variable assignment which coincides with ζ except that it assigns the element a to the variable x. Thus:

- $\zeta[x \mapsto a](v) = a$ if $v = x$
- $\zeta[x \mapsto a](v) = \zeta(v)$ otherwise.

For a rule R and $n \geq 1$, we write R^n for the rule **seq** $R \ldots R$ **endseq** that iterates R n times.

Definition B.2 (Semantics of transition rules). *The semantics of a transition rule R of a given UML Machine A with base set X in a state S with*

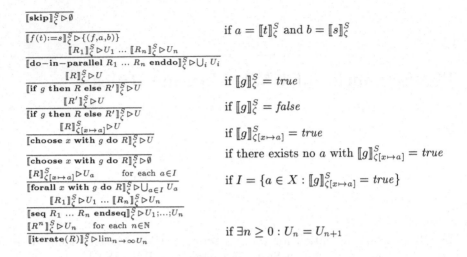

$$\overline{[\![\text{skip}]\!]^S_\zeta \triangleright \emptyset}$$

$$\overline{[\![f(t):=s]\!]^S_\zeta \triangleright \{(f,a,b)\}} \qquad \text{if } a = [\![t]\!]^S_\zeta \text{ and } b = [\![s]\!]^S_\zeta$$

$$\frac{[\![R_1]\!]^S_\zeta \triangleright U_1 \ \dots \ [\![R_n]\!]^S_\zeta \triangleright U_n}{[\![\text{do−in−parallel } R_1 \ \dots \ R_n \text{ enddo}]\!]^S_\zeta \triangleright \bigcup_i U_i}$$

$$\frac{[\![R]\!]^S_\zeta \triangleright U}{[\![\text{if } g \text{ then } R \text{ else } R']\!]^S_\zeta \triangleright U} \qquad \text{if } [\![g]\!]^S_\zeta = true$$

$$\frac{[\![R']\!]^S_\zeta \triangleright U}{[\![\text{if } g \text{ then } R \text{ else } R']\!]^S_\zeta \triangleright U} \qquad \text{if } [\![g]\!]^S_\zeta = false$$

$$\frac{[\![R]\!]^S_{\zeta[x \mapsto a]} \triangleright U}{[\![\text{choose } x \text{ with } g \text{ do } R]\!]^S_\zeta \triangleright U} \qquad \text{if } [\![g]\!]^S_{\zeta[x \mapsto a]} = true$$

$$\overline{[\![\text{choose } x \text{ with } g \text{ do } R]\!]^S_\zeta \triangleright \emptyset} \qquad \text{if there exists no } a \text{ with } [\![g]\!]^S_{\zeta[x \mapsto a]} = true$$

$$\frac{[\![R]\!]^S_{\zeta[x \mapsto a]} \triangleright U_a \qquad \text{for each } a \in I}{[\![\text{forall } x \text{ with } g \text{ do } R]\!]^S_\zeta \triangleright \bigcup_{a \in I} U_a} \qquad \text{if } I = \{a \in X : [\![g]\!]^S_{\zeta[x \mapsto a]} = true\}$$

$$\frac{[\![R_1]\!]^S_\zeta \triangleright U_1 \ \dots \ [\![R_n]\!]^S_\zeta \triangleright U_n}{[\![\text{seq } R_1 \ \dots \ R_n \text{ endseq}]\!]^S_\zeta \triangleright U_1;\dots;U_n}$$

$$\frac{[\![R^n]\!]^S_\zeta \triangleright U_n \qquad \text{for each } n \in \mathbb{N}}{[\![\text{iterate}(R)]\!]^S_\zeta \triangleright \lim_{n \to \infty} U_n} \qquad \text{if } \exists n \geq 0 : U_n = U_{n+1}$$

Fig. B.1. The semantics of UML Machine rules

respect to a variable assignment ζ is defined as an update set U such that $[\![R]\!]^S_\zeta \triangleright U$ can be derived in the calculus in Fig. B.1, if such a set exists. Otherwise, it is undefined.

Note that those rules from Sect. 7.1 whose semantics is not defined in Fig. B.1 can be defined in terms of those that are listed in Fig. B.1. Note also that there can be different update sets U such that $[\![R]\!]^S_\zeta \triangleright U$ is derivable in the calculus (because of the non-determinism introduced by the **choose with do** rule).

It is possible that the update set $[\![R]\!]^S_\zeta$ contains several updates for the same function name f. Then the updates have to be consistent in the following sense, otherwise the execution stops.

Definition B.3 (Consistent update set). *An update set U is called consistent if it satisfies the following property:*

$$\text{If } (f,(a_1,\dots,a_n),b) \in U \text{ and } (f,(a_1,\dots,a_n),c) \in U, \text{then } b = c.$$

Thus a consistent update set contains for each function and each argument tuple at most one value.

If an update set U is consistent, it can be fired in a given state. The result is a new state in which there may be function names the interpretations of which are changed according to U.

Definition B.4 (Firing of updates). *The result of firing a consistent update set U in a state S of the UML Machine A is a new state T of A satisfying the following two conditions for each function name $f \in \text{Voc}\, A$:*

- If $(f, (a_1, \ldots, a_n), b) \in U$, then $[\![f]\!]^T(a_1, \ldots, a_n) = b$.
- If there is no b with $(f, (a_1, \ldots, a_n), b) \in U$, then $[\![f]\!]^T(a_1, \ldots, a_n) = [\![f]\!]^S(a_1, \ldots, a_n)$.

Definition B.5 (Run of a UML Machine). *Let M be a UML Machine with vocabulary Σ, initial state S, and main rule name R. Let ζ be a variable assignment. A* run *$r \in \mathbf{Run}\, M$ of M is a finite or infinite sequence $S_0, S_1, \ldots$ of states for Σ such that the following conditions are satisfied:*

- $S_0 = S$.
- *For each $n \in \mathbb{N}$, if S_n is the last element of the sequence r then*
  - *for any update set U with $[\![R]\!]^{S_n}_\zeta \rhd U$, applying U leaves the state S_n unchanged, or*
  - *there exists an inconsistent update set U with $[\![R]\!]^{S_n}_\zeta \rhd U$.*
- *For each $n \in \mathbb{N}$, if S_n is not the last element of the sequence r, then there exists a consistent update set U with $[\![R]\!]^{S_n}_\zeta \rhd U$ in S_n such that S_{n+1} is the result of firing U, and such that $S_{n+1} \neq S_n$.*

C

Proofs

We give here proof sketches for the statements from Chaps. 5, 7, and 8. Note that the proofs for the statements in Chap. 5 are performed with respect to the formal definitions and results in Chaps. 7 and 8, rather than the informal exposition in Sect. 3.3, and are thus deferred to the end of this chapter. Note also that it is not intended to propose manual reasoning to establish security analysis results as in Chap. 5 in the context of security engineering with UMLsec in practice. Instead, tool support for analyzing UMLsec specifications should be used as discussed in Chap. 6. Manual proofs are presented here to demonstrate that UMLsec is suitable overall to express important security properties in a way that allows detailed formal security analysis.

C.1 UML Machines

Example

Fact 7.4. *For each sequence* $(I_1, \ldots, I_n)$, $[\![Sndr]\!](I_1, \ldots, I_n)$ *consists of those sequences* $(O_1, \ldots, O_n)$ *that fulfill the following conditions, for each* $i \in \{1, \ldots, n\}$:

- $O_i \subseteq \{\,transmit\,\}$.
- $\sharp(O_1 \uplus \ldots \uplus O_i) \leq \sharp(I_1 \uplus \ldots \uplus I_{i-1}) \backslash \{\,send\,\}$.
- *The conditions that*

$$\sharp(I_j \uplus \ldots \uplus I_{i-1}) - \sharp((I_j \uplus \ldots \uplus I_{i-1}) \backslash \{\,send\,\}) < i - j - 2 * \sharp(O_j \uplus \ldots \uplus O_{i-1})$$

for each $j < i$ *and that* $\sharp(O_1 \uplus \ldots \uplus O_{i-1}) < \sharp(I_1 \uplus \ldots \uplus I_{i-1}) \backslash \{\,send\,\}$ *imply* $\sharp O_i > 0$.

Proof. To see that the above characterization of the behavior of $[\![Sndr]\!](I_1, \ldots, I_n)$ is correct, one has to convince oneself that the given conditions are necessary and sufficient for a sequence $(O_1, \ldots, O_n)$ to be contained in $[\![Sndr]\!](I_1, \ldots, I_n)$, for any sequence $(I_1, \ldots, I_n)$.

We first consider necessity. The first condition is necessary, because $[\![Sndr]\!]()$ only outputs messages *transmit*, on any input. The second condition is necessary, because the UML Machine only outputs a message for each *send* that is received. The third condition is necessary because the UML Machine will output a message at execution round i provided that, firstly, there is still a *send* message in the input queue that has not yet prompted a *transmit* output, and, secondly, we have currState $= Send$, because any other input received apart from *send* messages has already been consumed.

To consider sufficiency of the conditions, suppose we are given sequences $(O_1, \ldots, O_n)$ and $(I_1, \ldots, I_n)$ such that the three conditions are fulfilled. Then $(O_1, \ldots, O_n)$ is contained in $[\![Sndr]\!](I_1, \ldots, I_n)$, because from the two sequences we can construct an internal behavior of the UML Machine *Sndr* with the sequence C_i of contents of currState which produces the sequence of outputs $(O_1, \ldots, O_n)$ given the sequence of inputs $(I_1, \ldots, I_n)$: for each i, if $O_i = \{\!\{transmit\}\!\}$ then $C_i = Send$, otherwise $C_i = Wait$.

C.2 Refinement

Fact 7.8. *(Delayed)* $\mathcal{E}$-$(\mathbf{i}, \mathbf{o})$-*refinement of UML Machines is a preorder for each set of events* $\mathcal{E} \subseteq$ **Events** *and tuples* $\mathbf{i}$ *and* $\mathbf{o}$ *of input and output names.*

Proof. We show that (delayed) $\mathcal{E}$-$(\mathbf{i}, \mathbf{o})$-refinement is reflexive for each set of events $\mathcal{E} \subseteq$ **Events** and tuples $\mathbf{i}$ and $\mathbf{o}$ of input and output names. For any UML Machine A, any set $\mathcal{E} \subseteq$ **Events**, tuples $\mathbf{i}$ and $\mathbf{o}$ of input and output names, and sequence $\mathbf{I}$ of event multi-sets, we have $[\![A]\!]_{\mathbf{i},\mathbf{o}}(\mathbf{I}) \frown \mathcal{E} \subseteq [\![A]\!]_{\mathbf{i},\mathbf{o}}(\mathbf{I}) \frown \mathcal{E}$ and $[\![A]\!]_{\mathbf{i},\mathbf{o}}(\mathbf{I}) \frown \mathcal{E} \underset{\sim}{\subseteq} [\![A]\!]_{\mathbf{i},\mathbf{o}}(\mathbf{I}) \frown \mathcal{E}$ since $\subseteq$ and $\underset{\sim}{\subseteq}$ are reflexive.

We show that (delayed) $\mathcal{E}$-$(\mathbf{i}, \mathbf{o})$-refinement is transitive for each set of events $\mathcal{E} \subseteq$ **Events** and tuples $\mathbf{i}$ and $\mathbf{o}$ of input and output names. Suppose we are given the UML Machines A, A', and A'', tuples $\mathbf{i}$ and $\mathbf{o}$ of input and output names, and a set $\mathcal{E} \subseteq$ **Events**, such that A' (delayed) $\mathcal{E}$-$(\mathbf{i}, \mathbf{o})$-refines A and A'' (delayed) $\mathcal{E}$-$(\mathbf{i}, \mathbf{o})$-refines A'. To show that A'' (delayed) $\mathcal{E}$-$(\mathbf{i}, \mathbf{o})$-refines A, suppose we are given a sequence $\mathbf{I} = I_1, \ldots, I_n$ of event multi-sets with $\bigcup_i \lfloor I_i \rfloor \subseteq \mathcal{E}$. We have to show that $[\![A'']\!]_{\mathbf{i},\mathbf{o}}(\mathbf{I}) \frown \mathcal{E} \subseteq [\![A]\!]_{\mathbf{i},\mathbf{o}}(\mathbf{I}) \frown \mathcal{E}$ and $[\![A'']\!]_{\mathbf{i},\mathbf{o}}(\mathbf{I}) \frown \mathcal{E} \underset{\sim}{\subseteq} [\![A]\!]_{\mathbf{i},\mathbf{o}}(\mathbf{I}) \frown \mathcal{E}$. By assumption, we know that we have $[\![A']\!]_{\mathbf{i},\mathbf{o}}(\mathbf{I}) \frown \mathcal{E} \subseteq [\![A]\!]_{\mathbf{i},\mathbf{o}}(\mathbf{I}) \frown \mathcal{E}$ and $[\![A'']\!]_{\mathbf{i},\mathbf{o}}(\mathbf{I}) \frown \mathcal{E} \subseteq [\![A']\!]_{\mathbf{i},\mathbf{o}}(\mathbf{I}) \frown \mathcal{E}$, and $[\![A']\!]_{\mathbf{i},\mathbf{o}}(\mathbf{I}) \frown \mathcal{E} \underset{\sim}{\subseteq} [\![A]\!]_{\mathbf{i},\mathbf{o}}(\mathbf{I}) \frown \mathcal{E}$ and $[\![A'']\!]_{\mathbf{i},\mathbf{o}}(\mathbf{I}) \frown \mathcal{E} \underset{\sim}{\subseteq} [\![A']\!]_{\mathbf{i},\mathbf{o}}(\mathbf{I}) \frown \mathcal{E}$. We can conclude by transitivity of $\subseteq$ and $\underset{\sim}{\subseteq}$.

Fact 7.10. *If the UMS* $\mathcal{A}'$ *is a refinement of the UMS* $\mathcal{A}$ *then the UML Machine* **Exec** $\mathcal{A}'$ *is a refinement of the UML Machine* **Exec** $\mathcal{A}$.

Proof. Suppose we are given UMSs $\mathcal{A}'$ and $\mathcal{A}$ such that $\mathcal{A}'$ is a refinement of $\mathcal{A}$. We need to show that the UML Machine $\mathcal{A}'$ is a refinement of the UML Machine $\mathcal{A}$.

The link structures of $\mathcal{A}$ and $\mathcal{A}'$ are the same by definition of refinement for UMSs. It is thus sufficient to show that each sequence of contents of the family of link queues $(\text{linkQu}_{\mathcal{A}'}(l))_{l \in \text{Links}_{\mathcal{A}'}}$ is also a sequence of contents of the family $(\text{linkQu}_{\mathcal{A}}(l))_{l \in \text{Links}_{\mathcal{A}}}$. This follows from the assumption that $\mathcal{A}'$ is a refinement of $\mathcal{A}$ and from the definition of refinement of UMSs, which implies that there are bijections b and $b_{\mathcal{C}}$ as in Definition 7.9 such that for each component $\mathcal{C} \in \text{Comp}_{\mathcal{A}}$ and activity $A \in \text{Act}_{\mathcal{C}}^{\mathcal{A}}$, the UML Machine of $b_{\mathcal{C}}(A)$ is a $(\mathbf{i}, \mathbf{o})$-refinement of the A Machine where $\mathbf{i} = \text{Att}_{\mathcal{C}}^{\mathcal{A}}$ and $\mathbf{o} = \mathbf{i} \cup \{\text{finished}_A\}$.

Fact 7.11. *Refinement of UMSs is a preorder.*

Proof. We show that refinement of UMSs is reflexive. For any UMS $\mathcal{A} = (\text{Comp}_{\mathcal{A}}, \text{Sched}_{\mathcal{A}}, \text{Links}_{\mathcal{A}}, \text{Msgs}_{\mathcal{A}})$, the identity functions $b \overset{\text{def}}{=} \text{id} : \text{Comp}_{\mathcal{A}} \to \text{Comp}_{\mathcal{A}}$ (and similarly the $b_{\mathcal{C}}$) fulfill the required conditions by Fact 7.8.

We show that refinement of UMSs is transitive. Suppose we are given UMSs $\mathcal{A} = (\text{Comp}_{\mathcal{A}}, \text{Sched}_{\mathcal{A}}, \text{Links}_{\mathcal{A}}, \text{Msgs}_{\mathcal{A}})$, $\mathcal{A}' = (\text{Comp}_{\mathcal{A}'}, \text{Sched}_{\mathcal{A}'}, \text{Links}_{\mathcal{A}'}, \text{Msgs}_{\mathcal{A}'})$, and $\mathcal{A}'' = (\text{Comp}_{\mathcal{A}''}, \text{Sched}_{\mathcal{A}''}, \text{Links}_{\mathcal{A}''}, \text{Msgs}_{\mathcal{A}''})$, such that $\mathcal{A}'$ *refines* $\mathcal{A}$ and $\mathcal{A}''$ *refines* $\mathcal{A}'$. Thus we have bijections $b : \text{Comp}_{\mathcal{A}} \to \text{Comp}_{\mathcal{A}'}$ and $b' : \text{Comp}_{\mathcal{A}'} \to \text{Comp}_{\mathcal{A}''}$ (and similarly for the $b_{\mathcal{C}}$) fulfilling the above conditions. To show that $\mathcal{A}''$ *refines* $\mathcal{A}$, we note that the bijection $b' \circ b : \text{Comp}_{\mathcal{A}} \to \text{Comp}_{\mathcal{A}''}$ (and similarly the $b_{\mathcal{C}}$) fulfills the conditions as well, by Fact 7.8.

Fact 7.12. *Suppose we are given a parameterized UMS $\mathcal{A}(\mathcal{Y}_1, \ldots, \mathcal{Y}_n)$, where the activity variable $\mathcal{Y}_i$ belongs to the component C_i, for each $i = 1, \ldots, n$, and that we are given UMSs $\mathcal{A}_i$ and $\mathcal{A}_i'$ for each i.*

If for each $i = 1, \ldots, n$, $\mathbf{Exec}\,\mathcal{A}_i'$ is a $(\mathbf{i}_i, \mathbf{o}_i)$-refinement of $\mathbf{Exec}\,\mathcal{A}_i$ where $\mathbf{i}_i = \text{Att}_{C_i}^{\mathcal{A}}$ and $\mathbf{o}_i = \mathbf{i}_i \cup \{\text{finished}_{\mathbf{Exec}\,\mathcal{A}_i}\}$ then $\mathcal{A}(\mathbf{Exec}\,\mathcal{A}_1', \ldots, \mathbf{Exec}\,\mathcal{A}_n')$ is a refinement of $\mathcal{A}(\mathbf{Exec}\,\mathcal{A}_1, \ldots, \mathbf{Exec}\,\mathcal{A}_n)$.

Proof. Suppose we are given a parameterized UMS $\mathcal{A}(\mathcal{Y}_1, \ldots, \mathcal{Y}_n)$, where the activity variable $\mathcal{Y}_i$ belongs to the component C_i, for each $i = 1, \ldots, n$, and that we are given UMSs $\mathcal{A}_i$ and $\mathcal{A}_i'$ for each i. Suppose that $\mathbf{Exec}\,\mathcal{A}_i'$ is a $(\mathbf{i}_i, \mathbf{o}_i)$-refinement of $\mathbf{Exec}\,\mathcal{A}_i$ where $\mathbf{i}_i = \text{Att}_{C_i}^{\mathcal{A}}$ and $\mathbf{o}_i = \mathbf{i}_i \cup \{\text{finished}_{\mathbf{Exec}\,\mathcal{A}_i}\}$, for each $i = 1, \ldots, n$. We have to show that $\mathcal{A}(\mathbf{Exec}\,\mathcal{A}_1', \ldots, \mathbf{Exec}\,\mathcal{A}_n')$ is a refinement of $\mathcal{A}(\mathbf{Exec}\,\mathcal{A}_1, \ldots, \mathbf{Exec}\,\mathcal{A}_n)$.

Firstly, we have $\text{Msgs}_{\mathcal{A}(\mathcal{A}_1, \ldots, \mathcal{A}_n)} = \text{Msgs}_{\mathcal{A}} = \text{Msgs}_{\mathcal{A}(\mathcal{A}_1', \ldots, \mathcal{A}_n')}$ by construction.

Secondly, we have the bijections mapping $\mathcal{A}_i$ to $\mathcal{A}_i'$ for each i and being the identity on the other activities; they fulfill the required conditions by supposition on the $\mathcal{A}_i$ and $\mathcal{A}_i'$.

Theorem 7.13. *Refinement of UMSs is a precongruence with respect to composition by system formation.*

Proof. This follows from Facts 7.11 and 7.12.

Corollary 7.15. *Equivalence of UMSs is a congruence with respect to composition by system formation.*

Proof. This follows from Theorem 7.13.

Theorem 7.17. *Each UMS $\mathcal{A}$ is a $\mathcal{I}d$-interface refinement of itself, where $\mathcal{I}d(\mathcal{Y}) \overset{\text{def}}{=} \mathcal{Y}$.*

For all UMSs $\mathcal{A}$, $\mathcal{A}'$, and $\mathcal{A}''$ such that $\mathcal{A}'$ is a $\mathcal{I}$-interface refinement of $\mathcal{A}$ and $\mathcal{A}''$ is a $\mathcal{I}'$-interface refinement of $\mathcal{A}'$, $\mathcal{A}''$ is a $\mathcal{I}' \circ \mathcal{I}$-interface refinement of $\mathcal{A}$, where $\mathcal{I}' \circ \mathcal{I}(\mathcal{Y}) \overset{\text{def}}{=} \mathcal{I}'(\mathcal{I}(\mathcal{Y}))$.

Proof. Suppose we have a UMS $\mathcal{A}$ and define $\mathcal{I}d(\mathcal{Y}) \overset{\text{def}}{=} \mathcal{Y}$. Then we have $\mathcal{I}d(\mathcal{A}) = \mathcal{A}$ which is a refinement of $\mathcal{A}$ by reflexivity of refinement (see Theorem 7.13). Thus $\mathcal{A}$ is a $\mathcal{I}d$-interface refinement of itself.

Suppose we have UMSs $\mathcal{A}$, $\mathcal{A}'$, and $\mathcal{A}''$ such that $\mathcal{A}'$ is a $\mathcal{I}$-interface refinement of $\mathcal{A}$ and $\mathcal{A}''$ is a $\mathcal{I}'$-interface refinement of $\mathcal{A}'$, and define $\mathcal{I}' \circ \mathcal{I}(\mathcal{Y}) \overset{\text{def}}{=} \mathcal{I}'(\mathcal{I}(\mathcal{Y}))$. Then we have $\mathcal{I}' \circ \mathcal{I}(\mathcal{A}) = \mathcal{I}'(\mathcal{I}(\mathcal{A}))$. By assumption, we know that $\mathcal{A}'$ is a refinement of $\mathcal{I}(\mathcal{A})$ and that $\mathcal{A}''$ is a refinement of $\mathcal{I}'(\mathcal{A}')$. By substitutivity of refinement, we derive that $\mathcal{I}'(\mathcal{A}')$ is a refinement of $\mathcal{I}'(\mathcal{I}(\mathcal{A}))$, and by transitivity of refinement, this implies that $\mathcal{A}''$ is a refinement of $\mathcal{I}'(\mathcal{I}(\mathcal{A}))$ (see Theorem 7.13). Thus $\mathcal{A}''$ is a $\mathcal{I}' \circ \mathcal{I}$-interface refinement of $\mathcal{A}$.

C.3 Rely-Guarantee Specifications

Theorem 7.19. *Suppose that the UML Machine A fulfills the rely-guarantee specification (R, G) where $R \frown \mathcal{E} = R$ and $G \frown \mathcal{E} = G$, and suppose $E = \{\mathbf{I} : \mathbf{I} \frown \mathcal{E} = \mathbf{I}\}$.*

If the UML Machine A' $\mathcal{E}$-refines A and A' fulfills the rely-guarantee specification (R, E) then A' fulfills the rely-guarantee specification (R, G).

If the UML Machine A' delayed $\mathcal{E}$-refines A, G is stutter-closed, and A' fulfills the rely-guarantee specification (R, E), then A' fulfills the rely-guarantee specification (R, G).

Proof. Suppose that the UML Machine A fulfills the rely-guarantee specification (R, G) and the UML Machine A' $\mathcal{E}$-refines A, with $R \frown \mathcal{E} = R$ and $G \frown \mathcal{E} = G$. We need to show that A' fulfills the rely-guarantee specification (R, G). Suppose we are given $\mathbf{I} \in R$. We need to show that $[\![A']\!](\mathbf{I}) \subseteq G$. By assumption on A, we know that $[\![A]\!](\mathbf{I}) \subseteq G$. By assumption on A', we have $[\![A']\!](\mathbf{I}) \subseteq [\![A']\!](\mathbf{I}) \frown \mathcal{E} \subseteq [\![A]\!](\mathbf{I}) \frown \mathcal{E}$. Thus we may conclude that $[\![A']\!](\mathbf{I}) \subseteq G$, as required, since $G \frown \mathcal{E} = G$.

The proof for delayed refinement is analogous, using the fact that G is stutter-closed to conclude that $[\![A']\!](\mathbf{I}) \subseteq G$ from the fact that $[\![A']\!](\mathbf{I}) \subsetneq [\![A]\!](\mathbf{I}) \subseteq G$.

C.4 Reasoning About Security Properties

Fact 7.21. *Suppose we are given a UMS $\mathcal{A}$, an adversary $adv \in \mathsf{Advers}_A(\mathcal{A})$ of type A, and an execution $\mathbf{e} \in \mathbf{Run}\,\mathcal{A}_{adv}$. Then after execution of $\mathbf{e}$, knows evaluates to $\mathcal{K}^{\mathbf{e}}_{adv}(\mathcal{A})$.*

Proof. Suppose the execution $\mathbf{e}$ of $\mathcal{A}_{adv}$ has been executed. We need to show that an expression E is in the set which is the value of knows after execution of $\mathbf{e}$ if and only if $E \in \mathcal{K}^{\mathbf{e}}_{adv}(\mathcal{A})$. This is, however, the case by definition of $\mathcal{K}^{\mathbf{e}}_{adv}(\mathcal{A})$.

Fact 7.22. *Given a UMS $\mathcal{A}$ and an adversary $adv \in \mathsf{Advers}_A(\mathcal{A})$ of type A, the set knows of $\mathcal{A}_{adv}$ evaluates to a subset of $\mathcal{K}_A(\mathcal{A})$, at any point.*

Proof. Suppose we are given a system $\mathcal{A}$ and an expression $E \in$ knows. We need to show that E evaluates to an element of $\mathcal{K}_A(\mathcal{A})$. Suppose we are given an adversary $adv \in \mathsf{Advers}_A(\mathcal{A})$ and an execution $\mathbf{e}$ of $\mathcal{A}_{adv}$. By Fact 7.21, we know that after execution of $\mathbf{e}$, E evaluates to an element of $\mathcal{K}^{\mathbf{e}}_{adv}(\mathcal{A})$. Therefore, E evaluates to an element of $\mathcal{K}_A(\mathcal{A})$, by definition of $\mathcal{K}_A(\mathcal{A})$.

Fact 7.23. *Given a UMS $\mathcal{A}$ with a name v and an adversary $adv \in \mathsf{Advers}_A(\mathcal{A})$ of type A, then during any run $\mathbf{e} \in \mathbf{Run}\,\mathcal{A}_{adv}$, the name v evaluates to an element of $\mathcal{I}_A(\mathcal{A}, v)$, at any point.*

Proof. Suppose we are given a UMS $\mathcal{A}$ with a name v, an adversary $adv \in \mathsf{Advers}_A(\mathcal{A})$ of type A, and an expression $E \in \mathbf{Exp}$ which is a value of the name v after an execution $\mathbf{e}$ of $\mathcal{A}$. We need to show that $E \in \mathcal{I}_A(\mathcal{A}, v)$. By the definition of $\mathcal{I}^{\mathbf{e}}_{adv}(\mathcal{A}, v)$, we know that $E \in \mathcal{I}^{\mathbf{e}}_{adv}(\mathcal{A}, v)$. Therefore, $E \in \mathcal{I}_A(\mathcal{A}, v)$, by definition of $\mathcal{I}_A(\mathcal{A}, v)$.

Fact 7.25. *Suppose we are given UMSs $\mathcal{A}$ and $\mathcal{B}$ such that $\mathcal{B}$ is a refinement of $\mathcal{A}$, and an adversary type A, such that the accessible knowledge for A in $\mathcal{B}$ is no larger than that in $\mathcal{A}$. Then the UMS $\mathcal{B}$ is a black-box refinement in presence of adversaries of type A of the UMS $\mathcal{A}$.*

Proof. Suppose we are given UMSs $\mathcal{B}$ and $\mathcal{A}$ such that $\mathcal{B}$ is a refinement of $\mathcal{A}$, and an adversary adv' of a given type A. We need to show that there exists an adversary adv the UML Machine $\mathcal{B}_{adv'}$ is a black-box refinement of the UML Machine $\mathcal{A}_{adv}$.

Since the link structures of $\mathcal{A}$ and $\mathcal{B}$ are the same by definition of refinement for UMSs, it is sufficient to show that each possible sequence of contents of the family $(\mathsf{linkQu}_\mathcal{B}(l))_{l \in \mathsf{Links}_\mathcal{B}}$ of multi-set names is also a possible sequence of contents of the family $(\mathsf{linkQu}_\mathcal{A}(l))_{l \in \mathsf{Links}_\mathcal{A}}$. This follows from the assumption that $\mathcal{B}$ is a refinement of $\mathcal{A}$ and from the definition of refinement of UMSs, which implies that there are bijections b and $b_\mathcal{C}$ as in Definition 7.9 such that for each component $\mathcal{C} \in \mathsf{Comp}_\mathcal{A}$ and activity $A \in \mathsf{Act}^{\mathcal{A}}_\mathcal{C}$, the UML Machine of $b_\mathcal{C}(A)$ is a $(\mathbf{i}, \mathbf{o})$-refinement of the A Machine where $\mathbf{i} = \mathsf{Att}^{\mathcal{A}}_\mathcal{C}$ and $\mathbf{o} = \mathbf{i} \cup \{\mathsf{finished}_A\}$.

Theorem 7.27. *A UMS $\mathcal{A}$ preserves the secrecy of E against adversaries of type A if and only if $E \notin \mathcal{K}_A(\mathcal{A})$.*

Proof. Suppose that we are given a UMS $\mathcal{A}$, an expression $E \in \mathbf{Exp}$, and an adversary type A.

Firstly, we show that if $\mathcal{A}$ preserves the secrecy of E against adversaries of type A then $E \notin \mathcal{K}_A(\mathcal{A})$. We proceed by contraposition. We assume that we have $E \in \mathcal{K}_A(\mathcal{A})$. We need to show that $\mathcal{A}$ does not preserve the secrecy of E against adversaries of type A. By definition of preservation of secrecy, it is sufficient to show that there is an adversary $adv \in \mathsf{Advers}_A(A)$, an input sequence $\mathbf{i}$, and a sequence $s \in [\![\mathcal{A}_{adv}]\!]_{\emptyset,\{\mathsf{knows}\}}(\mathbf{i})$ such that one of the knowledge sets in s contains E. By the assumption $E \in \mathcal{K}_A(\mathcal{A})$ and the definition of $\mathcal{K}_A(\mathcal{A})$, we know that we have $E \in \mathcal{K}_A^n(\mathcal{A})$ for some $n \in \mathbb{N}$. Thus there is an adversary adv and an execution $\mathbf{e}$ of length n such that $E \in \mathcal{K}_{adv}^{\mathbf{e}}(\mathcal{A})$. Thus $E \in \mathsf{knows}$ after the nth iteration of $\mathcal{A}_{adv}$.

Secondly, we show that if $E \notin \mathcal{K}_A(\mathcal{A})$ then $\mathcal{A}$ preserves the secrecy of E against adversaries of type A. Suppose that $E \notin \mathcal{K}_A(\mathcal{A})$. We need to show that $\mathcal{A}$ preserves the secrecy of E against adversaries of type A; that is, for every adversary adv of type A, input sequence $\mathbf{i}$, and sequence $s \in [\![\mathcal{A}_{adv}]\!]_{\emptyset,\{\mathsf{knows}\}}(\mathbf{I})$, the knowledge sets in s do not contain E. Suppose we are given such an adversary adv, input sequence $\mathbf{i}$, and a sequence $s \in [\![\mathcal{A}_{adv}]\!]_{\emptyset,\{\mathsf{knows}\}}(\mathbf{I})$. It follows from Fact 7.22 that the knowledge sets in s do not contain E, since we have $E \notin \mathcal{K}_A(\mathcal{A})$ by assumption on E.

Theorem 7.28. *If the UMS $\mathcal{A}$ preserves the secrecy of E from adversaries of type A and the UMS $\mathcal{B}$ (delayed) refines $\mathcal{A}$, such that the accessible knowledge for A in $\mathcal{B}$ is no larger than that in $\mathcal{A}$, then $\mathcal{B}$ preserves the secrecy of E from adversaries of type A given inputs in $\mathcal{E}$.*

Proof. Suppose we are given a UMS $\mathcal{A}$ that preserves the secrecy of a given expression E from adversaries of type A given inputs in $\mathcal{E}$ for $\mathcal{E} \subseteq \mathbf{Events}$. Suppose that the UMS $\mathcal{B}$ refines $\mathcal{A}$. We need to show that $\mathcal{B}$ preserves the secrecy of E from adversaries of type A given inputs in $\mathcal{E}$.

Suppose we are given an adversary $adv \in \mathsf{Advers}_B(A)$ and an execution $\mathbf{e}$ of $\mathcal{B}_{adv}$. Since $\mathcal{B}$ refines $\mathcal{A}$, we have $adv \in \mathsf{Advers}_A(A)$, and $\mathbf{e}$ is an execution of $\mathcal{A}_{adv}$, as far as observable to the adversary (up to stutter-equivalence, in the delayed case). Since $\mathcal{A}$ is assumed to preserve the secrecy of E, we conclude that $\mathcal{B}$ does, as well.

Theorem 7.29. *If the UMS $\mathcal{A}$ preserves the secrecy of E from adversaries of type A and the UMS $\mathcal{B}$ is a black-box refinement in presence of adversaries of type A of the UMS $\mathcal{A}$ then $\mathcal{B}$ preserves the secrecy of E from adversaries of type A.*

Proof. This directly follows from the Definition 7.24 of *black-box refinement in presence of adversaries*.

Theorem 7.31. *Each UMS $\mathcal{A}$ preserves the integrity of a variable v with respect to a set $E \subseteq \mathbf{Exp}$ of acceptable expressions against adversaries of type A if $\mathcal{I}_A(\mathcal{A}, v) \subseteq E$.*

Proof. Suppose that we are given a UMS $\mathcal{A}$, a variable v, a set $E \subseteq \mathbf{Exp}$ of acceptable expressions, and an adversary type A. We show that if $\mathcal{I}_A(\mathcal{A}, v) \subseteq E$ then $\mathcal{A}$ preserves the integrity of v respect to E against adversaries of type A. Suppose that $\mathcal{I}_A(\mathcal{A}, v) \subseteq E$. To show that $\mathcal{A}$ preserves the integrity of v with respect to E, it is sufficient to show that for every adversary adv of type A and every input sequence $\mathbf{i}$, v does not contain a value $a \notin E$ at any point. Suppose we are given such an adversary adv and an input sequence $\mathbf{i}$ such that at some point, v has the value a. By Fact 7.23 we can conclude that $a \in E$, by assumption on $\mathcal{I}_A(\mathcal{A}, v)$.

Theorem 7.32. *Suppose we are given UMSs $\mathcal{A}$ and $\mathcal{B}$. Suppose that $\mathcal{A}$ preserves the integrity of v with respect to a set $E \subseteq \mathbf{Exp}$ of acceptable expressions from adversaries of type A given inputs in $\mathcal{E}$ and that the UMS $\mathcal{B}$ is a $(\emptyset, \{v\})$-black-box refinement in presence of adversaries of type A of the UMS $\mathcal{A}$. Then $\mathcal{B}$ preserves the integrity of v with respect to E from adversaries of type A given inputs in $\mathcal{E}$.*

Proof. Suppose we are given a UMS $\mathcal{A}$ that preserves the integrity of a given expression v with respect to a set $E \subseteq \mathbf{Exp}$ of acceptable expressions from adversaries of type A given inputs in $\mathcal{E}$ for $\mathcal{E} \subseteq \mathbf{Events}$. Suppose that the UMS $\mathcal{B}$ $(\emptyset, \{v\})$-refines the UMS $\mathcal{A}$. We need to show that $\mathcal{B}$ preserves the integrity of v with respect to a set $E \subseteq \mathbf{Exp}$ of acceptable expressions from adversaries of type A given inputs in $\mathcal{E}$.

Suppose we are given $adv \in \mathsf{Advers}_\mathcal{B}(A)$ and an input sequence $\mathbf{i}$. We need to show that at no point of the execution of $\mathcal{B}_{adv}$ on the inputs $\mathbf{i}$, v takes on a value not contained in E.

Since $\mathcal{B}$ $(\emptyset, \{v\})$-refines the UMS $\mathcal{A}$. we have $adv \in \mathsf{Advers}_\mathcal{A}(A)$, and any value of v in $\mathcal{B}$ is also a value of v in $\mathcal{A}$. Since $\mathcal{A}$ is assumed to preserve the integrity of v, we conclude that at no point of the execution of $\mathcal{B}_{adv}$ on the inputs $\mathbf{i}$, v takes on a value not contained in E.

Theorem 7.34. *Suppose we are given UMSs $\mathcal{A}$ and $\mathcal{B}$. Suppose that $\mathcal{A}$ provides authenticity of v with respect to its origin o from adversaries of type A given inputs in $\mathcal{E}$ and that the UMS $\mathcal{B}$ is a $(\emptyset, \{v, o\})$-white-box refinement of the UMS $\mathcal{A}$, such that the accessible knowledge for A in $\mathcal{B}$ is no larger than that in $\mathcal{A}$. Then $\mathcal{B}$ provides authenticity of v with respect to its origin o from adversaries of type A given inputs in $\mathcal{E}$.*

Proof. Suppose we are given UMSs $\mathcal{A}$ and $\mathcal{B}$. Suppose that $\mathcal{A}$ provides authenticity of v with respect to its origin o from adversaries of type A given inputs in $\mathcal{E}$ and that the UMS $\mathcal{B}$ is a $(\emptyset, \{v, o\})$-refinement of the UMS $\mathcal{A}$.

We would like to show that $\mathcal{B}$ provides authenticity of v with respect to its origin o from adversaries of type A given inputs in $\mathcal{E}$, which means that for all $adv \in \mathsf{Advers}_\mathcal{B}(A)$ and each input sequence **i** whose multi-sets only contain elements in $\mathcal{E}$, at any point of the execution of $\mathcal{B}_{adv}$ on the inputs **i**, v takes on a value which appeared first within the execution outQu_o, of all output queues and link queues in $\mathcal{B}$.

Suppose we are given an adversary $adv \in \mathsf{Advers}_\mathcal{B}(A)$ and an input sequence **i** whose multi-sets only contain elements in $\mathcal{E}$. Since $\mathcal{B}$ is a $(\emptyset, \{v, o\})$-refinement of $\mathcal{A}$, we have $adv \in \mathsf{Advers}_\mathcal{A}(A)$. Since $\mathcal{A}$ provides authenticity of v with respect to its origin o from adversaries of type A given inputs in $\mathcal{E}$, we know that at any point of the execution of $\mathcal{A}_{adv}$ on the inputs **i**, v takes on a value which appeared first within the execution outQu_o, of all output queues and link queues in $\mathcal{A}$. Again, since $\mathcal{B}$ is a $(\emptyset, \{v, o\})$-refinement of $\mathcal{A}$, this means that that at any point of the execution of $\mathcal{B}_{adv}$ on the inputs **i**, v takes on a value which appeared first within the execution outQu_o, of all output queues and link queues in $\mathcal{B}$.

Fact 7.38. *For any expression $E \in \mathbf{Data} \cup \mathbf{Var} \cup \mathbf{Keys}$ and any set of expressions $\mathcal{E}$, E is independent of $\mathcal{E}$ if there exists no expression $E' \in \mathcal{E}$ such that E is a subexpression of E'.*

Proof. Suppose we are given E and $\mathcal{E}$ as above such that there exists no expression E' of which E is a subexpression. We show that E is independent of $\mathcal{E}$, that is E is not an element of the subalgebra $\mathcal{A}$ of **Exp** generated by $\mathcal{E}$. $\mathcal{A}$ is defined to be the subset of values **Exp** obtained by recursively applying all operations of **Exp** starting with the set $\mathcal{E}$.

For each set of expressions $A \subseteq \mathbf{Exp}$ let $p(A)$ be the property that there exists no expression E' in A such that E is a subexpression of E'. We prove inductively that $E \notin \mathcal{A}$ by showing that $p(\mathcal{E})$ holds and that the validity of $p(A)$ is preserved by applying the operations of **Exp** pointwise to A:

- We have $p(\mathcal{E})$ by assumption.
- Assuming $p(A)$, we show by contraposition that for all $a_1, a_2 \in A$, E is not a subexpression of $a_1 :: a_2$. Suppose E is a subexpression of $a_1 :: a_2$ for some $a_1, a_2 \in A$. Without loss of generality, suppose that E is not a subexpression of a_1. Thus there exists a term t_1 which is equal to a_1 in **Exp** such that E is not a subterm of t_1. However, by assumption, E is a subterm of $t_1 :: t_2$ for every term t_2 which is equal to a_2 in **Exp**. Since $E \in \mathbf{Data} \cup \mathbf{Var} \cup \mathbf{Keys}$ by assumption, E is thus a subterm of every such t_2, by definition of the equations in **Exp**. Thus, E is a subexpression of a_2, by definition of subexpression.
- Suppose $p(A)$ holds. Then for every $a \in A$, E is not a subexpression of $\mathbf{head}(a)$. If E was a subterm of every term h that is equal to $\mathbf{head}(a)$ in A, then E is also a subterm of every term t that is equal to a in A, because the head of every such term t is such an h. An analogous argument applies to $\mathbf{tail}(\_)$.
- The cases for $\{\_\}_\_$, $\mathcal{S}ign\_(\_)$, and $\mathcal{H}ash(\_)$ can be treated analogously to the one for $\_ :: \_$. For $\mathcal{D}ec\_(\_)$ and $\mathcal{E}xt\_(\_)$ one needs to choose a_1, a_2, t_1, t_2 such that t_1 and t_2 are minimal in length.

Fact 7.39. *For any expression $E \in$ **Data** $\cup$ **Var** $\cup$ **Keys** and any set of expressions $\mathcal{E} \subseteq$ **Data** $\cup$ **Var** $\cup$ **Keys**, E is independent of $\mathcal{E}$ if and only if $E \notin \mathcal{E}$.*

Proof. This follows from Fact 7.38 since for $E, E' \in$ **Data** $\cup$ **Var** $\cup$ **Keys**, E is a subexpression of E' only if $E = E'$.

Fact 7.40. *Suppose we are given an atomic value $d \in$ **Data** $\cup$ **Keys** in a UMS $\mathcal{A}$ which is fresh within a component $\mathcal{D}$ contained in $\mathcal{A}$, an adversary type A which does not have access to $\mathcal{D}$ and does not have d in its set $\mathcal{K}_A^p$ of previous knowledge, and an adversary adv of type A. Then during any run $\mathbf{e} \in$ **Run** $\mathcal{A}_{adv}$, if at any state S in $\mathbf{e}$ an output or link queue outside $\mathcal{D}$ contains d as a subexpressions, then there exists a state S' preceding S in $\mathbf{e}$ where $\mathsf{outQu}_{\mathcal{D}}$ contains d as a subexpressions.*

Proof. Suppose we are given an atomic value $d \in$ **Data** $\cup$ **Keys** in a UMS $\mathcal{A}$ which is fresh within a component $\mathcal{D}$ contained in $\mathcal{A}$, an adversary type A which does not have access to $\mathcal{D}$, and an adversary adv of type A. We would like to show that during any run $\mathbf{e} \in$ **Run** $\mathcal{A}_{adv}$, if at any state S in $\mathbf{e}$ an output or link queue outside $\mathcal{D}$ contains d as a subexpressions, then there exists a state S' preceding S in $\mathbf{e}$ where $\mathsf{outQu}_{\mathcal{D}}$ contains d as a subexpressions.

Assume that we a given a run $\mathbf{e} \in$ **Run** $\mathcal{A}_{adv}$ and the first state S in $\mathbf{e}$ such that $\mathsf{outQu}_{\mathcal{D}}$ or an output or link queue outside $\mathcal{D}$ contains d as a subexpression. It is sufficient to show that in S, d is contained in $\mathsf{outQu}_{\mathcal{D}}$ and not an output or link queue outside $\mathcal{D}$, as a subexpression. According to the behavior of UMSs defined in Sect. 7.2, d can only appear as a subexpression in $\mathsf{outQu}_{\mathcal{D}}$ or in an output or link queue outside $\mathcal{D}$ after being inserted in a link queue by the adversary or after being output by a part of $\mathcal{A}$. By assumption on the capabilities and previous knowledge of the adverary, and since S was assumed to be the first state of its kind, the first possibility is ruled out. By the freshness assumption on d, and again by the assumption on S, the possibility left is that in S, d is contained in $\mathsf{outQu}_{\mathcal{D}}$ and not an output or link queue outside $\mathcal{D}$, as a subexpression.

Theorem 7.42. *Suppose that the UML Machine A prevents down-flow (resp. up-flow) with respect to the set $H \subseteq$ **MsgNm** and that the UML Machine B refines A. Then B prevents down-flow (resp. up-flow) with respect to H.*

Proof. Suppose we are given UML Machines A, B and a set of message names $H \subseteq$ **MsgNm**, such that A prevents down-flow with respect to H and that B refines A.

We have to show that B prevents down-flow with respect to H. Suppose that we are given input sequences $\mathbf{i}, \mathbf{j}$ of event multi-sets and output sequences $\mathbf{o} \in [\![B]\!](\mathbf{i})$ and $\mathbf{p} \in [\![B]\!](\mathbf{j})$ with $\mathbf{i}_H = \mathbf{j}_H$. We have to show that $\mathbf{o}_H = \mathbf{p}_H$. Since B refines A, we know that $\mathbf{o} \in [\![A]\!](\mathbf{i})$ and $\mathbf{p} \in [\![A]\!](\mathbf{j})$. Since A prevents down-flow with respect to H, this implies that $\mathbf{o}_H = \mathbf{p}_H$.

The case for prevention of down-flow is analogous.

C.5 Formal Systems Development with UML

Fact 8.1. *During each given execution of a UML specification, each occurrence of a message is created at at most one location in the specification.*

Proof. We observe that the only ways in which a message can be newly introduced into the communication queues of the UMS is via a rule **ActionRuleSC**$_S(a)$ for a *call* or *send* action a or a rule **ActionRuleSD**(msg) for a message msg: there is no usage in the formal semantics of the macro tooutQu() except in these rules, the macro toinQu() is not used at all, and there are messages added directly to the multi-sets inQu, outQu, or linkQu(). Also, in the definition of the behavior of UMSs in terms of UML Machines in Sect. 7.2, no messages are newly added to the communication queues (but only transferred between the queues).

Thus to any occurrence m_i of a message m in any of the input, output, or link queues of the UMS modeling the specification at a given point of its execution, we can associate an occurrence l_i of a *call* or *send* action in a statechart or a message sent out in a sequence diagram, such that the occurrence m_i of m originated from the occurrence l_i of the action (for $i = 1, 2$). Conversely, each such occurrence l_i, when executed, adds a new occurrence m_i of m to the communication queues, by the definition of the associated action rule.

To see that each occurrence of a message is created at at most one location, it is sufficient to see that no occurrence of a message is removed during the execution of the UMS except when messages are consumed by its recipient.

For this we observe that in the formal semantics defined in this chapter, an occurrence of a message is only removed from the communication queues of a UML specification when it is consumed while it fires a transition at its recipient. Also, in the definition of the behavior of UMSs in terms of UML Machines in Sect. 7.2, no messages are removed from the communication queues (but only transferred between the queues).

Thus each occurence of a message is created at at most one location.

Fact 8.3. *(Delayed)* $\mathcal{E}$-$(\mathbf{i}, \mathbf{o})$-*black-box refinement of UML subsystems is a preorder for each set of events* $\mathcal{E} \subseteq$ **Events** *and tuples* $\mathbf{i}$ *and* $\mathbf{o}$ *of input and output names.*

Proof. This follows from Fact 7.8.

Fact 8.5. *The UML subsystem* S' *is a white-box refinement of the UML subsystem* S *then* S' *is also a black-box refinement of* S.

Proof. This follows from Fact 7.10.

Theorem 8.6. *White-box refinement of UML subsystems is a precongruence with respect to composition by subsystem formation.*

Proof. This follows from Theorem 7.13.

Corollary 8.8. *White-box equivalence of UML subsystems is a congruence with respect to composition by subsystem formation.*

Proof. This follows from Theorem 8.6.

Theorem 8.10. *Each UML subsystem S is a $\mathcal{I}d$-interface refinement of itself, where $\mathcal{I}d(\mathcal{Y}) \stackrel{\text{def}}{=} \mathcal{Y}$.*

For all UML subsystems S, S', and S'' such that S' is a $\mathcal{I}$-interface refinement of S and S'' is a $\mathcal{I}'$-interface refinement of S', S'' is a $\mathcal{I}' \circ \mathcal{I}$-interface refinement of S, where $\mathcal{I}' \circ \mathcal{I}(\mathcal{Y}) \stackrel{\text{def}}{=} \mathcal{I}'(\mathcal{I}(\mathcal{Y}))$.

Proof. This follows from Theorem 7.17.

Theorem 8.12. *Suppose that the UML subsystem S fulfills the rely-guarantee specification (R, G) and that $R \frown \mathcal{E} = R$ and $S \frown \mathcal{E} = S$.*

If the UML subsystem S' $\mathcal{E}$-black-box refines S then S' fulfills the rely-guarantee specification (R, G).

If the UML subsystem S' delayed $\mathcal{E}$-black-box refines A and G is stutter-closed then S' fulfills the rely-guarantee specification (R, G).

Proof. This follows from Theorem 7.19.

Fact 8.14. *Suppose we are given UML subsystems S and T such that T is a refinement of S, and an adversary type A. Then the UMS $\mathcal{B}$ is a black-box refinement in presence of adversaries of type A of the UMS $\mathcal{A}$.*

Proof. This follows from Theorem 7.25.

Theorem 8.16. *Suppose we are given UML subsystems S and T.*

If the UML subsystem S preserves the secrecy of E from adversaries of type A and T is a black-box refinement in presence of adversaries of type A, or T (delayed) refines S given adversaries of type A such that the accessible knowledge for A in $\mathcal{B}$ is no larger than that in $\mathcal{A}$, then T preserves the secrecy.

If S preserves the integrity of v with respect to a set $E \subseteq \mathbf{Exp}$ of acceptable expressions from adversaries of type A given inputs in $\mathcal{E}$ and T $(\emptyset, \{v\})$-black-box refines S then T preserves the integrity of v.

If S provides authenticity of v with respect to its origin o from adversaries of type A given inputs in $\mathcal{E}$ and T is a $(\emptyset, \{v, o\})$-black-box refinement of S such that the accessible knowledge for A in $\mathcal{B}$ is no larger than that in $\mathcal{A}$, then T $\mathcal{B}$ provides authenticity.

If S prevents down-flow (resp. up-flow) with respect to the set $H \subseteq$ $\mathbf{MsgNm}$ and T white-box refines S then T prevents down-flow (resp. up-flow) with respect to H.

Proof. The results in this theorem follow from the corresponding results on UMSs in Theorems 7.29, 7.28, 7.32, 7.34, and 7.42.

C.6 Secure Channels

Proposition 5.1. *The subsystem $\mathcal{C}$ preserves the secrecy of the variable* d *from adversaries of type* $A = $ default *with specified previous knowledge* $\mathcal{K}_A^p$, *given inputs from* **Data** $\setminus \mathcal{K}_A^p$.

Note that, intuitively, this proposition is obvious, because the adversary cannot read the channels. We give the proof to illustrate how to apply the formal framework.

Proof. We have to show that for every expression E which is a value of d at any point, $\mathcal{C}$ preserves the secrecy of E.

We use Theorem 7.27. Since an adversary of type default cannot access any of the components or links in $\mathcal{C}$, we have $\mathcal{K}_A(\mathcal{C}) = \mathcal{K}_A^0$ (because there is no read access), and d takes values only in **Exp** $\setminus \mathcal{K}_A^0$ (because there is no write access).

Thus for every expression E which is a value of d at any point, $\mathcal{C}$ preserves the secrecy of E, by definition of preservation of secrecy.

Proposition 5.2. *The subsystem $\mathcal{C}'$ is a delayed black-box refinement of $\mathcal{C}$ in presence of adversaries of type* $A = $ default *with*

$$\mathcal{K}_A^p \cap (\{\mathsf{K}_S^{-1}, \mathsf{K}_R^{-1}\} \cup \{\mathsf{k}_n, \{x :: n\}_{\mathsf{k}_n} : x \in \mathbf{Exp} \wedge n \in \mathbb{N}\}) = \emptyset$$

and for which $Sign_{\mathsf{K}_R^{-1}}(\mathsf{k}' :: m) \in \mathcal{K}_A^p$ *implies* $\mathsf{k}' = \mathsf{k}_m$ *for all* $m \in \mathbb{N}$ *and* $\mathsf{k}' \in \mathbf{Exp}$.

Proof. We have to show that for every adversary b of type A for the UMS $[\![\mathcal{C}']\!]$ there exists an adversary a of type A for the UMS $[\![\mathcal{C}]\!]$ such that the derived UML Machine **Exec** $[\![\mathcal{C}']\!]_b$ is a delayed black-box refinement of the UML Machine **Exec** $[\![\mathcal{C}]\!]_a$.

Note that $\mathcal{K}_A(\mathcal{C}')$ is contained in the algebra generated by $\mathcal{K}_A^0 \cup \{\{Sign_{\mathsf{K}_R^{-1}}(\mathsf{k}_i :: j)\}_{\mathsf{K}_S}\}$ and the expressions $\{\mathsf{d} :: n\}_{\mathsf{K}}$ for inputs d: Firstly, the adversary can obtain no certificate $\{\{Sign_{\mathsf{K}_R^{-1}}(k :: j)\}_{\mathsf{K}_S}\}$ for $k \neq \mathsf{k}_j$, because the Receiver object only outputs the certificates $\{Sign_{\mathsf{K}_R^{-1}}(\mathsf{k}_j :: j)\}_{\mathsf{K}_S}$ (for $j \in \mathbb{N}$) to the Internet. Secondly, the sender outputs only messages of the form $\{\mathsf{d} :: n\}_k$ to the Internet, for inputs d and any $k \in \mathbf{Keys}$ for which a certificate $\{Sign_{\mathsf{K}_R^{-1}}(k :: n)\}_{\mathsf{K}_S}$ has been received. Here k must be K_n since no other certificate can be produced (since the key K_R^{-1} is never transmitted). Note also that $\mathcal{K}_A^p = \mathcal{K}_A^0$ since there are no components accessed by the adversary.

Also, the values that an adversary for $\mathcal{C}'$ may insert into the Internet link may only delay the behavior of the two objects regarding outQu$_{\mathcal{C}'}$ since the adversary has no other certificate signed with K_R^{-1} and does not have access to the key K_R^{-1}, and because of the transaction numbers used. Thus any other value inserted is ignored by the two objects.

For any adversary b for $\mathcal{C}'$ we can thus derive an adversary a for $\mathcal{C}$ by omitting insert and read commands such that the UML Machine **Exec** $[\![\mathcal{C}']\!]_b$

is a delayed black-box refinement of the UML Machine **Exec** $[\![\mathcal{C}]\!]_a$ (since the outputs to outQu$_\mathcal{C}$ (resp. outQu$_{\mathcal{C}'}$) are stutter-equivalent).

Proposition 5.3. *The subsystem* $\mathcal{C}'$ *preserves the secrecy of the variable* d *from adversaries of type* $A =$ default *with*

$$\mathcal{K}^{\mathsf{p}}_A \cap (\{\mathsf{K}^{-1}_\mathsf{S}, \mathsf{K}^{-1}_\mathsf{R}\} \cup \{\mathsf{k}_n, \{x :: n\}_{\mathsf{k}_n} : x \in \mathbf{Exp} \wedge n \in \mathbb{N}\}) = \emptyset$$

and for which $Sign_{\mathsf{K}^{-1}_\mathsf{R}}(\mathsf{k}' :: m) \in \mathcal{K}^{\mathsf{p}}_A$ *implies* $\mathsf{k}' = \mathsf{k}_m$ *for all* $m \in \mathbb{N}$ *and* $\mathsf{k}' \in \mathbf{Exp}$.

Proof. Since $\mathcal{C}$ preserves the secrecy of the variable d from default adversaries given inputs from **Data** \ $\mathcal{K}^{\mathsf{p}}_A$ by Proposition 5.1 and $\mathcal{C}'$ is a delayed black-box refinement of $\mathcal{C}$ given default adversaries with $\mathcal{K}^{\mathsf{p}}_A \cap (\{\mathsf{K}^{-1}_\mathsf{S}, \mathsf{K}^{-1}_\mathsf{R}, \mathsf{K}\} \cup \{\{x :: n\}_\mathsf{K} : x \in \mathbf{Exp} \wedge n \in \mathbb{N}\}) = \emptyset$ and for which $Sign_{\mathsf{K}^{-1}_\mathsf{R}}(\mathsf{k}') \in \mathcal{K}^{\mathsf{p}}_A$ implies $\mathsf{K} = \mathsf{k}'$ by Proposition 5.2, we can conclude that $\mathcal{C}'$ preserves the secrecy of the variable d from default adversaries with $\mathcal{K}^{\mathsf{p}}_A \cap (\{\mathsf{K}^{-1}_{\mathsf{CA}}, \mathsf{K}^{-1}\} \cup \{\{x :: n\}_\mathsf{K} : x \in \mathbf{Exp} \wedge n \in \mathbb{N}\}) = \emptyset$ and for which $Sign_{\mathsf{K}^{-1}_{\mathsf{CA}}}(\mathsf{R} :: \mathsf{k}') \in \mathcal{K}^{\mathsf{p}}_A$ implies $\mathsf{K} = \mathsf{k}'$, given inputs from **Data** \ $\mathcal{K}^{\mathsf{p}}_A$, by Theorem 8.16.

C.7 A Variant of the Internet Protocol TLS

The Flaw

Theorem 5.4. *For given* C *and* i, *the UML subsystem* $\mathcal{T}$ *given in Fig. 5.3 does not preserve the secrecy of* s_i *from adversaries of type* $A =$ default *with* $\{\mathsf{K}_\mathsf{S}, \mathsf{K}_A, \mathsf{K}^{-1}_A\} \subseteq \mathcal{K}^{\mathsf{p}}_A$.

Proof. We show the existence of a successful attacker *adv*. We fix instances C and S with execution rounds i and j (where $\mathsf{S}_i = \mathsf{S}$) and denote the link between C and S as l_{CS}.

The adversary *adv* proceeds as follows:

- A message of the form S.init($\mathsf{N}_i, \mathsf{K}_\mathsf{C}, Sign_{\mathsf{K}^{-1}_\mathsf{C}}(\mathsf{C} :: \mathsf{K}_\mathsf{C})$) in l_{CS} is replaced by the message S.init($\mathsf{N}_i, \mathsf{K}_A, Sign_{\mathsf{K}^{-1}_A}(\mathsf{C} :: \mathsf{K}_A)$); that is, the public key K_C of C is replaced by the public key K_A of A at each occurrence and as the signature key.
- When S then sends back the message resp($\{Sign_{\mathsf{K}^{-1}_\mathsf{S}}(\mathsf{k}_j :: \mathsf{init}_1)\}_{\mathsf{K}_A}, Sign_{\mathsf{K}^{-1}_{\mathsf{CA}}}(\mathsf{S} :: \mathsf{K}_\mathsf{S})$), using K_A to encrypt the session key k_j, *adv* can obtain k_j and replace the message by resp($\{Sign_{\mathsf{K}^{-1}_\mathsf{S}}(\mathsf{k}_j :: \mathsf{init}_1)\}_{\mathsf{K}_\mathsf{C}}, Sign_{\mathsf{K}^{-1}_{\mathsf{CA}}}(\mathsf{S} :: \mathsf{K}_\mathsf{S})$).
- When C subsequently returns $\{\mathsf{s}_i\}_{\mathsf{k}_j}$, *adv* can extract the secret s_i (and forward the message).

An adversary machine that achieves this is defined as follows:

Rule Exec *adv* :
do − in − parallel
    if $\text{linkQu}_{\mathcal{T}}(l_{\text{CS}}) = \{\!\!\{e\}\!\!\} \wedge \mathbf{msgnm}(e) = \text{S.init}$
        then $\text{linkQu}_{\mathcal{T}}(l_{\text{CS}}) := \{\!\!\{\text{S.init}(\mathbf{Arg}_1(e), \mathsf{K}_A,$
                    $Sign_{\mathsf{K}_A^{-1}}(\mathbf{fst}(\mathcal{E}xt_{\mathbf{Arg}_2(e)}(\mathbf{Arg}_3(e))) :: \mathsf{K}_A))\}\!\!\}$
    if $\text{linkQu}_{\mathcal{T}}(l_{\text{CS}}) = \{\!\!\{e\}\!\!\} \wedge \mathbf{msgnm}(e) = \text{C.resp}$ **then**
        do − in − parallel
                $\text{linkQu}_{\mathcal{T}}(l_{CS}) := \{\!\!\{\text{C.resp}(\{Sign_{\mathsf{K}_A^{-1}}(\mathbf{Arg}_1(e))\}_{K_C}, \mathbf{Arg}_2(e))\}\!\!\}$
                $local := \{\!\!\{\mathbf{fst}(\mathcal{E}xt_{K_S}(\mathcal{D}ec_{\mathsf{K}_A^{-1}}(\mathbf{Arg}_1(e))))\}\!\!\}$
        enddo
    if $\text{linkQu}_{\mathcal{T}}(l_{\text{CS}}) = \{\!\!\{e\}\!\!\} \wedge \mathbf{msgnm}(e) = \text{S}.xchd$ **then**
        $secret := \{\!\!\{\mathcal{D}ec_{local}(\mathbf{Arg}_1(e))\}\!\!\}$
enddo

Thus the adversary gets to know the secrets $\mathsf{C.s}_i$.

The Fix

Theorem 5.5. *Suppose we are given a particular execution of the repaired TLS variant subsystem $\mathcal{T}'$ (including all clients and servers), a client C, and a number I with $\mathsf{S} = \mathsf{S}_I$, and suppose that the server S is in its Jth execution round in the current execution when C in its Ith execution round initiates the protocol (that is, $\mathsf{C}.\mathsf{i} = I$ and $\mathsf{S}.\mathsf{j} = J$). Then this execution of $\mathcal{T}'$ preserves the secrecy of $\mathsf{C.s}_I$ against adversaries of type $A = \mathsf{default}$ whose previous knowledge $\mathcal{K}_A^{\mathsf{p}}$ fulfills the following conditions:*

- *we have*

$$\Big(\{\mathsf{C.s}_I, \mathsf{K}_\mathsf{C}^{-1}, \mathsf{K}_\mathsf{S}^{-1}\} \cup \{\mathsf{S.k}_j : j \geq J\}$$

$$\cup \{\{Sign_{\mathsf{K}_\mathsf{S}^{-1}}(X :: \mathsf{C.N}_I :: \mathsf{K}_\mathsf{C})\}_{\mathsf{K}_\mathsf{C}} : X \in \mathbf{Keys}\}\Big) \cap \mathcal{K}_A^{\mathsf{p}} = \emptyset$$

- *for any $X \in \mathbf{Exp}$, $Sign_{\mathsf{K}_\mathsf{C}^{-1}}(\mathsf{C} :: X) \in \mathcal{K}_A^{\mathsf{p}}$ implies $X = \mathsf{K}_\mathsf{C}$, and*
- *for any $X \in \mathbf{Exp}$, $Sign_{\mathsf{K}_{\mathsf{CA}}^{-1}}(\mathsf{S} :: X) \in \mathcal{K}_A^{\mathsf{p}}$ implies $X = \mathsf{K}_\mathsf{S}$.*

Proof. We use Theorem 7.27 from Sect. 7.5.2. We show the following claim.

Claim. *For each knowledge set $\mathcal{K}^{\mathsf{e}}_{adv}(\mathcal{A})$ for an adversary adv of type A after an overall execution $\mathbf{e}$ of $\mathcal{T}'$, whose previous knowledge $\mathcal{K}_A^{\mathsf{p}}$ satisfies the conditions in the above statement of the theorem, there exists a subalgebra X_0 that is minimal with respect to the subset relation among the subalgebras X of $\mathbf{Exp}$ fulfilling the following two conditions,[1] such that X_0 contains $\mathcal{K}^{\mathsf{e}}_{adv}(\mathcal{A})$.*
    Firstly, the following condition (1) is required to hold:

---

[1] $\mathcal{K}^{\mathsf{e}}_{adv}(\mathcal{A})$ is not contained in *every* such subalgebra X, because the actual messages exchanged may differ depending on the adversary behavior.

$$\mathcal{K}^{\mathsf{p}}_A \cup \Big\{ \mathsf{c}.\mathsf{N}_i, \mathsf{K}_c, \mathcal{S}ign_{\mathsf{K}_c^{-1}}(\mathsf{c} :: \mathsf{K}_c) : i \in \mathbb{N} \wedge \mathsf{c} \in \mathsf{Client} \Big\}$$

$$\cup \Big\{ \mathcal{S}ign_{\mathsf{K}_{\mathsf{CA}}^{-1}}(\mathsf{s} :: \mathsf{K}_s) : \mathsf{s} \in \mathsf{Server} \wedge (\mathsf{s} = \mathsf{S} \Rightarrow \mathsf{K}_s = \mathsf{K}_S) \Big\}$$

$$\cup \Big\{ \{\mathsf{c}.\mathsf{s}_i\}_k : k \in \mathbf{Keys} \wedge i \in \mathbb{N} \wedge \mathsf{c} \in \mathsf{Client}$$

$$\wedge \exists K \in \mathbf{Keys}, E \in \mathbf{Exp}, E' \in X$$

$$\Big(\mathcal{S}ign_{\mathsf{K}_{\mathsf{CA}}^{-1}}(E) \in X \wedge \mathbf{fst}(E) = \mathsf{c}.\mathsf{S}_i \wedge \mathbf{snd}(E) = K$$

$$\wedge \mathcal{E}xt_K(\mathcal{D}ec_{\mathsf{K}_c^{-1}}(E')) = (k, \mathsf{c}.\mathsf{N}_i, \mathsf{K}_c) \Big) \Big\}$$

$$\subseteq X.$$

Condition (2) requires that for each $j \in \mathbb{N}$ *and* $\mathsf{s} : \mathsf{Server}$ *and for an associated fixed key* $k_{j,s} \in \mathbf{Keys} \cap X$, *a fixed expression* $x_{j,s} \in \mathbf{Exp}$, *and a fixed nonce* $n_{j,s} \in \mathbf{Data} \cap X$ *with* $\mathcal{S}ign_{k_{j,s}^{-1}}(x_{j,s} :: k_{j,s}) \in X$,[2] *we have*

$$\{ \mathcal{S}ign_{\mathsf{K}_s^{-1}}(\mathsf{s}.\mathsf{k}_j :: n_{j,s} :: k_{j,s}) \}_{k_{j,s}} \in X.$$

Note that in the second condition, it can be the case that $k_{j,s}^{-1} \in \mathcal{K}^{\mathsf{e}}_{adv}(\mathcal{A})$, but then $k_{j,s} \neq \mathsf{K}_c$ for any client c (because $\mathsf{K}_C^{-1} \notin \mathcal{K}^{\mathsf{e}}_{adv}(\mathcal{A})$ since $\mathsf{K}_c^{-1} \notin \mathcal{K}^{\mathsf{p}}_A$ and K_c^{-1} is never sent out), and c will notice that something is wrong in the corrected protocol (and because the counter j is increased, the adversary cannot make the server publish another signature with the same k_j and the correct K_C).

Proof of claim. Intuitively, the above claim holds because each knowledge set $\mathcal{K}^{\mathsf{e}}_{adv}(\mathcal{A})$ is by definition the subalgebra of the algebra of expressions $\mathbf{Exp}$ built up from $\mathcal{K}^{\mathsf{p}}_A$ in interaction with the protocol participants during the protocol run e. To argue in more detail, we have to consider what knowledge the adversary can gain from interaction with the protocol participants. From the first message of a client c, the adversary can learn the expressions $\mathsf{c}.\mathsf{N}_i$, K_c, and $\mathcal{S}ign_{\mathsf{K}_c^{-1}}(\mathsf{c} :: \mathsf{K}_c)$. From the first message of a server s, the adversary can firstly learn $\mathcal{S}ign_{\mathsf{K}_{\mathsf{CA}}^{-1}}(\mathsf{s} :: \mathsf{K}_s)$. Secondly, for each encryption key $K \in \mathbf{Keys}$ in the knowledge of the adversary such that the adversary knows $\mathcal{S}ign_{K^{-1}}(x :: K)$ for some $x \in \mathbf{Exp}$, and for each N known to the adversary, the adversary learns $\{\mathcal{S}ign_{\mathsf{K}_s^{-1}}(\mathsf{s}.\mathsf{k}_j :: vN :: K)\}_K \in X$, but only a unique such expression for a given server s, protocol run e, and transaction number j, because the transaction number j is increased as long as the protocol is iterated (this is reflected by the fact that X_0 is required to be minimal). From the second message from a client c, for each encryption key $K \in \mathbf{Keys}$ such that

- $\mathcal{S}ign_{\mathsf{K}_{\mathsf{CA}}^{-1}}(E)$ is known to the adversary for an $E \in \mathbf{Exp}$ with $\mathbf{fst}(E) = \mathsf{c}.\mathsf{S}_i$ and $\mathbf{snd}(E) = K$, and such that

---

[2] Note that condition (1) guarantees the existence of these unique expressions associated with each $j \in \mathbb{N}$ and $\mathsf{s} : \mathsf{Server}$.

- there exists $E' \in \mathbf{Exp}$ which is known to the adversary and such that $\mathcal{E}xt_{\mathsf{K}}(\mathcal{D}ec_{\mathsf{K}_c^{-1}}(E')) = (\mathsf{k}, \mathsf{c}.\mathsf{N}_i, \mathsf{K}_c)$ for some $\mathsf{k} \in \mathbf{Keys}$,

the adversary learns $\{\mathsf{c}.\mathsf{s}_i\}_{\mathsf{K}} \in X$.

Since there are no other messages sent out by the specified system, the claim holds by the definition of the adversary knowledge as the algebra generated by the exchanged messages and the initial adversary knowledge. This completes proof of the claim.

Thus it is sufficient to show that $\mathsf{C}.\mathsf{s}_I \notin X_0$ for every X_0 defined above, because $\mathcal{K}_A(\mathcal{A}) \stackrel{\mathrm{def}}{=} \bigcup_{adv,e} \mathcal{K}_{adv}^e(\mathcal{A})$ is contained in the union of all such X_0 by the above argument. We aim for a contradiction by fixing such an X_0 and assuming that $\mathsf{C}.\mathsf{s}_I \in X_0$. X_0 is defined to be a minimal subalgebra satisfying the conditions (1) and (2) above. Recall that from the definition of the algebra of expressions $\mathbf{Exp}$ in Sect. 3.3.3 as a free algebra it follows that $\mathsf{C}.\mathsf{s}_I$ is different from any other expression not containing it, since no equation with such an expression is defined. In particular, we have $\mathsf{C}.\mathsf{s}_I \neq \mathsf{c}.\mathsf{s}_i$ for any client c and number i with $\mathsf{c} \neq \mathsf{C}$ or $i \neq I$. Thus the only occurrence in the conditions defining X_0 in a minimal way, where $\mathsf{C}.\mathsf{s}_I$ may be introduced as a subterm, is in the requirement that X_0 contains $\{\mathsf{C}.\mathsf{s}_I\}_{\mathsf{k}}$ for each key $\mathsf{k} \in \mathbf{Keys}$ for which there exist $\mathsf{K} \in \mathbf{Keys}, E \in \mathbf{Exp}, E' \in X_0$ such that

$$Sign_{\mathsf{K}_{\mathsf{CA}}^{-1}}(E) \in X_0 \wedge \mathbf{fst}(E) = \mathsf{S} \wedge \mathbf{snd}(E) = \mathsf{K}$$
$$\wedge \mathcal{E}xt_{\mathsf{K}}(\mathcal{D}ec_{\mathsf{K}_c^{-1}}(E')) = (\mathsf{k}, \mathsf{C}.\mathsf{N}_I, \mathsf{K}_{\mathsf{C}})$$

in condition (1). The assumption $\mathsf{C}.\mathsf{s}_I \in X_0$ thus implies that there exists a key $\mathsf{k} \in \mathbf{Keys}$ for which there exist $\mathsf{K} \in \mathbf{Keys}, E \in \mathbf{Exp}, E' \in X_0$ such that

$$Sign_{\mathsf{K}_{\mathsf{CA}}^{-1}}(E) \in X_0 \wedge \mathbf{fst}(E) = \mathsf{S} \wedge \mathbf{snd}(E) = \mathsf{K}$$
$$\wedge \mathcal{E}xt_{\mathsf{K}}(\mathcal{D}ec_{\mathsf{K}_c^{-1}}(E')) = (\mathsf{k}, \mathsf{C}.\mathsf{N}_I, \mathsf{K}_{\mathsf{C}}).$$

By definition of X_0 and assumption on $\mathcal{K}_A^{\mathsf{p}}$, the condition $Sign_{\mathsf{K}_{\mathsf{CA}}^{-1}}(E) \in X_0 \wedge \mathbf{fst}(E) = \mathsf{S} \wedge \mathbf{snd}(E) = \mathsf{K}$ implies that $\mathsf{K} = \mathsf{K}_{\mathsf{S}}$ (since any expression of this form in $\mathcal{K}_A^{\mathsf{p}}$ must satisfy this, and also any such expression introduced in X_0). Similarly, $E' \in X_0$ with $\mathcal{E}xt_{\mathsf{K}_{\mathsf{S}}}(\mathcal{D}ec_{\mathsf{K}_c^{-1}}(E')) = (\mathsf{k}, \mathsf{C}.\mathsf{N}_I, \mathsf{K}_{\mathsf{C}})$ implies $\mathsf{k} = \mathsf{S}.\mathsf{k}_j$ for some j, because $E' \notin \mathcal{K}_A^{\mathsf{p}}$ by assumption on the previous adversary knowledge $\mathcal{K}_A^{\mathsf{p}}$, because $\mathsf{K}_{\mathsf{S}}^{-1}$ is never communicated, and because the expression $\{Sign_{\mathsf{K}_{\mathsf{S}}^{-1}}(\mathsf{S}.\mathsf{k}_j :: \mathsf{n}_{j,s} :: \mathsf{k}_{j,s})\}_{\mathsf{k}_{j,s}}$ (in condition (2)) is the only expression with a subterm of the form $Sign_{\mathsf{K}_{\mathsf{S}}^{-1}}(\mathsf{k} :: \mathsf{n}_{j,s} :: \mathsf{k}_{j,s})$ that is introduced (and we can also conclude that $\mathsf{n}_{j,s} = \mathsf{C}.\mathsf{N}_I$ and $\mathsf{k}_{j,s} = \mathsf{K}_{\mathsf{C}}$ in this term). Furthermore, we can conclude $j \geq J$ by the assumption that S is in its Jth execution round when C is in its Ith round, and by the requirement that the $\mathsf{C}.\mathsf{N}_i$ should be fresh (that is, each distinct from any other occurring value). Thus by assumption on the previous adversary knowledge $\mathcal{K}_A^{\mathsf{p}}$, we have $\mathsf{S}.\mathsf{k}_j \notin \mathcal{K}_A^{\mathsf{p}}$ since $j \geq J$, and thus the adversary must have learned $\mathsf{S}.\mathsf{k}_j$ in a protocol interaction. By the freshness assumption on $\mathsf{S.k}_j$, the only message containing $\mathsf{S.k}_j$ is a term of the form $\{\mathcal{S}ign_{\mathsf{K}_\mathsf{S}^{-1}}(\mathsf{S.k}_j :: n_{j,s} :: \mathsf{k}_{j,s})\}_{\mathsf{k}_{j,s}}$. By condition (2) and the minimality of X_0, we know that $n_{j,s} = \mathsf{C.N}_\mathsf{I}$ and $\mathsf{k}_{j,s} = \mathsf{K}_\mathsf{C}$ for any such term by the above observation. Therefore, this term has to be decrypted with $\mathsf{K}_\mathsf{C}^{-1}$ in order to get the $\mathsf{S.k}_j$. The only protocol participant that possesses $\mathsf{K}_\mathsf{C}^{-1}$ and that could thus provide this service for the adversary is C (since the other participants do not have $\mathsf{K}_\mathsf{C}^{-1}$ in their initial knowledge, and $\mathsf{K}_\mathsf{C}^{-1}$ is never exchanged). However, none of the values in $\{\mathcal{S}ign_{\mathsf{K}_\mathsf{S}^{-1}}(\mathsf{S.k}_j :: \mathsf{C.N}_I :: \mathsf{K}_\mathsf{C})\}_{\mathsf{K}_\mathsf{C}}$ is ever sent out to the network by C. Thus we must conclude that $\mathsf{K}_\mathsf{C}^{-1} \in \mathcal{K}_A^p$, which contradicts the initial assumption about $\mathcal{K}_A^p$.

One can see as follows that the adversary knowledge before each *iteration* of the system satisfies these conditions as well:

(1) In the Ith execution round of the client C, no data of the form $X.s_i$ is output except $\mathsf{C.s}_I$, which, as the theorem shows, is kept secret from the adversary. The secret keys $\mathsf{K}_\mathsf{C}^{-1}, \mathsf{K}_\mathsf{S}^{-1}$ (for each C, S) are never output at all. The key $\mathsf{S.K}_J$ is only sent out during the Jth executing round of S, and it follows from the above theorem that in that round, the key is not leaked to the adversary (because otherwise the adversary would gain knowledge of $\mathsf{C.s}_I$ by decrypting the contents of the xchd message). Similarly, an expression of the form $\{\mathcal{S}ign_{\mathsf{K}_\mathsf{S}^{-1}}(X :: \mathsf{C.N}_I :: \mathsf{K}_\mathsf{C})\}_{\mathsf{K}_\mathsf{C}}$ (for $X \in \mathbf{Keys}$) is only output in the Ith execution round of C (and is of no use in any later round).

(2) For any $X \in \mathbf{Exp}$, $\mathcal{S}ign_{\mathsf{K}_\mathsf{C}^{-1}}(\mathsf{C} :: X)$ is sent out only for $X = \mathsf{K}_\mathsf{C}$ (and $\mathsf{K}_\mathsf{C}^{-1}$ is not sent out at all).

(3) For any $X \in \mathbf{Exp}$, $\mathcal{S}ign_{\mathsf{K}_\mathsf{CA}^{-1}}(\mathsf{S} :: X)$ is sent out only for $X = \mathsf{K}_\mathsf{S}$ (and $\mathsf{K}_\mathsf{CA}^{-1}$ is not sent out at all).

Corollary 5.6. *Any execution of $\mathcal{T}'$ over all clients and servers and all execution rounds preserves the secrecy of each $\mathsf{C.s}_I$ (for $\mathsf{C} : \mathsf{Client}$ and $1 \leq I \leq \mathsf{I}$) against adversaries of type $A = \mathsf{default}$ whose previous knowledge $\mathcal{K}_A^p$ before the overall execution of $\mathcal{T}'$ fulfills the following conditions:*

- *we have*

$$\left(\{\mathsf{K}_\mathsf{c}^{-1}, \mathsf{K}_\mathsf{s}^{-1}, \mathsf{c.s}_i, \mathsf{s.k}_j, \{\mathcal{S}ign_{\mathsf{K}_\mathsf{s}^{-1}}(X :: \mathsf{c.N}_i :: \mathsf{K}_\mathsf{c})\}_{\mathsf{K}_\mathsf{c}} : \right.$$

$$\left. \mathsf{c} : \mathsf{Client} \wedge \mathsf{s} : \mathsf{Server} \wedge 1 \leq i \leq \mathsf{I} \wedge 1 \leq j \wedge X \in \mathbf{Keys}\}\right) \cap \mathcal{K}_A^p = \emptyset,$$

- *for any $X \in \mathbf{Exp}$ and any $\mathsf{c} : \mathsf{Client}$, $\mathcal{S}ign_{\mathsf{K}_\mathsf{c}^{-1}}(\mathsf{c} :: X) \in \mathcal{K}_A^p$ implies $X = \mathsf{K}_\mathsf{c}$, and*
- *for any $X \in \mathbf{Exp}$ and any $\mathsf{s} : \mathsf{Server}$, $\mathcal{S}ign_{\mathsf{K}_\mathsf{CA}^{-1}}(\mathsf{s} :: X) \in \mathcal{K}_A^p$ implies $X = \mathsf{K}_\mathsf{s}$.*

Proof. Suppose we are given an execution $\mathbf{e}$ of $\mathcal{T}'$, a client C, and a number I. Then we have $\mathsf{S}_I = \mathsf{S}$ for a server S, and within the execution $\mathbf{e}$, at the point where $C.i = I$, we have $S.j = J$ for a number J. Since the conditions on the previous adversary knowledge in the current corollary imply those of the previous theorem, we can thus directly apply the theorem.

C.8 Common Electronic Purse Specifications

C.8.1 Purchase Transaction

Vulnerability

Theorem 5.7. $\mathcal{P}$ *does not provide* merchant security *against* insider *adversaries with* $\{Sign_{K_{CA}^{-1}}(ID_{C'} :: K_{C'}), K_{C'}^{-1}\} \subseteq \mathcal{K}_A^{P}$.

Proof. We show the existence of a successful attacker adv. We assume that the adversary has a certificate $Sign_{K_{CA}^{-1}}(ID_{C'} :: K_{C'})$ and the corresponding private key $K_{C'}^{-1}$ (this should of course not be linked to the identity of the adversary to avoid identification). We write l_{CP} (resp. l_{PD}) for the link between C and P (resp. P and D). $l_{AP'}$ is a link between the attacker and the PSAM P'. Thus:

Rule Exec adv :
if $linkQu_{\mathcal{P}}(l_{CP}) = \{\!\{e\}\!\} \wedge \mathbf{msgnm}(e) = P.Ccert$
 then
    $linkQu_{\mathcal{P}}(l_{AP'}) := linkQu_{\mathcal{P}}(l_{CP});$
    $linkQu_{\mathcal{P}}(l_{CP}) := \{\!\{P.Ccert(ID_{C'}, K_{C'}, Sign_{K_{CA}^{-1}}(ID_{C'} :: K_{C'}))\}\!\}$
 else
   if $linkQu_{\mathcal{P}}(l_{CP}) = \{\!\{e\}\!\} \wedge \mathbf{msgnm}(e) = C.Deb$
    then $m := \mathbf{fst}(\mathcal{D}ec_{K_{C'}^{-1}}(\mathbf{Arg}_2(e)));$
   if $linkQu_{\mathcal{P}}(l_{AP'}) = \{\!\{e\}\!\} \wedge \mathbf{msgnm}(e) \in \{C.Pcert, C.Deb\}$
    then $linkQu_{\mathcal{P}}(l_{CP}) := linkQu_{\mathcal{P}}(l_{AP'});$
   if $linkQu_{\mathcal{P}}(l_{CP}) = \{\!\{e\}\!\} \wedge \mathbf{msgnm}(e) = P'.Resp$
   then do $-$ **in** $-$ **parallel**
    $linkQu_{\mathcal{P}}(l_{AP'}) := linkQu_{\mathcal{P}}(l_{CP})$
    $linkQu_{\mathcal{P}}(l_{DP}) := \{\!\{D.Disp(m)\}\!\}$
 enddo

Note that again we give a simplified presentation of the UML Machine for increased readability. For example, according to the definition of an adversary in Sect. 7.5, the command $linkQu_{\mathcal{P}}(l_{AP'}) := linkQu_{\mathcal{P}}(l_{CP})$ has to be realized by using commands of the form $read_{l_{CP}}(m) \equiv m := linkQu_{\mathcal{P}}(l_{CP})$ and $insert_{l_{AP'}}(e) \equiv linkQu_{\mathcal{P}}(l_{AP'}) := linkQu_{\mathcal{P}}(l_{AP'}) \uplus \{\!\{e\}\!\}$, in a suitable iteration.

We explain how the attacker UML Machine proceeds. If a message with name P.Ccert is sent over l_{CP}, the adversary copies it to $l_{AP'}$ and replaces it in l_{CP} by $P.Ccert(ID_{C'}, K_{C'}, Sign_{K_{CA}^{-1}}(ID_{C'} :: K_{C'}))$. Otherwise, if a message with name C.Deb is sent over l_{CP}, the adversary extracts the amount $\mathbf{fst}(\mathcal{D}ec_{K_{C'}^{-1}}(\mathbf{Arg}_2(e)))$ from it and stores it in m. A message with name C.Pcert or C.Deb in $l_{AP'}$ is copied to l_{CP}. If l_{CP} consists of a message with name P'.Resp, the content of l_{CP} is copied to $l_{AP'}$ and the message D.Disp(m) is sent to l_{DP}.

The above condition of *merchant security* is clearly violated: when executing $\mathcal{P}$ in the presence of *adv*, D receives the value M_{NT}, but P is not in possession of $Sign_{K_C^{-1}}(ID_C :: ID_P :: M_{NT} :: NT)$.

Proposed Solution

Proposition 5.8. *$\mathcal{P}'$ provides secrecy of K_C^{-1}, K_P^{-1} and integrity of K_C^{-1}, K_C, K_{CA}, ID_C, K_P^{-1}, K_P, M_{NT}, SK_{NT}, NT (meaning that the adversary should not be able to make the atttributes take on values previously known only to him) against insider adversaries with $\mathcal{K}_A^p \cap \{K_C^{-1}, K_P^{-1}\} = \emptyset$.*

Proof. For an adversary to gain knowledge of K_C^{-1}, K_P^{-1}, the adversary would have to read these expressions from one of the two communication links. We therefore have to consider, if at any point any of the two expressions is communicated over any of the two communication links. According to the specification, none of the values is output by any of the protocol participants at any time. Therefore secrecy of K_C^{-1}, K_P^{-1} is provided since these values are never sent outside the smart cards (which under the current threat scenario are assumed to be impenetrable).

For the adversary to violate the integrity of any of the attributes K_C^{-1}, K_C, K_{CA}, ID_C, K_P^{-1}, K_P, M_{NT}, SK_{NT}, the adversary would have to cause their values to take on an atomic value in **Data**^{a}, during the interaction with the protocol participants. In particular, their values would have to change. From the protocol specification, we can see that the value of none of these attributes is changed at all during the execution of the protocol. Thus their integrity is preserved.

Similarly, for the adversary to violate the integrity of the attribute NT, the adversary would have to cause its value to take on an atomic value in **Data**^{a}, during the interaction with the protocol participants. From the protocol specification, we can see that the value of NT is changed only to take on values of the form 0, $0 + 1$, $0 + 1 + 1$, etc., all of which are not in **Data**^{a}. Thus the integrity of NT is preserved.

Theorem 5.9. *Consider adversaries of type $A = $ insider with*

$$\mathcal{K}_A^p \cap \Big(\{K_C^{-1}, K_P^{-1}, K_{CA}^{-1}\} \cup \{SK_{NT} : NT \in \mathbb{N}\}$$
$$\cup \{Sign_{K_P^{-1}}(E) : E \in \mathbf{Exp}\} \cup \{Sign_{K_C^{-1}}(E) : E \in \mathbf{Exp}\}$$
$$\cup \{Sign_{SK_{NT}}(E) : E \in \mathbf{Exp} \wedge NT \in \mathbb{N}\} \Big) = \emptyset$$

and such that for each $X \in \mathbf{Exp}$ with $Sign_{K_{CA}^{-1}}(X :: K) \in \mathcal{K}_A^p$, $X = ID_C$ implies $K = K_C$ and $X = ID_P$ implies $K = K_P$. The following security guarantees are provided by $\mathcal{P}'$ in the presence of adversaries of type A:

Cardholder security: For all $\mathsf{ID_C}$, $\mathsf{ID_P}$, $\mathsf{M_{NT}}$, NT, $\mathsf{K_C^{-1}}$ *such that* $\mathsf{K_C}$ *is valid for* $\mathsf{ID_C}$, *if* P *is in possession of* $Sign_{\mathsf{K_C^{-1}}}(\mathsf{ID_C :: ID_P :: M_{NT} :: NT})$ *then* C *is in possession of* $Sign_{\mathsf{K_P^{-1}}}(\mathsf{M_{NT} :: SK_{NT} :: ID_P :: ID_C :: NT})$ *(for some* $\mathsf{SK_{NT}}$ *and* $\mathsf{K_P^{-1}}$ *such that the corresponding key* $\mathsf{K_P}$ *is valid for* $\mathsf{ID_P}$ *).*

Merchant security: Each time D *receives the value* $\mathsf{M_{NT}}$, P *is in possession of* $Sign_{\mathsf{K_{CA}^{-1}}}(\mathsf{ID_C :: K_C})$ *and* $Sign_{\mathsf{K_C^{-1}}}(\mathsf{ID_C :: ID_P :: M_{NT} :: NT})$ *for some* $\mathsf{ID_C}$, $\mathsf{K_C^{-1}}$, *and a new value* NT.

Card issuer security: After each completed purchase transaction, let S *be the sum of all* $\mathsf{M_{NT}}$ *in the sequence consisting of the processed elements of the form* $Sign_{\mathsf{K_C^{-1}}}(\mathsf{ID_C :: ID_P :: M_{NT} :: NT})$ *(with possibly varying* $\mathsf{ID_C}$, $\mathsf{ID_P}$, *and* $\mathsf{K_C^{-1}}$, *such that the corresponding key* $\mathsf{K_C}$ *is valid for* $\mathsf{ID_C}$ *and where the* NT *are mutually distinct for fixed* C *). Also, let* S' *be the sum of all* $\mathsf{M'_{NT'}}$ *in the sequence of processed* $Sign_{\mathsf{K_{P'}^{-1}}}(\mathsf{M'_{NT'} :: SK'_{NT'} :: ID_{C'} :: ID_{P'} :: NT'})$ *(with possibly varying* $\mathsf{ID_{C'}}$, $\mathsf{ID_{P'}}$, *and* $\mathsf{K_{P'}^{-1}}$, *such that the corresponding key* $\mathsf{K_{P'}}$ *is valid for* $\mathsf{ID_{P'}}$, *and where the* $\mathsf{NT'}$ *are mutually distinct for fixed* $\mathsf{C'}$ *). Then* S *is no greater than* S'.

Proof

Cardholder security: We proceed by contraposition. Suppose that (for any $\mathsf{SK_{NT}}$, $\mathsf{K_P^{-1}}$ such that the corresponding key $\mathsf{K_P}$ is valid for $\mathsf{ID_P}$) C is not in possession of $Sign_{\mathsf{K_P^{-1}}}(\mathsf{M_{NT} :: SK_{NT} :: ID_P :: ID_C :: NT})$. We would like to show that for every $\mathsf{K_C^{-1}}$ such that the corresponding key $\mathsf{K_C}$ is valid for $\mathsf{ID_C}$, P is not in possession of $Sign_{\mathsf{K_C^{-1}}}(\mathsf{ID_C :: ID_P :: M_{NT} :: NT})$. We fix such $\mathsf{ID_C}$, $\mathsf{K_C}$, and $\mathsf{K_C^{-1}}$.

We consider:

- the joint knowledge set $\mathcal{K}$ of all participants except C (that is, the objects P and D, and any given adversary, which according to the threat scenario are not able to penetrate the smart card on which C resides) and
- the knowledge set $\mathcal{K}_C$ of C.

Claim. $\mathcal{K}$ *is contained in every subalgebra* X *of* **Exp** *containing*

$$\mathbf{Keys} \setminus \{\mathsf{K_C^{-1}}\} \cup \mathcal{K}_A^p \cup \mathbf{Data}\ \cup$$
$$\Big\{ \{Sign_{\mathsf{K_C^{-1}}}(\mathsf{ID_C :: id_P :: m :: nt})\}_{\mathsf{sk}},$$
$$Sign_{\mathsf{sk}}(\mathsf{m ::} \{Sign_{\mathsf{K_C^{-1}}}(\mathsf{ID_C :: id_P :: m :: nt})\}_{\mathsf{sk}}) :$$
$$\mathsf{id_P, k_P, m, sk, nt}, E \in \mathcal{K}_C \wedge Sign_{\mathsf{K_{CA}^{-1}}}(\mathsf{id_P :: k_P}) \in \mathcal{K}_C$$
$$\wedge \mathcal{E}xt_{\mathsf{k_P}}(E) = \mathsf{m :: sk :: id_P :: ID_C :: nt} \Big\}.$$

Note that $Sign_{\mathsf{sk}}(\mathsf{m ::} \{Sign_{\mathsf{K_C^{-1}}}(\mathsf{ID_C :: id_P :: m :: nt})\}_{\mathsf{sk}})$ is actually redundant, but included for explicitness. Note also that it is not claimed that $\mathcal{K}$ is actually the intersection of such algebras. For example, any of the above algebras (and thus their intersection) contains the key K_{CA}^{-1}, although $\mathcal{K}$ does not. The latter fact is nevertheless used in the proof (below when using the claim). A similar remark applies to terms of the form $Sign_{K_{CA}^{-1}}(\text{ID}::\text{K})$. Note that $\mathcal{K}$ contains SK_{NT}, but not K_C^{-1} (as shown below).

The above claim holds because the knowledge set $\mathcal{K}$ is by definition the subalgebra of the algebra of expressions **Exp** built up from the initial knowledge by the protocol participants except C and any adversary in interaction with C. We thus have to consider what knowledge the other participants can gain from interaction with C. The expressions learned from the first message from C are contained in X because X is assumed to contain all keys $K \in \textbf{Keys} \setminus \{K_C^{-1}\}$, and all data in **Data**. The expressions learned from the second message from C are contained in X because X is assumed to contain $\{Sign_{K_C^{-1}}(\text{ID}_C::\text{id}_P::m::nt)\}_{sk}$ and $Sign_{sk}(m::\{Sign_{K_C^{-1}}(\text{ID}_C::\text{id}_P::m::nt)\}_{sk})$ for all $\text{id}_P, k_P \in \mathcal{K}_C$ with $Sign_{K_{CA}^{-1}}(\text{id}_P::k_P) \in \mathcal{K}_C$ and $m, sk, nt, E \in \mathcal{K}_C$ with $\mathcal{E}xt_{k_P}(E) = m :: sk :: \text{id}_P :: \text{ID}_C :: nt$, and because C must receive the values $\text{id}_P, k_P, Sign_{K_{CA}^{-1}}(\text{id}_P::k_P), m, sk, nt, E$ before sending out the messages $\{Sign_{K_C^{-1}}(\text{ID}_C::\text{id}_P::m::nt)\}_{sk}$ and $Sign_{sk}(m :: \{Sign_{K_C^{-1}}(\text{ID}_C::\text{id}_P::m::nt)\}_{sk})$.

In particular, we have $K_C^{-1} \notin \mathcal{K}$, because the initial knowledge of P, D, and the adversary does not include K_C^{-1}, and it (or anything it could be derived from) is not transmitted.

Under the above assumption that $Sign_{K_P^{-1}}(\text{M}_{NT}::\text{SK}_{NT}::\text{ID}_P::\text{ID}_C::\text{NT}) \notin \mathcal{K}_C$ (for any SK_{NT}, K_P^{-1} such that the corresponding key K_P is valid for ID_P), we prove that such a subalgebra X with $Sign_{K_C^{-1}}(\text{ID}_C::\text{ID}_P::\text{M}_{NT}::\text{NT}) \notin X$ exists. Let X be the **Exp** subalgebra generated by

$$G := \textbf{Keys} \setminus \{K_C^{-1}\} \cup \textbf{Data} \cup$$
$$\{\{Sign_{K_C^{-1}}(\text{id}_C::\text{id}_P::m::nt)\}_{sk},$$
$$Sign_{sk}(m::\{Sign_{K_C^{-1}}(\text{id}_C::\text{id}_P::m::nt)\}_{sk}) :$$
$$(\text{id}_C, \text{id}_P, m, nt) \neq (\text{ID}_C, \text{ID}_P, \text{M}_{NT}, \text{NT})\}.$$

By construction, X fulfills the above conditions, using the fact that the adversary does not have access to K_{CA}^{-1} (since it is not in the adverary's initial knowledge and it (or anything it could be derived from) is never transmitted) and thus does not have access to terms of the form $Sign_{K_{CA}^{-1}}(\text{id}_P::k_P)$ unless k_P is valid for id_P. Also, we have $Sign_{K_C^{-1}}(\text{ID}_C::\text{ID}_P::\text{M}_{NT}::\text{NT}) \notin X$.

Thus we have $Sign_{K_C^{-1}}(\text{ID}_C::\text{ID}_P::\text{M}_{NT}::\text{NT}) \notin \mathcal{K}$.

Merchant security: Each time D receives the value M_{NT}, P is in possession of $Sign_{K_{CA}^{-1}}(\text{ID}_C::\text{K}_C)$ and $Sign_{K_C^{-1}}(\text{ID}_C::\text{ID}_P::\text{M}_{NT}::\text{NT})$ for some ID_C, K_C^{-1}, and a new value NT.

By the specification of P (and the assumption of a secure communication link between P and D), D receives the value M_{NT} only after P has checked the conditions in its part of the protocol; that is, P is in possession of $Sign_{K_{CA}^{-1}}(id_C :: k_C)$ and $Sign_{K_C^{-1}}(id_C :: ID_P :: M_{NT} :: NT)$ for some id_C. Newness of NT in this expression is guaranteed since P creates the value itself by incrementing it between different runs of the protocol, and because the value is prevented from rolling over.

Card issuer security: This follows from the proof of *cardholder security*.

C.8.2 Load Transaction

Vulnerabilities

Theorem 5.10. $\mathcal{L}$ *does not provide* load acquirer security *against adversaries of type* insider *with* $\{cep, lda, m_n\} \subseteq \mathcal{K}_A^p$.

Proof. An attacker may proceed as follows. The attack assumes a threat scenario where the attacker may be (or collaborate with) the card issuer. Thus it suffices to give a modification of the card issuer behavior that achieves the goal of the attack, that is to successfully complete the protocol and to possess a signature of the form ml_n but with the changed amount $\tilde{m}$ in the end. The following modified card issuer specification J simply stores $Sign_{r'}(cep'' :: nt'' :: lda'' :: \tilde{m} :: s1'' :: hc'_{nt} :: hl' :: h2l')$ instead of ml' in the logging object CLog:

Rule Exec J :
case currState$_I$ **of**
    Init: **do trans**$_I$(Load, (cep, lda, m, nt, s1, R, ml, hl, h2l),
                valid(cep) $\wedge$ $\mathcal{E}xt_{K_{CI}}$(s1) = cep :: lda :: m :: nt
                  $\wedge$ $\mathcal{E}xt_{\mathcal{D}ec_{K_{LI}}(R)}$(ml) = cep :: nt :: lda :: m :: s1 ::
                         $\mathcal{H}ash$(lda :: cep :: nt :: rc$_{nt}$) :: hl :: h2l;
         L.RespL($Sign_{K_{CI}}$(cep :: n1 :: s1 :: hl)), Load;
         L.RespL(0), Fail)
    Load: **do trans**$_I$(Comp, (cep, lda, m, nt, r2l, s3), *true*;
               i.llog(cep, lda, m, nt, r, $\tilde{m}$l, r2l), Final; ,)
    Fail: **do trans**$_I$([], [], *true*; i.llog(cep, lda, 0, nt, r, $\tilde{m}$l, 0), Final; ,)
    Final: **do** finished := *true*

Here we use the macro

$\tilde{m}l \equiv Sign_r(cep :: nt :: lda :: \tilde{m} :: s1 :: hc_{nt} :: hl :: h2l)$

Proposed solution

Proposition 5.11. $\mathcal{L}'$ *provides* secrecy *of* $K_{CI}, K_L^{-1}, K_I^{-1}$ *and* integrity *of* K_{CI}, K_L^{-1}, K_I^{-1}, cep, nt, rc$_{nt}$, lda, n, rl$_n$, r2l$_n$, m_n *(meaning that the adversary should not be able to make the atttributes take on values previously known only to him) against* insider *adversaries with* $\mathcal{K}_A^p \cap \{K_{CI}, K_L^{-1}, K_I^{-1}\} = \emptyset$.

Proof. Secrecy is evident since these values are never sent outside the smart cards (which are under the current threat scenario assumed to be impenetrable).

Similarly, integrity of K_{CI}, K_L^{-1}, K_I^{-1}, cep, rc_{nt}, lda, rl_n, $r2l_n$, m_n is evident since these values are not changed during the execution of the specification. Note that the secure definition of m_{nt} (which is outside the current specification) again relies on a secure connection between the terminal where the cash is entered and the LSAM. Also, the creation of the random values rc_{nt}, rl_n, $r2l_n$ is outside the current scope. Finally, integrity of nt (resp. n) in the sense of Sect. 4.1.2 follows from the fact that the card (resp. the LSAM) changes the value of nt (resp. n) during the protocol irrespective of the behavior of the environment.

Theorem 5.12. *In the presence of adversaries of type $A =$ insider with*

$$\mathcal{K}_A^p \cap \{K_{CI}, K_L^{-1}, K_I^{-1}\} \cup \{rc_{nt} : nt \in \mathbb{N}\} \cup \{rl_n, r2l_n : n \in \mathbb{N}\} = \emptyset$$

the following security guarantees are provided by $\mathcal{L}'$:

Cardholder security: For any message Clog(lda, m, nt, s2, rl) *sent to* c : CLog, *if* $m \neq 0$ *(that is, the card seems to have been loaded with m) then* $rl \neq 0$ *and*

$$\mathcal{E}xt_{K_{CI}}(s2) = cep :: nt :: \mathcal{S}ign_{K_{CI}}(cep :: lda :: m :: nt) ::$$
$$\mathcal{H}ash(lda :: cep :: nt :: rl)$$

holds (that is, the card issuer certifies rl *to be a valid proof for the transaction). For any two messages* Clog(lda, m, nt, s2, rl) *and* Clog(lda′, m′, nt′, s2′, rl′) *sent to* c : CLog, *we have* $nt \neq nt'$.

Load acquirer security: Suppose that we have $ml_n \in \mathcal{K}$ *and* $rl_n \in \mathcal{K}$ *where* $ml_n = \mathcal{S}ign_{K_L^{-1}}(cep :: nt :: lda :: m_n :: s1 :: y :: hl_n :: h2l_n)$ *with* $hl_n = \mathcal{H}ash(lda :: cep :: nt :: rl_n)$ *and* $h2l_n = \mathcal{H}ash(lda :: cep :: nt :: r2l_n)$, *for some* cep, nt, s1, *and* y. *Then at the end of an execution of* L *either of the following two conditions hold:*

- *a message* Llog(cep, lda, m_n, nt, x) *has been sent to* l : LLog *(which implies that* L *has received and retains* m_n *in cash) or*
- *a message* Llog(cep, lda, 0, nt, x) *has been sent to* l : LLog, *for some x (that is, the load acquirer assumes that the load failed and returns the amount* m_n *to the cardholder), and we have* $x' \in \mathcal{K}_L$ *and* $z \in \mathcal{K}$ *with* $z = \mathcal{S}ign_{K_I^{-1}}(cep :: lda :: m_n :: nt :: y')$ *where* $y' = \mathcal{H}ash(lda :: cep :: nt :: x')$ $= y$ *(that is, the load acquirer can prove that the load was aborted).*

Card issuer security: For each message Clog(lda, m, nt, s2, rl) *sent to* c : CLog, *if* $m \neq 0$ *and*

$$\mathcal{E}xt_{K_{CI}}(s2) = cep :: nt :: \mathcal{S}ign_{K_{CI}}(cep :: lda :: m :: nt) ::$$
$$\mathcal{H}ash(lda :: cep :: nt :: rl)$$

holds for some lda, *then the card issuer has a valid signature* ml_n *corresponding to this transaction.*

Proof.

Cardholder security: Suppose that the message $\mathsf{Clog}(\mathsf{lda}, \mathsf{m}, \mathsf{nt}, \mathsf{s2}, \mathsf{rl})$ has been sent to $\mathsf{c} : \mathsf{CLog}$, where $\mathsf{m} \neq 0$. We need to show that $\mathsf{rl} \neq 0$ and that

$$\mathcal{E}xt_{\mathsf{K}_{\mathsf{Cl}}}(\mathsf{s2}) = \mathsf{cep} :: \mathsf{nt} :: \mathcal{S}ign_{\mathsf{K}_{\mathsf{Cl}}}(\mathsf{cep} :: \mathsf{lda} :: \mathsf{m} :: \mathsf{nt}) :: \mathcal{H}ash(\mathsf{lda} :: \mathsf{cep} :: \mathsf{nt} :: \mathsf{rl})$$

holds. By assumption, the connection between $\mathsf{C} : \mathsf{Card}$ and $\mathsf{c} : \mathsf{CLog}$ is secure (since the objects are on the same smart card). This implies that C actually sent the message $\mathsf{Clog}(\mathsf{lda}, \mathsf{m}, \mathsf{nt}, \mathsf{s2}, \mathsf{rl})$. According to the specification of C, this can only happen if $\mathsf{rl} \neq 0$ and if $\mathcal{E}xt_{\mathsf{K}_{\mathsf{Cl}}}(\mathsf{s2}) = \mathsf{cep} :: \mathsf{nt} :: \mathsf{s1} :: \mathsf{hl}$ holds, where $\mathsf{s1} = \mathcal{S}ign_{\mathsf{K}_{\mathsf{Cl}}}(\mathsf{cep} :: \mathsf{lda} :: \mathsf{m} :: \mathsf{nt})$ and $\mathsf{hl} = \mathcal{H}ash(\mathsf{lda} :: \mathsf{cep} :: \mathsf{nt} :: \mathsf{rl})$.

Suppose the two messages $\mathsf{Clog}(\mathsf{lda}, \mathsf{m}, \mathsf{nt}, \mathsf{s2}, \mathsf{rl})$ and $\mathsf{Clog}(\mathsf{lda}', \mathsf{m}', \mathsf{nt}', \mathsf{s2}', \mathsf{rl}')$ have been sent to $\mathsf{c} : \mathsf{CLog}$. We need to show that $\mathsf{nt} \neq \mathsf{nt}'$. Again, by the threat scenario we can conclude that C sent the two messages to c. Suppose without loss of generality that $\mathsf{Clog}(\mathsf{lda}, \mathsf{m}, \mathsf{nt}, \mathsf{s2}, \mathsf{rl})$ was sent first. According to the statechart specification for C, C reaches the final state immediately afterwards. According to the overall activity diagram given in the specification, C starts a new protocol run only after nt is incremented (and rolling over is not possible). Thus we have $\mathsf{nt}' \geq \mathsf{nt} + 1$, in particular $\mathsf{nt} \neq \mathsf{nt}'$.

Load acquirer security: Suppose that we have $\mathsf{ml}_\mathsf{n} \in \mathcal{K}$ and $\mathsf{rl}_\mathsf{n} \in \mathcal{K}$ where $\mathsf{ml}_\mathsf{n} = \mathcal{S}ign_{\mathsf{K}_{\mathsf{L}}^{-1}}(\mathsf{cep} :: \mathsf{nt} :: \mathsf{lda} :: \mathsf{m}_\mathsf{n} :: \mathsf{s1} :: y :: \mathsf{hl}_\mathsf{n} :: \mathsf{h2l}_\mathsf{n})$ with $\mathsf{hl}_\mathsf{n} = \mathcal{H}ash(\mathsf{lda} :: \mathsf{cep} :: \mathsf{nt} :: \mathsf{rl}_\mathsf{n})$ and $\mathsf{h2l}_\mathsf{n} = \mathcal{H}ash(\mathsf{lda} :: \mathsf{cep} :: \mathsf{nt} :: \mathsf{r2l}_\mathsf{n})$, for some cep, nt, $\mathsf{s1}$, and y, and that a message $\mathsf{Llog}(\mathsf{cep}, 0, \mathsf{nt}, x)$ has been sent to $\mathsf{l} : \mathsf{LLog}$, for some x. We need to show that there exist $x' \in \mathcal{K}_\mathsf{L}$ and $z \in \mathcal{K}$ with $z = \mathcal{S}ign_{\mathsf{K}_{\mathsf{l}}^{-1}}(\mathsf{cep} :: \mathsf{lda} :: \mathsf{m}_\mathsf{n} :: \mathsf{nt} :: y')$ where $y' = \mathcal{H}ash(\mathsf{lda} :: \mathsf{cep} :: \mathsf{nt} :: x') = y$.

By the assumed threat scenario, the communication link between L and l is secure (and according to the specification only L can send messages to l). This implies that the message $\mathsf{Llog}(\mathsf{cep}, 0, \mathsf{nt}, x)$ to $\mathsf{l} : \mathsf{LLog}$ originated at L. According to the specifications of L, this implies that L previously received a message $\mathsf{RespC}(\mathsf{s3}, x')$ with $x' = x$, $x' \neq 0$, and such that $\mathcal{H}ash(\mathsf{lda} :: \mathsf{cep} :: \mathsf{nt} :: x') = y'$ for a value y' received in the message $\mathsf{Respl}(\mathsf{cep}, \mathsf{nt}, \mathsf{s1}, y')$ previously in the same protocol run, and such that for the second argument of the message $\mathsf{RespL}(\mathsf{s2}, z)$ received immediately before $\mathsf{RespC}(\mathsf{s3}, x')$, $\mathcal{E}xt_{\mathsf{K}_{\mathsf{l}}}(z) = \mathsf{cep} :: \mathsf{lda} :: \mathsf{m}_\mathsf{n} :: \mathsf{nt} :: y'$ holds (in particular we have $x', z \in \mathcal{K}_\mathsf{L}$).

Card issuer security: Suppose that the message $\mathsf{Clog}(\mathsf{lda}, \mathsf{m}, \mathsf{nt}, \mathsf{s2}, \mathsf{rl})$ was sent to $\mathsf{c} : \mathsf{CLog}$, where $\mathsf{m} \neq 0$ and $\mathcal{E}xt_{\mathsf{K}_{\mathsf{Cl}}}(\mathsf{s2}) = \mathsf{cep} :: \mathsf{nt} :: \mathcal{S}ign_{\mathsf{K}_{\mathsf{Cl}}}(\mathsf{cep} :: \mathsf{lda} :: \mathsf{m} :: \mathsf{nt}) :: \mathcal{H}ash(\mathsf{lda} :: \mathsf{cep} :: \mathsf{nt} :: \mathsf{rl})$ holds for some lda. We need to show that the card issuer has a valid signature ml_n corresponding to this transaction.

From the specification of C we see that C has received the message $\mathsf{Credit}(\mathsf{s2}, \mathsf{rl})$ just before in the same protocol run, and that $\mathcal{E}xt_{\mathsf{K}_{\mathsf{Cl}}}(\mathsf{s2}) = \mathsf{cep} :: \mathsf{nt} :: \mathsf{s1} :: \mathsf{hl}$ holds, where $\mathsf{s1} := \mathcal{S}ign_{\mathsf{K}_{\mathsf{Cl}}}(\mathsf{cep} :: \mathsf{lda} :: \mathsf{m} :: \mathsf{nt})$ and $\mathsf{hl} := \mathcal{H}ash(\mathsf{lda} :: \mathsf{cep} :: \mathsf{nt} :: \mathsf{rl})$. Since the key K_{Cl} is kept secret by C and I (see Proposition 5.11), we may conclude that I created $\mathsf{s2}$. According to the specification of I, this can only be the case if $\mathsf{ml} \in \mathcal{K}_{\mathsf{I}}$ with $\mathcal{E}xt_{\mathsf{K}_{\mathsf{L}}}(\mathsf{ml}) = \mathsf{cep} :: \mathsf{nt} :: \mathsf{lda} :: \mathsf{m} :: \mathsf{s1} :: \widehat{\mathsf{hc}}_\mathsf{nt} :: \mathsf{hl} :: \mathsf{h2l}$.

References

[Aba00]   M. Abadi. Security protocols and their properties. In F.L. Bauer
            and R. Steinbrüggen, editors, *Foundations of Secure Computation*,
            pages 39–60. IOS Press, Amsterdam, 2000. 20th International Summer
            School, Marktoberdorf, Germany.

[ABKL93]   M. Abadi, M. Burrows, C. Kaufman, and B. Lampson. Authentication
            and delegation with smart-cards. *Science of Computer Programming*,
            21(2):93–113, 1993.

[Abr90]   S. Abramsky. A generalized Kahn principle for abstract asynchronous
            networks. In *Mathematical foundations of programming semantics
            (New Orleans, LA, 1989)*, pages 1–21. Springer, Berlin Heidelberg New
            York, 1990.

[AdBD+02]   J.Ø. Aagedal, F. den Braber, T. Dimitrakos, B.A. Gran, D. Raptis,
            and K. Stølen. Model-based risk assessment to improve enterprise
            security. In *6th International Enterprise Distributed Object Computing
            Conference (EDOC 2002)*, pages 51–62. IEEE Computer Society, New
            York, 2002.

[AFG02]   M. Abadi, C. Fournet, and G. Gonthier. Secure implementation of
            channel abstractions. *Information and Computation*, 174(1):37–83,
            2002.

[AG99]   M. Abadi and A.D. Gordon. A calculus for cryptographic protocols:
            The spi calculus. *Information and Computation*, 148(1):1–70, January
            1999.

[AGM00]   S. Abramsky, D.M. Gabbay, and T.S.E. Maibaum, editors. *Hand-
            book of logic in computer science*, volume 1–5, pages xii+827. The
            Clarendon Press, New York, 1992–2000.

[AGMO04]   S. Abramsky, D.R. Ghica, A.S. Murawski, and C.-H.L. Ong. Applying
            game semantics to compositional software modeling and verification.
            In K. Jensen and A. Podelski, editors, *10th International Conference
            on Tools and Algorithms for the Construction and Analysis of Systems
            (TACAS 2004)*, volume 2988 of *Lecture Notes in Computer Science*,
            pages 421–435. Springer, Berlin Heidelberg New York, 2004.

[AJ01]   M. Abadi and J. Jürjens. Formal eavesdropping and its computational
            interpretation. In N. Kobayashi and B.C. Pierce, editors, *Theoretical
            Aspects of Computer Software (4th International Symposium, TACS*

2001), volume 2215 of *Lecture Notes in Computer Science*, pages 82–94. Springer, Berlin Heidelberg New York, 2001.

[AJP95]   M. Abrams, S. Jajodia, and H. Podell, editors. *Information security: an integrated collection of essays.* IEEE Computer Society Press, Silver Springs, MD, 1995. Download at http://www.acsac.org/secshelf/book001/book001.html.

[AJSW00]   N. Asokan, P. Janson, M. Steiner, and M. Waidner. State of the art in electronic payment systems. *Advances in Computers*, 53:425–449, 2000.

[AK96]   R. Anderson and M. Kuhn. Tamper resistance – a cautionary note. In *USENIX Workshop on Electronic Commerce*, pages 1–11, 1996.

[AKS96]   T. Aslam, I. Krsul, and E. Spafford. Use of a taxonomy of security faults. In *19th National Information Systems Security Conference (NISSC)*, pages 551–560, 1996.

[AL91]   M. Abadi and L. Lamport. The existence of refinement mappings. *Theoretical Computer Science*, 82(2):253–284, May 1991.

[AL93]   M. Abadi and L. Lamport. Composing specifications. *ACM Transactions on Programming Languages and Systems 15*, 1:73–132, January 1993.

[Ald01]   A. Aldini. Probabilistic information flow in a process algebra. In K. G. Larsen and M. Nielsen, editors, *12th International Conference on Concurrency Theory (CONCUR 2001)*, volume 2154 of *Lecture Notes in Computer Science*, pages 152–168. Springer, Berlin Heidelberg New York, 2001.

[AN96]   M. Abadi and R. Needham. Prudent engineering practice for cryptographic protocols. *IEEE Transactions on Software Engineering*, 22(1):6–15, January 1996.

[And94]   R. Anderson. Why cryptosystems fail. *Communications of the ACM*, 37(11):32–40, November 1994.

[And99]   R. Anderson. The formal verification of a payment system. In M. Hinchey and J. Bowen, editors, *Industrial-Strength Formal Methods in Practice*, pages 43–52. Springer, Berlin Heidelberg New York, 1999.

[And01]   R. Anderson. *Security Engineering: A Guide to Building Dependable Distributed Systems.* John Wiley & Sons, New York, 2001.

[And02]   R. Anderson. Two remarks on public key cryptology. Technical Report UCAM-CL-TR-549, University of Cambridge, 2002.

[APG95]   M. Abrams, H. Podell, and D. Gambel. Security engineering. In Abrams et al [AJP95], chapter 14, pages 330–349. Download at http://www.acsac.org/secshelf/book001/book001.html.

[APS99]   V. Apostolopoulos, V. Peris, and D. Saha. Transport layer security: How much does it really cost? In *Conference on Computer Communications (IEEE Infocom)*, pages 717–725. IEEE Computer Society, New York, March 1999.

[AR00a]   M. Abadi and P. Rogaway. Reconciling two views of cryptography (The computational soundness of formal encryption). In J. van Leeuwen, O. Watanabe, M. Hagiya, D. Mosses P. and T. Ito, editors, *Theoretical Computer Science, International Conference IFIP TCS 2000*, volume 1872 of *Lecture Notes in Computer Science*, pages 3–22. Springer, Berlin Heidelberg New York, 2000.

[AR00b]   E. Astesiano and G. Reggio. Formalism and method. *Theoretical Computer Science*, 236:3–34, 2000.

[Arc01]   ArcSecure. http://www.arcsecure.de, February 2001.

[AS85]   B. Alpern and F. Schneider. Defining liveness. *Information Processing Letters*, 21(4):181–185, October 1985.

[AW03]   K. Alghathbar and D. Wijesekera. Consistent and complete access control policies in use cases. In Stevens [Ste03b], pages 373–387.

[BAN89]   M. Burrows, M. Abadi, and R. Needham. A logic of authentication. *Proceedings of the Royal Society, Series A*, 426(1871):233–271, December 1989. Also appeared as SRC Research Report 39 and, in a shortened form, in *ACM Transactions on Computer Systems 8*, 1:18–36 (February 1990).

[BB03]   E. Boiten and M. Bujorianu. Exploring UML development through unification. In Jürjens et al [JRFF03], pages 47–62.

[BBD$^+$03] C. Bodei, M. Buchholtz, P. Degano, F. Nielson, and H. R. Nielson. Automatic validation of protocol narration. In *16th IEEE Computer Security Foundations Workshop (CSFW-16 2003)*, pages 126–140. IEEE Computer Society, New York, 2003.

[BBH$^+$03] R. Breu, K. Burger, M. Hafner, J. Jürjens, G. Popp, G. Wimmel, and V. Lotz. Key issues of a formally based process model for security engineering. In *16th International Conference "Software & Systems Engineering & their Applications" (ICSSEA 2003)*, 2003.

[BCR00]   E. Börger, A. Cavarra, and E. Riccobene. Modeling the dynamics of UML State Machines. In Y. Gurevich, P. Kutter, M. Odersky, and L. Thiele, editors, *Abstract State Machines. Theory and Applications*, volume 1912 of *Lecture Notes in Computer Science*, pages 223–241. Springer, Berlin Heidelberg New York, 2000.

[BCR04]   E. Börger, A. Cavarra, and E. Riccobene. On formalizing UML state machines using ASM. *Information & Software Technology*, 46(5):287–292, 2004.

[BD00]   C. Bolton and J. Davies. Using relational and behavioural semantics in the verification of object models. In Smith and Talcott [ST00], pages 163–182.

[BDCL$^+$01] A. Bondavalli, M. Dal Cin, D. Latella, I. Majzik, A. Pataricza, and G. Savoia. Dependability analysis in the early phases of UML based system design. *Journal of Computer Systems Science and Engineering*, 16:265–275, 2001.

[BDL03]   D. Basin, J. Doser, and T. Lodderstedt. Model driven security for process-oriented systems. In *Proceedings of the 8th ACM Symposium on Access Control Models and Technologies (SACMAT 2003)*, pages 100–109. ACM, New York, 2003.

[BDNN01]   C. Bodei, P. Degano, F. Nielson, and H. R. Nielson. Security analysis using flow logics. In G. Paun, G. Rozenberg, and A. Salomaa, editors, *Current Trends in Theoretical Computer Science*. World Scientific, 2001.

[BdVS02]   P. Bonatti, S. De Capitani di Vimercati, and P. Samarati. An algebra for composing access control policies. *ACM Transactions on Information and System Security*, 5(1):1–35, February 2002.

[Bel98]   S. M. Bellovin. Cryptography and the internet. In H. Krawczyk, editor, *Advances in Cryptology - CRYPTO '98*, volume 1462 of *Lecture Notes in Computer Science*, pages 46–55. Springer, Berlin Heidelberg New York, 1998.

[BFPR02]   A. Bossi, R. Focardi, C. Piazza, and S. Rossi. Transforming processes to check and ensure information flow security. In H. Kirchner and C. Ringeissen, editors, *9th International Conference on Algebraic Methodology and Software Technology (AMAST 2002)*, volume 2422 of *Lecture Notes in Computer Science*, pages 271–286. Springer, Berlin Heidelberg New York, 2002.

[BG03]   J. Barros and L. Gomes. Actions as activities and activities as Petri nets. In Jürjens et al [JRFF03], pages 129–135.

[BGH+97]   R. Breu, R. Grosu, F. Huber, B. Rumpe, and W. Schwerin. Towards a precise semantics for object-oriented modeling techniques. In J. Bosch and S. Mitchell, editors, *Object-Oriented Technology, ECOOP 1997 Workshop Reader*, volume 1357 of *Lecture Notes in Computer Science*. Springer, Berlin Heidelberg New York, 1997.

[BGH+98]   R. Breu, R. Grosu, F. Huber, B. Rumpe, and W. Schwerin. Systems, views and models of UML. In M. Schader and A. Korthaus, editors, *The Unified Modeling Language – Technical Aspects and Applications*, pages 93–109. Physica-Verlag, Heidelberg, 1998. 1st UML Workshop of the GROOM GI-Arbeitskreis.

[BHH+97]   R. Breu, U. Hinkel, C. Hofmann, C. Klein, B. Paech, B. Rumpe, and V. Thurner. Towards a formalization of the unified modeling language. In M. Aksit and S. Matsuoka, editors, *ECOOP'97 - Object-Oriented Programming*, volume 1241 of *Lecture Notes in Computer Science*, pages 344–366. Springer, Berlin Heidelberg New York, 1997.

[BHP+97]   M. Broy, F. Huber, B. Paech, B. Rumpe, and K. Spies. Software and system modeling based on a unified formal semantics. In M. Broy and B. Rumpe, editors, *Requirements Targeting Software and Systems Engineering (RTSE '97)*, volume 1526 of *Lecture Notes in Computer Science*, pages 43–68. Springer, Berlin Heidelberg New York, 1997.

[BJMF02]   M. Boger, M. Jeckle, S. Mueller, and J. Fransson. Diagram Interchange for UML. In Jézéquel et al [JHC02], pages 398–411.

[BKL02]   G. Brose, M. Koch, and K.-P. Löhr. Integrating access control design into the software development process. In *Integrated Design and Process Technology (IDPT)*, 2002.

[Bla04]   B. Blanchet. Automatic proof of strong secrecy for security protocols. In *2004 IEEE Symposium on Security and Privacy*, pages 86–100. IEEE Computer Society, New York, 2004.

[Blo02]   B. Blobel. Aspects of modeling using the examples of Electronic Health Records (EHRs). In *CORAS workshop*, 2002. Part of International Conference on Telemedicine (ICT2002).

[BMM99]   S. Brackin, C. Meadows, and J. Millen. CAPSL interface for the NRL protocol analyzer. In *Application-Specific Systems and Software Engineering Technology (ASSET 1999)*. IEEE Computer Society, New York, 1999.

[BMV03]   D. A. Basin, S. Mödersheim, and Luca Viganò. An on-the-fly model-checker for security protocol analysis. In Snekkenes and Gollmann [SG03], pages 253–270.

[Boe81]   B.W. Boehm. *Software Engineering Economics*. Prentice Hall, Englewood Cliffs, NJ, 1981.

[Boo91]   G. Booch. *Object-Oriented Design With Applications*. Benjamin/Cummings, Redwood City, CA, 1991.

[BP04]   R. Breu and G. Popp. Actor-centric modeling of user rights. In Wermelinger and Margaria [WM04], pages 165–179.

[BR97]   G. Bella and E. Riccobene. Formal analysis of the Kerberos authentication system. *Journal of Universal Computer Science*, 3(12):1337–1381, December 1997.

[BR98]   G. Bella and E. Riccobene. A realistic environment for crypto-protocol analyses by ASMs. In U. Glasser, editor, *5th International Workshop on Abstract State Machines (ASM)*, pages 127–138, 1998. Part of INFORMATIK 1998.

[Bre01]   R. Breu. *Objektorientierter Softwareentwurf - Integration mit UML*. Springer, Berlin Heidelberg New York, 2001.

[Bro86]   M. Broy. A theory for nondeterminism, parallelism, communication, and concurrency. *Theoretical Computer Science*, 45:1–61, 1986.

[Bro97]   M. Broy. Compositional refinement of interactive systems. *Journal of the ACM*, 44(6):850–891, 1997.

[Bro98]   M. Broy. A functional rephrasing of the assumption/commitment specification style. *Formal Methods in System Design*, 13(1):87–119, 1998.

[Bro00]   M. Broy. Algebraic specification of reactive systems. *Theoretical Computer Science*, 239(1):3–40, 2000.

[Bro01]   M. Broy. Toward a mathematical foundation of software engineering methods. *IEEE Transactions on Software Engineering*, 27(1):42–57, 2001.

[BS00]   E. Börger and J. Schmid. Composition and submachine concepts for sequential ASMs. In P. Clote and H. Schwichtenberg, editors, *Computer Science Logic (CSL 2000)*, volume 1862 of *Lecture Notes in Computer Science*, pages 41–60. Springer, Berlin Heidelberg New York, 2000.

[BS01]   M. Broy and K. Stølen. *Specification and Development of Interactive Systems*. Springer, Berlin Heidelberg New York, 2001.

[BS03]   M. Broy and R. Steinbrüggen. *Modellbildung in der Informatik*. Springer, Berlin Heidelberg New York, 2003.

[BV99]   B. Bokowski and J. Vitek. Confined types. In *14th Annual ACM SIGPLAN Conference on ObjectOriented Programming Systems, Languages, and Applications (OOPSLA 1999)*, pages 82–96, 1999.

[BW00]   M. Broy and M. Wirsing. Algebraic state machines. In T. Rus, editor, *8th International Conference on Algebraic Methodology and Software Technology (AMAST 2000)*, volume 1816 of *Lecture Notes in Computer Science*, pages 89–188. Springer, Berlin Heidelberg New York, 2000.

[Cas03]   Castor. Castor library. Available at http://castor.exolab.org, June 2003.

[Cav00]   A. Cavarra. *Applying Abstract State Machines to Formalize and Integrate the UML Lightweight Method*. PhD thesis, DMI, Universitá di Catania, 2000.

[CC01]   Common Criteria. http://csec.nist.gov/cc/, 2001.

[CCG+03]   S. Chaki, E. M. Clarke, A. Groce, S. Jha, and H. Veith. Modular verification of software components in C. In *25th International Conference on Software Engineering (ICSE 2003)*, pages 385–395. IEEE Computer Society, New York, 2003.

[CEP01]   CEPSCO. Common Electronic Purse Specifications, 2001. Business
            Requirements Version 7.0, Functional Requirements Version 6.3, Tech-
            nical Specification Version 2.3, available from http://www.cepsco.
            com.

[CER]   CERT Coordination Center (CERT/CC) http://www.cert.org.

[Chu93]   L. Chung. Dealing with security requirements during the develop-
            ment of information systems. In *5th International Conference on Ad-
            vanced Information Systems Engineering (CAiSE 1993)*, pages 234–
            251. Springer, Berlin Heidelberg New York, 1993.

[CKM+99]   S. Cook, A. Kleppe, R. Mitchell, B. Rumpe, J. Warmer, and A. Wills.
            Defining UML family members using prefaces. In Ch. Mingins and
            B. Meyer, editors, *Proceedings of Technology of Object-Oriented Lan-
            guages and Systems (TOOLS Pacific 1999)*. IEEE Computer Society,
            New York, 1999.

[CLM+03]   S. Cigoli, P. Leblanc, S. Malaponti, D. Mandrioli, M. Mazzucchelli, and
            A. Morzenti. An experiment in applying UML 2.0 to the development
            of an industrial critical application. In Jürjens et al [JRFF03], pages
            19–34.

[Coo00]   S. Cook. The UML family: Profiles, prefaces and packages. In Evans
            et al [EKS00], pages 255–264.

[CRS04]   A. Cavarra, E. Riccobene, and P. Scandurra. A framework to simulate
            uml models: moving from a semi-formal to a formal environment. In
            H. Haddad, A. Omicini, R. L. Wainwright, and L. M. Liebrock, editors,
            2004 ACM Symposium on Applied Computing (SAC), pages 1519–
            1523, 2004.

[CW96]   E. Clarke and J. Wing. Formal methods: State of the art and future
            directions. *ACM Computing Surveys*, 28(4):626–643, 1996.

[DB00]   J. Derrick and E. Boiten. Refinement of objects and operations in
            Object-Z. In Smith and Talcott [ST00], pages 257–277.

[DB01]   J. Derrick and E. Boiten. *Refinement in Z and Object-Z: Foundations
            and advanced applications*. Formal Approaches to Computing and In-
            formation Technology. Springer, Berlin Heidelberg New York, 2001.

[DBG01]   J. Dushina, M. Benjamin, and D. Geist. Semi-Formal Test Generation
            with Genevieve. In *38th Design Automation Conference (DAC)*, pages
            617–622. ACM, New York, 2001. Download at http://www.dac.com.

[DEG01]   Degas, 2001. http://www.omnys.it/degas.

[DF93]   J. Dick and A. Faivre. Automating the generation and sequencing of
            test cases from model-based specifications. In *Formal Methods Eu-
            rope (FME) 1993: Industrial-Strength Formal Methods*, volume 670 of
            Lecture Notes in Computer Science, pages 268–284. Springer, Berlin
            Heidelberg New York, 1993.

[DFG00]   A. Durante, R. Focardi, and R. Gorrieri. A compiler for analyzing
            cryptographic protocols using noninterference. *ACM Transactions on
            Software Engineering and Methodology*, 9(4):488–528, 2000.

[DFS98]   P. Devanbu, P. Fong, and S. Stubblebine. Techniques for trusted soft-
            ware engineering. In *20th International Conference on Software Engi-
            neering*, pages 126–135, 1998.

[DGH02]   K. Diethers, U. Goltz, and M. Huhn. Model checking UML statecharts
            with time. In Jürjens et al [JCF+02], pages 35–52.

[DHS03]   A. Darvas, R. Hähnle, and D. Sands. A theorem proving approach to analysis of secure information flow. In Gorrieri [Gor03], pages 111–120. Available at http://www.dsi.unive.it/IFIPWG1_7/WITS2003/program-wits03.htm.

[Dij68]   E. W. Dijkstra. Stepwise program construction. published as [Dij82], February 1968.

[Dij82]   E. W. Dijkstra. Stepwise program construction. In Selected Writings on Computing: A Personal Perspective, pages 1–14. Springer, Berlin Heidelberg New York, 1982.

[DRR+02]   T. Dimitrakos, B. Ritchie, D. Raptis, J. Ø. Aagedal, F. den Braber, K. Stølen, and S. H. Houmb. Integrating model-based security risk management into ebusiness systems development: The CORAS approach. In J. Monteiro, P. Swatman, and L. Tavares, editors, Second IFIP Conference on E-Commerce, E-Business, E-Government (I3E 2002), volume 233 of IFIP Conference Proceedings, pages 159–175. Kluwer Academic, Dordrecht, 2002.

[DS00a]   J. Derrick and G. Smith. Structural refinement in Object-Z/CSP. In W. Grieskamp, T. Santen, and B. Stoddart, editors, Integrated Formal Methods (IFM 2000), volume 1945 of Lecture Notes in Computer Science, pages 194–213. Springer, Berlin Heidelberg New York, 2000.

[DS00b]   P. Devanbu and S. Stubblebine. Software engineering for security: A roadmap. In The Future of Software Engineering, pages 227–239, 2000. Special Volume of the International Conference on Software Engineering (ICSE 2000).

[DY83]   D. Dolev and A. Yao. On the security of public key protocols. IEEE Transactions on Information Theory, IT-29(2):198–208, 1983.

[Eck95]   C. Eckert. Matching security policies to application needs. In J. H. P. Eloff and S. H. von Solms, editors, 11th International Conference on Information Security (SEC 1995), pages 237–254. Chapman & Hall, London, 1995.

[Eck98]   C. Eckert. Tool-supported verification of cryptographic protocols. In 14th International Information Security Conference (SEC 1998). Chapman & Hall, London, 1998.

[Eck03]   C. Eckert. IT-Sicherheit – Konzepte, Verfahren, Protokolle. Oldenbourg, München, 2nd edition, 2003.

[EFLR99]   A. Evans, R. B. France, K. Lano, and B. Rumpe. Meta-modeling semantics of UML. In H. Kilov, B. Rumpe, and I. Simmonds, editors, Behavioral Specifications of Businesses and Systems. Kluwer Academic, Amsterdam, 1999.

[eHe03]   ehealth project webpages. http://www.dimdi.de/de/ehealth/karte, 2003.

[EHHS00]   G. Engels, J. Hausmann, R. Heckel, and S. Sauer. Dynamic metamodeling: A graphical approach to the operational semantics of behavioral diagrams in UML. In Evans et al [EKS00], pages 323–337.

[EKS00]   A. Evans, S. Kent, and B. Selic, editors. The Unified Modeling Language: Advancing the Standard (UML 2000), volume 1939 of Lecture Notes in Computer Science. Springer, Berlin Heidelberg New York, 2000.

[EM97]   C. Eckert and D. Marek. Developing secure applications: A systematic approach. In *13th International Conference on Information Security (SEC 1998)*, pages 267–279. Chapman & Hall, London, 1997.

[ERW81]   B. Fernandez E. C. Summers R. and C. Wood. *Database Security and Integrity*. Systems Programming Series. Addison-Wesley, Reading, MA, February 1981.

[FELR98]   R. B. France, A. Evans, K. Lano, and B. Rumpe. The UML as a formal modeling notation. *Computer Standards & Interfaces*, 19:325–334, 1998.

[Fer98]   E. B. Fernandez. A holistic view of internet security, 1998. Tutorial notes.

[Fer99]   E. B. Fernandez. Coordination of security levels for internet architectures. In *International Workshop on Database and Expert Systems Applications (DEXA 1999)*, pages 837–841, 1999.

[FG95]   R. Focardi and R. Gorrieri. A taxonomy of security properties for process algebras. *Journal of Computer Security*, 3(1):5–34, 1995.

[FG97]   R. Focardi and R. Gorrieri. The compositional security checker: A tool for the verification of information flow security properties. *IEEE Transaction of Software Engineering*, 23(9):550–571, September 1997.

[FGG97]   R. Focardi, A. Ghelli, and R. Gorrieri. Using non interference for the analysis of security protocols. In H. Orman and C. Meadows, editors, *DIMACS Workshop on Design and Formal Verification of Security Protocols*, 1997. Available at http://dimacs.rutgers.edu/ Workshops/Security/program2/program.html.

[FGM03]   R. Focardi, R. Gorrieri, and F. Martinelli. A comparison of three authentication properties. *Theoretical Computer Science*, 291(3):285–327, 2003.

[FH97]   E. B. Fernandez and J. C. Hawkins. Determining role rights from use cases. In *Workshop on Role-Based Access Control*, pages 121–125. ACM, New York, 1997.

[FHH⁺03]   R. B. France, H. Hermanns, H. Hußmann, A. Knapp, B. Selic, and J. Jürjens. What's wrong with uml for critical systems design ? In Jürjens et al [JRFF03]. Panel session.

[FJ02]   E. B. Fernandez and J. Jürjens. A holistic view of secure systems development: Using patterns and UML. In *17th International Conference on Information Security (SEC 2002)*. International Federation for Information Processing (IFIP), 2002. Half-day tutorial.

[FKG⁺02]   R. Fredriksen, M. Kristiansen, B.A. Gran, K. Stølen, T.A. Opperud, and T. Dimitrakos. The CORAS framework for a model-based risk management process. In S. Anderson, S. Bologna, and M. Felici, editors, *21st International Conference on Computer Safety, Reliabiltiy and Security (SAFECOMP 2002)*, volume 2434 of *Lecture Notes in Computer Science*, pages 94–105. Springer, Berlin Heidelberg New York, 2002.

[FMMMP02] E. Fernández-Medina, A. Martínez, C. Medina, and M. Piattini. UML for the design of secure databases: Integrating security levels, user roles, and constraints in the database design process. In Jürjens et al [JCF⁺02], pages 93–106.

[Fow04]   M. Fowler. *UML Distilled*. Addison-Wesley, Reading, MA, third edition, 2004.

[FP01]   E. B. Fernandez and R. Y. Pan.   A pattern language for secu-
             rity models.   In *Conference on Pattern Languages of Programs
             (PLoP 2001)*, 2001.   http://jerry.cs.uiuc.edu/~plop/plop2001/
             accepted_submissions/accepted-papers.html.

[FPR00]   M. Fontura, W. Pree, and B. Rumpe. UML-F: A modeling language
             for object-oriented frameworks. In E. Bertino, editor, *14th European
             Conference on Object-Oriented Programming (ECOOP 2000)*, volume
             1850 of *Lecture Notes in Computer Science*, pages 63–82. Springer,
             Berlin Heidelberg New York, 2000.

[Gas88]   M. Gasser. *Building a secure computer system.* Van Nostrand Rein-
             hold, New York, 1988.

[GB99]   S. Goldwasser and M. Bellare. Lecture notes on cryptography. Summer
             Course "Cryptography and Computer Security" at MIT, 1999.

[GCS91]   J. Graham-Cumming and J. Sanders. On the refinement of noninter-
             ference. In *Computer Security Foundations Workshop (CSFW)*, pages
             35–42, 1991.

[Gen03]   Gentleware. http://www.gentleware.com, 2003.

[GFR02]   G. Georg, R. B. France, and I. Ray.   An aspect-based approach to
             modeling security concerns. In Jürjens et al [JCF+02], pages 107–120.

[GFR03]   G. Georg, R. B. France, and I. Ray.   Creating security mechanism
             aspect models from abstract security aspect models. In Jürjens et al
             [JRFF03], pages 35–46.

[GHJV95]   E. Gamma, R. Helm, R. Johnson, and J. Vlissides. *Design Patterns
             – Elements of Reusable Object-Oriented Software.* Addison-Wesley,
             Reading, MA, 1995.

[GHJW03]   J. Grünbauer, H. Hollmann, J. Jürjens, and G. Wimmel. Modelling and
             verification of layered security protocols: A bank application. In *Com-
             puter Safety, Reliability, and Security (SAFECOMP 2003)*, volume
             2788 of *Lecture Notes in Computer Science*, pages 116–129. Springer,
             Berlin Heidelberg New York, 2003.

[GHR03]   J. D. Guttman, A. L. Herzog, and J. D. Ramsdell. Information flow in
             operating systems: Eager formal methods. In Gorrieri [Gor03], pages
             81–90. Available at http://www.dsi.unive.it/IFIPWG1_7/WITS2003/
             program-wits03.htm.

[GI98]   Gesellschaft für Informatik. *28th Annual Conference of the German
             Society of Computer Science.* Technical Report, Magdeburg University,
             1998.

[GKW02]   D. Gollmann, G. Karjoth, and M. Waidner, editors. *7th European Sym-
             posium on Research in Computer Security (ESORICS 2002)*, volume
             2502 of *Lecture Notes in Computer Science*. Springer, Berlin Heidel-
             berg New York, 2002.

[GL97]   F. Germeau and G. Leduc. Model-based design and verification of
             security protocols using LOTOS. In H. Orman and C. Meadows, ed-
             itors, *DIMACS Workshop on Design and Formal Verification of Se-
             curity Protocols*, 1997.   Available at http://dimacs.rutgers.edu/
             Workshops/Security/program2/program.html.

[GM82]   J. Goguen and J. Meseguer. Security policies and security models.
             In *Symposium on Security and Privacy (S&P)*, pages 11–20. IEEE
             Computer Society, New York, 1982.

[GM84]   J. Goguen and J. Meseguer. Unwinding and inference control. In *Symposium on Security and Privacy (S&P)*, pages 75–87. IEEE Computer Society, New York, 1984.

[GMM03]   P. Giorgini, F. Massacci, and J. Mylopoulos. Requirement engineering meets security: A case study on modelling secure electronic transactions by VISA and Mastercard. In I.-Y. Song, S. W. Liddle, T. W. Ling, and P. Scheuermann, editors, *22nd International Conference on Conceptual Modeling (ER 2003)*, volume 2813 of *Lecture Notes in Computer Science*, pages 263–276. Springer, Berlin Heidelberg New York, 2003.

[GNY90]   L. Gong, R. Needham, and R. Yahalom. Reasoning about belief in cryptographic protocols. In *Symposium on Security and Privacy (S&P)*, pages 234–248. IEEE Computer Society, New York, 1990.

[Gol96]   D. Gollmann. What do we mean by entity authentication? In *Symposium on Security and Privacy (S&P)*, pages 46–54, 1996.

[Gol99]   D. Gollmann. *Computer Security*. John Wiley & Sons, New York, 1999.

[Gol00]   D. Gollmann. On the verification of cryptographic protocols – a tale of two committees. In S. Schneider and P. Ryan, editors, *Workshop on Security Architectures and Information Flow*, volume 32 of *Electronic Notes in Theoretical Computer Science*. Elsevier, Amsterdam, 2000.

[Gol03a]   D. Gollmann. Analysing security protocols. In A. Abdallah, P. Ryan, and S. Schneider, editors, *Formal Aspects of Security (FASec 2002)*, volume 2629 of *Lecture Notes in Computer Science*, pages 71–80. Springer, Berlin Heidelberg New York, 2003.

[Gol03b]   D. Gollmann. Authentication by correspondence. *IEEE Journal on Selected Areas in Communications*, 21(1):88–95, January 2003.

[Gol03c]   D. Gollmann. Facets of security. In C. Priami, editor, *Global Computing. Programming Environments, Languages, Security, and Analysis of Systems, IST/FET International Workshop, (GC 2003)*, volume 2874 of *Lecture Notes in Computer Science*, pages 192–202. Springer, Berlin Heidelberg New York, 2003.

[Gon98]   L. Gong. Java^{TM} Security Architecture (JDK1.2). http://java.sun.com/j2se/1.4.2/docs/guide/security/spec/security-spec.doc.html, October 1998.

[Gon99]   L. Gong. *Inside Java 2 Platform Security – Architecture, API Design, and Implementation*. Addison-Wesley, Reading, MA, 1999.

[GOR02]   S. Gürgens, P. Ochsenschläger, and C. Rudolph. Role based specification and security analysis of cryptographic protocols using asynchronous product automata. In *DEXA Workshops 2002*, pages 473–482. IEEE Computer Society, New York, 2002.

[Gor03]   R. Gorrieri, editor. *Workshop on Issues in the Theory of Security (WITS'03)*. IFIP WG 1.7, ACM SIGPLAN, and GI FoMSESS, 2003. Available at http://www.dsi.unive.it/IFIPWG1_7/WITS2003/program-wits03.htm.

[GPP98]   M. Gogolla and F. Parisi-Presicce. State diagrams in UML: A formal semantics using graph transformations. In M. Broy, D. Coleman, T. Maibaum, and B. Rumpe, editors, *Workshop on Precise Semantics for Software Modeling Techniques (PSMT 1998)*, pages 55–72. TU München, TUM-I9803, 1998.

[GSG99]   S. Gritzalis, D. Spinellis, and P. Georgiadis. Security protocols over open networks and distributed systems: Formal methods for their analysis, design, and verification. *Computer Communications Journal,* 22(8):695–707, 1999.

[GSS00]   W. Grieskamp, T. Santen, and B. Stoddart, editors. *2nd International Conference on Integrated Formal Methods (IFM 2000),* volume 1945 of *Lecture Notes in Computer Science.* Springer, Berlin Heidelberg New York, 2000.

[Gur95]   Y. Gurevich. Evolving algebras 1993: Lipari guide. In E. Börger, editor, *Specification and Validation Methods,* pages 9–36. Oxford University Press, Oxford, 1995.

[Gur97]   Y. Gurevich. Draft of the ASM Guide. Technical Report CSE-TR-336-97, University of Michigan, EECS Department, May 1997.

[Gut00]   J. Guttman. Security goals: Packet trajectories and strand spaces. In R. Focardi and R. Gorrieri, editors, *Foundations of Security Analysis and Design (FOSAD 2000),* volume 2171 of *Lecture Notes in Computer Science.* Springer, Berlin Heidelberg New York, 2000. Summer school lectures.

[HBVL97]   T. Hillenbrand, A. Buch, R. Vogt, and B. Lochner. WALDMEISTER – high-performance equational deduction. *Journal of Automated Reasoning,* 2(18):265–270, 1997.

[HdBLS02]   S. H. Houmb, F. den Braber, M. S. Lund, and K. Stølen. Towards a UML profile for model-based risk assessment. In Jürjens et al [JCF⁺02], pages 79–92.

[Hei99]   C. Heitmeyer. Formal methods for developing software specifications: Paths to wider usage. In H. R. Arabnia, editor, *International Conference on Parallel and Distributed Processing Techniques and Applications (PDPTA 1999),* pages 1047–1053, 1999.

[Hei01]   C. Heitmeyer. Applying "practical" formal methods to the specification and analysis of security properties. In V. I. Gorodetski, V. A. Skormin, and L. J. Popyack, editors, *International Workshop on Mathematical Methods, Models and Architectures for Computer Networks Security (MMM-ACNS 2001),* volume 2052 of *Lecture Notes in Computer Science,* pages 84–89. Springer, Berlin Heidelberg New York, 2001.

[Her03]   P. Herrmann. Formal security policy verification of distributed component-structured software. In H. König, M. Heiner, and A. Wolisz, editors, *23rd IFIP WG 6.1 International Conference on Formal Techniques for Networked and Distributed Systems (FORTE 2003),* volume 2767 of *Lecture Notes in Computer Science,* pages 257–272. Springer, Berlin Heidelberg New York, 2003.

[HF97]   J. C. Hawkins and E. B. Fernandez. Extending use cases and interaction diagrams to develop distributed system architecture requirements. Technical Report TR-CSE-97-47, Department of Computer Science & Engineering, Florida Atlantic University, 1997.

[HG97]   D. Harel and E. Gery. Executable object modeling with statecharts. *Computer,* 30(7):31–42, 1997.

[HG02]   K. Hansen and I. Gullesen. Utilizing UML and patterns for safety critical systems. In Jürjens et al [JCF⁺02], pages 147–154.

[HH03a]   R. Heldal and F. Hultin. Bridging model-based and language-based security. In Snekkenes and Gollmann [SG03], pages 235–252.

[HH03b]   S. H. Houmb and K. Hansen. Towards a UML profile for model-based risk assessment of security critical systems. In Jürjens et al [JRFF03], pages 95–104.

[Hit01]   R. Hite. Oral communication, May 2001.

[HJ03a]   S. Höhn and J. Jürjens. Automated checking of SAP security permissions. In *6th Working Conference on Integrity and Internal Control in Information Systems (IICIS)*. International Federation for Information Processing (IFIP), Kluwer Academic, Dordrecht, 2003.

[HJ03b]   S. H. Houmb and J. Jürjens. Developing secure networked web-based systems using model-based risk assessment and UMLsec. In *10th Asia-Pacific Software Engineering Conference (APSEC 2003)*, page 488ff. IEEE Computer Society, New York, 2003.

[HK98]   M. Hitz and G. Kappel. Developing with UML – goodies, pitfalls, workarounds. In J. Bézivin and P.-A. Muller, editors, *UML 1998 – Beyond the Notation*, volume 1618 of *Lecture Notes in Computer Science*, pages 9–20. Springer, Berlin Heidelberg New York, 1998.

[HMR$^+$98] F. Huber, S. Molterer, A. Rausch, B. Schätz, M. Sihling, and O. Slotosch. Tool supported specification and simulation of distributed systems. In *International Symposium on Software Engineering for Parallel and Distributed Systems*, pages 155–164, 1998.

[HNS97]   S. Helke, T. Neustupny, and T. Santen. Automating test case generation from Z specifications with Isabelle. In J. Bowen, M. Hinchey, and D. Till, editors, *Proceedings of the Z Users Conference (ZUM 1997): The Z Formal Specification Notation*, volume 1212 of *Lecture Notes in Computer Science*, pages 52–71. Springer, Berlin Heidelberg New York, 1997.

[Hoa72]   C. A. R. Hoare. Proof of correctness of data representations. *Acta Informatica*, 1:271–282, 1972.

[Hoa85]   C. A. R. Hoare. *Communicating Sequential Processes*. Prentice Hall, Englewood Cliffs, NJ, 1985.

[Hoa96]   C. A. R. Hoare. How did software get so reliable without proof? In M.-C. Gaudel and J. Woodcock, editors, *Formal Methods Europe 1996 (FME): Industrial Benefit and Advances in Formal Methods*, volume 1051 of *Lecture Notes in Computer Science*, pages 1–17. Springer, Berlin Heidelberg New York, 1996.

[Hol03]   G. Holzmann. *The Spin Model Checker*. Addison-Wesley, 2003.

[HPS01]   M. Heisel, A. Pfitzmann, and T. Santen. Confidentiality-preserving refinement. In *Computer Security Foundations Workshop (CSFW)*, pages 295–306. IEEE Computer Society, New York, 2001.

[HTB03]   R. Hawkins, I. Toyn, and I. Bate. An approach to designing safety critical systems using the Unified Modelling Language. In Jürjens et al [JRFF03], pages 3–18.

[Huß01]   H. Hußmann, editor. *4th International Conference on Fundamental Approaches to Software Engineering (FASE)*, volume 2029 of *Lecture Notes in Computer Science*. Springer, Berlin Heidelberg New York, 2001.

[Jan02]   D. Jansen. Probabilistic UML statecharts for specification and verification: A case study. In Jürjens et al [JCF$^+$02], pages 121–132.

[JBR98]   I. Jacobsen, G. Booch, and J. Rumbaugh. *The Unified Software Development Process*. Addison-Wesley, Reading, MA, 1998.

[JCF⁺02]   J. Jürjens, V. Cengarle, E. B. Fernandez, B. Rumpe, and R. Sandner, editors. *Critical Systems Development with UML (CSDUML 2002)*, TU München Technical Report TUM-I0208, 2002. UML 2002 satellite workshop proceedings.

[JFS04]   J. Jürjens, E. B. Fernandez, and R. Sandner. Critical systems development with UML-like languages. *Journal on Software and Systems Modeling*, 2004. Special section, to be published.

[JG03]   J. Jürjens and J. Grünbauer. Critical systems development with UML: Overview with automotive case-study. In *4th International Conference on Software Engineering, Artificial Intelligence, Networking, and Parallel/Distributed Computing (SNPD 2003)*, pages 512–517. International Association for Computer and Information Science (ACIS), 2003.

[JH03]   J. Jürjens and S. H. Houmb. Development of safety-critical systems and model-based risk analysis with UML. In *Dependable Computing*, volume 2847 of *Lecture Notes in Computer Science*, pages 364–365. Springer, Berlin Heidelberg New York, 2003.

[JH04]   J. Jürjens and S. K. Houmb. Risk-driven development of security-critical systems using UMLsec. Kluwer Academic, Dordrecht, 2004. Book chapter to be published (book title pending).

[JHC02]   J.-M. Jézéquel, H. Hußmann, and S. Cook, editors. *5th International Conference on the Unified Modeling Language (UML 2002)*, volume 2460 of *Lecture Notes in Computer Science*. Springer, Berlin Heidelberg New York, 2002.

[JHK03]   D. N. Jansen, H. Hermanns, and J.-P. Katoen. A QoS-oriented extension of UML statecharts. In Stevens [Ste03b], pages 76–91. 6th International Conference.

[JK03]   J. Jürjens and T. Kuhn. Mobile web-based applications with UML: Concepts and tools. In *International Conference WWW/Internet 2003*. International Association for Development of the Information Society (IADIS), 2003. Half-day tutorial.

[JKS95]   S. Jajodia, B. Kogan, and R. Sandhu. A multilevel-secure object-oriented data model. In Abrams et al [AJP95]. Download at http://www.acsac.org/secshelf/book001/book001.html.

[Jon72]   C. B. Jones. Formal development of correct algorithms: An example based on Earley's recogniser. In *ACM Conference on Proving Assertions about Programs*, volume 7 of *SIGPLAN Notices*, pages 150–169, 1972.

[Jon87]   B. Jonsson. *Compositional Verification of Distributed Systems*. PhD thesis, Department of Computer Systems, Uppsala University, 1987. Technical Report DoCS 87/09.

[JPW02]   J. Jürjens, G. Popp, and G. Wimmel. Towards using security patterns in model-based system development. In *7th European Conference on Pattern Languages of Programs (EuroPLoP 2002)*, 2002. Security Focus Group.

[JPW03]   J. Jürjens, G. Popp, and G. Wimmel. Use case oriented development of security-critical systems. In *Workshop on Distributed Objects and Components Security (DOCsec 2003)*. Object Management Group (OMG), 2003. Also appeared in *Information Security Bulletin* 8:51–56, 2003.

[JRFF03] J. Jürjens, B. Rumpe, R. B. France, and E. B. Fernandez, editors. *Critical Systems Development with UML (CSDUML 2003)*, number TUM-I0317 in TU München Technical Report, 2003. UML 2003 satellite workshop proceedings.

[JS04a] J. Jürjens and P. Shabalin. Automated verification of UMLsec models for security requirements. In J.-M. Jézéquel, H. Hußmann, and S. Cook, editors, *UML 2004 – The Unified Modeling Language*, volume 2460 of *Lecture Notes in Computer Science*, pages 412–425. Springer, Berlin Heidelberg New York, 2004.

[JS04b] J. Jürjens and P. Shabalin. XML-based analysis of UML models for critical systems development. In *Advances in UML and XML Based Software Evolution*. IDEA Group Publishing, 2004. To be published.

[JS04c] J. Jürjens and Pasha Shabalin. A foundation for tool-supported critical systems development with UML. In *11th Annual IEEE International Conference on the Engineering of Computer Based Systems (ECBS 2004)*, Brno, Czech Republic, May 24–26 2004. IEEE Computer Society, New York.

[JSA+04] J. Jürjens, P. Shabalin, E. Alter, A. Gilg, S. Höhn, D. Kopjev, M. Lehrhuber, S. Meng, M. Schwaiger, G. Kokavecz, S. Schwarzmüller, and S. Shen. UMLsec tool, 2004. Accessible through a webinterface via [Jür04]. Available as open-source.

[Jür00] J. Jürjens. Secure information flow for concurrent processes. In C. Palamidessi, editor, *CONCUR 2000 (11th International Conference on Concurrency Theory)*, volume 1877 of *Lecture Notes in Computer Science*, pages 395–409. Springer, Berlin Heidelberg New York, 2000.

[Jür01a] J. Jürjens. Abstracting from failure probabilities. In *Second International Conference on Application of Concurrency to System Design (ACSD 2001)*, pages 53–64. IEEE Computer Society, New York, 2001.

[Jür01b] J. Jürjens. Composability of secrecy. In V. Gorodetski, V. Skormin, and L. Popyack, editors, *International Workshop on Mathematical Methods, Models and Architectures for Computer Networks Security (MMM-ACNS 2001)*, volume 2052 of *Lecture Notes in Computer Science*, pages 28–38. Springer, Berlin Heidelberg New York, 2001.

[Jür01c] J. Jürjens. Developing secure systems with UMLsec – from business processes to implementation. In D. Fox, M. Köhntopp, and A. Pfitzmann, editors, *Verläßliche IT-Systeme 2001 (VIS 2001)*, DuD-Fachbeiträge. Vieweg, Wiesbaden, 2001.

[Jür01d] J. Jürjens. Formal development and verification of security-critical systems with UML. In *Workshop on Automated Verification of Critical Systems (AVoCS 2001)*, Oxford, 2001. Published as OUCL Technical Report PRG-RR-01-07. Available at ftp://ftp.comlab.ox.ac.uk/pub/Documents/techreports/RR-01-07.ps.gz.

[Jür01e] J. Jürjens. Modelling audit security for smart-card payment schemes with UMLsec. In M. Dupuy and P. Paradinas, editors, *Trusted Information: The New Decade Challenge*, pages 93–108. International Federation for Information Processing (IFIP), Kluwer Academic, Dordrecht, 2001. Proceedings of the *16th International Conference on Information Security (SEC 2001)*.

[Jür01f]   J. Jürjens. On a problem of Gabriel and Ulmer. *Journal of Pure and Applied Algebra*, 158:183–196, 2001.

[Jür01g]   J. Jürjens. Secrecy-preserving refinement. In *International Symposium on Formal Methods Europe (FME)*, volume 2021 of *Lecture Notes in Computer Science*, pages 135–152. Springer, Berlin Heidelberg New York, 2001.

[Jür01h]   J. Jürjens. Secure Java development with UMLsec. In B. De Decker, F. Piessens, J. Smits, and E. Van Herrenweghen, editors, *Advances in Network and Distributed Systems Security*, pages 107–124. International Federation for Information Processing (IFIP) TC-11 WG 11.4, Kluwer Academic, Dordrecht, 2001. Proceedings of the *First Annual Working Conference on Network Security (I-NetSec 2001)*.

[Jür01i]   J. Jürjens. Towards development of secure systems using UMLsec. In H. Hußmann, editor, *4th International Conference on Fundamental Approaches to Software Engineering (FASE)*, volume 2029 of *Lecture Notes in Computer Science*, pages 187–200. Springer, Berlin Heidelberg New York, 2001. Also Oxford University Computing Laboratory TR-9-00 (November 2000), http://web.comlab.ox.ac.uk/oucl/publications/tr/tr-9-00.html.

[Jür01j]   J. Jürjens. Transformations for introducing patterns – a secure systems case study. In *Workshop on Transformations in UML (WTUML, ETAPS 2001 Satellite Event)*, 2001.

[Jür02a]   J. Jürjens. A UML statecharts semantics with message-passing. In Lamont et al [LHPP02], pages 1009–1013.

[Jür02b]   J. Jürjens. Critical systems development with UML. In *Forum on Design Languages (FDL 2002)*. European Electronic Chips & Systems design Initiative (ECSI), 2002. Invited talk.

[Jür02c]   J. Jürjens. Encapsulating rules of prudent security engineering. In B. Christianson, B. Crispo, J. A. Malcolm, and M. Roe, editors, *Security Protocols*, volume 2467 of *Lecture Notes in Computer Science*, pages 95–101. Springer, Berlin Heidelberg New York, 2002. 9th International Workshop. Transcript of discussion on pages 102–106.

[Jür02d]   J. Jürjens. Formal semantics for interacting UML subsystems. In B. Jacobs and A. Rensink, editors, *5th International Conference on Formal Methods for Open Object-Based Distributed Systems (FMOODS 2002)*, pages 29–44. International Federation for Information Processing (IFIP), Kluwer Academic, Dordrecht, 2002.

[Jür02e]   J. Jürjens. Methodische Entwicklung sicherer CORBA-Anwendungen. In P. Horster, editor, *Enterprise Security*. IT-Verlag, Sauerlach, 2002.

[Jür02f]   J. Jürjens. *Principles for Secure Systems Design*. PhD thesis, Oxford University Computing Laboratory, 2002.

[Jür02g]   J. Jürjens. Secure systems development with UML – applications to telemedicine. In *CORAS Public Workshop*, 2002. International Conference on Telemedicine (ICT 2002). Invited talk.

[Jür02h]   J. Jürjens. UMLsec – presenting the profile. In *6th Annual Workshop on Distributed Objects and Components Security (DOCsec 2002)*. Object Management Group (OMG), 2002. Half-day tutorial.

[Jür02i]   J. Jürjens. UMLsec: Extending UML for secure systems development. In Jézéquel et al [JHC02], pages 412–425.

[Jür02j]   J. Jürjens. Using UMLsec and goal-trees for secure systems development. In Lamont et al [LHPP02], pages 1026–1031.

[Jür03a]   J. Jürjens. Algebraic state machines: Concepts and applications to security. In M. Broy and A. Zamulin, editors, *Andrei Ershov 5th International Conference "Perspectives of System Informatics" (PSI 2003)*, volume 2890 of *Lecture Notes in Computer Science*, pages 338–343. Springer, Berlin Heidelberg New York, 2003.

[Jür03b]   J. Jürjens. Critical systems development with UML and model-based testing, 2003. Tutorials at SAFECOMP 2003, ICSTEST-E 2003, SE 2004. Download of material at http://www4.in.tum.de/~juerjens/csdumltut.

[Jür03c]   J. Jürjens. Developing safety- and security-critical systems with UML. In *DARP workshop*, 2003. Invited talk.

[Jür03d]   J. Jürjens. Developing safety-critical systems with UML. In Stevens [Ste03b], pages 360–372.

[Jür03e]   J. Jürjens. Developing secure enterprise applications with UML. In *Fourth Workshop on UML for Enterprise Applications*. Object Management Group (OMG), 2003. Half-day tutorial.

[Jür03f]   J. Jürjens. FoMSESS webpages. Working Group on Formal Methods and Software Engineering for Safety and Security (FoMSESS) of the German Computer Society (GI). Website at http://www4.in.tum.de/~fomsess, 2003.

[Jür03g]   J. Jürjens. Model-based security with UMLsec. In *UML Forum Tokyo*, 2003. Invited talk.

[Jür04]   J. Jürjens. UMLsec webpage, 2002-04. Accessible at http://www.umlsec.org. Protected content can be accessed as user: Reader, with password: Ihavethebook.

[Jür04a]   J. Jürjens. Componentware for critical systems. *Journal of Object Technology*, 2004. To be published.

[Jür04b]   J. Jürjens. Critical Systems Development with UML, 2004. Series of about 30 tutorials at international conferences 2002–04. Further information and download of material at http://www4.in.tum.de/~juerjens/csdumltut.

[Jür04c]   J. Jürjens. Developing high-assurance secure systems with UML: An electronic purchase protocol. In *Eighth IEEE International Symposium on High Assurance Systems Engineering (HASE 2004)*, pages 231–240. IEEE Computer Society, New York, 2004.

[Jür04d]   J. Jürjens. Developing security-critical applications with UMLsec – a short walk-through. *Novatica*, 168, March/April 2004.

[Jür04e]   J. Jürjens. Developing Security-Critical Systems with UML, 2004. Series of tutorials at 30 international conferences including OMG DOCsec 2002, IFIP SEC 2002, ETAPS 2003, OMG Workshop On UML for Enterprise Applications 2003, Formal Methods Symposium 2003, ASE 2003, FMOODS 2003, ECOOP 2004, and WCC 2004. Download of material at http://www4.in.tum.de/~juerjens/csdumltut.

[Jür04f]   J. Jürjens. Foundations for designing secure architectures. In *First International Workshop on Views On Designing Complex Architectures (VODCA 2004)*, Bertinoro, 2004.

[Jür04g]   J. Jürjens. Logic for security. In *Spring School "Logic in Computer Science"*, Venezia, 2004. Graduate school on Logic in Informatics, Munich.

[Jür04h]   J. Jürjens. Playing the devil's advocate: Testing real-time systems. In *Conference on Software Testing (ICSTEST-E 2004)*, Bilbao, 2004.

[Jür04i]   J. Jürjens. Security in UML. In *4th International School on Foundations of Security Analysis and Design (FOSAD 2004)*, 2004.

[Jür04j]   J. Jürjens. Standards and processes for modelbased engineering of safety- and security-critical systems. In *23rd International Conference on Computer Safety, Reliability, and Security (SAFECOMP 2004)*, Lecture Notes in Computer Science. Springer, Berlin Heidelberg New York, 2004. Full-day tutorial.

[Jür04k]   J. Jürjens. Tools for Critical Systems Development with UML. In *19th International Conference on Automated Software Engineering (ASE 2004)*. IEEE Computer Society, New York, 2004.

[Jür05]   J. Jürjens. Security modeling with UML. Universidad Carlos III de Madrid, 2005.

[JW01a]   J. Jürjens and G. Wimmel. Formally testing fail-safety of electronic purse protocols. In *16th International Conference on Automated Software Engineering (ASE 2001)*, pages 408–411. IEEE Computer Society, New York, 2001.

[JW01b]   J. Jürjens and G. Wimmel. Security modelling for electronic commerce: The Common Electronic Purse Specifications. In B. Schmid, K. Stanoevska-Slabeva, and V. Tschammer, editors, *Towards the E-Society: E-Commerce, E-Business, and E-Government*, pages 489–506. International Federation for Information Processing (IFIP), Kluwer Academic, Dordrecht, 2001. First IFIP Conference on E-Commerce, E-Business, and E-Government (I3E 2001).

[JW02]   J. Jürjens and G. Wimmel. Specification-based testing of firewalls. In D. Bjørner, M. Broy, and A. Zamulin, editors, *Andrei Ershov 4th International Conference "Perspectives of System Informatics" (PSI 2001)*, volume 2244 of *Lecture Notes in Computer Science*, pages 308–316. Springer, Berlin Heidelberg New York, 2002.

[KAH99]   J. Kirby, M. Archer, and C. Heitmeyer. Applying formal methods to an information security device: An experience report. In *4th IEEE International Symposium on High Assurance Systems Engineering (HASE 1999)*, pages 81–88. IEEE Computer Society, New York, 1999.

[Kar00]   G. Karjoth. Java and mobile code security – an operational semantics of Java 2 access control. In *Computer Security Foundations Workshop (CSFW)*, pages 224–232, 2000.

[Kem89]   R. A. Kemmerer. Analyzing encryption protocols using formal verification techniques. *IEEE Journal on Selected Areas in Communications*, 7(4):448–457, May 1989.

[KER99]   S. Kent, A. Evans, and B. Rumpe. UML semantics FAQ. In A. Moreira and S. Demeyer, editors, *Object-Oriented Technology, ECOOP 1999 Workshop Reader*, volume 1743 of *Lecture Notes in Computer Science*, pages 33–56. Springer, Berlin Heidelberg New York, 1999.

[KG98]   L. Kassab and S. Greenwald. Towards formalizing the Java Security Architecture in JDK 1.2. In Quisquater et al [QDMG98], pages 191–207.

294   References

[KK04]   R. Kilian-Kehr. Can formal verification become mainstream in soft-
            ware engineering ? In J. Jürjens, editor, *FoMSESS 2004*, 2004. Second
            Workshop of the Working Group on Formal Methods and Software En-
            gineering for Safety and Security (FoMSESS) of the German Computer
            Society (GI). Available at http://www4.in.tum.de/~fomsess.
[KN98]   V. Kessler and H. Neumann. A sound logic for analysing electronic
            commerce protocols. In Quisquater et al [QDMG98], pages 345–360.
[Kna99]   A. Knapp. A formal semantics for UML interactions. In R. B. France
            and B. Rumpe, editors, « *UML* » *'99: Second International Conference
            on The Unified Modeling Language*, volume 1723 of *Lecture Notes in
            Computer Science*, pages 116–130. Springer, Berlin Heidelberg New
            York, 1999.
[KPP02]   M. Koch and F. Parisi-Presicce. Access control policy specification in
            UML. In Jürjens et al [JCF+02], pages 63–78.
[KRFL04]   D.-K. Kim, I. Ray, R. B. France, and Na Li. Modeling role-based
            access control using parameterized UML models. In Wermelinger and
            Margaria [WM04], pages 180–193.
[Krü00]   I. H. Krüger. *Distributed System Design with Message Sequence Charts*.
            PhD thesis, Institut für Informatik, TU München, 2000.
[Krü02]   I. H. Krüger. Towards precise service specification with UML and
            UML-RT. In Jürjens et al [JCF+02], pages 19–34.
[KW01]   A. Kleppe and J. Warmer. Unification of Static and Dynamic Seman-
            tics of UML. Technical report, Klasse Objecten, NL, 2001. Download
            at http://www.klasse.nl/english/uml/uml-semantics.html.
[KW04]   R. Küsters and T. Wilke. Automata-based analysis of recursive cryp-
            tographic protocols. In V. Diekert and M. Habib, editors, *21st An-
            nual Symposium on Theoretical Aspects of Computer Science (STACS
            2004)*, volume 2996 of *Lecture Notes in Computer Science*, pages 382–
            393. Springer, Berlin Heidelberg New York, 2004.
[Lam73]   B. W. Lampson. A note on the confinement problem. *Communications
            of the ACM*, 16(10):613–615, 1973.
[LB73]   L. J. LaPadula and D. E. Bell. Secure computer systems: A math-
            ematical model. Technical report, The MITRE Corporation, 1973.
            Reprinted in *Journal of Computer Security*, 4:239–263, 1996.
[LBD02]   T. Lodderstedt, D. Basin, and J. Doser. SecureUML: A UML-based
            modeling language for model-driven security. In Jézéquel et al [JHC02],
            pages 426–441.
[LGS01]   U. Lang, D. Gollmann, and R. Schreiner. Verifiable identifiers in mid-
            dleware security. In *17th Annual Computer Security Applications Con-
            ference*, pages 450–459. IEEE Computer Society, New York, 2001.
[LHPP02]   G. B. Lamont, H. Haddad, G. Papadopoulos, and B. Panda, editors.
            Proceedings of the 2002 Symposium of Applied Computing (SAC).
            ACM Press, 2002.
[LLK+02]   W. Längst, A. Lapp, K. Knorr, H.-P. Schneider, J. Schirmer, D. Kraft,
            and U. Kiencke. CARTRONIC-UML models: Basis for partially au-
            tomated risk analysis in early development phases. In Jürjens et al
            [JCF+02], pages 3–17.
[LMM03]   L. Lavazza, A. Morzenti, and S. Morasca. A dual language approach
            to the development of time-critical systems with UML. In Jürjens et al
            [JRFF03], pages 113–120.

[Lot97]   V. Lotz. Threat scenarios as a means to formally develop secure systems. *Journal of Computer Security 5*, pages 31–67, 1997.

[Lot00]   V. Lotz.   Formally defining security properties with relations on streams. *Electronic Notes in Theoretical Computer Science*, 32, 2000. DERA/RHUL Workshop on Secure Architecture and Information Flow, 1999.

[Low95]   G. Lowe. An attack on the Needham-Schroeder public-key authentication protocol. *Information Processing Letters*, 56(3):131–133, November 1995.

[Low96]   G. Lowe. Breaking and fixing the Needham-Schroeder public-key protocol using FDR. *Software Concepts and Tools*, 17(3):93–102, 1996.

[Low98]   G. Lowe. Casper: A compiler for the analysis of security protocols. *Journal of Computer Security*, 6(1–2):53–84, 1998.

[LP99]   J. Lilius and I. Porres. Formalising UML state machines for model checking. In R. B. France and B. Rumpe, editors, *The Unified Modeling Language (UML 1999)*, volume 1723 of *Lecture Notes in Computer Science*, pages 430–445. Springer, Berlin Heidelberg New York, 1999.

[LR97]   G. Lowe and B. Roscoe. Using CSP to detect errors in the TMN protocol. *IEEE Transactions on Software Engineering*, 23(10):659–669, 1997.

[LW94]   B. Liskov and J. Wing. A behavioral notion of subtyping. *ACM Transactions on Programming Languages and Systems*, 16(6):1811–1841, November 1994.

[Man01]   H. Mantel. Preserving information flow properties under refinement. In *Symposium on Security and Privacy (S&P)*, pages 78–93, 2001.

[Man02]   H. Mantel. On the composition of secure systems. In *2002 IEEE Symposium on Security and Privacy*, pages 88–101. IEEE Computer Society, New York, 2002.

[MCF87]   J. K. Millen, S. C. Clark, and S. B. Freedman. The Interrogator: Protocol security analysis. *IEEE Transactions on Software Engineering*, SE-13(2):274–288, February 1987.

[McG98]   G. McGraw. Testing for security during development: Why we should scrap penetrate-and-patch. *IEEE Aerospace and Electronic Systems*, April 1998.

[McL94]   J. McLean. Security models. In J. Marciniak, editor, *Encyclopedia of Software Engineering*. John Wiley & Sons, New York, 1994.

[McL96]   J. McLean. A general theory of composition for a class of "possibilistic" properties. *IEEE Transactions on Software Engineering*, 22(1):53–67, 1996.

[McM93]   K. L. McMillan. *Symbolic Model Checking*. Kluwer Academic, Boston, 1993.

[Mea91]   C. Meadows. A system for the specification and analysis of key management protocols. In *Symposium on Security and Privacy (S&P)*, pages 182–195, 1991.

[Mea92]   C. Meadows. Using traces based on procedure calls to reason about composability. In *Symposium on Security and Privacy (S&P)*, pages 177–188. IEEE Computer Society, New York, 1992.

[Mea95]   C. Meadows. Formal verification of cryptographic protocols: A survey. In J. Pieprzyk and R. Safavi-Naini, editors, *Asiacrypt 1994*, volume

917 of *Lecture Notes in Computer Science*, pages 135–150. Springer, Berlin Heidelberg New York, 1995.

[Mea96]   C. Meadows. The NRL Protocol Analyzer: An overview. *Journal of Logic Programming*, 26(2):113–131, 1996.

[Mea00]   C. Meadows. Open issues in formal methods for cryptographic protocol analysis. In *DARPA Information Survivability Conference and Exposition (DISCEX 2000)*, pages 237–250. IEEE Computer Society, New York, 2000.

[Mer02]   S. Merz. From diagrams to semantics – and back (invited talk). In Jürjens et al [JCF⁺02].

[MGM03]   H. Mouratidis, P. Giorgini, and G. A. Manson. Integrating security and systems engineering: Towards the modelling of secure information systems. In J. Eder and M. Missikoff, editors, *15th International Conference on Advanced Information Systems Engineering (CAiSE 2003)*, volume 2681 of *Lecture Notes in Computer Science*, pages 63–78. Springer, Berlin Heidelberg New York, 2003.

[MH98]   P. Malacaria and C. Hankin. Generalised flowcharts and games. *Lecture Notes in Computer Science*, 1443:363–??, 1998.

[MIB98]   M. Maia, V. Iorio, and R. Bigonha. Interacting Abstract State Machines. In GI [GI98], pages 37–49.

[Mic01]   Microsoft TechNet. Information about virus-infected hotfixes, April 25 2001. Available at http://www.microsoft.com/technet/security/topics/virus/vihotfix.mspx.

[Mil71]   R. Milner. An algebraic definition of simulation between programs. In *2nd International Joint Conference on Artificial Intelligence (IJCAI 1971)*, pages 481–489, 1971.

[Mil89]   R. Milner. *Communication and Concurrency.* Prentice Hall, New York, 1989.

[MIL⁺97]   M. Moser, O. Ibens, R. Letz, J. Steinbach, C. Goller, J. Schumann, and K. Mayr. SETHEO and E-SETHEO – The CADE-13 Systems. *Journal of Automated Reasoning (JAR)*, 18(2):237–246, 1997.

[ML02]   R. Marcano and N. Levy. Transformation rules of OCL constraints into B formal expressions. In Jürjens et al [JCF⁺02], pages 147–154.

[MMS97]   J. Mitchell, M. Mitchell, and U. Stern. Automated analysis of cryptographic protocols using Murφ. In *Symposium on Security and Privacy (S&P)*, pages 141–151. IEEE Computer Society, New York, 1997.

[MOF02]   Object Management Group. *MOF 1.4 Specification*, April 2002. Available at http://www.omg.org/technology/documents/formal/mof.htm.

[MS00]   É. Meyer and T. Santen. Behavioural conformance verification in an integrated approach using UML and B. In Grieskamp et al [GSS00], pages 358–379.

[MS03]   H. Mantel and A. Sabelfeld. A unifying approach to the security of distributed and multi-threaded programs. *Journal of Computer Security*, 11(4):615–676, 2003.

[MvOV96]   A. Menezes, P. van Oorschot, and S. Vanstone. *Handbook of Applied Cryptography.* CRC Press, Boca Raton, FL, 1996. Download at http://www.cacr.math.uwaterloo.ca/hac.

[NEP01]   NEPTUNE, 2001. http://neptune.irit.fr.

[Net03]   Netbeans project.   Open source. Available from `http://mdr.netbeans.org`, 2003.

[NNS02]   F. Nielson, H. R. Nielson, and H. Seidl. Normalizable horn clauses, strongly recognizable relations, and spi. In M. V. Hermenegildo and G. Puebla, editors, *9th International Symposium on Static Analysis (SAS 2002)*, volume 2477 of *Lecture Notes in Computer Science*, pages 20–35. Springer, Berlin Heidelberg New York, 2002.

[NPW02]   T. Nipkow, L. C. Paulson, and M. Wenzel. *Isabelle/HOL - A Proof Assistant for Higher-Order Logic*. Springer, Berlin Heidelberg New York, 2002.

[NS78]   R. Needham and M. Schroeder. Using encryption for authentication in large networks of computers. *Communications of the ACM*, 21(12):993–999, 1978.

[NSU03]   Novosoft NSUML project.   Available from `http://nsuml.sourceforge.net/`, 2003.

[Off95]   J. Offutt. Practical mutation testing. In *12th International Conference on Testing Computer Software*, 1995.

[ÖP00]   G. Övergaard and K. Palmkvist. Interacting subsystems in UML. In Evans et al [EKS00], pages 359–368.

[OXL99]   J. Offutt, Y. Xiong, and S. Liu. Criteria for generating specification-based tests. In *5th IEEE Conference on Engineering of Complex Computer Systems (ICECCS 1999)*, page 119ff. IEEE Computer Society, New York, 1999.

[Pat02]   A. Pataricza. From the general resource model to a general fault modeling paradigm? In Jürjens et al [JCF+02], pages 163–170.

[Pau98a]   L. C. Paulson. Inductive analysis of the Internet protocol TLS (transcript of discussion). In B. Christianson, B. Crispo, W. S. Harbison, and M. Roe, editors, *Security Protocols*, volume 1550 of *Lecture Notes in Computer Science*, pages 13–23. Springer, Berlin Heidelberg New York, 1998. 6th International Workshop.

[Pau98b]   L. C. Paulson. The inductive approach to verifying cryptographic protocols. *Journal of Computer Security*, 6(1–2):85–128, 1998.

[Pet02]   L. Petre. Control systems development: A case study. In Jürjens et al [JCF+02], pages 171–180.

[PJWB03]   G. Popp, J. Jürjens, G. Wimmel, and R. Breu. Security-critical system development with extended use cases. In *10th Asia-Pacific Software Engineering Conference (APSEC 2003)*, pages 478–487. IEEE Computer Society, New York, 2003.

[PMP01]   Z. Pap, I. Majzik, and A. Pataricza. Checking general safety criteria on UML statecharts. In U. Voges, editor, *SAFECOMP 2001*, volume 2187 of *Lecture Notes in Computer Science*, pages 46–55. Springer, Berlin Heidelberg New York, 2001.

[Pol92]   W. T. Polk. Automated tools for testing computer systems vulnerability. In *NIST Special Publications*. National Institute of Standards and Technology, December 1992.

[PR94]   B. Paech and B. Rumpe. A new concept of refinement used for behaviour modelling with automata. In M. Naftalin, B. T. Denvir, and M. Bertran, editors, *FME 1994: Industrial Benefit of Formal Methods*, volume 873 of *Lecture Notes in Computer Science*, pages 154–174.

Springer, Berlin Heidelberg New York, 1994. Second International
Symposium of Formal Methods Europe.

[PS97]   J. Peleska and M. Siegel. Test automation of safety-critical reactive
systems. *South African Computer Jounal*, 19:53–77, 1997.

[PW00]   B. Pfitzmann and M. Waidner. Composition and integrity preservation
of secure reactive systems. In *7th ACM Conference on Computer and
Communications Security (CCS 2000)*, pages 245–254, 2000.

[QDMG98]   J.-J. Quisquater, Y. Deswarte, C. Meadows, and D. Gollmann, editors.
European Symposium on Research in Computer Security (ESORICS),
volume 1485 of *Lecture Notes in Computer Science*. Springer, Berlin
Heidelberg New York, 1998.

[RACH00]   G. Reggio, E. Astesiano, C. Choppy, and H. Hußmann. Analysing UML
active classes and associated state machines – A lightweight formal
approach. In T. S. E. Maibaum, editor, *Fundamental Approaches to
Software Engineering (FASE 2000)*, volume 1783 of *Lecture Notes in
Computer Science*, pages 127–146. Springer, Berlin Heidelberg New
York, 2000.

[RCA00]   G. Reggio, M. Cerioli, and E. Astesiano. An algebraic semantics
of UML supporting its multiview approach. In D. Heylen, A. Nij-
holt, and G. Scollo, editors, *Algebraic Methods in Language Processing
(AMiLP 2000)*, number 16 in International Twente Workshop on Language Technology (TWLT). University of Twente, NL, 2000. Algebraic
Methodology and Software Technology (AMAST) Workshop.

[RCA01]   G. Reggio, M. Cerioli, and E. Astesiano. Towards a rigorous semantics
of UML supporting its multiview approach. In Hußmann [Huß01],
pages 171–186.

[RE00]   W. Rankl and W. Effing. *Smart Card Handbook*. John Wiley & Sons,
New York, 2000. 2nd edition.

[RFBLO01]   D. Riehle, S. Fraleigh, D. Bucka-Lassen, and N. Omorogbe. The architecture of a UML virtual machine. In *ACM SIGPLAN Conference on Object-Oriented Programming Systems, Languages and Applications (OOPSLA 2001)*, volume 36 (11) of *SIGPLAN Notices*, pages
327–341. ACM, New York, November 2001.

[RFLG03]   I. Ray, R. B. France, N. Li, and G. Georg. An aspect-based approach to
modeling access control concerns. *Information & Software Technology*,
2003. To be published.

[Ric03]   R. Richardson. 2003 CSI/FBI computer crime and security survey.
Technical report, Computer Security Institute, San Francisco, May
2003. Available at http://www.gocsi.com/forms/fbi/pdf.html.

[RJB99]   J. Rumbaugh, I. Jacobson, and G. Booch. *The Unified Modeling Language Reference Manual*. Addison-Wesley, Reading, MA, 1999.

[RJW+03]   J. Romberg, J. Jürjens, G. Wimmel, O. Slotosch, and G. Hahn. AUTO-
FOCUS and the MoDe Tool. In *3rd International Conference on Appli-
cation of Concurrency to System Design (ACSD 2003)*, pages 249–250.
IEEE Computer Society, New York, 2003.

[RLKF03]   I. Ray, N. Li, D.-K. Kim, and R. B. France. Using parameterized
UML to specify and compose access control models. In *6th Working
Conference on Integrity and Internal Control in Information Systems
(IICIS)*. International Federation for Information Processing (IFIP),
Kluwer Academic, Dordrecht, 2003.

[RS98]   P. Ryan and S. Schneider. An attack on a recursive authentication protocol. *Information Processing Letters*, 65:7–10, 1998.

[RS01]   A. Rosenthal and E. Sciore. Administering permissions for distributed data: Factoring and automated inference. In *Conference on Data and Application Security*, pages 91–104. International Federation for Information Processing (IFIP), 2001.

[RSG⁺01] P. Ryan, S. Schneider, M. Goldsmith, G. Lowe, and B. Roscoe. *The Modelling and Analysis of Security Protocols: the CSP Approach.* Addison-Wesley, Reading, MA, 2001.

[Rum96]   Bernhard Rumpe. *Formale Methodik des Entwurfs verteilter objektorientierter Systeme.* PhD thesis, TU München, 1996.

[Rum02]   B. Rumpe. Executable modeling with UML. A vision or a nightmare? In *Issues & Trends of Information Technology Management in Contemporary Associations*, pages 697–701, Seattle, 2002. Idea Group Publishing, London.

[Rum04]   B. Rumpe. *Modellierung mit UML.* Springer, Berlin Heidelberg New York, 2004.

[RV01]   A. Riazanov and A. Voronkov. Vampire 1.1 (system description). In R. Goré, A. Leitsch, and T. Nipkow, editors, *First International Joint Conference on Automated Reasoning (IJCAR 2001)*, volume 2083 of *Lecture Notes in Computer Science*, pages 376–380. Springer, Berlin Heidelberg New York, 2001.

[RW99]   G. Reggio and R. Wieringa. Thirty one problems in the semantics of UML 1.3 dynamics. In *Rigorous Modelling and Analysis of the UML: Challenges and Limitations*, 1999. OOPSLA 1999 workshop.

[RWW94]   A. Roscoe, J. Woodcock, and L. Wulf. Non-interference through determinism. In D. Gollmann, editor, *3rd European Symposium on Research in Computer Security (ESORICS 1994)*, volume 875 of *Lecture Notes in Computer Science*, pages 33–53. Springer, Berlin Heidelberg New York, 1994.

[SBCJ97]   P. Samarati, E. Bertino, A. Ciampichetti, and S. Jajodia. Information flow control in object-oriented systems. *IEEE Transactions on Knowledge and Data Engineering*, pages 524–537, August 1997.

[SC01]   P. F. Syverson and I. Cervesato. The logic of authentication protocols. In *Foundations of Security Analysis and Design (FOSAD 2000)*, volume 2171 of *Lecture Notes in Computer Science*, pages 63–136, 2001.

[Sch96]   S. Schneider. Security properties and CSP. In *IEEE Symposium on Security and Privacy (S&P)*, pages 174–187, 1996.

[Sch97]   J. Schumann. Automatic verification of cryptographic protocols with SETHEO. In W. McCune, editor, *14th International Conference on Automated Deduction (CADE-14)*, volume 1249 of *Lecture Notes in Computer Science*, pages 87–100. Springer, Berlin Heidelberg New York, 1997.

[Sch98]   W. Schönfeld. Interacting Abstract State Machines. In GI [GI98], pages 22–36.

[Sch99a]   F. Schneider, editor. *Trust in Cyberspace.* National Academy Press, Washington, DC, 1999. Available at http://www.nap.edu/readingroom/books/trust.

[Sch99b]   J. Schumann. PIL/SETHEO: A tool for the automatic analysis of authentication protocols. In N. Halbwachs and D. Peled, editors, *11th*

International Conference on Computer Aided Verification (CAV '99), volume 1633 of *Lecture Notes in Computer Science*, pages 500–504. Springer, Berlin Heidelberg New York, 1999.

[Sch00]   W. Schulte. Why doesn't anyone use formal methods? In Grieskamp et al [GSS00], pages 297–298.

[Sch01]   J. M. Schumann. *Automated Theorem Proving in Software Engineering*. Springer, Berlin Heidelberg New York, 2001.

[Sch03a] M. Schumacher. *Security Engineering with Patterns – Origins, Theoretical Models, and New Applications*, volume 2754 of *Lecture Notes in Computer Science*. Springer, Berlin Heidelberg New York, 2003.

[Sch03b] M. A. Schwaiger. Tool-supported analysis of business processes and SAP permissions, 2003. Study project, TU München.

[SCW00]   S. Stepney, D. Cooper, and J. Woodcock. *An Electronic Purse: Specification, Refinement, and Proof*. Oxford University Computing Laboratory, 2000. Technical Monograph PRG-126.

[Sel03]   B. Selic. The use of modeling techniques in safety-critical system design (invited talk). In Jürjens et al [JRFF03], pages 1–2.

[SG03]   E. Snekkenes and D. Gollmann, editors. *8th European Symposium on Research in Computer Security (ESORICS 2003)*, volume 2808 of *Lecture Notes in Computer Science*. Springer, Berlin Heidelberg New York, 2003.

[SH99]   B. Schätz and F. Huber. Integrating formal description techniques. In J. M. Wing, J. Woodcock, and J. Davies, editors, *World Congress on Formal Methods in the Development of Computing Systems (FM 1999)*, volume 1709 of *Lecture Notes in Computer Science*, pages 1206–1225. Springer, Berlin Heidelberg New York, 1999.

[Sha99]   A. Shamir. Crypto predictions. In *3rd International Conference on Financial Cryptography (FC 1999)*, 1999.

[SHP02]   T. Santen, M. Heisel, and A. Pfitzmann. Confidentiality-preserving refinement is compositional – sometimes. In Gollmann et al [GKW02], pages 194–211.

[SKM01]   T. Schäfer, A. Knapp, and S. Merz. Model checking UML state machines and collaborations. In S. D. Stoller and W. Visser, editors, *Workshop on Software Model Checking*, volume 55(3) of *Electronic Notes in Theoretical Computer Science*. Elsevier, Amsterdam, 2001. Satellite event of the 13th International Conference on Computer-Aided Verification (CAV 2001)

[SP99]   P. Stevens and R. Pooley. *Using UML: software engineering with objects and components*. Addison-Wesley Longman, Reading, MA, 1999.

[SR98]   B. Selic and J. Rumbaugh. Using UML for modeling complex real-time systems. Available at http://www-106.ibm.com/developerworks/rational/library/, 1998.

[SS75]   J. Saltzer and M. Schroeder. The protection of information in computer systems. *Proceedings of the IEEE*, 63(9):1278–1308, September 1975.

[SS94]   R. Sandhu and P. Samarati. Access control: Principles and practice. *IEEE Communications Magazine*, 32(9):40–48, 1994.

[SS01]   G. Sutcliffe and C. Suttner. The tptp problem library for automated theorem proving, 2001. Available at http:\\www.tptp.org.

[SSB01]   R. Stärk, J. Schmid, and E. Börger. *Java and the Java virtual machine – definition, verification, validation.* Springer, Berlin Heidelberg New York, 2001.

[SSRB00]   D. C. Schmidt, M. Stal, H. Rohnert, and F. Buschmann. *Pattern-oriented Software Architecture*, volume 2. John Wiley & Sons, New York, 2000. Patterns for Concurrent and Networked Objects.

[ST00]   S. F. Smith and C. L. Talcott, editors. *4th International Conference on Formal Methods for Open Object-Based Distributed Systems (FMOODS 2000)*, volume 177 of *IFIP Conference Proceedings*. International Federation for Information Processing (IFIP), Kluwer Academic, Dordrecht, 2000.

[Ste01a]   P. Stevens. On use cases and their relationships in the Unified Modelling Language. In Hußmann [Huß01], pages 140–155.

[Ste01b]   P. Stevens. A revolution in UML tool use? Tool adaptation, extension and integration using XMI. UML 2001 tutorial, 2001.

[Ste03a]   P. Stevens. Small-scale XMI programming; a revolution in UML tool use? *Journal of Automated Software Engineering*, 10(1):7–21, 2003. Kluwer.

[Ste03b]   P. Stevens, editor. *The Unified Modeling Language (UML 2003)*, volume 2863 of *Lecture Notes in Computer Science*. Springer, Berlin Heidelberg New York, 2003. 6th International Conference.

[Stø01]   K. Stølen. A framework for risk analysis of security critical systems. In *Supplement of the 2001 International Conference on Dependable Systems and Networks (DSN 2001)*, pages D4–D11, 2001.

[Stö03]   H. Störrle. Assert and negate and refinement in UML-2 interactions. In Jürjens et al [JRFF03], pages 79–94.

[SvO94]   P. Syverson and P. van Oorschot. On unifying some cryptographic protocol logics. In *IEEE Symposium on Security and Privacy*, pages 14–28, 1994.

[SW97]   A. Schürr and A. Winter. Formal definition and refinement of UML's module/package concept. In J. Bosch and S. Mitchell, editors, *Object-Oriented Technology (ECOOP'97 Workshop Reader)*, volume 1357 of *Lecture Notes in Computer Science*, pages 211–215. Springer, Berlin Heidelberg New York, 1997.

[SW00]   G. Stenz and A. Wolf. E-SETHEO: An automated[3] theorem prover. In R. Dyckhoff, editor, *Automated Reasoning with Analytic Tableaux and Related Methods (TABLEAUX 2000)*, volume 1847 of *Lecture Notes in Computer Science*, pages 436–440. Springer, Berlin Heidelberg New York, 2000.

[TFHG99]   F. J. Thayer Fábrega, J. C. Herzog, and J. D. Guttman. Strand spaces: Proving security protocols correct. *Journal of Computer Security*, 7(1), 1999.

[The01]   The Register. Microsoft security fixes infected with funlove virus, April 25 2001. Available at http://www.theregister.co.uk/2001/04/25/microsoft_security_fixes_infected.

[TS02]   J. Tenzer and P. Stevens. Modelling recursive calls with UML state diagrams. In M. Pezzè, editor, *Fundamental Approaches to Software Engineering (FASE 2003)*, volume 2621 of *Lecture Notes in Computer Science*, pages 135–149. Springer, Berlin Heidelberg New York, 2002.

[UML03]   Object Management Group. *OMG Unified Modeling Language Spec-ification v1.5*, March 2003. Version 1.5. OMG Document formal/03-03-01.

[vdB02]   M. von der Beeck. A structured operational semantics for UML-statecharts. *Software and System Modeling*, 1(2):130–141, 2002.

[Ver03]   Verisoft project webpages. http://www.verisoft.de, 2003.

[vKSZ03]   J. van Katwijk, B. Sanden, and J. Zalewski. A study of new approaches to evaluate real-time software architectures for safety-critical systems. In Jürjens et al [JRFF03], pages 121–128.

[VM98]   J. Voas and G. McGraw. *Software Fault Injection: Inoculating Pro-grams Against Errors*. John Wiley & Sons, New York, 1998.

[VM02]   J. Viega and G. McGraw. *Building Secure Software*. Addison-Wesley, Reading, MA, 2002.

[vOL02]   D. von Oheimb and V. Lotz. Formal security analysis with interacting state machines. In Gollmann et al [GKW02], pages 212–228.

[VP03]   D. Varro and A. Pataricza. Automated formal verification of model transformations. In Jürjens et al [JRFF03], pages 63–78.

[VWW02]   M. Vetterling, G. Wimmel, and A. Wisspeintner. Secure systems de-velopment based on the common criteria. In *10th International Sym-posium on the Foundations of Software Engineering (FSE-10)*, pages 129–138. ACM, New York, 2002.

[Wal00]   M. Walker. On the security of 3GPP networks. In B. Preneel, editor, *Advances in Cryptology – EUROCRYPT*, volume 1807 of *Lecture Notes in Computer Science*, pages 102–103. Springer, Berlin Heidelberg New York, 2000.

[Wat02]   B. Watson. Non-functional analysis for UML models. In *Real-Time and Embedded Distributed Object Computing Workshop*. OMG, July 15–18, 2002. http://www.omg.org/news/meetings/workshops/RT_2002_Workshop_Presentations/03-1_Watson_Non-FunctionalAnalysis.pdf.

[WBH⁺02]   C. Weidenbach, U. Brahm, T. Hillenbrand, E. Keen, C. Theobald, and D. Topić. Spass version 2.0. In *18th International Conference on Automated Deduction (CADE-18)*, volume 2392 of *Lecture Notes in Computer Science*, pages 275–279. Springer, Berlin Heidelberg New York, 2002.

[Weh02]   H. Wehrheim. Checking behavioural subtypes via refinement. In B. Ja-cobs and A. Rensink, editors, *5th International Conference on For-mal Methods for Open Object-Based Distributed Systems (FMOODS 2002)*, pages 79–94. International Federation for Information Process-ing (IFIP), Kluwer Academic, Dordrecht, 2002.

[Wei95]   C. Weissman. Penetration testing. In Abrams et al [AJP95], chap-ter 11, pages 269–296.

[Wei99]   C. Weidenbach. Towards an automatic analysis of security protocols in first-order logic. In H. Ganzinger, editor, *16th International Conference on Automated Deduction (CADE-16)*, volume 1632 of *Lecture Notes in Computer Science*, pages 314–328, 1999.

[WF98]   D. S. Wallach and E. W. Felten. Understanding Java stack inspection. In *IEEE Symposium on Security and Privacy (S&P)*, page 52ff, 1998.

[Whi00]   J. Whittle. Formal approaches to systems analysis using UML: An overview. *Journal of Database Management*, 11(4):4–13, 2000.

[Wir71]   N. Wirth.   Program development by stepwise refinement.   *Communications of the ACM*, 14(4):221–227, April 1971.   Available at http://www.acm.org/classics/dec95.

[WJ02]   G. Wimmel and J. Jürjens.   Specification-based test generation for security-critical systems using mutations. In *International Conference on Formal Engineering Methods (ICFEM)*, volume 2495 of *Lecture Notes in Computer Science*, pages 471–482. Springer, Berlin Heidelberg New York, 2002.

[WM04]   M. Wermelinger and T. Margaria, editors. *Fundamental Approaches to Software Engineering (FASE 2000)*, volume 2984 of *Lecture Notes in Computer Science*. Springer, Berlin Heidelberg New York, 2004.

[WS02]   A. Wasowski and P. Sestoft. Compile-time scope resolution for state-charts transition. In Jürjens et al [JCF⁺02], pages 133–146.

[WW01]   G. Wimmel and A. Wißpeintner. Extended description techniques for security engineering. In M. Dupuy and P. Paradinas, editors, *Trusted Information: The New Decade Challenge*, page 469ff. International Federation for Information Processing (IFIP), Kluwer Academic, Dordrecht, 2001. 16th International Conference on Information Security (SEC 2001).

[XLL03]   Zhongfu Xu, J. Luethi, and A. Lehmann. Predicting software performance based on UML models during the unified software development process. In Jürjens et al [JRFF03], pages 105–112.

[XMI02]   Object Management Group. *OMG XML Metadata Interchange (XMI) Specification*, January 2002.

[ZG02]   P. Ziemann and M. Gogolla. An extension of OCL with temporal logic. In Jürjens et al [JCF⁺02], pages 53–62.

Index